# COACHING AND PERFORMANCE MANAGEMENT

*Developing and Inspiring Leaders*

**Bahaudin G. Mujtaba**

ILEAD Academy, LLC
Davie, Florida

© Bahaudin G. Mujtaba (2008). *Coaching and Performance Management: Developing and Inspiring Leaders.*

Cover Design By: Cagri Tanyar

ISBN-10: 0-9774211-4-7

ISBN-13: 978-0-9774211-4-5


1. SPO061000: Sports & Recreation: Coaching - General
2. BUS030000: Business & Economics: Human Resources & Personnel Management
3. BUS046000: Business & Economics: Motivational


Printed in the United States of America by ILEAD Academy, LLC.




ILEAD Academy, LLC
Davie, Florida. United States
www.ileadacademy.com

# Peer Review Statements

As a recent graduate and a first time business owner, I suddenly found myself faced with the challenge of managing a diverse group of individuals. Neither dental school nor residency had prepared me for the trials and tribulations to come, and being the youngest member of the team did not help either. Luckily, I landed myself a copy of Dr. Bahaudin Mujtaba's "*Coaching and Performance Management: Developing and Inspiring Leaders*," which proved to be a Godsend. I highly recommend this exceptionally written and organized book to any leader in any walk of life, young or old, experienced or inexperienced. Dr. Mujtaba's book provided me with the tools and insight to build rapport and camaraderie among my staff and taught me invaluable skills such as effective communication, conflict management, and effectively executing performance evaluations (something I previously dreaded!). I certainly value this book as I know it will continue to guide and mold me in the years to come. Many thanks to Dr. Mujtaba for making this book available to us entrepreneurs, and on a job well done!

> – *Dr. Anissa Ahmadi, Pediatric Dentist, Fort Myers, Florida*

This book has it all! Bahaudin has written an all-inclusive book that is must reading for any professional or executive who wants to grow people. He provides an excellent general context for coaching along with some special coaching situations which make this a value-added book. His treatment of listening as the key to successful coaching is right on target. The supplemental exercises and cases makes this book an excellent toolkit for trainers and professors who wish to maximize learning about one of the most important management skills of the 21st century. This book is all you will need to know about coaching and being a successful coach.

> – *Dr. Robert C. Preziosi, Human Resources Chair*

This book is an excellent combination of theory and practice – useful, practical, and essential information for managers who aspire for their employees to excel, and for educators at the undergraduate and graduate levels. In addition to traditional topics on leadership, Dr. Mujtaba successfully addresses more difficult current issues in leadership including work-life balance, disruptive behavior, and alternative work arrangements. The book artfully includes cases and exercises to assist the reader in better developing coaching skills. Highly recommended!

> – *Dr. Les Carter, Entrepreneurship Chair, St. Edward's University*

This book is a wonderful resource for current and aspiring managers. Bahaudin takes key managerial topics and presents them in a vivid concise manner that makes this book outstanding for both undergraduate and graduate students. The numerous examples from top business leaders, the cases and exercises in the back, and the great quotes throughout make this an excellent book. I strongly recommend it.

> – *Dr. Jeffrey J. Fountain, Assistant Professor of Sport and Recreation Management*

Bahaudin, in his book *"Coaching and Performance management: Developing and Inspiring Leaders"*, uses personal anecdotes and real-life examples from a compendium of sources to make this an excellent combination of theory and practice. The book has a wide appeal and will be invaluable to the reader in developing their leadership skills and becoming a successful coach, a coaches' coach.

— Mr. Joe Pineda, Assistant Dean of External Affairs - Office of Development

The book *"Coaching and Performance Management: Developing and Inspiring Leaders"* contains extensive information that guides the reader in developing his/her leadership skills. The book not only explains the concepts presented in a thorough and factual manner, but also offers practical application of the same. I liked the combination of concepts, cases, exercises, and questions that add to the learning experience and allow one to further his/her understanding. The author clearly has a grasp of the subtle aspects of coaching and that is what makes this book stand out. The focus was on the relationship between the coach and the person being coached. This approach emphasizes what can be accomplished by perfecting one's interpersonal communication skills, and it exposes the reader to simple but powerful ways to achieve this. Today's business is conducted in a culturally diverse environment and participants cannot afford to overlook the need for effective interaction.

— *Mrs. Marikay Concannon, Academic Adviser; M.S. Mental Health Counseling*

Bahaudin Mujtaba has opened up a substantially untapped source for better utilizing the performance management concept and the influence of coaching. The genius of Mujtaba's book is recognizing the natural integration of these two principles and the impact upon the organization's human condition.

— *Dr. William J. Harrington, Professor of Human Resources Management*

Bahaudin has written a useful and practical book for managers and leaders about human capacity and development of trusting relationships. The content and principles of coaching stated in this book form a solid foundation for developing and inspiring extraordinary performance. This book is a practical tool for today's managers and team leaders to become effective and skilled coaches in order for their employees, peers, and teams to be achievement-oriented every day. All entrepreneurs, managers and leaders would benefit from reading and applying the concepts discussed in this book. I highly recommend it.

— *Dr. Nilofar Jamasi, Dentist in Central Florida*

## * * * **Dedication** * * *

*This book is dedicated to leaders who make good use of
their coaching skills to enhance innovation,
creativity and performance for all. May
the force be with their heads,
hearts, and
habits.*

☆

*

*

*

*

*

*

# TABLE OF CONTENTS

# Preface

*Coaching and Performance Management: Developing and Inspiring Leaders* is about enhancing human capacity and development. In this book, coaching is focused on developing a trusting relationship with others, as well as on clarifying expectations and goals, thereby leading to specific action plans for their achievement. Coaching is not an innate skill, but rather it is learned. It occurs through one's life personally and professionally. Effective coaching is the process of letting people know that what they do matters. Furthermore, it is about being sincere, specific, and to the point about both good and poor performance so others can take personal responsibility for their achievements. From this perspective, coaching is, and it can be, one of the most important functions managers perform because it communicates performance levels, expectations, importance of the tasks and responsibilities, and a caring attitude. The skills and behaviors of effective coaches are presented and thoroughly discussed. This book is appropriate for current and aspiring managers, leaders, scholars, and training and development professionals.

This book defines *coaching* as the continuous process of conversational collaborations and interactions aimed at assisting others to unlock and realize their full potential one task and one skill at a time, and at a pace appropriate for the person being coached. The essence of coaching is unlocking people's potential, through rich, two-way interactions as well as stimulating questions, so people can maximize their own performance. Effective coaches accept the challenge of developing their colleagues and employees knowing that the growth and development journey is a continuous process, and that learning how to learn and develop are the real goals for both the coach and the coachee.

The author has used the concepts discussed in this book both nationally and internationally with academic and practitioner audiences to help increase their awareness of performance management, coaching, influence, and leadership skills. As such, the concepts, cases, and exercises are relevant to today's work environment and can easily fit most leadership and management courses, seminars, and employee development workshops. Leadership and management trainers, corporate universities, colleges or professors wishing to adopt this book or any of its chapters may contact the publisher or the author for receiving the available supplementary facilitator's materials such as the electronic power point files for presentation, chapter summaries for usage with lectures and online postings, test questions for discussions or exams, and/or instructor thoughts or supplementary material for exercises. The instructor's resources comes electronically using Microsoft Power Point, Word, and other files; as such, they can be adjusted by each educator and facilitator for his or her lectures, training and presentations.

*******************

"We are led to believe a lie - When we see with and not through the eye."

*******************

# Acknowledgements

I thank my family members, colleagues and friends for their coaching (guidance and valuable input) in the review of this material as well as for generously sharing their thoughts, suggestions, writings, and other contributions on coaching, performance management, and leadership related issues in this book.

The following individuals are especially thanked for their review, editing, guidance, mentorship, and coaching of the author, and contributions in this book:

- Anissa Ahmadi
- Barbara A. Alston
- Carolina (Maria) Ayala
- Barry Barnes
- Charlie Blackwell
- Solange Beckford
- Thomas J. Byrnes
- Daniel Cantillo
- Frank Cavico
- Reccia N. Charles
- Lamoy Coburn
- Marikay Concannon
- Richard Conwell
- Steven D. Cooke
- Bonita (Bonnie) L. Durazo
- Vickie Cox Edmondson
- Claire Fair
- Peter Finley
- Jeffrey Fountain
- Donna Galla
- Fernanda Gazmuri
- Jane Gibson
- Rafael Gonzalez
- B. Cassandra Grant
- Kim Greenfest
- Regina A. Greenwood,
- Patricia (Trish) M. Hagan
- William Harrington
- Gina Harris
- Roger (Mack) M. Hinson
- Nilofar Jamasi
- William Lauffer
- Eleanor Marschke
- Simone Maxwell
- Belqis Majboor
- Terrell G. Manyak
- Jean McAtavey
- Mary Ann Moore
- Ghulam Mujtaba
- Lisa Mujtaba
- Mustafa G. Mujtaba
- Jay Martin
- Timothy McCartney
- Donovan A. McFarlane
- Keith S. Meredith
- Edward F. Murphy, Jr.
- Bina Patel
- Joseph Pineda
- Maria M. Pinto
- Randolph Pohlman
- Robert Preziosi
- Anisa Qadir
- Brian E. Renaud
- Jaime A. Ruiz-Gutierrez,
- Tronia Smith
- Arnel Onesimo O. Uy
- Ramon J. Venero
- Stefanie D. Wilson
- Felix Young

It has been said that each petal on the shamrock can bring a wish your way,
If you wish for good health, good luck, and happiness every day!
May your blessings outnumber the shamrocks that grow,
And may trouble avoid you wherever you go!
~Irish Blessing

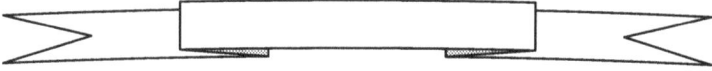

If you choose to purposely live, be, and serve as an effective
coach each day, this could be the single most important
initiative in your life. With coaching, you can chisel
the type of character you want to be through your
day—to—day thinking, feelings, words, and
behaviors. So, consciously reflect upon
your feelings, thoughts, words, and
actions as they determine your
character and destiny
as an effective
coach.

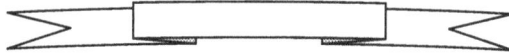

# CHAPTER 1

## Coaching and Management

Effective coaching, leadership and management are one and the same. Coaching is an effective method of leading people and managing processes and resources. In today's complex and competitive business environment, firms and managers must do everything they can to recruit and retain talented and experienced employees. Furthermore, organizational leaders must do everything that they can to make sure their employees are not underutilized, error prone, and dissatisfied with their daily assignments. Underutilized, error prone and dissatisfied employees can become a burden to the organization and cause further unwanted employee turnover. This is why it is important for today's team leaders, supervisors, managers, and executives to become effective and skilled coaches in order for their colleagues and employees to be achievement-oriented every day. Becoming an effective coach requires internalizing the idea of being and living as an influential leader through value-based thinking, strategic planning, consistently caring behavior, trust and relationship building, and continuous learning and growth. If you choose to purposely live and serve as an effective coach, this could be the single most important initiative both in your personal and professional lives. Through coaching, you can chisel the type of person you want to be through your day-to-day thinking, feelings, words, and behaviors. So, consciously reflect upon your feelings, thoughts, words, and actions as they determine your character and destiny.

> Be careful of your *thoughts*, for your thoughts become your words.
> Be careful of your *words*, for your words become your actions.
> Be careful of your *actions*, for your actions become your habits.
> Be careful of your *habits*, for your habits become your character.
> Be careful of your *character*, for your character becomes your *destiny*.
> (*Universal Proverb*)

This author's mother often emphasized an Afghan proverb which states that "One should do good acts and throw it in the river." This basically means do good acts for others in society, but don't expect anything in return; however, because of your compassionate and considerate acts, you can be certain that the world will generously reward you for your kindheartedness, goodwill, munificence, and benevolence. What she is saying is that the world will give our rewards according to the services we provide, the people we associate with, and the environment we choose to settle in or accept. In other words, the world is like a giant mirror which reflects what it sees. Furthermore, the human mind is like a magnet, subconsciously pulling some things while pushing others away. Therefore, what we perceive and receive in this world in our personal and professional work environments is largely a reflection of our own internal beliefs and expressed attitudes. Life tends to give us what we consistently attract through our thoughts, feelings and behaviors. So, if a person is thinking, acting and talking negatively then his or her world is likely to echo back negative reflections. If we consistently think, act and talk with enthusiasm, a positive mindset, and optimism, then we are likely to attract positive individuals, friends, rewards, and desirable outcomes. Therefore, the world is a reflection of our thoughts, feelings, and behaviors. The key to long-term happiness and success for each individual, at least to some extent, seems to be a function of positive thoughts, feelings, attitudes, and responses to the environment. Since positive attitude and optimistic mindsets can be contagious, coaches and performance managers must be living role-models for their colleagues, employees and industry peers if they are to effectively and strategically influence performance.

Some people expect to become a leader or manager simply by obtaining a certificate or acquiring new knowledge. While gaining a certificate of expertise or new knowledge are often prerequisites to successfully initiating and completing a project, they are no longer enough without strategic action, application and continuous improvement. Someone who knows how to read but has never read anything useful will probably not benefit much from this skill unless he or she actually uses this knowledge, skill and ability toward a specific purpose or objective that enhances his or her life or those of others in society. One cannot and should not expect to become a skilled leader or manager simply by acquiring a title or position of authority in one's department, institution or government. One cannot and should not expect to become a skilled leader or manager in the work environment simply by obtaining and earning a college degree or the title of "business master" as that is only the beginning. Last but not least, one cannot and should not expect to become a skilled leader or manager simply by gaining a certificate or knowledge since information and comprehension of complex subjects or phenomenon without application is not much better than never having been exposed to such wisdom. However, one can become a skilled leader or manager by acquiring the coaching skills that are necessary to excel beyond one's current ability and capacity to influence and lead others toward better performance standards.

Hank Aaron's, the baseball star, work philosophy was to: "Always to keep swinging. Whether I was in a slump or feeling badly or having trouble off the field, the only thing to do was keep swinging." Effective coaches and performance managers keep on exploring new ideas, better means of positively influencing others and helping people grow as human beings. When it comes to obtaining the prestigious status or character of a coach, one does not need to always be "*A Cautious Man.*" If you have the slightest opportunity or an interest in leading and influencing others through proper management techniques, then go for it and become a coach; begin being one!

*The Cautious Man*:
Once there was a very cautious man
Who never loved, laughed or cried.
    He never risked, he never lost
    He never won nor ever tried.
And one day when he passed away
His insurance was denied.
    For since he never really lived
    They claimed he never really died.
        (*Unknown*)

Being and becoming an effective leader through coaching skills is a good idea, and remember that "Good ideas are not adopted automatically; they must be driven into practice with courageous patience," as stated by Hyman Rickover, Naval Admiral and father of the nuclear submarine. Today's coaches (managers and supervisors) must be courageous, value and goal-driven, persistent, and caring human beings in an often competitive and "dog-eat-dog" work environment. Furthermore, today's managers and supervisors have been said to have the most difficult job in the organization as they must effectively balance work and resources to achieve the stated objectives amid widespread competition. In most organizations, the transition from an employee to the role of manager is often stressful and full of obstacles and challenges. In many cases, there are few resources available to alleviate the challenges associated with the transition and provide the knowledge and skills necessary to instill confidence in the new leaders and their associates. Acquiring and improving managerial skills is not just for "business" nor always the responsibility of business, but it is for managers in all types of organizations and the manager's personal responsibility. All managers and supervisors should learn the values, skills, and behaviors of admirable coaches. Then, they must envision themselves as talented and caring coaches and begin being one. As a supervisor or manager, if you can perceive and believe that you can be a great coach, then you can certainly achieve it. Begin being one, and others will follow!

> You are in charge of your feelings, beliefs, and actions. And you teach others how to behave toward you. While you cannot change other people, you can influence them through your own behaviors and actions. By being a living role model of what you want to receive from others, you create more of what you want in your life (Eric Allenbaugh).

By consistently expecting the best from everyone and demonstrating a positive attitude toward their capacity or potential for high performance, you can be a great role model in doing what you enjoy the most. Oprah Winfrey, the popular Talk Show Host, said that "I've come to believe that each of us has a personal calling that's as unique as a fingerprint - and that the best way to succeed is to discover what you love and then find a way to offer it to others in the form of service, working hard, and also allowing the energy of the universe to lead you." Of course, offering your services or expertise to others in the form of coaching those who need it most is an excellent way to make your legacy live on beyond physically performing what you enjoy doing most. William Arthur Ward has been quoted as having said: "Flatter me, and I may not believe you. Criticize me, and I may not like you. Ignore me, and I may not forgive you. Encourage me, and I may not forget you." So, be a coach and encourage others to become their best. After all, life is about doing one's best and reaching for stars. As someone once answered the question of "what is life?" If it is a challenge, be prepared and prepare others to meet it; and if it is a puzzle, then solve it.

> *What is Life?*
> Life is a challenge... meet it
> Life is a gift... accept it
> Life is an adventure... dare it
> Life is a sorrow... overcome it
> Life is a tragedy... face it
> Life is a duty... perform it
> Life is a game... play it
> Life is a mystery... unfold it
> Life is a song... sing it
> Life is an opportunity... take it
> Life is a journey... complete it
> Life is a promise... fulfill it
> Life is a beauty... praise it
> Life is a struggle... fight it
> Life is a goal... achieve it
> Life is a puzzle... solve it
> (*Unknown*)

## Introduction to Coaching

Since the beginning of time, the human struggles and wisdom have enabled the specie to survive and prosper in almost everything it did. While survival is not the ultimate goal, one must successfully maintain this goal till the end to achieve prosperity in life. Choosing to survive is often complemented with other worthwhile dreams and goals in one's personal and professional lives. Someone once said that:

> There are times when one may be left to survive the repercussions of the behaviors of another. Behaviors which one in no way anticipated,…nor encouraged. Robbed of one's past…present…and future, the soul forfeits the dreams…the aspirations…and the ambitions that had previously sustained its existence. Choosing to survive demands one learn to bear an insufferable grief, bringing a stoicism…enabling one to endure (Unknown).

Survival and prosperity require not only the effective coaching of one's personal affairs, but also positively and situationally influencing the motivation of others in one's department or vicinity toward predetermined and worthwhile goals in a fair and ethical manner. For managers and organizational leaders, survival means retaining their ranks and preventing their organizations from becoming complacent or bankrupt. Such efforts toward professional survival require effective management and leadership skills; in other words, in today's workplace, survival requires that managers and leaders become strong coaches if they are to effectively lead their people and organizations toward prosperity and industry competitiveness.

According to *The Cluetrain Manifesto: The End of Business as Usual* (a 2001 book written by Christopher Locke, Rick Levine, Doc Searls, and David Weinberger), the "Command-and-control management styles both derive from and reinforce bureaucracy, power tripping, and an overall culture of paranoia." If leaders do not desire bureaucracy, power tripping and a culture of paranoia in their organizations, then they must search for a better alternative than a "command and control" style of leading and managing. Of course, there are many critical variables and reasons that are causing a paradigm shift from a culture of managing by force to an environment of leading by increasing each employee's commitment to the purpose of the organization as well as through empowerment and collaboration. According to studies, a good number of twenty-first century managers (about 57% as per the statistics provided by Bacon and Spear, 2003) believe that today's firms are not developing employees effectively or as quickly as needed to help them be highly productive and remain competitive. What is also true is that over half of employees who seek job opportunities elsewhere do so because they are not experiencing sufficient development and learning growth in their current jobs. In the mean time, many top executives and managers believe that their human resources happen to be their most important asset in the firm, and their managers need to be stronger experts (both functionally and interpersonally) if they are too effectively meet the demands of the new business environment.

Due to the changing demographics of the business world, such as increased competition and advanced technologies, organizations are discovering that traditional tactics of management are no longer enough to remain competitive. Some senior managers are focused on creating an organizational culture where ordinary employees are capable of extraordinary performance. These leaders and managers recognize that this type of a culture would be difficult for their competitors to easily duplicate. Consequently, for the creation of an effective organizational culture, coaching is becoming recognized and practiced as an effective tool to increase morale, performance and the bottom line through the success of each individual associate. For example, studies have shown that a majority of employees who received coaching in their jobs say that it improved their job performance and professional success. In organizations where coaching is effectively practiced as a management style, the bottom-line performance is two to three times better than the traditional "command-and-control" type of organizations. Furthermore, it has been proven that employee commitment increases when there is a strong, positive relationship between the manager and his/her employees. These types of relationships are developed best as a result of effective coaching.

Effective relationship-oriented coaching creates more knowledgeable and competent employees, reduces errors and rework, and greatly assists in bringing new changes to the culture. Both effective and ineffective managers tend to know what makes a good coach. The difference lies in being able to transfer this knowledge into goal-oriented actions with employees to increase their performance and success. Effective coaching skills make a manager's job easier as it enables greater delegation, leaving him/her time to take on bigger, more strategic projects. It builds the manager's reputation as a developer of people, while increasing productivity since everyone will know the expectations and the fact that what they do matters. It can also develop trust and a good relationship between managers and employees. Last but not least, good coaching skills can increase creativity, innovation, morale, and teamwork since everyone will feel safe working in an inclusive environment.

So what is coaching? Simply stated, *coaching* is about developing a trusting relationship with your people so you can jointly clarify expectations and departmental goals thereby leading to specific action plans for their achievement. As such, there are many situations where coaching skills will be very effective, such as: reinforcing good performance, motivating employees to new heights and peak performance levels, orienting a new employee into the department or organization, providing new knowledge to individuals about changes and tactics, training a new skill for a new task that needs performing, clarifying expectations and correcting poor performance, increasing the self confidence of an employee about the task or new responsibilities and challenges, and other such responsibilities as conducting a performance review.

Coaching is not an innate skill, but rather it is learned. It occurs through one's life personally and professionally. Effective coaching is the process of letting people know that what they do matters to you and to the organization. Furthermore, it is about letting them know that you are there to help them be the best they can be as their success is important because it matters to you. It is also about being sincere, specific and to the point about both good and poor performance so others can take personal responsibility for their achievements. From this perspective, coaching is and can be one of the most important functions managers perform because it communicates performance levels, expectations, importance of the tasks and responsibilities, and it communicates a caring attitude. The following are some elements involved in coaching.

1.  Planning.
2.  Being positive.
3.  Communicating clearly.
4.  Respecting others and their individualities.
5.  Making others feel comfortable.
6.  Being culturally sensitive.
7.  Avoiding value judgments.
8.  Using effective listening skills.
9.  Staying focused on tasks and goals.
10. Having high expectations.
11. Supporting and encouraging others.
12. Following up, adapting, adjusting, and communicating as needed.

Coaching involves the above-stated elements and more that are discussed and emphasized in this book. Managers and leaders have gotten where they are because somebody bent down and helped them use these coaching skills. So, now it is time for them to be there for others and effectively educate and coach aspiring managers and leaders toward maximum productivity. Of course, everything that a leader does to help employees grow should be done (or coached) with care and a focus on the development of trust and a long-term relationship. In other words, coaches and leaders must be compassionate and people-oriented. Boyatzis, Melvin and Blaize (2006) stated that:

> One purpose of management education is to develop people to be leaders of organizations and institutions for the future. The manner in which we approach the development of leaders is largely dependent on our concept of leadership. Leader sustainability is adversely affected by the psychological and physiological effects of chronic power stress associated with the performance of the leadership role...When leaders experience compassion through coaching the development of others, they experience psycho-physiological effects that restore the body's natural healing and growth processes, thus enhancing their sustainability...Leaders should emphasize coaching as a key part of their role and behavioral habits (2006, p. 8).

Boyatzis, Melvin and Blaize mention that for today's leaders and managers to sustain themselves over a long period of time, the human response to stress should be ameliorated, improved, or restructured. They argue that the "practice of coaching others for their development can have this effect; coaching, along with the experience of compassion, should ameliorate the negative physiological and psychological effects of power stress; in this way, coaching with compassion is likely to enhance a leader's sustainability" (Boyatzis, Melvin and Blaize, 2006, p. 12). Boyatzis, Melvin and Blaize (2006) also discuss that mandated coaching programs often lead to compliance and other administrative responsibilities that can increase the level of stress. Mandated coaching programs (when compared to voluntary coaching processes through influence and participatory collaborations) do not seem to elicit compassion on the part of the coach and may actually cause undue hardship and stress. As such, coaching with compassion requires an effective and caring relationship between the coach and his or her employees or the person that is being coached. Boyatzis, Melvin and Blaize conclude that "coaching with compassion may provide the platform for sustainable leadership effectiveness and an effective approach for developing leaders—to teach them how to effectively engage and develop other leaders" (2006, p. 18). In order for coaching with compassion to take place, managers and leaders must truly and sincerely care for their employees and others around them, instead of simply viewing them as a burden and responsibility. In other words, coaching with compassion requires that leaders have a positive mindset and believe that employees want to work and are excited to learn, grow and develop to their highest capacity.

"*Managers lose talent when they neglect to coach their staffs*" is the title of Carol Hymowitz's article that was published on the Wall Street Journal on March 19, 2007. Hymowitz says that "Rather than worry so much about the war for talent in today's tight job market, executives ought to focus on the waste of talent in their ranks...many don't spend nearly enough time making sure the people under them learn and grow on the job." Many firms are filled with bored, underutilized and overqualified employees who are not doing a good job as a result of their boredom or they are looking for a new company. According to Hymowitz (2007), "A whopping 70% of U.S. employees say they feel either '*not engaged*' or '*actively disengaged*' at work." Research shows that organizations and departments with a large number of dissatisfied employees tend to have "more absenteeism and lower productivity—as well as 51% higher turnover rates than those with engaged employees" (Hymowitz, 2007). Engaged employees tend to be working for managers, leaders and coaches who are spending a large percentage of time assisting their employees be successful at their jobs. These managers make sure that their employees' strengths are being used and they provide the needed resources so associates can achieve their expected performance levels. Hymowitz says that "Most people-focused managers have innate coaching skills or worked for a boss who masterfully mentored them." Managers should work on being role-models of effective coaching and they should engage as well as encourage all employees to develop the talent of their people as to make the organization more competitive through its human resources. In academia, all educators, advisors, and doctoral dissertation committee members tend to fall in this category of mentors and coaches to their students. Furthermore, school administrators also fall in the category of coaches, as they can help each faculty and staff member continuously grow by providing them with the needed resources and guidance. Dr. Randolph Pohlman, Dean for the School of Business and Entrepreneurship at Nova Southeastern University, states that "One of the most important jobs of a leader is to create an environment in the organization where people can thrive and grow" (Personal Communication, April 02, 2007). Creating such an environment where people can thrive and grow is the essence of effective coaching.

**Coaching Application and Relevance**

*Coaching*, in this book, is defined as the continuous process of conversational collaborations and interactions aimed at assisting others unlock and realize their full potential one task and one skill at a time, and at a pace appropriate for the person being coached. According to Professor David Clutterbuck, coaching consultant, "If you know where the conversation is going to go, you are acting as a consultant or facilitator, not as a coach. A genuine coaching conversation creates its own direction and meaning. While both coach and coachee bring expertise of different kinds, what emerges is something beyond and different to their collective knowledge before the conversation began" (Clutterbuck Associates Newsletter, January 26, 2007). According to this book and many experts, the essence of coaching is unlocking people's potential, through rich, two-way interactions as well as stimulating questions, so people can maximize their own performance. Effective coaches accept the challenge of developing their colleagues and employees knowing that the growth and development journey is a continuous process, and that learning how to learn and develop are the real goals for both the coach and the coachee. Effective coaches are those that work with others by describing the problem (as they see it), helping the employee or colleague see the problem, clarifying standards and expectations, encouraging and helping one in generating possible solutions, agreeing on a specific action plan, and following up as needed to make sure the problem is solved and performance enhanced. Effective coaches, through proper planning and skill, help others go through these procedures without them knowing that it was a process made up of several steps.

According to Dr. Robert Preziosi, management and leadership consultant, one can increase his or her leadership and coaching impact using *TARRITP*: tenacity, adaptability, respect, resilience, initiative, tolerance, and patience (Personal Communication, February 11, 2007 at the Graduation Ceremony in Nassau, Bahamas). While showing tenacity, adaptability, respect, resilience, initiative, tolerance, and patience can certainly improve one's influence, to be an effective coach one must also be a self-motivator and a great friend to others, while being surrounded by admired personal and professional colleagues. One must also understand that having great friends, starts by being one. Coaches must be great friends and they must self-motivate themselves to socialize and achieve their goals. Bernard Berkowitz is quoted as having said that "It is up to us to give ourselves recognition. If we wait for it to come from others, we feel resentful when it doesn't, and when it does, we may well reject it." So, coaches must be self-motivated and they should serve as friends and caring relatives to their employees, colleagues and others who look up to them. As stated by Dr. Amanullah, being a friend is above all relations:

> A friend is like father who scolds you,
> like mother who hugs you,
> like sister who teases you,
> like brother who fights you,
> in short combine all worldly relations
> you will have a friend, and that is what makes a friend above all relations.

Effective friendship and coaching interactions are about increasing the manager's leadership influence, understanding people as individuals, and building productive human relationships in the workplace. During a New Year (*Naowruz*) carnival in Kabul, Afghanistan, a six-year boy asked a balloon salesperson if the small, bluish-looking balloon would go up if it is was released into the air. The boy's favorite color had been blue and, due to his small body size and "country-style" drawl and pronunciation, he felt a little out of place among his "city" peers. The balloon salesperson looked at the little boy, who was associating the size and color of the balloon with his life, and said "Son, it is not the color or the size of the balloons that matter or make a difference. It is what is inside that makes them go up." Then he released the little bluish-appearing balloon that the little boy was pointing to and, surely, it went way up into the air just like the big ones. Effective coaching is about applying the principles implied in what this balloon salesperson was saying. It is the strategic coaching of managers, as well as the goal-oriented efforts and hard work of each employee that make a difference in their success or achievement of high performance on the job. Effective coaching and performance management is about being objective, sensitive, clear, specific, and building a trusting relationship with each individual to help him or her get where the individual is headed.

There is a story about an officer and an enlisted member and their conversation which did not produce an effective outcome. As the story goes, a man was flying a hot air balloon and realized he is lost. He reduces the air balloon's height and spots a man down below. He lowers the balloon further and shouts, "Excuse me, can you help me? I promised my friend I would meet him half an hour ago, but I don't know where I am." The man below says, "Yes. You are in a hot air balloon, hovering approximately 30 feet above this field. You are between 40 and 42 degrees north latitude, and between 58 and 60 degrees west longitude." "You must be an "enlisted" member," says the man. "I am," replies the enlisted member, "How did you know?" "Well," says the balloonist, "everything you have told me is technically correct, but I have no idea what to make of your information, and the fact is I am still lost." The man below says, "You must be an officer." "I am," replies the balloonist, "but how did you know?" "Well," says the enlisted member, "you don't know where you are, or where you are going. You have made a promise which you have no idea how to keep, and you expect me to solve your problem. The fact is you are in the exact same position you were in before we met, but now it is somehow turning to be my fault." As can be seen from the story of the enlisted member and the officer, coaching is not just applied in the workplace since the skills of being clear, concise and goal-directed are applicable in almost every aspect of life.

While coaching is not limited to the workplace, most books, similar to this one, tend to apply its principles in the professional work environment. Staying focused in the workplace, as a common denominator, allows for specific industry and organizational examples and applications for reflection and discussion purposes. In the mean time, one must realize that the material is applicable to all situations where one has an opportunity to influence others. The following pages provide examples for relevancy of how coaching can be of assistance in different industries and organizations where managers and leaders deal with various performance and behavioral challenges on a day-to-day basis.

### *Coaching and the Larger Perspective[1]*

In their article, *Alignment Coaching: A Broader Perspective on Business Coaching*, John Lazar and William Bergquist propose an important, unique focus of coaching: improving performance by "making sense of one's life and the fundamental values and meaning that get expressed through choice and action" (Bergquist & Lazar, 2004). In the course of the article, they distinguish alignment coaching from performance and executive coaching, describe four types of alignment coaching, and use a case study to illustrate alignment coaching and its impact.

There are situations where traditional executive or performance business coaching is not generating the desired results. Altering the specific behaviors or decisions that are affected by these coaching efforts fail to generate the expected improvements. Factors that may be contributing to sub-par improvements may include "lack of motivation, ambivalent behavior, depression, resignation, resentment, (or) distrust" (Bergquist & Lazar, 2004). For significant improvement, a deeper level of understanding must be sought. According to Bergquist and Lazar, "This gets to where people live and make sense of their lives: their underlying values, beliefs, expectations, and attitudes." Therefore, alignment coaching is likely to be more effective with executive and performance management coaching. These authors present four types of alignment coaching: spiritual, philosophical, ethical, and life and career coaching. *Spiritual coaching* focuses on the bringing about of "discernment" by the coachee. This comes about after, "reflective inquiry into and appreciation of

---

[1] Contributed by Trish Hagan (M.D.), Nova Southeastern University.

the major, transcendental forces that 1) call on us to improve the quality of our lives, our community, and our society; 2) provide meaning and context for our complex and unfathomable life experiences; and 3) provide an institutional base of set ceremonial activities that enable us to express our deepest longings and life joys" (Bergquist and Lazar, 2004). *Philosophical coaching* is similar to spiritual, but focuses on the secular side of life. Philosophical coaches encourage and assist an individual to probe deeply into his or her underlying beliefs and to reflect on how these underlying assumptions and beliefs relate to and impact his or her perceptions and actions in all aspects of life (Bergquist and Lazar, 2004). According to Bergquist and Lazar, *ethical coaching* specifically helps individuals, "identify and clarify their own values and ethical stances and to identify ways they align with (and betray) those values and ethics." Finally, *life and career* coaching looks at the "entire life experience of the individual" and focuses on the important goals and aspirations of the individual. Distinct from performance and executive coaching, alignment coaching can enhance these other areas of coaching.

Bergquist and Lazar provide the example of "Tom," the president of family-owned business who was struggling with work-life balance. In Tom's case, "the life-coaching approach provided an opportunity to recognize and identify the full range of life domains and their concerns, then ensure that work was appreciated within that context, rather than vice versa" (Bergquist and Lazar, 2004). Together with his coach, Tom identified seven areas that needed attention and projects within each area. Over the course of a year, Tom saw progress and greater satisfaction in each of his areas despite some very difficult situations developing during that time period. The authors note that during his year of coaching Tom faced puzzles, issues with clear solutions; problems, situations that are multidimensional and lack a clear solution; and, mysteries, happenings that are out of one's control. As a result of the coaching process, Tom was frequently able to analyze problems as well as create and solve puzzles. Puzzles were then amenable to performance coaching which ensured an efficient solution to those issues. Alignment coaching was especially helpful when Tom was addressing mysteries. Understanding those issues beyond his control in the context of what was fundamentally important to him allowed for better utilization of resources and less stress about the outcomes. In their article and through the case example, Bergquist and Lazar create a persuasive argument that alignment coaching can improve performance, employee satisfaction and enhance other types of coaching.

Zeus and Skiffington introduced the concept of executive coaching by stating that, "Executive coaching is an individualized, one-to-one relationship designed to assist executives in developing and enhancing their professional effectiveness and on-the-job performance" (Zeus and Skiffington, 2002). Bergquist and Lazar supplement the idea of executive coaching by including alignment coaching. In today's business climate with increasing stress from lack of work-life balance among employees, issues with retention, difficulties with business ethics and difficulty developing leaders, paying close attention to alignment coaching as well as executive coaching would serve the individual and the organization well.

In her article *Fighting for Balance*, Julia Chang stated that, "In a recent poll by online career site Monster.com, 81% of workers said they were not happy with their work/life balance" (Chang, 2005). In another article, *Workable Solutions*, Paula

Allen (2004) states that the cost to organizations that fail to address these issues includes "increased health benefit costs, increased absenteeism, increased employee assistance program usage and increasing employee disengagement." Leaders who struggle with work-life balance issues can have an even more profound impact on their organization since they are entrusted to "motivate and inspire others, managing their own moods and associated behaviors and thereby setting the tone and climate for how work gets done. When leadership falters or fails, that result is suboptimal performance for the leader, the leadership team, and the enterprise" (Bergquist & Lazar, 2004). Using coaching to help leaders look at their own fundamental values and meaning and how to best express those through choice and action would likely help decrease the work-life dichotomy. Understanding one's spiritual, philosophical, ethical, and life/career thoughts makes for a better platform for decisions that are in alignment between life and work and pay appropriate respect to both. Alignment coaching, as the example in the article by Bergquist and Lazar illustrated, can be very helpful with overcoming work-life imbalance, resulting in improved satisfaction in both areas.

Satisfied workers tend to stay with an organization for a longer period of time. High achieving, high performing, dissatisfied workers tend to leave a company, creating a huge void that must be filled. Replacing these key employees is expensive and time consuming and diverts resources away from other productive activities. In a survey conducted by the Pittsburgh-based business consulting firm, "Key Group found that 18 percent of workers plan to switch jobs this year specifically to bring a better work-life balance to their lives" (Kinsman, 2006). Looking at values alignment as a way to combat this costly problem is only logical. The Enron and Worldcom scandals illustrate the importance of having values alignment among executives in an organization. Understanding an individual's and an organization's ethics and values and having alignment between them would prevent these unfortunate situations from occurring in the future. Working through ethical issues and developing a strong foundation in one's own ethical opinions could be a valuable focus of alignment coaching for each new leader. Many organizations, such as Youth-Land[2], Publix Super Markets and many others, have traditionally attempted to develop leaders from within the company. As part of that professional development, it would seem valuable to provide some alignment coaching in addition to the performance and executive coaching. Ensuring that values and goals are aligned provides for a strong foundation for the future leaders of an organization. The clearer the goals and path are to all involved, the more productivity can be expected and more satisfaction for all.

### *Coaching versus Mentoring[3]*

Edward Sketch (2001), the director of education, training and development at Ford Motor Co., addressed the topic of mentoring and its importance for coaching. Let us start with the basics. So, what is coaching? Coaching is a one-on-one, face-to-face teaching, learning, and counseling relationship designed to develop job-related

---

[2] Youth-Land Healthcare Pros (YLHPs) is a hypothetical firm used to demonstrate real-world scenarios.
[3] Contributed by *Brian Renaud, Nova Southeastern University.*

knowledge and skills and improve performance. Coaching usually involves a continuous flow of instructions, comments, and suggestions from coach to employee - listening, questioning, relating learning to the learner's experience, and providing guided practice (Tracey, 2002, p. 84). What is mentoring? According to Edmund and Noon, mentoring is the process whereby a senior employee takes an active role in developing a junior colleague. Typically this occurs at managerial level or amongst professions. In this case, the mentor provides advice on how the mentee can develop his or her skills, competencies, knowledge, and experience in order to progress along a successful career path. As well as giving advice, the mentor might also prove useful in providing contacts that help the mentee to engage in the process of networking (Edmund and Noon, 2001, p. 220).

Sketch (2001) differentiates the two concepts of coaching and mentoring. Coaching deals with improving performance, it focuses on developing and selecting options for behavior modification to improve organizational performance and is task-oriented. Mentoring deals with personal transitions, it addresses the individual's identity in the organization and focuses on options and exploration that is not necessarily tied to organizational performance. While both may appear to be very different, the responsibilities of the coach and mentor will overlap; both skills result in the improvement of the organization and the individual. Managers often discuss the impact of retention (customer and employee) on the organization and both concepts can play an important role in improving retention. Aside from retention, they also enhance performance, improve productivity and provide training. For mentoring and coaching to be effective, individuals must be committed to the end goal. A strong relationship must exist between both parties, and for that to happen there must be a clear understanding of what each party hopes to gain from the process. Both ideas allow individuals to better understand themselves as well as their expectations and goals and work on their strengths and weaknesses.

JP Morgan Partners (NYC) uses both coaching and mentoring programs and the programs are open to all of its employees. The programs were instituted after a loss of talent occurred, while the company went through a number of mergers. Since the implementation of the programs, employee turnover has dropped considerably, to 2%, among the employees they have identified as key, while the competition has 25-30% turnover. Edward Sketch has worked with 18 mentees in the past 20 years and 80% of them have reached levels equal to or higher than his own. Manchester Consulting data for 2001 states that coaching provides an average return on investment (ROI) of $100,000, with many companies exceeding an ROI of $500,000. Besides a substantial ROI, companies enjoy better relationships among co-workers, increased job satisfaction and greater commitment to the organization.

## *Coaching for Improved Work Performance[4]*

Ferdinand Fournies (1987) discussed the steps coaches should take to analyze the need for coaching to occur. Fournies is the president of Fournies & Associates, a management-consulting firm that specializes in training programs.

---

[4] Contributed by Bonita Durazo, Nova Southeastern University.

Fournies is an author, lecturer and a former professor of management training in the Graduate Schools of Business of Columbia and Fairleigh Dickinson Universities.

The first step in the coaching process is to identify the unsatisfactory performance. This may seem an unnecessary step, as most times the manager will notice the unsatisfactory result as a clue that performance needs to improve. It is important to make the distinction of what the coachee is doing wrong or what he/she is not doing right. From this point, coaches and employees must analyze to determine what needs to be done differently so the result will change. Asking the employee to try harder or work "smarter" will not be enough. If the employee is coming in late each day, is the employee leaving too late in the morning or driving too slow? Merely asking the employee to be on time will not change the result, even if the employee agrees that the performance is unsatisfactory.

Often, the performance issue is a behavior that all employees do but a particular employee is doing it more than everyone else. When the manager notices this occurring, the manager conducts a work sampling. For example, a manager notices that every time she walks through the department, employee X is not at her desk. The manager does a sampling of walking through the work area several different times a day to prove or disprove the belief that employee X takes excessive breaks. This sampling will validate the behavior of Employee X.

Another step in the analysis process is to determine if the performance issue is worth the manager's time. Issues that do not relate to the performance and results of the job may not be appropriate coaching opportunities. A night janitor that does not have a happy disposition and works alone, but gets the job done well and on time may not need coaching to improve his/her attitude. It is not the manager's responsibility to manage and control every aspect of the person in and outside of work.

Evaluation should be related to the employee's understanding of the expectations of the position. Do the workers know what is expected, what satisfactory performance looks like? One way to determine the employee's understanding is simply to ask him/her. Asking an employee the expectations of the job as well as their understanding of the problem when there is unsatisfactory performance will open up communication. The coach should ask direct questions like, "Do you know how many accounts you are required to work each day? Do you know how many times you were late last week? Do you know how many absences are acceptable under the policy?" Openly discussing the employee's understanding of the job allows both the coach and coachee an understanding of where the breakdown has occurred. It is critical to the coaching process that the manager has let the employee know what is to be done, how it is to be done, when it is to be done, and the due date for completion. Setting up these expectations up front will avoid some coaching difficulties in the future.

Once the employee knows what, how, and when, the manager evaluates and monitors the employee's success in the position. If unsatisfactory performance occurs and the manager determines coaching is needed, the coach evaluates any obstacles to the employee's success. Does the employee know how to do the job? Does the employee need training? Does the employee need different or additional tools to do the job? Is the employee physically able to do the work?

The manager must remove any obstacle facing the employee that is beyond their control. This means providing training, tools or time to perform the tasks. If unsatisfactory performance continues after these efforts, the manager must analyze to determine if the employee could do the work if he/she wanted to by asking these questions: Does the employee know the performance is unsatisfactory? Does the employee know what is supposed to be done and when? Are there any obstacles beyond his or her control? Does the employee know how to do it? Did the manager reinforce the ideas that negative consequence does not follow performance? After this final evaluation, the coach must determine if the employee is the right fit for the job and the department. In such cases, the result may be a warning, suspension, transfer, or termination (Fournies, 1987).

Fournies outlines basic steps for setting up the coaching opportunity. In a busy office, being reminded of these simple steps is an efficient way of capturing the opportunity and setting up coaching for the most benefit to each individual. In preparing for coaching and influencing, these practical steps set up the scenario used.

An example of the use of this analysis is a review of productivity numbers in an accounts receivable department. In the review of the monthly reports, it was noticed that the accounts were not being worked as thoroughly as they should have been. This resulted in slowed cash reimbursement that affected the office's collection incentive bonus for all staff. The manager took the sampling of accounts and found that the strongest collector was not working the accounts appropriately. Accounts were then reviewed individually with the collector to show how the accounts should be worked and the unsatisfactory performance evidenced on the account. The collector immediately indicated she was not comfortable with some of the new procedures. The manager provided training and follow up. The employee now knows what is expected as it relates to working the accounts, knows how to work them and knows the deadlines for completion.

When does a behavior warrant a coaching discussion? In the case of a production driven department, several factors need consideration when reviewing interruptions to the workday. An example is reviewing the use of the telephone for personal calls. How much is too much personal phone call time? Should we allow excessive phone use when there is a life-changing event in a person's life (buying a house or getting married)? Some employees complain that they are very restricted in their daily job. If they complete their tasks on time, should excessive infractions of policies be overlooked? This may begin to muddy the expectations in the employee's mind if behaviors are overlooked. If the employee is able to get the minimal expectation completed with time to spare, how do we encourage the employee to keep striving to exceed the minimum expectations? The coaching opportunity turns from punitive, punishing for excessive phone usage, to a positive encouragement to strive for a higher standard.

### Coaching the Alpha Male[5]

Ludeman and Erlandson (2004) discuss in their article, *Coaching the alpha male,* the characteristics and identification of the alpha male. Kate Ludeman is the

---

[5] Contributed by Roger "Mack" Hinson (M.D.), Nova Southeastern University.

founder and CEO of Work Ethic in Carpinteria, California. Eddie Erlandson is a senior vice president at Worth Ethic, and the former chief of staff at St. Joseph Mercy Hospital in Ann Arbor, Michigan. Together they have coached more than 1,000 senior executives. They are the authors of *Radical Change, Radical Results* (Dearborn Trade Publishing, 2003). They note that the majority of senior executives qualify as alpha males under their taxonomy. Alpha males rise to their positions of power based on their innate intelligence and their action-oriented personalities. They are motivated by success and feel driven to produce results. These very characteristics that have served them so well over the course of their careers are often the characteristics that begin to cause interference in the alpha male's continued development. The authors note that alpha males "take extraordinarily high levels of performance for granted" (Ludeman and Erlandson, 2004). The constant pressure that the alpha male exerts on his work associates wears on them over time. The need of the alpha male for the rapid processing of information leads them to have difficulty with listening. Listening is often a meaningless ritual as the alpha male has usually decided on a course of action. The lack of listening skills not only antagonizes coworkers, but it robs the alpha male of the advice of other parties.

Alpha males often have the attitude that they know best. This self-assuredness and external assertiveness about their correctness is often very intimidating. This intimidation makes coworkers uneasy and erodes the sense of teamwork that should ideally exist. This situation also increases the likelihood that time and energy will be spent navigating around the alpha male in order to avoid conflicts with the omniscient alpha male. It is important to note that alpha males are generally very data driven. This is essential to understand in coaching them and important to understand in otherwise dealing with the alpha male. Numbers tend to impress them more than feelings. Feelings and emotions are looked at with disfavor by the alpha male. A tightly reasoned, data rich presentation is more likely to meet with the approval of the alpha male as opposed to an emotional appeal. This lack of emotion is inwardly driven. Alpha males are not terribly introspective as a group and they often deny feelings and emotions within them with subsequent predictable consequences such as anger and lashing out. Ludeman and Erlandson note three traps that a coach can fall into: coming across as too passive; too much secrecy; and kowtowing. The coach must be equally as data driven as the alpha male. He or she cannot be viewed as emotional and weak by the alpha male. This will generate a lack of respect fatal to any coaching attempt. Secrecy defeats the purpose of the coaching. One of the main effects of coaching an alpha male is the development of the ability to demonstrate or model new and inclusive behaviors. If the coworkers cannot see any improvement or changes, then the coaching is irrelevant. The coach must also be viewed as an equally powerful peer of the alpha male. If there is no respect for the coach, there is unlikely to ultimately be any coaching accomplished. Ludeman and Erlandson conclude by noting five steps toward alpha growth: admit vulnerability, accept responsibility, connect with underlying emotions, balance the positive with critical feedback, and become aware of patterns (Ludeman and Erlandson, 2004). The first three steps, admitting vulnerability, accepting responsibility, and connecting with underlying emotions both underline the usual alpha male's lack of introspection and self-awareness. Any coaching process that aims to produce external change must first address these internal issues. Feedback about how an alpha male is perceived by his coworkers and feedback about how the coaching process is effecting change is essential for a successful coaching interaction. The feedback should relate the good, but the hard truths that exist should not be minimized. It is only through the realization of the difficulties that they can be overcome. Finally, pattern recognition allows the alpha male to perceive when he is defaulting to a tried and true alpha behavior and understand how this behavior may or may not be constructive in a certain situation.

Ludeman and Erlandson's article is of much practical value to leaders in healthcare organizations. By definition, most physicians have something, if not a lot, of the alpha male within them. Physicians, for example, often wield immense influence and power within their organizations. They have sought out a career in which action and decision-making are crucial. The decisions are at times life and death ones. It requires a confident, responsible, and driven person to do this sort of job. These characteristics are necessary in measure, but they can often present problems if demonstrated inappropriately. Most physicians occupy a spectrum on the alpha male scale. At one end are the typically collaborative doctors who are directive only when necessary. But even amongst these doctors, there often is an expectation that "if I'm working this hard, others should be as well." The consequence of this attitude is often frustration and irritation at the work habits of coworkers. The preoccupation with getting results often means that the alpha doctor is not a terribly good listener. Their mind is racing ahead in the conversation. They think about other topics or what they are going to say instead of really listening to the other person. It often conveys disregard or arrogance. At the other end of the spectrum is the disruptive physician. They often display their alpha maleness in full color to everyone with whom they work. The behavior usually impedes the productivity of the alpha male.

In *Coaching the alpha male* article, the authors mention many important approaches for influencing or coaching an alpha doctor or an alpha professional in any workplace. It points out the value in physician leadership. The alpha doctor will use the excuse that "he does not understand what I do" with a non-physician coach. It allows the physician coach equal footing in the coaching interaction. It was also a quite practical approach to describe the alpha male coaching process in terms of internal and external facets. The primary goal of coaching a disruptive physician is to change his/her behavior. *Coaching the alpha male* article points out repeatedly that until the internal focus is adjusted and more self-awareness created, there will not be a persistent external change in behavior. It requires honest discussions about the alpha doctor's behaviors and the effect of these behaviors on coworkers. Insistence on accountability of the alpha doctor not just for his behavior, but for the ripple effect of his behavior on others is a major tool to demonstrate why the behavior must be changed. Beneficial behavior change is the external proof to others of the alpha male's commitment to the team and organization.

## Gaining People's Trust during Acquisitions[6]

Many of today's successful organizations have experienced phenomenal growth, enabling them to continue investing in and realizing tremendous benefits through economies of scale in such areas as improved recruitment, increased investment in research and education, stronger infrastructures in terms of technology and human resources as well as other fiduciary strengths. Through joint ventures, mergers, and acquisitions, some organizations are able to experience continuous growth throughout the United States, Europe, and Asian markets. Continuous growth, joint ventures and acquisitions tend to bring change, stress, and morale issues that managers and coaches must deal with on a regular basis. Furthermore, in their day-to-day operations, there can be many more obstacles that must be overcome as managers attempt to align their organization's culture and motivation with their desired objectives as they seek improvements in productivity, quality of service, and a competitive advantage in the industry. This short section explores the premise that an invaluable factor impacting the success of a joint venture, merger or acquisition is management's ability to garner employee trust. It explores a variety of factors which impact management's perceived trustworthiness, emphasizing the value of effective and honest communication.

A prominent source of stress in any workplace is change, and nothing guarantees change more than an acquisition. Employees contend with stress stemming from a wide range of concerns initially generated by the announcement of their organization's acquisition. Although their resulting behavior is influenced by a variety of factors, research has shown that there are methods associated with proper managerial behaviors that engender success by effectively communicating and addressing a common source of difficulties: fears stemming from the uncertainty of employment.

The commitment and willingness of employees to collaborate in developing a productive working relationship hinges upon the perceived trustworthiness of management. It is important to note that although perceptions of management's trustworthiness after an acquisition are influenced by situational and personal factors, understanding the synthesis of these perceptions is integral in designing plans for integration of the acquired entity. Nikandrou, Papalexandris and Bourantas argue that perceptions are affected by "the way acquired employees perceive communication regarding the acquisition, the nature of the interpersonal relations with "new" employees, the uncertainty associated with the acquisition and employee tolerance to change" (Nikandrou, Papalexandris & Bourantas, 2000). The authors propose and support through their research that management benefits through frequent communication with employees before, during, and after the acquisition. Not all details can be communicated, but merely inquiring after or expressing their concern for employees will positively impact the perception employees have of their new management. For management to have a lasting and profound impact on the perception of their trustworthiness, however, communication must always be open and sincere, as well as relevant to the employees' concerns. If such efforts are undertaken, the potential for a successful integration is much higher.

---

[6] Contributed by Jay Martin, Nova Southeastern University.

Frequent and honest communication will demonstrate integrity, but management needs to also develop quality relationships with members of the acquired entity. Solid relations between employees engender a collaborative work environment (as opposed to a competitive one) and inspire the view that management is committed to group cohesion. These perceptions will bolster the trustworthiness of management, positively impacting motivation and commitment of employees from the acquired entity.

Perhaps the most difficult aspect of integrating an acquired entity is responding to uncertainty. Abilities and opinions about uncertainty in any given situation differs from individual to individual; however, any lack of clarity or communication of management's intentions will undermine efforts to successfully integrate employees into the company's culture and operations. Again, communication with acquired employees has been shown to reduce uncertainty which will in turn create a more favorable environment to embrace change.

A critical consideration is the impact that the speed of change imparts upon the acquired employees. Depending upon the situation, different considerations need to be addressed to achieve the greatest success. Nikandrou, Papalexandris and Bourantas note that although the perception of management imposing changes is not optimal, in any acquisition there is an expectation of change that should be met within the limits of the situation. The key here seems to be the level and quality of communications and relationships that exist at the time changes are implemented. Of course, change for its own sake is not justifiable and management must ensure that their integrity and trustworthiness is unassailable during this transitional period.

The issues and concerns raised are critical for management's consideration when acquiring another entity if they are to successfully incorporate the acquisition's existing employees into their culture and workforce. Developing the opportunity and coordinating the efforts aimed at an acquisition is important, but the development and implementation of an effective integration plan is critical to capture the expected value of the acquisition.

Are the developed integration plans robust, appropriately addressing the concerns noted in the article by Nikandrou, Papalexandris and Bourantas? If not, where and why do the perceived disconnects exist? How do acquired employees perceive their relevant value to the acquiring entity? Is this perception impacting their productivity? Could communications before acquisition be improved to facilitate the integration of the acquired entity? If not, could communications be improved or accelerated at the time of acquisition to address fears spawned by uncertainty amongst the acquired entity's employees? These are relevant questions that all coaches, managers and leaders in every industry should explore and answer in order for their firms or organizations to develop high performing workers and successfully compete in today's business environment.

## Approaching Destructive Behavior[7]

The article by Andre Delbecq (2001) has specific relevance to the identification, evaluation, and management of highly trained professionals with

---

[7] Contributed by Keith S. Meredith (M.D.), Nova Southeastern University.

destructive behavior. Gaining a specific competence in this area, whether coaching the individual with destructive behavior or coaching an executive to gain skill to do so, is crucial to minimizing the negative impact this type of personality has on an organization. To emphasize this, Delbecq remarks in his commentary: "The evil individual sucks the life juices from the organizational group by unusually destructive behavior, crippling the group in such a way that all positive spirit is lost" (2001, p. 222). Delbecq states that during his years of addressing senior managers in executive seminars, he was struck by the frequency with which he was taken aside and asked to address the impact that remarkable individuals with powerfully disruptive influences have on change. These individuals were seen as "a singular and destructive force in their organization whose behavior was outside their normal experience as senior executives" (Delbecq, 2001, p. 221). Fully eighty-eight percent of the senior executives he queried expressed that at least once in their leadership tenure they encountered a personality they would loosely describe as "evil." Most of these executives also believed that they intuitively recognized this aberrant personality sooner than they had facts to support this insight; reacted too late to their presence; and felt poorly equipped to deal with them because traditional policies and procedures were inadequate.

A colleague is fond of saying: "Sanctimony is the last refuge of the defenseless" (Roger Hinson, personal communication, 2006). In this quip, Dr. Hinson has nicely described the position these personalities take. Especially in the medical profession, where the focus on patient care is an unquestioned value, much negativity can be levied in the name of patient outcome. These individuals are commonly quite brilliant and destructively divisive; they tend to use a fairly narrow range of self-determined perspective to assess the value of actions and group directions and to separate groups into supporters and non-supporters. They are vigorous politicians and rarely show their destructive and controlling tendencies upward. If this individual happens to be an administrator, they use carefully managed resource allocation to gain and keep power.

According to Delbecq, the disingenuous behavior common to these individuals is rarely appreciated by leadership until damage has already occurred. This appears to be true because these individuals rarely become apparent to leadership. Their initial impact is on peers and colleagues by subverting innovation and change. This subversion is not so much the natural resistive reaction to change that most feel as it is a clear attempt to thwart change management with the intention of creating failure. In this atmosphere co-workers become fearful of creativity and innovation and choose instead to become self-protective. The greater good of the organization and its customers become secondary to self-preservation. Delbecq describes affected organizational units as being "composed of combat fatigued refugees" (Delbecq, 2001, p. 223). The attuned leader should be aware of inconsistent behaviors (differing upward from downward); watch for changing unit morale; and investigate unraveling change dynamics and loss of team innovation. Delbecq quotes a particularly relevant paper which describes the attributes of the disruptive physician. In this paper Pfifferling says "the disruptive physician or professional undermines practice morale, heightens turnover in the organization, steals from productive activities, increases the risks for ineffective or substandard practice, and causes distress among colleagues" (Pfifferling, 1999, p. 58).

The development of a proactive approach to this potentially destructive force is where the importance of coaching becomes clear. Action taken to develop the culture that immediately identifies and marginalizes these individuals will avoid unit chaos and limit encroachment upon morale and productivity. Establishing mutually agreed upon behavioral norms that define collegial behavior, decision making processes and values will develop the culture that creates non-negotiable behavioral expectations and one of personal accountability. In addition to this, early recognition and action is necessary to avoid the appearance that norms are negotiable. As soon as there is the appearance of norm violation tolerance, the individual who, by his or her behavior, establishes the new norms becomes the *de facto* leader.

In developing the skills needed to recognize and address the type of damaging behavior described by Delbecq resides one of the many competencies a coach may bring to an executive or professional in any workplace. The mitigation of the damage possible by such an individual will easily create a positive return on investment.

## *Summary*

Coaching and performance management is about continuous and strategic collaboration, commitment and communication among all the parties involved to meet the needs of one's clients, customers, employees, and bosses and thereby gain a competitive advantage. In the 2006 Annual Employee Appreciation Day (December 13, 2006) at Nova Southeastern University to an audience of approximately 1,500 employees, President Ray Ferrero mentioned that he has advised all NSU administrators to make the coming year a year of the three Cs: collaboration, commitment and communication. President Ferrero, as an effective coach, encouraged all NSU leaders and program managers to follow the same advice and continuously collaborate with their people, jointly commit to quality work and communicate with each other effectively to resolve the day to day obstacles. Dr. Abraham Fischler, founder of NSU, who was being honored for his forty years of service to the University, mentioned that President Ferrero and Nova Southeastern University have been successful in the last decade due to the quality of continuous collaboration, commitment and communication among managers, faculty members, and their departmental staff. He further encouraged everyone in the audience to continue this process of effective collaboration, commitment and communication as it is the essence of effective leadership, performance and coaching.

While presidents, directors and other organizational leaders can certainly serve as formal and informal coaches to thousands of their people in the organization, ultimately it is the manager that can work on a one-to-one basis with his or her individual employees. While interacting on a one-to-one basis, a manager/coach should dig deeper into his or her employee's abilities and see the person's performance possibilities and capacities to perform bigger and better things. Coaches understand the expression that "Only those who can see the invisible can do the impossible." These coaches and managers should understand the financial, personal, professional, and motivational needs of their employees.

After being interviewed by the school administration and various senior level "coaches," a colleague mentioned that an "eager teaching prospect" said the following:

> Let me see if I've got this right. You want me to go into that room with all those kids, and fill their every waking moment with a love for learning, and I'm supposed to instill a sense of pride in their ethnicity, modify their disruptive behavior, observe them for signs of abuse and even censor their T-shirt messages and dress habits.
>
> You want me to wage a war on drugs and sexually transmitted diseases, check their backpacks for weapons of mass destruction, and raise their self esteem.
>
> You want me to teach them patriotism, good citizenship, sportsmanship, fair play, how to register to vote, how to balance a checkbook, and how to apply for a job. I am to check their heads for lice, maintain a safe environment, recognize signs of anti-social behavior, make sure all students pass the state exams, even those who don't come to school regularly or complete any of their assignments.
>
> Plus, I am to make sure that all of the students with disabilities get an equal education regardless of the extent of their mental or physical abilities. I am to communicate regularly with the parents by letter, telephone, newsletter and report card.
>
> All of this I am to do with just a piece of chalk, a computer, a few books, a bulletin board, a big smile AND on a starting salary that qualifies my family for food stamps! You want me to do all of this and then you tell me to further increase my performance without any financial incentives! Are you kidding me? (Anonymous; electronic communication on December 2006).

Leaders and managers should understand that effective coaches focus on the fairness of their work schedules, talent requirements, and compensation strategies. Coaching is a function of each leader and manager, not just human resource professionals. Even the role of the Human Resources (HR) department is now shifting, and that means that the roles and responsibilities of HR professionals are changing each day as they become more involved in strategic initiatives of the company. Increasingly complex organizational needs are placing high demands on the HR function and the ability to integrate the basic HR disciplines is essential to success. The coaching concepts can give one the knowledge and skills to excel not only as a manager, but also as a human resource professional as well. With human resource professionals becoming a strategic partner in each organization, it is important to understand what strategic HR actually means. *Strategic human resource management* refers to the organizational use of all employees as long-term partners of the firm, including those in the human resources department, to gain and/or keep a competitive advantage against competitors in the industry. Of course, human resource professionals are also responsible for the training and development of all their managers and employees. The training process should be viewed both narrowly and broadly as it is often tied to a variety of organizational purposes. In a limited sense, training provides employees with specific, identifiable knowledge and skills for use in their present jobs. Development, on the other hand, is broader in scope and focuses on individuals gaining new capabilities useful for both present and future jobs. Human resource professionals are also responsible for making sure people are paid well. In regard to compensation strategies, employers must be reasonably competitive with several types of compensation to attract and retain competent employees. Besides fair and lucrative compensation packages, today's employees expect their employers to provide work environments that are safe, secure, and healthy. Effective performance management programs and systems, using the material discussed in this book, can increase the likelihood that employees will perform their jobs well and become productive members of the organization.

Effective coaches can increase the performance of their organizations, teams and employees by showing appreciation and the creation of a motivational work environment for everyone. The following are some statements and languages of gratitude that have been used in employee appreciation plaques and certificates that can be adopted or duplicated by coaches and managers when appropriate.

- *Thank you; you are a great success.* On the other side of the door to failure is the key to success. Just insert it in the lock and give it a turn and a push. All it takes is a little effort. You are our key to success. Every day, you turn and push, and make the door to success open wide. Thank you for your creativity, push and hard work on the team.
- *Thank you; way to go.* Some people just love their jobs. They come to work every day with smiles on their faces, always wanting to do their best, without thinking about external rewards. Often, these people never realize how much they are appreciated. You are one of these people, so we're letting you know, in no uncertain terms, how valuable you are to our company. Thank you for all that you do to help the team.
- *Thank you; you are phenomenal.* You are constantly stretching your mind, reaching for greatness and lifting yourself higher and higher until you touch the stars. Your effort and dedication show in everything you do, and your continual perseverance to achieve excellence makes you a valuable member of this department and company. We appreciate your quality work. Thank you for all that you do.
- *You are a shining star.* In the night sky, there always seems to be one star shining brighter than most. Even though there are hundreds of stars in the sky, this one stands out. Its twinkle is truer, its gleam is greater. This one is extra special because it shines through even in the darkest night. You are a shining star. We appreciate all your hard work.
- *You are a star.* The thing people notice most about a star is how brightly it shines. The brighter the star, the more it stands out from all the other stars in the sky. Of all the stars in the universe, we're glad YOU chose to shine in our company. We appreciate you and your contributions.
- *Thank you for your great "SERVICE."*
  - *S* is the support you provide; your loyalty is true.
  - *E* is for eagerness; your great attitude shines through.
  - *R* is for reaching; you always aim high.
  - *V* is for value; your worth goes beyond the sky.

- ○ *I* is for ideas; you help our company grow.
- ○ *C* is for conviction; it means more than you could know.
- ○ *E* is for excellence in everything you do.

Put it all together, and we happily get YOU! Thank you for your dedicated service to this team and organization.

## *Discussion Questions*

1. What are the most difficult aspects of coaching?
2. Is coaching the job of human resource managers? Discuss.
3. What can coaches and managers do to provide an inspirational work environment for their employees? Discuss.
4. What is strategic human resource management? How is it different from traditional human resource management practices? Discuss.
5. What kind of person in what kind of role would be most effective as an alignment coach? What kind of background would you want to see? Would it be better if that person was an outside consultant or a company employee?
6. Should coachees be assigned mentors to aid in their growth and development or is the coaching relationship sufficient?
7. Openness about the need for changes in behavior and openness about the change process can demonstrate to coworkers and the organization that the alpha male is working to improve his interactions. How much openness and transparency is enough? Is there a limit to what should be shared with a larger group, if so, how do you know what this limit is? Is there a downside to openness and transparency in coaching the alpha male?
8. Have you identified an individual in your immediate world who behaves in a destructive fashion? If so, what were the characteristics that brought him/her to your attention and what steps can you take to lessen his/her negative impact? Do you feel you currently possess the skills to deal with this scenario?
9. Why is it important for companies and their managers to be involved in effective coaching and performance management practices?
10. Identify one person (worker, colleague or friend) that you need to coach. Determine how you are going to approach him or her regarding the coaching situation. How are you going to describe the problem or expectations to this person? What are you going to say to get his/her agreement about the problem and improving it? What are some possible solutions that you and the person can agree upon?

# CHAPTER 2

## Performance Management

Many organizations, managers and leaders are working diligently to make sure their organizations perform and stay competitive in today's global workplace. They understand that true long-term competitiveness can only come from the best use of their available resources in the organization. Organizations must make effective use of their human, financial, physical, capital, and other such available resources if they are to be, and remain, competitive in their industries. While most organizations promote the idea that their people resources are their most important asset, few firms truly put sufficient emphasis on the development of this important and mission-critical asset. In other words, a number of these organizations simply provide "lip-service" about people being their most important asset. If managers and leaders of these firms are truly caring about their most important asset, their people, then they should also be serious about the growth, development and productivity of each worker in the firm. This might require a substantial and dramatic investment in performance management and disciplined coaching related programs. Someone once said that about one-half of life is luck and the other half is discipline; the discipline is the important half, for without discipline one would not know what to do with luck. Similarly, performance management is basically a disciplined process of discovering, identifying, recognizing, measuring, aligning, and strategically developing the performance capabilities of an organization's human resources asset toward worthwhile and predetermined goals.

H. Wayne Huizenga, who as a coach and an entrepreneur has been called a visionary leader, agrees that it is the capacity and capability of the organization's human resources that makes them do well and outshine their competitors. In the Super Bowl XLI Diversity Business Forum that was held on February 1, 2007 at the Miniaci Performing Arts Center of Nova Southeastern University, Mr. Huizenga said that the secret to his success and his organization's achievement has been the recruitment, hiring and development of great talent. The job of a great coach and an effective performance manager is exactly that: to recruit, hire, develop, and retain a talented group of individuals that can transform the organization's existing status from ordinary production and ranks to extraordinary performance by taking advantage of available opportunities through creative means. In this regard, performance management requires that coaches hire and surround themselves with talented individuals. Mr. Huizenga mentioned that hiring and retaining top talent is one trait of effective leadership, and the other important characteristic of successful leaders and entrepreneurs is that they are not afraid of "smart" people; rather, they are able to listen and learn from these professional experts. Effective coaches encourage and support the creativity of talented individuals to help them achieve their personal and professional dreams. The Diversity Business Forum was moderated by Jason Jackson and the panel members also included other great performance managers such as Cris Carter, Bernie J. Kosar Jr., Robert Porcher, and Lesley Visser who has been a successful Sports Reporter for CBS television network. All of these celebrities have performed well individually and, due to their ability to effectively work with others and communicate their vision, they are able to help their colleagues perform extraordinarily toward a brighter future. Their conclusion at the forum was that successful leaders, coaches and performance managers need to be open-minded, persistent about their dreams, goal-driven, great communicators and listeners, do what makes sense to them based on the situation, and they should also be polite to others. Furthermore, great performance managers must also be socially responsible and ethical in all of their dealings.

Besides being socially responsible, another important responsibility for today's managers, leaders, and coaches is to not only engage employees using their strengths and expertise, but to also engage them physically and mentally in their organizational tasks. Studies (Hymowitz, 2007; Welbourne, 2007) have consistently shown that a majority of today's workers are not effectively engaged at work; perhaps the blame falls with the managers, coaches, leaders, and the employees themselves. According to Teresa Welbourne (2007), president and chief executive officer of eePulse Inc., employee engagement in the twenty-first century workplace is one of the key topics in management because it is necessary for achieving higher and competitive organizational performance. Welbourne estimates that only about 14% to 30% of employees are actively engaged at work. Dr. Welbourne states that "In today's environment, where the employee contract has evolved considerably, the process by which we expect engagement to happen needs to be fully understood so that managers can change contract terms or other context issues to enable full employee engagement." In Welbourne's role-based performance model, she attempts to identify the types of employee behaviors that are needed to drive performance. Welbourne offers five key roles that employees tend to occupy at work: 1-Core job-holder role, or what's in the job description; 2-Entrepreneur role that involves coming up with innovative ideas; 3-Team member role, which includes working with others; 4-Career role to improve skills and knowledge; and 5-Organizational member role to undertake tasks that benefit the company. The goal for managers, leaders and coaches is to develop a firm's human resources by involving them in as many of their roles as possible so that the organization's culture cannot be easily replicated by their competition. Of course, the role models for being active, learning and developing should be the firm's managers, leaders and coaches if they are to create an environment where employees are actively engaged in their work and departmental achievements.

Observations and studies tend to show that today's managers are extremely busy with their long work hours and busy work schedules. As such, many managers are reporting low personal energy and some are even struggling to keep pace with their work loads and management roles as they feel exhausted, distracted and confused (Welbourne, 2007). If managers and leaders, the company's role models, are feeling overwhelmed, then they should also know that their behaviors are contagious and observing employees will probably feel much worse. Such feelings can lead to further fatigue, low morale, and lack of effective performance in the department. Managers and coaches can increase employee engagement in their organizations by having a work environment where engaged associates are appropriately and fairly rewarded as per their efforts. Of course, since employee engagement by itself is not always enough for high performance, managers and leaders must be the role models of what they expect from their employees. Since there is no panacea to quickly and actively engage employees, managers and coaches need to have an effective performance management system that starts at the top of the organization and moves its way throughout the business through fair and appropriate reward mechanisms.

### What is Performance Management?

Twenty-first century organizations and their leaders must understand and realize that their most important asset in achieving long-term success is not necessarily their technologies, but this competitive edge and the key to success lies in their people. This is why continuous coaching and developing of each person in the organization is so critical in today's competitive workplace. Coaching and developing people are important elements of a holistic paradigm for the growth and development of organizations through effective performance management systems. Professor Herman Aguinis, in his book entitled *Performance Management*, defined performance management as the "continuous process of identifying, measuring, and developing the performance of individuals and teams and aligning performance with the strategic goals of the organization" (2007, p. 2). This definition emphasizes that an effective performance management program requires continuous feedback and improvement processes for the development of people. Aguinis states that "A system that involves employee evaluations once a year without an ongoing effort to provide feedback and coaching so that performance can be improved is not a true performance management system" (2007, p. 3). Furthermore, according to Aguinis, a performance management program that does not explicitly make clear the employee's contribution to the goals of the organization is not a true performance management system. Aguinis highlights that a true performance management system makes the following contributions with regard to employee performance, morale and organization (2007, pp. 4-6):

1. Motivation for performance increases.
2. Self-esteem of each employee increases.
3. Managers gain more information about their employees on a regular basis.
4. The definition of jobs and various tasks become clearer.
5. Self-insight and growth opportunities are enhanced.
6. Various administrative actions are more fair and relevant.
7. The organization's goals are clear to everyone.
8. Employees are more competent.
9. There is a better protection from lawsuits.
10. There is better and timely differentiation between good and poor performers.

11. The manager's perception of an employee's performance is communicated more clearly on a regular basis.
12. Change is facilitated more effectively.

Aguinis mentions the following characteristics as important ingredients of an ideal performance management system: strategic congruence, thoroughness, practicality, meaningfulness, specificity, identification of effective and ineffective performance, reliability, validity, acceptability and fairness, inclusiveness, openness, correctability, standardization, and ethicality (2007, p. 17). The successful implementation of a comprehensive performance management system can provide everyone the direction and support they need to enhance and improve their productivity and standards on a regular basis. Besides serving as important input or feeders to the organization's developmental efforts, performance management programs can also provide information for effective workforce planning and compensation projections. A comprehensive performance management program allows managers to gain relevant and timely insights into their employees' goals, desires and abilities, thereby enabling them to execute better motivational strategies and fairer evaluation methods for each person as per his or her performance. For employees, a comprehensive performance management program can clarify their jobs, the expectation of managers from them, as well as the perception of managers regarding their performance for each task and responsibility. A good comprehensive performance management program also provides relevant and timely information for those who need training, the type of training, and how they should be rewarded for meeting departmental and organizational goals. In addition, a comprehensive performance management program is an ongoing and never-ending process. According to Aguinis, a good performance management process includes six related components: prerequisites, performance planning, performance execution, performance assessment, performance review, and performance renewal and re-contracting (2007, p. 41).

According to James Rollo (2001), performance management is the process of continuously attracting, developing, and retaining talented employees. In his pocket guide book, entitled *Performance Management*, he provides supervisors, work groups, and human resource professionals with easy-to-use processes and forms for planning, supporting, counseling, mentoring, appraising, and recognizing employee performance. By reading this guide, one can learn how to effectively set measurable goals, build competencies, coach and mentor, conduct performance appraisals, and recognize accomplishments. One purpose of performance management in regard to people development is that effective coaching can build an employee's confidence and commitment while resolving performance and attitude problems on a just-in-time basis.

### Trends in Performance Management

The outcomes of an effective and comprehensive performance management program should be satisfied and productive employees, better bottom-line profits, and a better competitive position in the market or industry. Traditionally, performance management programs have been devalued due to the fact that most organizations viewed it as a single or "stand alone" initiative, rather than a strategic tool to enhance performance and achieve organizational productivity. Some people have viewed performance management programs as "touchy feely" initiatives that simply do not add much value to the organization, while others have seen it as being out of touch from the needs of an organization's human resource asset. Other reasons for the "devalued" view of performance management programs can be attributed to the view that it is considered as extra work to complete the required forms, its perception that it is part of some legal requirement by the human resource department, lack of proper training for understanding the process and its core elements, and the fact that often employees and managers are not included in the initial design and implementation processes.

According to James Rollo (2001), the new trends toward a comprehensive performance management program is that it is now designed by, and for, managers and their employees. Since managers and employees do not want to spend too much time with useless paperwork, the forms and processes are often planned as per their needs and in simple formats. The new trends in comprehensive performance management program include the fact that groups and teams are now taking the ownership of processes that are designed and agreed upon for their use. The new processes designed for comprehensive performance management programs are used not only by the managers and employees but also by others in the organization to make better decisions through the Human Resource Management Department. Another important trend in today's performance management programs is that the processes are linked to measurable results for the individual, department, and organization. In other words, managers and employees are now consumers of the results produced and created by the integrative and comprehensive performance management programs. Such data, and many of these forms and processes, are also available for use by managers and employees through cyberspace technologies in the organization's websites, or intranets that can be accessed by a firm's associates.

### Benefits of Performance Management

Modern organizations are constantly in search of appropriate tools and processes for the recruitment, staffing, development, and retention of competent professionals at least costs to their bottom-line profits. Many are discovering that a comprehensive performance management program can help them effectively deal with the accelerated rate of organizational change for quickly identifying and developing the needed competencies in their employees. Rollo (2001) mentions the following benefits for an effective and comprehensive performance management program:

1. Clarifies the core skills needed for the tasks to be achieved successfully.
2. Provides metrics for individuals and teams to regularly assess their own skills.
3. Creates an environment where each person can have and own his/her own personal skill development plan.
4. Encourages developmental training programs.
5. Clarifies the skills and competencies needed to effectively perform a task.

Furthermore, a comprehensive performance management program allows each employee to take a leadership role for his/her performance and develop his/her skills on a continuous basis. A comprehensive performance management program should develop employees' leadership and communication skills, expose them to other functional areas and tasks, provide opportunities for colleagues to meet each other and acquire new technical and business expertise, help everyone become more confident about their tasks and jobs, build employee ownership with regard to their tasks and final products, create a more empowering work environment, reduce employee turnover and social loafing, and free up more time for managers to focus on other long-term strategic initiatives.

### Performance Management Skills

A performance management program should be comprehensive and inclusive of a system's view of the organization. In other words, a performance management program must take a holistic view of the firm and should lead to a learning organization. An effective performance management program exists and functions to identify, develop, coach, and utilize the talents of each individual in the organization. Coaching in this sense means *assessing* the needs of each individual, *counseling* him or her toward higher performance, *training* or *supporting* the individual by providing the needed resources and "know-how" to successfully complete each task, and *encouraging* or *mentoring* the person to become more and grow as a human being. In a performance management program, the job of the coach could be summed-up with such adjectives as: assessing, counseling, training, supporting, encouraging, and mentoring to name a few. This coaching should be a part of the comprehensive performance management program that includes performance assessment, performance plans, teamwork, communication, goal setting, performance appraisals and employee discipline, and recognition programs. Such a comprehensive and integrative performance management program can be proactive and responsive to the needs of the individual employee as well as the objectives of the organization. While there are many experts and skills that should be involved in a comprehensive performance management program, the most critical skill that is required from all managers and leaders is that of coaching. Aguinis mentions that:

> Performance management systems are not likely to help employees develop and improve their performance if managers do not have the necessary skills to help employees accomplish these goals. Such skill include being able to serve as coaches, to observe and document performance accurately, to give both positive and negative feedback, and to conduct useful and constructive performance review discussion (2001, p. 197).

According to Aguinis, coaching is a continuous process of collaborations between the manager and his/her employees where the superior takes an active role in their performance. This coaching process involves directing employees, motivating them to achieve the stated goals and standards, and providing the right incentives through an effective and fair reward program. In this sense, coaching is an ongoing, day-to-day activity in observing employee performance, correcting poor behavior and results, and rewarding good performance. Aguinis mentions that coaching involves giving advice, providing guidance, giving support, increasing employees' confidence, and helping them gain greater competence through knowledge and skill acquisition in their area of responsibility. Aguinis (2007, p. 198) writes that coaching can assist managers to turn feedback into results by establishing development objectives, communicating effectively, motivating employees, documenting performance, giving timely feedback, diagnosing performance problems, and developing employees on a regular basis.

According to author James Rollo (2001), "The single most powerful component of a Performance Management System is the coaching of employees by the supervisor and other individual mentors" (p. 89). Rollo states that:

> Coaching is at the heart of caring for an individual's success as a person and as an employee. It is taking the time to listen, provide direction, counsel, teach, and challenge. Above all, coaching is showing a sincere commitment to the individual. Coaching goes beyond personal employee growth. Results-oriented coaching contributes to meeting organizational needs. Providing career direction in the context of organizational needs enables the employee to plan how he or she can further contribute to the organizational long-term goals. Tutoring and skill transfer are done in the context of how these skills are to be applied to business initiatives. By linking coaching to organizational needs, the coaching process becomes mutually beneficial to the individual and the organization (Rollo, 2001, p. 89).

James Rollo (2001, p. 91) offers four types of coaching which can be applied by organizational leaders, managers and employees as part of a comprehensive performance management program. The four complimentary and at times overlapping coaching types are:

1. *Counseling.* Through counseling, coaches can create awareness of changes in the employee's feelings, attitudes and behaviors that are negatively impacting the work done by him or her or others in the process.
2. *Teaching.* Teaching and tutoring is the process of transferring skills and knowledge to the employee as per the individual's needs.
3. *Mentoring.* Coaches can serve as mentors to provide a better perspective to the associate about his/her current organizational fit and possible future contributions to the firm.
4. *Challenging.* Coaches can challenge their associates to eliminate performance gaps and stagnations in meeting individual or departmental objectives.

There are many situations that require an intervention or coaching from managers and organizational leaders where counseling, teaching, mentoring, and challenging the employee can be beneficial. A manager should provide coaching, if and, when a person asks for advice or help, performance is not up to standard, there is an unresolved conflict, a person's attitudes and behaviors are negatively impacting the work environment, there is an opportunity to improve morale or performance, there is a new task or skill that needs to be performed, and when an individual requires more information to successfully get his or her job completed. Coaches need to have excellent listening skills if they are to effectively assess when and what type of coaching is required for their colleagues and employees. Listening is a skill that requires active attention to the speaker, his or her environment, his or her body language and other non-verbal messages, and the confirmation of what is being heard and understood. In other words, listening is a skill and it should be perfected by managers and leaders so they can serve as effective coaches. Rollo (2001) recommends that in order for one to become an effective listener, one must believe that listening to others is worth the time and energy. Therefore, one must truly believe that listening can provide more information about the person or is helpful for better communication and relationship development. Even if one does not believe that listening to a person can lead to better understanding, letting the other person speak and truly hearing him or her can certainly lead to a better relationship with the person.

## Performance Appraisals

An important element of any comprehensive performance management program is to have an effective performance appraisal process. Wendell L. French (2007, p. 359) defines performance management programs or systems as a process where "companies ensure that employees are working toward organizational goals." A comprehensive or systemic view of performance management programs would include strategic planning, departmental responsibility, promotional patterns, compensation plans, succession planning and development, education and training development, performance appraisals, and employee discipline components. Performance appraisals, as one component of an effective performance management program, is defined as "the formal, systematic assessment of how well employees are performing their jobs in relation to established standards and the dialogue about that assessment with employees" (French, 2007, p. 359). The way and manner in which appraisal systems are implemented and how the results are communicated with employees and managers can affect morale, the department's work environment, and the productivity and performance of the organization. Performance appraisals and standards are now more likely to be tied to specific outcomes such as customer satisfaction, production levels of products being produced, the quality of products being produced, and the skill development of employees in relation to their jobs.

A *performance appraisal* is basically a formal interaction between the manager and employee to discuss the employee's achievements, progress, performance gaps, and developmental plans for the future. Performance appraisals can be formal or informal. *Informal appraisals* between employees, team leaders, senior colleagues, and their managers take place on a continuous basis as they interact with and through each other to produce products or serve their customers. *Formal appraisals* tend to be more strategic, standardized, periodic, and become a part of an employee's historical records in the company. It is important that managers recognize the importance of ongoing and standardized formal performance appraisals. Managers should not wait for the standardized and periodic performance appraisal periods to discuss performance challenges with their employees. Appraisals, even on a formal basis, should be ongoing and continuous. Of course, the purpose of the ongoing and continuous appraisal process should be task-specific and developmental.

While performance appraisals tend to have their evaluation goals, they must also emphasize the coaching and developmental objectives as well. French (2007, p. 360) cites the work of Michael Beer and mentions that evaluation goals can include: giving feedback to employees so they are aware of their work and performance status; developing valid data for compensation and promotion decisions and a means of effectively communicating such assessments; and helping managers make retention and termination decisions for a fair disciplinary process. On the other side, coaching and development goals can include the following (French, 2007, p. 360):

1. Guiding and directing employees to improve their current and future performance.
2. Increasing employees' commitment to the organization through strategic and succession planning.
3. Providing motivation through support, encouragement and appropriate incentives.
4. Enhancing employees' relationship with their superiors.
5. Proactively assessing and diagnosing personal and professional challenges facing the individual or organization.

The goals of all performance appraisals, evaluative and developmental, are to create competent employees with the right behaviors, skills and attributes to efficiently achieve the stated organizational objectives. If appraisals are mainly and primarily used for evaluation of the employee regarding pay, promotion, discipline, discharge, and layoffs, then such a process is likely to produce anxiety for employees and managers. However, if performance appraisals and evaluations are mainly used to develop employees and enhance their potential to do more, learn more, and achieve more, then it is more likely to achieve its objectives and lead to a productive and trusting work environment. A high level of trust between employees and their bosses regarding the managers' best interest about the well-being of their associates can lead to more effective and open communication as well as the achievement of the organization's goals in a much more productive manner.

A performance appraisal process allows both the manager and the employee to clarify their understandings and expectations about the job and plans for the future. Historically, performance appraisals have been one-sided where the manager provides a numerical assessment of the employee's performance over the last six months or year. Traditionally, many firms' performance appraisal processes have included such a rating process as a 5 for excellent work, 4 for above average, 3 for average, 2 for below average, and 1 for unacceptable performance with regard to customer service, attendance, teamwork, communication, cooperative, initiative, and other such elements. Such numerical assessments are often unclear, subjective, and of little value to the future development of the employee, especially when conducted without much quality interaction between the manager and employee. If a performance appraisal process is to be an effective element of a comprehensive performance management program, it must be clear, objective, developmental, and continuous.

Rollo (2001) emphasizes that an effective performance appraisal process should reinforce both individual and team performance. According to Rollo, "the intent of a dual appraisal process is to reinforce the importance of an individual's looking beyond self-accomplishment to how he or she contributes to the work group's goals" (p. 105). According to Rollo, performance appraisal systems that have both an individual and work group component tend to:

1. Create accountability for meeting the stated performance expectations.
2. Link individual and work group performance outcomes to the goals of the organization.
3. Provide appreciation and recognition to both the individual as well as the work group for job well done.
4. Identify skill areas that need to and should be developed.
5. Create the basis for performance improvement interactions.
6. Reinforce the importance of individual contribution to the group.
7. Provide a basis for compensation and promotion decisions.
8. Lay the foundation for future developmental plans for the individual and group goals.
9. Provide motivation for continuous improvement.

### Performance Appraisal Elements and Process

According to most experts, an effective performance appraisal system should provide a sense of purpose, empowerment, vision of what needs to be done, incentive for achieving the outcomes, and ownership in the process. Rollo (2001, p. 107) states the following elements as being essential for an effective performance appraisal process:

- *Purposeful.* Clearly define the purpose of the process for both the manager and employee.
- *Shared ownership.* Design the appraisal process and forms with input from managers and employees who are going to be using them. Such involvement from the outset can create relevance as well as ownership.
- *Practical.* Create processes, tasks and forms that are easy to use and understand. The criteria for evaluation must be specific and measurable. Furthermore, the major aspects of the employee's job should be reflected in the appraisal form.
- *Trained.* Effective training should be conducted for managers and employees to explain the purpose, process, roles, and the forms. Furthermore, training in the areas of effective communication and evaluation should be provided to create confidence and competence on the part of both employees and their managers.
- *Expectation-based.* Base the performance appraisal on a planned and documented set of expectations. This requires a planning discussion and interaction at the beginning of the process to clarify and agree upon the objectives, resources, and evaluation criteria.
- *Linked to rewards.* Clarify and reinforce the link between performance appraisal and some form of reward and recognition.
- *Promoted.* Promote the importance of performance appraisals through role models and integrity using the company's senior leaders. Senior leaders should talk about the process and use it with their direct associates.

Managers should remember that an effective performance appraisal process should involve both the supervisor and employee. It is a two-way discussion, interaction, and planning process to achieve a certain outcome that is beneficial to the employee and the organization. The performance appraisal process can greatly impact the relationship of managers with their employees. As such, managers should properly prepare and plan for it in order to create a high level of trust with their employees. Managers should remember that about 85% of the problems that do happen in their firms tend to be process related and not necessarily caused by people. So, if the process is fixed, the problems are likely to disappear. On the other side, about 15% of the problems are caused by people. In such cases, proper assessment of people-oriented skills and training needs through a gap analysis can be an initial stage. Then, training should be developed and implemented as part of the performance appraisal process. The link between the expected performance and reward should be clarified at the initial discussion among employees and managers. Overall, managers should base the performance appraisal process on planned and clarified objectives, roles, and mutually agreed-upon ratings. Managers should also avoid assessing everyone equally across the board. In other words, managers should take the time to plan the process, discriminate between excellent and mediocre performance, and genuinely assess each person's work while staying focused on the employee's future development as per his or her job requirements and personal dreams. An employee should not be surprised during the evaluation process. More importantly, the performance appraisal process should be future-oriented and developmental. In an ongoing and continuous performance appraisal process, employees are usually not unpleasantly surprised by the rating in the assessment of their work. Managers should do everything they can to avoid unpleasant surprises and continuous coaching can be a great solution to this dilemma. Of course, effective coaches and managers can use a discipline without punishment concept to meet desired performance objectives.

Performance appraisals are about both assessment of performance standards and growth / development of the employee. Whatever procedures are used in the performance appraisal processes, the focus should be on the assessment of duties performed, the standards established, and the future growth and development of the employee's skills to achieve what is agreed upon. The following procedures and steps can be used by managers to assess and coach an employee's performance (adopted from French, 2007, p. 379):

1. Prepare the employee by scheduling the session in advance. Both the manager and employee should assess the subordinate's performance in advance and come to the session prepared.
2. Establish a fair atmosphere so both individuals can communicate freely. Managers should try to put the employee at ease and make sure there are no interruptions during the scheduled time.
3. Mention the purpose of the session at the outset of the process. Make sure the employee understands this and is clear on the necessity of it.
4. Encourage the employee to participate. Employees can describe their own achievements and verbally assess their performance.

5. Understand or agree on the assessment of current performance as per the established goals by the organization or manager.
6. Agree on a future performance goal or goals. Make sure the standard or performance goals are clear to both the employee and manager.
7. Create a development plan. Discuss a plan for the employee to gain new skills, and managers should provide the resources and tools or suggest how they can be acquired.
8. Finalize a written and formal document that can be used to reach the stated goals and to assess achievement levels in the future appraisal sessions. Copies should be distributed to the employee, managers and the appropriate person in the human resource department as needed.

While the immediate boss is usually involved in facilitating the review, appraisals can be conducted by managers, employees, peers, customers, suppliers, vendors, and/or a combination of relevant stakeholders through a 360-degree process. Whatever processes or procedures are used, managers should ensure that employees are involved in their own performance assessment and development planning. Performance appraisal procedures can be helpful for managers and each organization should create a standardized process for everyone in the firm. When conducted effectively, performance appraisals become a part of the performance management systems for an organization by integrating and aligning each employee's goals with those of the organization. Since the assessment is often the responsibility of immediate managers and supervisors, the human resource department should provide sufficient training and development workshops to help them effectively plan for, conduct and implement individualized performance appraisals for their employees and colleagues.

### Performance Appraisal Quotations

You have heard of the statement "If you can't say anything nice, say nothing at all." Of course, while politeness is a good characteristic for every leader, managers and coaches have a responsibility to politely and constructively provide relevant feedback to their employees so they can learn from their work and grow. Dr. Randolph Pohlman states that "Not telling an employee that something is a problem so he or she can fix it, thrive and grow is not nice either" (Personal Communication, April 02, 2007). The key to effective coaching and performance management is to regularly provide appropriate and honest feedback to all employees in a professional and constructive manner.

The following quotes are actual statements made on employee performance evaluations. Such statements, verbally or in a written format, should be avoided as they do not lead to effective development of performance because they are derogatory, sarcastic and not behavior or performance based.

- ♥ Works well only when under constant supervision and when cornered like a rat in a trap.
- ♥ His men would follow him anywhere but only out of morbid curiosity.
- ♥ This employee is not so much of a has-been, but more of a definite won't be.

- ❤ Since my last report, he has reached rock bottom and has started to dig.
- ❤ He would be out of his depth in a parking lot puddle.
- ❤ She sets low personal standards and consistently fails to achieve them.
- ❤ This employee should go far, and the sooner he gets started, the better.
- ❤ This employee is depriving the village of an idiot.
- ❤ Not the sharpest knife in the drawer.
- ❤ He has a room temperature IQ.
- ❤ He has a photographic memory but with the lens cover glued on.
- ❤ She is a prime candidate for natural deselection.
- ❤ Bright as Alaska in December.
- ❤ Donated his brain to science before he was done using it.
- ❤ Gates are down, lights are flashing, but the train isn't coming.
- ❤ Has two brains; one is lost and the other is out looking for it.
- ❤ If brains were taxed, he would get a rebate.
- ❤ If he were anymore stupid, he would have to be watered twice a week.
- ❤ If you give him a penny for his thoughts, you'd get change.
- ❤ If you stand close enough to him, you can hear the ocean.
- ❤ Some drink from the fountain of knowledge, he's only gargled.
- ❤ Was left on the tilt-a-whirl a bit too long as a baby.
- ❤ Wheel is turning, but the hamster is dead.

While the above statements are ridiculous, opinionated, and not necessarily developmental, managers and supervisors must provide effective and timely feedback to their employees. With few exceptions here and there, there is really no good reason for managers to worry about passing on negative or constructive feedback about an employee's performance. Employees have a right to know what managers and coaches think about their work and overall performance.

Things are not always fair in this world and employee discipline programs are likely to be full of subjective assessments and opinions. Yes, these are not good reasons for not doing them or being afraid of doing them. Someone once said that "Expecting the world to treat you fairly because you are a good person is a little like expecting the bull not to attack you because you are a vegetarian." So, it is understandable that some good employees may receive fair and, at times, below standard evaluations. Thus, there is no reason to worry about evaluation or be afraid of the process. As Confucius put it, "The man of wisdom is never of two minds; the man of benevolence never worries; and the man of courage is never afraid."

## Small Business Management[8]

Coaches are needed in both small and large businesses. It takes a great coach to manage a small business and lead its people to effectively compete with their larger competitors. Small businesses are a vital part of the economy and the global transition taking place in the new digital age. The benefits which small businesses have accorded to individuals and society are numerous, and so are the opportunities and

---

[8] Contributed by Donovan A. McFarlane, St. Thomas University.

challenges which they now face. One of the most stringent challenges confronting small businesses and small business owners is the problem of failure resulting from inadequate funding and managerial ineffectiveness, among competition and high volatility in the local-global market. Becoming a successful small business owner is not an easy task and the thousands of small businesses failing annually attest to this fact. A small business owner must be a skillful entrepreneur who is extremely versed in strategic thinking, innovative-market orientation, technological savvy, and have a market-leadership approach to doing business. The small business owner must think big and take giant steps despite his or her limited corporate stature.

Bamford and Bruton (2006) have written a small, but powerful book with just the above considerations in mind. This book is an efficiently written compilation of sound business stratagems, which the authors describe as a text "for individuals who wish to understand the process involved in starting a new small business." However, its scope extends wider than this as it offers comprehensive knowledge and skills through real world examples, case studies and exercises, video cases, summaries, discussion questions, and end of chapter vignettes relating real-world stories. This makes *Small Business Management: a Framework for Success* a very "practical guide to the issues and concerns with starting a small business." Besides being a practical guide for those interested in acquiring superior knowledge about the small business process, *Small Business Management: a Framework for Success* is a fully integrative and interactive book for entrepreneurs, managers, coaches, and college level courses in small business management. Managers and coaches that are performance-oriented, will find this book useful in effectively running their businesses.

Bamford and Bruton have subdivided *Small Business Management* into a five-step analytical approach: Part 1: Laying the Groundwork for a Small Business; Part 2: Due Diligence on the Business Idea; Part 3: Establishing the Business; Part 4: Building the Business; and Part 5: Other Issues. This type of organizational structuring of the text and small business issues facilitate easy comprehension as the reader immediately recognizes the path towards any initial success in the small business world.

The first part of the text; Laying the Groundwork for a Small Business consists of three chapters; *Chapter one* as an introduction explores the history of small business in the United States, the nature and characteristics of small business owners, the benefits which small businesses bring to society, small business and global economy, and the definitions of small businesses in the 21$^{st}$ century. *Chapter two* examines the small business owner by looking at founders, entrepreneurial potential, reasons for becoming and forming small businesses, and the support available, as well as the small business owner's passion for business. *Chapter three,* deals with idea generation and initial evaluation of a business idea, opportunity identification, and the targeting of specific opportunities.

The second part of *Small Business Management*; Due Diligence on the Business Idea has three interesting chapters dealing with the external environmental analysis (chapter 4), the development of the business mission and strategy (chapter 5), and the analysis of cash flow and other financial information (chapter 6). In these chapters, the individual learns how to define both industry and customers, conduct industry research and develop competitive advantage, develop mission statements, as well as understand and develop cash flows and other financial tools.

The third part of the book deals with the establishment of the business venture, looking at the legal issues involved, operations, key issues and funding, and accounting tasks. The fourth part of *Small Business Management* examines the three activities relevant in building the business: marketing, human resources and finance. Practical recommendations and knowledge are provided on employee hiring, retention and monitoring. The marketing plan, an important tool for the new business to grow, is also discussed in relation to customer and target market goals, along with factors of promotion, pricing and sales management. The finance section looks at measurement and performance tools for small business owners. These include ratio analysis, sensitivity analysis, and deviation analysis. Part five of the text deals with other issues; chapters 13 and 14 look at exit/harvest/turnaround, steps in selling and closing a small business, and the franchising and purchasing of existing business as alternatives to starting a business from scratch.

Overall, Bamford and Bruton have written a well-organized book with practical and sensible recommendations and knowledge for the aspiring managers, coaches, small business owners, and business students. This book is a framework for managers, coaches, academic teachings, and real world success!

## Earl G. Graves as a Performance Manager[9]

Over the past few years and decades, many people have served as effective coaches and performance managers through their personal achievements. These individuals can serve as formal and informal coaches and mentors to those who are aspiring to such heights. Young entrepreneurs and aspiring business leaders should identify successful coaches and mentors and follow in their footsteps. A starting place would be to understand their biographies and achievements by reading what they have done, said, and written. Identifying coaches as well as books and coaching material can be a daunting task, particularly if the learner is one of the first and only persons in his/her demographics to hold a role in the organization. One book that could help learners, especially minorities, develop and better contribute to the organization is *How to Succeed in Business without Being White: Straight Talk on Making It in America*, written in 1997 by Earl G. Graves, publisher of *Black Enterprise* and CEO of Earl Graves LTD.

A legend in American business, Graves' experiences as an entrepreneur and director on the boards of such organizations as AMR (the parent company of American Airlines), Aetna, Chrysler Corp., Federated Department Stores Inc., Rohm & Haas, Howard University, the Associates of Harvard University's Graduate School of Business, and vice president of relationships/marketing on the executive board of the National Office of the Boy Scouts of America allows him to offer unique and insightful recommendations that can improve the performance of individuals, Blacks in particular, regardless if they are executives, managers, professionals, or

---

[9] Earl G. Graves' book review is contributed by Vickie Cox Edmondson, The University of Alabama at Birmingham.

entrepreneurs. His alma mater, Morgan State University, honored him by naming its school of business the Earl G. Graves School of Business and Management.

The book begins with a few of Graves' recollections of some of the teachings of his father whom he describes as strict disciplinarian, a hard worker with entrepreneurial instincts. He also recollects some of the problems and racial situations he faced as a young Black man aspiring to become an entrepreneur. Moreover, he discusses some of the public policy efforts that were put into place to aid Blacks and members of other ethnic groups who own business enterprises.

He points out that due to the changing social climate and the introduction of laws protecting the civil rights of people of color, racism was subdued in the seventies. He argues that things are considerably tougher today than they were when he started his first endeavor, *Black Enterprise*. Graves explains how his salespeople spend about 30 percent of their time overcoming what he calls the "nuisance factor" in which they must explain to prospective customers why they should target and sell to people of color. However, Graves maintains that while racism is definitely a problem in trying to do business, it can be dealt with if Blacks use their wit and determination. Graves wrote: "I am an equal opportunist. I want smart black people who work hard to have the same opportunities as smart white people who work hard...The racists will say, why should blacks get preferential treatment? Why should we allow you to become millionaires?" Some people's response to these questions might be "why we don't want to be given anything." As minorities, Graves says that "We only want the opportunity to run the race wearing the same track shoes they wear, rather than combat boots." Graves sets forth some specific recommendations for people of color who want to succeed in the business world:

1. Business first. Graves maintains that Blacks won't make it if they go into every presentation or interview feeling they have to convince people that African Americans are wonderful people.
2. Don't deal with the subordinates if you can get to the chief executive.
3. Sell to their needs, not to yours.
4. Storm the castle. Find a way to get to the decision-makers.
5. Never forget that business is personal.
6. Latch on to a guardian angel.
7. Do not sell your soul.
8. If you are selling the Black consumer market, sell its buying power, not your social consciousness.
9. Get involved in your community.
10. Work on developing a commanding presence.
11. Don't get frustrated because you can't hit the ball out of the park every time.

Perhaps the greatest contribution of this book is the chapter on no-nonsense networking. Graves understands the importance of networking and maintains that it is one of the best tools for competing in the White-dominated business world. Graves defines networking as nothing less than developing relationships with people who can help you and whom in turn, you can help. He goes as far as to say that Blacks have an obligation to help. However, he criticizes the way that most Black business people network (i.e. merely exchanging business cards at social gatherings). He argues that the most valuable form of networking cannot be done without investing in relationships. He provides the following guidelines for networking and building those relationships:

1. Relax. Don't try too hard.
2. Listen at least half as much as you talk.
3. Find a common interest; don't assume it is you.
4. Do not strive to be impressive; instead, try to leave a positive impression.
5. Make a graceful exit. Stick around as long as you have something to contribute.
6. Follow through. A telephone call or a note, or even an e-mail message is appropriate.
7. Practice networking etiquette.
8. Acknowledge networking favors.
9. Don't forget the personal touch. It is necessary to nurture the relationship beyond business.

Not only does Earl Graves provide some guidelines on how to network, but he also discusses some of the problems that Blacks encounter when trying to build relationships. He reveals how he and another prominent Black entrepreneur who owned a competing magazine were able to work out their differences. Finally, he advises Blacks to network with their checkbook by supporting organizations that support the Black community.

Although Graves discusses some of the strategies that Blacks should consider when starting a career including what career opportunities to consider, he argues that the key to Black wealth is ownership. He offers some sound recommendations to Blacks who want to start their own businesses. He discusses the importance of planning for business success and developing and revising (when necessary) a well-thought-out business plan. He gives some practical advice on financing and growing the venture. Moreover, he discusses the importance of succession planning and growing entrepreneurs within the family to ensure business continuation.

Finally, Graves discusses the responsibility that Blacks in business have to take care of their business ventures. He argues that Blacks in business must look out for one another, regardless of their position in the organization. Here is a list of things Graves said Blacks can do to help those coming up behind or working beside them:

1. Be an opportunity spotter. Let others know of job and business opportunities.
2. Be a quiet champion for fair treatment.
3. Monitor charitable contributions by their business or corporation.
4. Try to help others understand the value of sharing responsibilities for fairness.
5. Stand together.
6. Do not be afraid to take a stand.

A major strength of this book is that its author, Earl G. Graves, takes the time to write about his experiences. Rarely do insider businessmen with the success record of this author write books on self-help. The openness and candor with which he wrote this book is to be applauded. Most people do not learn these tips until they have tried and failed many times.

A primary weakness is one that is to be expected in a book by an author with the success of Graves. As mentioned in *Fortune* regarding Graves and other pioneers in the struggle, Earl Graves has a huge ego and it permeates the book. However, it takes a huge ego in order to accomplish the things Graves has accomplished and what he hopes others will accomplish.

Without question, the tips provided by Graves apply not only to people of color, but to most entrepreneurs and business people. But people of color, who have generally distributed their products within their respective communities, will find this book particularly useful because it clearly states some of the particular difficulties they will most likely face and should be prepared to overcome. *How to Succeed in Business without Being White* should be a required reading for all young people who are aspiring to be entrepreneurs and those who want to advance in the corporate world. Moreover, business persons who do or plan to do a substantial amount of business with Black businesses would also benefit from Graves' contribution. Graves is a good role model and mentor for each aspiring coach, performance manager, and entrepreneur.

**Mentoring New Employees**

Performance can be managed effectively through role-modeling as well as formal and informal mentoring programs. In today's twenty-first century global business environment, effective mentoring of staff and colleagues enhances internal business relationships, perceived career success, organizational commitment, overall performance, and the reduction of turnover. When an organization invests monetarily into a person, it is best to establish a relationship with that person to ensure that he/she is receiving optimal support. This is even more important for international assignments, diverse groups, and for those who deal with others in multinational environments. Many businesses have paid the high price of losing key personnel due to the lack of an effective mentoring and socialization program regarding the culture of the organization and the countries involved. One main goal of mentoring is to support the new employee through effective socialization and indoctrination practices.

Coaching, which is task-oriented, deals with improving performance, and it focuses on developing and selecting options for behavior modification to enhance performance. Mentoring deals with personal transitions, it addresses the individual's identity in the organization and focuses on options and exploration that is not necessarily tied to organizational performance. Some of the responsibilities of the coach and mentor do overlap. Coaching usually involves a continuous flow of instructions, comments, and suggestions from coach to employee. Mentoring is the process whereby a senior employee takes an active role in developing a junior colleague.

At a general level, the term mentor applies to a person who helps another become familiarized with an organization's culture, people and tasks in order to function effectively, and/or progressively move upward on the ladder of success, as defined by the internal culture. Depending on the assigned mentor and his/her influence in the organization, mentoring relationships can greatly enhance a person's growth and advancement opportunities. Mentoring can be formal or informal. Informal mentorship programs are natural connections that bond two or more individuals together based on some similarity, liking for each other, or common goals. On the other side, formal mentoring programs are developed purposefully by managers or the organization to partner a new employee with a veteran employee in the organization. Some common forms of mentorship include peer mentorship, supervisor/subordinate mentorship, and third party mentorship where the new employee is assigned an outside coach. Regardless of format or level of formality, mentoring programs tend to focus on familiarizing the new employee with the organization, career development opportunities, and psychological well-being while learning the ropes and politics of the culture, and role modeling.

Businesses also invest considerable monetary resources to hire people with the same attributable cultural values as the institution. People seek normalcy which aspires to specific affective, cognitive, and behavioral patterns based on their level of cognitive dissonance. For example, as new employees enter a company, they seek to have commonality within their environment, which will reduce the level of anxiety within the new organization. If new employees' perceive they have the same values with the company they are entering, the level of cognitive dissonance will be lower. Of course, people with the same nuances will benefit the organization because of similarities in values, beliefs and work behaviors which can lead to higher productivity and better teamwork. The socialization process within an organization is a very important function which establishes the foundation of affective job satisfaction and organizational commitment for the new employee. The employee must be able to adapt to his/her new work environment by assessing the organization's internal capabilities and to derive one's full capacity within this new environment. Successful socialization processes allow new employees to effectively understand their place within this environment. An effective socialization process creates value for the organization by escalating the process of a new hire to become proficient on the job more quickly, thus increasing overall effectiveness for the organization.

Great mentors can use the skills of great coaches to lead associates to better performance before, during and after the socialization process. As such, mentors should acquire the skills needed to coach employees for good performance, bad performance, and for no performance. As mentioned before, effective coaching is a continuous process of conversational collaborations and interactions aimed at assisting new and veteran employees unlock and realize their full potential one task or one skill at a time, and at a pace appropriate for the person being coached. The essence of mentoring and coaching is unlocking an employee's potential, through stimulating questions and clear guidance as needed, so they can maximize their own performance.

Mentors and coaches should expect patience and demonstrate it as well. Someone once said that "Patience is something you admire in the driver behind you, but not in one ahead." It is important that mentors and coaches be role models of their important behavioral expectations for everyone else in their vicinity and beyond. Overall, coaches and mentor should remember to treat everyone with kindness and compassion every day:

Beginning today, treat everyone you meet as if they were going to be dead by midnight. Extend to them all the care, kindness, and understanding you can muster, and do it with no thought of any reward. Your life will never be the same again (Og Mandino).

Besides treating everyone with care and compassion, mentors and coaches also need to have a positive attitude and optimistic expectations of everyone else. They need to inspire and motivate others. Mentors and coaches should intrinsically motivate themselves by seeing every day as a "new day" and a "new start" for themselves, their employees and their colleagues.

### A New Day
This is the beginning of a new day.
I have been given this day to use as I will.

I can waste it, or use it.
I can make it a day long to be remembered for its joy, its beauty and its achievements, or it can be filled with pettiness.

What I do today is important because I am exchanging a day of my life for it.
When tomorrow comes this day will be gone forever, but I shall hold something which I have traded for it.

It may be no more than a memory, but if it is a worthy one I shall not regret the price.
I want it to be gain not loss, good not evil, success not failure.
*Author Unknown*

### Summary
This chapter discussed some aspects of an integrative performance management program that organizations, managers and leaders can use to make sure their firms perform and stay competitive in today's global workplace. Organizational leaders and coaches should understand that true long-term competitiveness can best be achieved through the productive use of their human resources. Of course, it is also important that organizations make effective use of their human, financial, physical, capital, and other such available resources as well if they are to be, and remain, competitive in their industries.

The performance success of a person and an organization is often determined through effective leadership and efficient management. During his presentation on June 25, 2006, at the Society for Human Resource Management (SHRM) conference, the retired General Colon Powell, of the United States, emphasized that to effectively lead, coaches and managers need to focus on those individuals who actually get the work done and get those who are standing by moving. General Powell said that if a manager or coach has a sense of purpose and direction, this will become contagious among his/her peers, colleagues and employees. General Powell believes that coaches and managers need to nurture and take care of their people so they are appreciated and their performance is recognized and valued on a regular basis. The fact is that effective coaches tend to set high standards to meet and exceed the stated goals and objectives. According to General Powell, effective coaches and leaders are honest and truthful; they look reality in the eye and face the facts, while strategically planning to move forward. Strategically moving forward requires that managers and coaches plan on maintaining a motivational work environment. Furthermore, managers, coaches, and leaders must also be perceived by their followers as people of integrity and great character. General Powell's retired colleague, General Norman Schwarzkopf, said that effective "leadership is a potent combination of strategy and character; if you must be without one, be without the strategy." Strategy implementation becomes much easier and simpler when a leader is respected for his/her character.

Coaches and managers must take personal responsibility for the morale of their people and department. As presented by many experts in the field, morale is the nature of a relationship between employees and the organization. Morale reflects the nature of the department and reveals the heart of an organization at its best or worst depending on the outcome of the assessment. Effective coaches should keep their finger on the pulse of the organization and measure morale on a regular basis. Managers and coaches must have the ability to create a sense of pride among employees about the organization and its objectives. Managers and coaches must also recruit, retain, develop, and motivate a high-performance workforce if they are to be productive and efficient in their individual positions, tasks and departments. The number of years employees stay in an organization is directly linked to the type of relationship they maintain with their superiors. Managers and coaches can motivate and increase organizational morale by engaging all employees in the mission and vision of the firm. Engaging[10] everyone in the organization requires ongoing and effective strategic planning, appreciation, communication, and employee recognition programs. Coaches can "*LEAD*" by:

- *Learning* about the needs and wants of their people on a continuous basis.
- *Educating* and "*empowering*" their people about the mission, vision and objectives of the organization and department. Empowering, at its best, comes with proper education, training, development, responsibility, and the authority to get the job done. Through effective and timely education, true empowerment and enthusiasm will be the natural results in a given department or organization.
- *Acknowledging* and "*appreciating*" the contributions of all employees on an individual basis.
- *Demanding* high performance and total integrity from everyone in the organization.

Demanding high performance has many implications related to the concept of self-fulfilling prophecy, and it basically means that coaches will most likely see the type of performance that they communicate and expect from their employees. The

---

[10] See Mujtaba (2007), *Cross Cultural Management and Negotiation Practices*, ILEAD Academy, LLC.

suggestions, stated throughout this book, offer coaching ideas so managers can be successful in achieving their stated outcomes synergistically with and through each employee. The effective use of the skills and suggestions provided can create high performing, happy and satisfied employees. As stated by Mahatma Gandhi, "Happiness is when what you think, what you say, and what you do are in harmony." Effective coaching is about creating harmony in one's head (thoughts), heart (feelings), and habits (behaviors) about each employee and his or her ability to perform. Besides being consistent in one's own communication by sending the message of high performance expectations through one's head, heart and habits, coaches must also attempt to create regularity of commitment in their employee's head, heart and habits if they are to lead to long-term success and high performance. As presented in the *Workforce Diversity Management* book (Llumina Press, 2007):

➢ *Head* implies continuous cognitive learning about each situation, thinking objectively based on current facts, awareness of universal principles, and knowledge generation.

➢ *Heart* implies the consistent controlling of one's feeling, basing it on objective facts, and aligning it with universal values. It means basing one's feeling for long-term impact, rather than short term satisfaction of personal desires that are linked to revenge, vengeance, payback, or retribution.

➢ *Habits* should be linked to one's objective feelings and universal principles. It means ensuring that one's day-to-day behaviors are aligned with one's universal principles of right and wrong, personal or professional values, and knowledge-based and goal-oriented feelings.

Mentors and coaches have the responsibility of consistently demonstrating a positive attitude through their head, heart and habits on a continuous basis if they are to create a motivational work environment and inspire others. Mentors and coaches should also understand that when employees and mentees know their work makes a difference in a specific manner, then productivity is likely to rise and so will their level of job satisfaction and organizational commitment. The training video entitled *"Would I Inspire Me?"* asks the following question: What does it take to inspire a work group to greater commitment and productivity? Experts conclude that, for long-term inspiration, it is not the trait of charisma. Rather, it is behavior that any well-intentioned leader can emulate, as demonstrated through the examples presented in the video. The "Would I Inspire Me?" program provides coaches and managers with practical ways to make the work life more meaningful, productive, and rewarding for themselves and their colleagues. The program concludes that the best way to inspire one's employees, colleagues and team members seem to at least include the following steps:

1. *Communicating why work is important.* Use real world examples and express genuine enthusiasm.

2. *Acknowledging the contribution of every employee and looking for reasons to praise them.* Manager and coaches need to convey accomplishments to employees, co-workers and superiors.

3. *Supporting employees and team members.* Pitch in as a team member and remove obstacles that may get in the way of the team's success.

4. *Creating opportunities for growth.* Coaches and managers should go beyond job descriptions and must be aware of each person's personal and professional goals if they are to provide effective and individualized motivational incentives.

In one respect, coaches are teachers and facilitators. As such, coaches should spend sufficient time with their associates, explain their expectations thoroughly, assure others of a brighter future, care for each person, help employees get to where they should be headed, encourage everyone, and reward associates incrementally for a job well done. In summary, coaches must:

- Take time.
- Explain.
- Assure.
- Care.
- Help.
- Encourage.
- Reward.

### Discussion Questions

1. What is coaching? What is mentoring? What is the difference between coaching and mentoring? Discuss.
2. What is performance management? How can it help organizations make better use of their human resources asset? Discuss.
3. What are the various components of a holistic performance management program? In other words, what types of functions and tasks are often included in such a program if they are to be effective and provide a competitive advantage for the firm? Discuss the benefits of a holistic performance management program.
4. What is a performance appraisal process? What are some examples of effective and not so effective performance appraisals that you have experienced or heard of in today's workplace? Discuss two personal examples.
5. Who should be involved in performance appraisals and why?
6. Should performance appraisals take place once a year or more often? Discuss your thoughts, logic and reasons.
7. What are some of the skills and expertise that are needed in a comprehensive performance management program?
8. Can aspiring entrepreneurs and small businesses use performance management skills to become better coaches? Discuss.
9. Who are some of the most effective coaches and performance managers that you have seen in the last few decades? Mention two individuals that you think are great role models of effective coaches and performance managers. Discuss what makes them effective role models (or effective coaches and performance managers).

# CHAPTER 3

## Influencing and Leadership Skills

Coaching is a continuous process of conversational collaborations and interactions aimed at assisting others unlock and realize their full potential, one task and skill at a time, and at a pace appropriate for the person being coached. This definition encompasses most of the elements for successful coaching and influencing. Coaching must be continuous as it involves a regular feedback loop of unlearning what does not work, changing the status quo, and relearning as per the current needs of an employee or the organization. Successful coaching is an interactive and collaborative exchange between the coach and coachee. Through this exchange process, the coach must build an environment of trust. Through this trust, the coachee will be free to take the risk to try new ideas and change behaviors. The primary goal of coaching is to improve individual performance. This improved performance has an obvious direct impact on the organization's profit and competitiveness. Organizations today are in a state of perpetual change. Coaching encourages employees to manage these changes by developing new skills and enhancing their existing ones. Thus, the organization's ability to succeed in a changing world marketplace provides the competitive edge needed to succeed in today's work environment. In order for managers to become effective coaches and leaders, they need a repertoire or toolbox of influencing skills. This chapter discusses the art of influencing others as managers, leaders and coaches either in the workplace or in the community.

### The Influence of Coaching

Perry Zeus and Suzanne Skiffington state that coaching is "a methodology for creating more effective conversations, for assessing and reformulating values and goals, and reaching solutions" (2005, p. 2). According to Zeus and Skiffington, coaching has two directional approaches. The first one is *inward-looking*; it is an assessment of one's strengths and weaknesses and it requires a rigorous self-assessment in order to understand how one reacts to external events. The second directional approach is one that is *future-oriented*. Coaches can help coachees think about possible future events and then develop strategies to best cope with these events. The process of coaching influence involves an assessment of the coachee's internal characteristics and the utilization of this knowledge to build upon one's strengths to develop better behaviors and actions in response to projected and anticipated future events.

A coach-coachee interaction and influencing process, according to experts, can be broken down into at least three phases of building: trust building, self-awareness building, experiential and strengths building. Trust is the most essential and basic element of coaching. It must exist for both the coach and the coachee. The coach must trust that the coachee is open and committed to the interaction and learning experience. The coachee must trust that the coach has his or her best interest at heart and that the coach is committed to a constructive and nonjudgmental evaluation and teaching process. If trust does not exist, then the second phase of building self-awareness cannot happen. The process of building self-awareness is critical to a successful coaching interaction. If one does not understand what one's own values and goals are, or what one's strengths and weaknesses are, it is impossible to develop refinements of strengths and to minimize weaknesses. It requires a rigorous, unblinking, self-examination. Honest, self-evaluation leads to awareness and understanding of one's values, habits and behaviors. The successful coach guides the coachee through this process. Once a coachee clarifies his/her values and goals and she/he has thoroughly examined her/his own strengths and weaknesses, the coach is then able to guide the coachee through a process of using this knowledge to build upon his/her experience and professional strengths to meet personal and organizational challenges.

Effective coaching provides a positive mechanism for promoting behaviors that are beneficial to the organization. How is the influence through coaching different from mentoring? No one would argue that mentoring is unnecessary. If you have mentors, why have coaches? It is important to differentiate coaching from mentoring. Mentoring is just as essential as coaching in an organization. There are, however, differences between mentoring and coaching. The differences are subtle, but real. Mentoring is about capacity building, guidance and "showing a person the way" toward a brighter future, while coaching is about managing performance and enhancing performance-related standards. Mentoring is guided, task-oriented or experience-derived teaching. There is an element of teaching or mentoring in all coaching, but coaching focuses not necessarily on specific situations, but on identification of strengths and tools that allow coachees to handle a wide variety of current and future performance-related challenges. Coaching is a much more standard-based approach to situationally influencing behavior and performance. Coaching is therefore essential to promoting behaviors that best serve the values and goals of an organization.

## Being True to Yourself[11]

Effective leaders and coaches must be true to themselves if they are to influence and lead others. One way for each person to be true to him- or herself is to clarify his/her values. Professionals are hearing more and more about values. Values are getting increasing recognition as being important for management; however in the

---

[11] Book review provided by Donna Galla, Nova Southeastern University. Review completed for the *Journal of Applied Management and Entrepreneurship.*

2006 book, entitled *True to Yourself: Leading a Values-Based Business,* Mark Albion stresses the importance for a business owner's long-term plan to be influenced by core values. Mark has personal experience as a business owner practicing leadership and socially responsible values. These values of the owner integrate into their business and community and reach as far globally as the company supply chain is involved.

Having your own business is one way to make an impact as "a force for social change" by knowing what your values are and always practicing them in every business transaction. The book is replete with examples of successful business owner/entrepreneurs that grew their business and their ideals by supporting their chosen cause and enhancing their personal standing in their community.

Albion's book is different from others because of the methodology the author offers. It is the leadership philosophy to practice compassion and social responsibility of resources. By answering the questions outlined in the book one can get in touch with one's own values and refine a course in life whether it be job related or on a more personal level. The questions act as a catalyst to help each individual begin to get in touch with what is important to them. Everyone has had the experience of close friends or family members who want to give their advice and expect it to be followed; however, for each individual to be successful they must get in touch with what is important to them. Basically it never pays to stray from honest values no matter what your endeavor. The questions act as a means of transformation to help you focus on your strengths in order to lead with clearly directed values. Everyone knows someone that did not walk their talk. Not surprisingly employees of a business can sense the values of a CEO no matter if she/he spends time with them or not. Clearly spoken and unspoken values also are important to the vision and mission of a company as demonstrated by the examples in Albion's book.

As a CEO you need to understand how your ideals and relationship with others in your company impact your culture and bottom line. For example do you have a program for your employees to benefit from the company's growth through stock options?

In this book, coaches learn values-based leaders negotiate; however, they do not retreat from their values. Instead they work with each person, company growing trust and relationships. As the author explains, people care about what you know and about how much you care about them. Compassion extends to how you treat everyone. But one might ask how do you keep on track? Albion suggests checking your values and company direction on a regular basis.

The term "values" refers to seeing your values as an important part of who you are. The author instructs us to connect to the business allowing no separation in policy or practice between how you act and how the business operates. Again to assist with this process Albion has specific questions as follows:

1. How do you see what your company does as an outgrowth of you and your interests?
2. What are the specific ways you transmit your values and communicate them to others?
3. What do you do when values-based decisions have conflicting goals?

4.  How do you reevaluate your role in keeping your values and creating market value? This last one corresponds with the author's premise of having multiple objectives beyond profitability.

The author gives one example of a time when he asked a venture-capitalist for backing for his business. He was turned down; the reason: The author sounded brainy and the capitalist did not feel any heart, any real commitment to what the company was going to do. Jane Hileman, founder of American Reading Company (ARC), grew her company from $5 million in the first three years to $13 million in sales. In January 2005, Random House became a minority shareholder. Jane attributes this success to being 100 percent committed to her mission of getting inner city kids to read. Her program is now in 650 schools and 26 states.

Regarding values the book outlines three truths: 1) Bring all of you to work- your values produce unique value. 2) Study the humanities and get service experience. 3) Expect your values to evolve. Perhaps the most unique section is "*Walk toward the Talk*," giving myths and truths for the business owner. One truth that stands out is: Your most important work, is building an organization, which cannot be measured. The myth: what matters most is what you can measure; my job is to increase sales as the owner.

Overall, this book is appropriate for all coaches and business leaders in all levels of the company. At first glance the book may seem to target a CEO/owner of a business, however, that would be a mistake. Rather, employees at all ranks and everyone with a stake in the company can benefit from this book. Lastly, this book should be read more than once or on a quarterly basis to ensure the principles are understood and integrated into one's daily decision-making routine to enhance performance and effectively influence others.

## Influence and Persuasion

*Influencing* or persuading, in this book, is defined as the art of moving people to action toward a predetermined course or vision that is of value to everyone involved. Influencing is different from manipulation as the later often does not consider the development of a long-term relationship or trust with the other party. Vengel mentions that "When it comes to getting other people to get the job done, nothing succeeds like the art of influence" (2001, p. 2). In today's work environment, coaches and leaders must have the ability to influence others to embrace common goals. With these shared goals, behaviors are congruent to the values that achieve the desired results. According to Alan Vengel (2000, p. 5), *influencing* is the art of persuading others over whom we have no direct authority. In today's management climate, organizations are flatter, technology-driven, and made up of more self-directed teams. In order to be effective and successful, there is the need to learn techniques that will permit goal achievement with the assistance of others through skillfully applied methods of influence. These approaches should incorporate a thorough understanding of the influence situation, a clear appreciation for the needs of the other(s) over whom influence is sought, a determination of the type of influence energy needed, gaining command of the communication style of both parties, and creating an influence strategy. Perhaps most importantly, effective influencing is about developing and maintaining positive relationships or rapport with one's colleagues and employees.

Influencing is the ability to achieve goals through the willing and committed work of others. It is an essential skill-set in today's workplace considering the erosion of vertical hierarchical structures that have resulted in more collaborative and team-oriented organizations. Even someone with authority to dictate actions would be better served utilizing influencing skills to encourage the individual's willing investment and commitment in an action. Although there are many skills that can be learned, it is essentially leading or managing employees and coworkers as whole human beings rather than any stereotype. If an organizational culture is imbued with influencing practices, the organization itself will benefit as a collaborative, team-oriented and accountable workforce develops. Tension is reduced and work can be more enjoyable for each effected employee. In attempting to gain approval and successfully implement a program or change, influencing skills utilized throughout the process will engender greater success. Dr. Paul Hersey and Dr. Ron Campbell's 2004 book states that "Leadership is the activity of influencing people to strive willingly for group objectives." Robert Tannenbaum, Irving Weschler, and Fred Massarik define leadership as the "…interpersonal influence exercised in a situation and directed, through the communication process, toward the attainment of a specialized goal or goals" (Hersey and Campbell, 2004).

Vengel states that influencing is "using a precise system of behavioral skills … to move others to action" (Vengel, 2002, p. 1). There are at least two ways of getting another person to do something. One might force people to do something, in essence, taking the decision making authority away. Or the other person will make the decision, because one grants them the authority or one "sells" them on the idea. The first option can be utilized successfully to produce a desired behavior. For instance, medical doctors' position as physicians and leaders within an intensive care unit is a relevant example. They are viewed as leaders and in possession of authority. There are times when the exercise of this type of influence is useful and justified. An example would be a code situation where there is no time to discuss matters and there are very specific actions that must be performed in a rapid fashion. However, these times are fairly rare. The difficulty with many physician leaders is that they generalize this type of authoritarian behavior to the non-critical, much more common situations. This type of influencing behavior may lead to the destruction of relationships. The second option is much more common. Again in reference to the situation for physicians in a critical care unit, they often do not have direct authority over other members of the unit staff. The nurses do not work for the physicians, nor do the respiratory therapists. Persuasion of the nursing and ancillary care staff must be done with care as their cooperation is critical for the delivery of optimum patient care. It is far too common the case that this influencing interaction goes awry interfering with the desired behavior and performance. This is greatly important on a personal level and it matters even more on an organizational level. The inability to successfully influence others to behave or perform tasks that accomplish one's goals may mean failure to accomplish organizational goals as well. The inability to influence others often creates organizational stalemate and frustration.

If gentle persuasion is often the preferred method of influencing others, how does one best do it? Vengel states that an influence situation can be broken down into two basic elements: your goal and the other person's goal (2000, p. 17). Clarity about your own goal is critical. It is necessary to understand how your goal might affect the other person and the organization. It is also essential to understand the other person and his/her goals. One must understand how the other person might feel about the situation, what factors might motivate him/her to change a specific behavior. Getting to know the other person is possibly the most important and most difficult concept in influencing someone else's behavior. Facts are necessary to determine what is important to the other person. More importantly, developing and understanding context for this interpretation of the other person's wants and needs is critical.

Like coaching, influencing can be very important in organizations. Coaches influence their coachees. Managers often influence their employees to be great performers and model associates. Employees, on the other hand, influence one another, as well as their superiors and customers. Simply stated, influence is the ability to move others to action. Influencing allows individuals to get certain results from others without destroying their relationships. Influencing is important to individuals seeking results whether or not they have legitimate authority. Experts state that "Learning effective influence skills to win the willing commitment of others gives us the edge we need to get what we want and build more productive business relationships—even when we have the so-called authority to enforce rather than cultivate compliance" (Vengel, 2001, p. 5). Effective influencing skills allow people to the get work done faster, as well as reduce conflict and stress, while demonstrating that one is a team player and a flexible negotiator. All of these objectives lead to a more effective work performance.

Within organizations, individuals can be put in a position of having to influence "up," "down," or "laterally" to accomplish a goal. They may be attempting to influence another individual or an entire group. The influencer may seek to motivate an individual to complete a specific task. He or she may have a new idea to develop or strategy to implement. An organizational change may need a champion to become successful. In each of these scenarios, it is essential for the individual who wishes to exert influence to be cognizant of not only his or her goal, but the goal and mindset of others who he or she needs to influence. This allows the individuals exerting the influence to plan the most persuasive strategy. They then must look to use the right actions and communication style to accomplish their goal. Influencing skills are particularly necessary in the current work environment because, modern organizations tend to be flatter, more collaborative, team-oriented in their decision-making, and less overtly dependent on a formal chain of command. Good influencing skills by managers are rewarded through stronger working relationships with employees. Given the importance of the manager-employee relationship in the retention of employees, developing good influencing skills in their managers would greatly help organizations with employee retention. As highlighted before, managers, leaders and coaches can get their work more efficiently when they exert influence, and it would serve them well to learn good, effective influencing skills.

In its simplest form, *influencing* can be seen as the ability to affect persons or events. Professional people today proactively spend some of their time trying to manage conflict and influence their staff, colleagues, managers, clients, and suppliers, inside and outside the organization. For coaches and leaders to be successful, they must have the ability to influence people over whom they have little to no direct or formal authority. Within the organization, typical influence challenges include improving performance, resolving conflict and differences of opinion, motivating, giving direction, selling ideas, competing for limited resources, and negotiating. The ability to influence is paramount to individual and organizational success. Whether we view a coach from an athletic perspective or a corporate perspective, both coach and leader roles involve followers. You cannot coach or lead without followers. Zeus and Skiffington (2005, p. 38) point out a number of competencies that both the coach and leader share, including the following:

- Leaders and coaches commit to building trusting and authentic relationships.
- Leaders and coaches are aware of their blind spots.
- Leaders and coaches allow others freedom, power and choice.
- Leaders and coaches generate possibilities for action and involvement.
- Leaders and coaches generate new conversations.
- Leaders and coaches allow others to be responsible for their own moods and interpretations.
- Leaders and coaches invent the future.

The leader/coach empowers others to take action when he/she feels it is necessary. Through empowerment and collaboration the leader/coach is able to tap into the employee's motivation. Effective leaders/coaches do not rely so much on position power as they do on personal force which comes through their relationships and as such they align the individual's goals with those of the organization. Effective managers and leaders become influential through training; as a result, their leadership effectiveness is raised to new levels through coaching. According to some individuals, corporate America is full of managers and executives that are not effective coaches. One may argue that by virtue of the ability of organizations in general to continue moving forward or exist they must have some level of effective leadership. Zeus and Skiffington state that "Progressive, success-oriented managers recognize that a culture of coaching is needed to shift the paradigm of management from one of authority and control to one of a committed, responsible partnership" (2005, p. 38)

### *The "Push" and "Pull" Behaviors*

There are perhaps thousands of ways that people are influenced by various factors in the society as they go through a socialization process from birth till death. Of course, the socialization influence during one's early childhood years tend to be very influential and long-lasting in life. While many elements and factors that influence people during their childhood years tend to be out of their control, some of these elements are under their full control during adulthood. As an adult, one must take full responsibility for his/her behaviors. Furthermore, as an adult, one can condition himself/herself to take ownership of certain behaviors that, when consistently repeated, will bring one more influence over others.

Vengel (2000) discussed two key behaviors that tend to drive the success of one's influence: Push energy and Pull energy. When you are trying to impress another person about a product or service that you are offering, then you are using the

Push strategy for influencing him/her. *Push behaviors* require that you assertively state your point of view and get your ideas heard by the other person. One can use Push behaviors by being assertive (not necessarily aggressive) and making suggestions. On the other hand, when people are drawn to you or your products and services because they believe in you or the product, then this is the power of Pull energy. *Pull behaviors* require summarizing, clarifying and actively listening by asking questions to draw the other person into the discussion, topic, or interaction. Pull behaviors, when used consistently with one's associates, can lead to better understanding, rapport with others, a high level of trust, and more commitment on the part of the employee. While one can assert and suggest for Push behaviors, summarize and ask questions for Pull behaviors, the combination of Push/Pull behaviors can take place by offering incentives for others to be drawn to what is being said or sold, while making the process easier for them to get it. Vengel recommends that coaches use Push behaviors when they know what they want, have good reasons with which to make a case, and when they believe a direct approach is needed. Coaches can use the Pull behaviors when they want to build a relationship with their employees, when they want commitment from others, and when additional information is needed to complete a task or achieve the end-result. Furthermore, coaches should use the Push/Pull strategy when they want to achieve extraordinary results and have rich interactions.

Vengel points out that the "Push energy is direct, forceful and persuasive;" it is not about being aggressive, but rather being assertive and offering specific steps toward a better end or conclusion. On the other side, Vengel points out that, "Pull energy is inclusive and involving," which requires listening through asking open-ended questions to engage people in the process of conversation. And, the "Push/Pull energy is a blend of the best of both Push and Pull energy," which is meant for situations when one needs to be direct and forceful as well as inclusive, motivational and considerate of others simultaneously. Coaches can use the Push and Pull behaviors or a combination of them to more effectively influence others. Coaches can be assertive, make suggestions, summarize, clarify, actively listen, ask questions, and offer incentives to influence their colleagues and employees.

### *Influencing Techniques*[12]

Power, influence and leadership are inextricably intertwined. Although power is invisible, it is an ever present attribute in the influence one has on another (Hughes et al., 2002). In 1959, French and Raven identified five bases of power used to motivate and influence others in any situation. They categorized their power sources as expert, referent, reward, legitimate, and coercive. Later, behavioral scientists such as Paul Hersey and Marshal Goldsmith added other sources of power, such as information, connection, etc. French and Raven hypothesized that certain applications of power produce greater force of influence. They found referent power has the greatest range. Coercive and reward power are dependent on the follower's conformity since coercive power breeds contempt, while reward power encourages

---

[12] Originally published in *Workforce Diversity Management: Challenges, Competencies and Strategies,* 2007, Llumina Press.

results. If coercive power, for example, is legitimate, there will be less resistance. French and Raven also theorized that some types of power are not applicable to all situations. It is left to the influencer to determine which behavior will have the greatest impact on the respondent. People who hold power can use a variety of influence tactics to modify behavior and produce desired effects. Although "power is the capacity to cause change, influence is the degree of actual change in a target person's attitudes, value, beliefs, or behaviors" (Hughes et al., 2002, p. 108). Influence tactics refer to the mode used to change those behaviors.

Influence is an important motivator because it "concentrates on interpersonal contact and communication" (Bruins, 1999, p. 1). Contacts and communication can lead to belongingness, security, and social acceptance, as reflected in Maslow's research. A breakdown in influence can result in negative consequences such as lack of self-esteem and powerlessness. French and Raven understood the connection between power and influence and created The Power/Interaction Model of Interpersonal Influence. This model describes the rational decision making process used by leaders who tend to weigh the costs and benefits of power bases before using one of them to influence a target individual (Bruins, 1999). Kipnis followed this research with the development of The Power Act Model. Simply stated, this model explains that the choice of influence is dependent upon the power bases one possesses, the willingness to use this power, against the expected resistance by using this influence tactic (Bruins, 1999). Before a tactic is applied, the leader must understand the reason behind possible resistance and diagnose which tactic to use. With such understanding, the leader can abandon, modify, or use a stronger influence tactic depending upon resistance.

In 1982, Kipnis and Schmidt outlined nine influence tactics most often used by agents trying to affect change. The tactics included rational persuasion, inspirational appeals, consultation, integration, personal appeals, exchange, coalition tactics, pressure tactics, and legitimizing tactics. These tactics can be grouped into three categories: hard tactics which use authority and position power; soft tactics which rely upon personal power; and rational persuasion using logic (Hughes et al., 2002).

*Rational persuasion* uses logical arguments and facts to influence others. Like expert and information power, it will appeal to followers who perceive data and knowledge as important factors in motivation. Thus, it can be used with any follower readiness level.

*Inspirational appeals* target emotions and are often used in religious situations. These appeals may work best with referent or legitimate power, but may backfire if people believe the influencer is taking advantage of the follower.

*Consultation* is used to collaborate on an activity. This tactic is best used with referent power and situations with high relationship affiliation. Empowered and encouraged individuals will display high performance.

*Integration* is a tactic to get the follower in a good mood before making a request. It can be used at any follower readiness level by any leadership level and in any situation. It may be more effective with high levels of referent or connection power.

*Personal appeals* are favors requested based on friendship. This style would be more effective on those with high levels of referent and reward power and those with high relationship needs.

*Exchange* targets trade of favors or information. It can be used with almost any power except coercive. Thus, it can be used with all leadership styles and readiness levels. However, people at lower readiness levels may not have anything to exchange.

*Coalition tactics* are used to get a group of people to influence another's behavior. An example of coalition tactics could be an intervention for a compulsive gambler or an alcoholic. This tactic may require expert, legitimate, or position power to make others understand the significance of the event. Referent and personal power may appeal to the cause. The particular situation will determine which type of leadership style and readiness level is most appropriate for this tactic.

*Pressure tactics* relate to coercive power and use punishment and fear as motivators. These tactics will be effective on people with low readiness levels. However, these tactics will only prove effective on people who perceive the tactic to be punishing.

*Legitimizing tactics* occur when position power is used to influence. Some people will be motivated based on power and status. This tactic is best used on followers with moderate readiness levels.

Clearly, there are synergies between power bases, influence tactics, leadership styles, and follower readiness levels. Kipnis and Schmidt determined that hard tactics like legitimizing or pressure are used when the influencer has the upper hand, when resistance is expected, or when the new behavior is not accepted by an organization (Hughes et al., 2002). Soft tactics like integration are used when the influencer is at a disadvantage, expects resistance or when the influencer will benefit. Rational tactics like exchange and rational appeal are often used when the leader and follower have equal power. Authoritarian and task-oriented leaders use harder tactics, while democratic and relationship leaders often use softer tactics and rational appeals (Clark, 2000). To be sure, any tactic must be executed correctly in order to achieve the desired result. Further, the tactic, power base, leadership style, follower readiness, and situation are distinct areas that must be identified before any influence can be applied appropriately.


### Communication Styles: Authoritarian, Analyzer, Visionary, or Supporter

The way one communicates verbally and nonverbally can assist in influencing others. People tend to automatically "size you up" and have a first impression, of who you are in the first ten seconds of meeting you, through your physical appearance and non-verbal messages. And the way you communicate with others can have a great impact on your level of influence with them and whether the first impression is confirmed or disconfirmed. Vengel (2000), in his book entitled *The Influence Edge,* mentions four styles of communication (the authoritarian, the analyzer, the visionary, and the supporter) that coaches can use to help them better communicate and influence others, not just by *what* they say, but by *how* they say it.

According to Alan Vengel, the *authoritarian* prefers to be in control, makes decisions quickly, focuses on the task at hand, is face-paced, prefers brief, well-organized communication, and wants to be in charge. They are likely to make such statements as "What is the bottom line?", "Get to the point," and "Put it in a memo." The *analyzer* prefers to deal with facts and confirmed information, makes careful and logical decisions, tends to have a slow pace, is reluctant to decide without having all of the facts at hand, and wants to be "in the know." They are likely to say such things as "I need more time and information to make a decision," "Can you show me the evidence?" and "We need to do our research before moving on." The *visionary* individuals prefer to see things holistically and deal with the big picture, make decisions impulsively, focus on ideas rather than little details, want to share the vision with everyone, tend to be fast-paced, and want to be in the middle of every major issue. They are likely to say such things as "Change is good," "From my perspective, here is how it can happen," and "Let us see the end goal or the big picture." The *supporter* prefers to deal with other individuals, sees the relationship when making decisions, tends to be more cautious when making decisions that involve other people, often seeks input from multiple parties, and wants to be "in the loop." They are likely to say such things as "Perhaps there is another way to look at it," "Everyone should voice their thoughts and perspectives," and "Tell me what you think and how can I help you or your team." Are you more likely to use the authoritarian, the analyzer, the visionary, or the supporter style of communication? Effective coaches tend to consciously choose their communication styles as per the needs of the situation and the person they are trying to influence. Therefore, one day they might use the authoritarian and the analyzer styles of communication, while with others they might use the visionary and the supporter styles as their dominant forms based on its relevancy for the situation.

### *Rapport Building: Visual, Auditory or Kinesthetic*

Effective coaches also work on building better rapport with others through visual, auditory and kinesthetic strategies. Building rapport with others is a very important element in effectively influencing them. Vengel (2000) defines *rapport* as the "magical dynamic between two people that 'click' that makes it a joy and a pleasure to interact with another person as a colleague, friends, lover…or sometimes, as a combination of all three." Rapport, as stated by Vengel, is "the ability to sustain good communication with the other person, even when you strongly disagree on an issue." Building a rapport with an employee or a colleague should be initiated by the coach. He or she must initiate and commit to strategically sustaining the rapport building process. Besides using an appropriate communication style to build better rapport with another person, coaches can also use visual, auditory and kinesthetic techniques to build a better relationship with others. Vengel states that human beings tend to perceive the world, process information and communicate mainly using their principle senses of vision, hearing, and feeling. If coaches communicate with others in the language of the other person's preference or dominant style (meaning "talking their talk," "being at their pace" and "speaking their language"), they will build greater understanding and build better rapport with them. This will provide a better probability of influencing them positively. Vengel (2000, pp. 93-99) states that you can determine a person's dominant preferred communication system or pattern by the word they use on a regular basis.

*Visual people* think and see concepts through the creation of pictures and writing of their thoughts. They select pictures from their memory to make sense out of what is being said or presented. Visual people primarily use words such as "look," "see," and "picture." Visual people can also recall shapes, photos, maps, and colors with a good level of detail. Visual people are often affected by the color of the room, and the way things are structured around them in an office or a conference room. Some of the words and phrases used by visual people might include the following:

- Envision
- Clear
- Hidden
- Appears to me
- In light of
- Makes a scene
- Mind's eye
- Plainly see
- Up front
- View

- Graphic
- Notice
- Get a perspective on
- Looks like
- Mental image
- Paint a picture
- See to it
- Well-defined
- In view of

*Auditory people* think by creating an internal dialogue or by intrapersonally communicating with themselves. Speaking well is important to them and they tend to primarily use words such as "call," "discuss," and "sounds good." Auditory people are able to recall what someone said to them months and years later, and they can become somewhat disoriented with too much environmental noise. Some of the common words and phrases that auditory individuals might use can include:

- Petition
- Resonant
- Loud
- Shout
- Request
- Afterthought
- Call on
- Earful
- Give an account of
- Grant an audience
- Voice an opinion
- Within hearing range

- Ringing
- Told
- Silent
- Talk
- Ask
- Clearly expressed
- Described in detail
- Express yourself
- Give me your ears
- Hidden message
- Well-informed
- Word for word

*Kinesthetic people* tend to think by clarifying how they feel and by getting in touch with their feelings more often than others. They walk and move around while thinking or talking and use words such as "touch," "feel," and" contract" in their conversations. Kinesthetic people rarely forget their feelings or how they were made to feel and they tend to publicly express their emotions. Some of the words and phrases that kinesthetic individuals might use can include the following:

- Feel
- Hurt
- Graceful
- Irritated
- Cool
- Calm
- Collected
- Floating on thin air
- Get a load of this
- Know-how

- Light-headed
- Pressure
- Get the point
- Sensual
- Problem
- Firm foundation
- Get in touch with
- Hand-in-hand
- Too much hassle

Based on the above information on the three communication modes discussed by experts like Tony Robbins, the motivational speaker and performance consultant, as well as authors like Alan Vengel (2000), do you think you are a visual, auditory or kinesthetic person? Which of the three modes best reflect your way of speaking and thinking? Once you have determined your dominant style of thinking and speaking, that tends to be your common rapport building strategy for others.

Now, how do you build rapport with others that you are trying to influence? First and foremost, you need to determine their manner of speaking and thinking. Which of the three modes best reflect this person's mode of speaking and thinking? Is he or she a visual, an auditory or a kinesthetic person? Once you have determined this person's dominant style of thinking and speaking, then you can adjust your mode of communication with this person by "mirroring" him or her through the usage of the same words as his or her approach. If the person is a visual communicator, then use more words and phrases from the visual communicator's category as this is the best mode of building rapport with this individual. If the person is an auditory communicator, then use more words and phrases from the auditory communicator's category as this is the best mode of building rapport with this individual. If the person is a kinesthetic communicator, then use more words and phrases from the kinesthetic communicator's category as this is the best mode of building rapport with this individual. The key is to adjust your communication style to his or her preferred mode of language and this will greatly assist in rapport building and, thus, influencing.

## The Power in Charming Others

Rapport building and influencing people is not an easy task and nobody is born with innate qualities of leading and charming others. However, the skills of influencing and charming others are demonstrated every day through the work and writings of many great coaches in this world. In their beautifully written short, 2006 book, entitled *The Power of Charm: How to win anyone over in any situation*, Brian

Tracy and Ron Arden mention that "charm" is gained through the consistent use of specific skills by effective coaches and leaders. In other words, charm can be learned and every coach, manager, and human being can benefit from the skills associated with the term charm. In their book, Tracy and Arden offer the principles and concepts that are often associated with magnetic attraction and charismatic influence that all coaches and managers should master. Brain Tracy, who "is one of the world's top success coaches," has spent his entire life learning and coaching others about success and performance. Ron Arden is a former actor who is now a "top-flight coach of professional speakers."

*The Power of Charm* offers tools and skills that can help coaches win more friends and influence over people, negotiate more effectively, and get better deals in the workplace. The consistent and effective use of the principles discussed can earn managers, leaders and coaches a certain level of trust, support, respect, loyalty, and affection. Through the use of real-life examples and practical exercises, readers will learn about:

- Listening effectively by pausing, questioning, and paraphrasing.
- Making better eye contact.
- Using head tilts and nods to signal interest and convey warmth.
- Mastering body language to project confidence and inspire trust from others.
- Putting others at ease with a smile and laughter.
- Offering verbal reassurances and using silence advantageously.
- Breaking the habits of using such verbal bridges as "umm" and "er."
- Being an engaging speaker.
- Carefully steering the discussion toward a new topic.
- Avoiding conflict while being firm on one's position.
- Getting in step and creating rapport with others.

*The Power of Charm* offers many great tips for managers and coaches to make a great first impression, gaining an advantage over one's competitors, and socializing more effectively in private and business settings. According to Tracy and Arden (2006), the single most important quality to possess when one is trying to win someone over is the ability to charm others. *Charming* is basically the ability to create and produce extraordinary rapport with others, and making them feel exceptionally good during each face-to-face meeting. Tracy and Arden explain that about 85% of each person's ability to succeed at anything depends on his/her ability to win people over, to convince him or her, in other words to charm him/her. Authors Tracy and Arden offer many secrets to make others feel special, including the Five A's of Charm which can be used by all coaches to be more charming:

- *Acceptance.* By smiling, you can give another person the attitude of "unconditional positive regard." You are telling others that you accept them as they are. Smiling and being happy at the presence of others make them feel good about themselves; they feel noteworthy. In return, they find you to be charming.
- *Appreciation.* Showing appreciation to others increases their self-esteem. One can make others feel more valuable and capable by saying "thank you" to every thing they do. Making others feel appreciated can bring more joy to

the manager and coach. Doing more good for others also means that you will like yourself more. The more you like yourself, in a modest manner of course, the more charming you will be to others.

- *Approval.* People naturally have a deep need for ongoing approval for their work and accomplishments. If you take advantage of such opportunities and express feelings of approval for others' achievements through timely and sincere praise, you will be more charming to them. Praise makes people feel good about themselves and you.
- *Admiration.* Giving others compliments that are timely and sincere makes them feel recognized. Take advantage of this opportunity by complimenting others on their clothing, punctuality, and other great qualities. Giving people sincere and timely compliments makes them feel good and in return they will find you more charming.
- *Attention.* Being acknowledged and listened to is the best way to make someone feel special. Give others your full attention by using good listening techniques, making eye contact, and using effective body language. Such acts of paying attention can make people special and, therefore, they will find you charming.

The concepts of acceptance, appreciation, approval, admiration, and attention can go a long way when one is trying to be charming and an effective manager or coach. One can start by simply greeting others as if one is truly thrilled to see them. Be delighted, excited and show gratitude when you see another person and when you are in his/her presence. Look at the person in detail and compliment him or her on something that you find charming about him or her. Attentively listen to what he or she has to say. Nod to the person to acknowledge the person and to confirm your understanding. Last but not least, be a slow talker. Being a slower talker is a trait that makes people more charming. Speak at a pace that might be a bit uncomfortable for you at first, but it might just be the right pace when conversing with others.

There are many others skills, such as strategically determining what one says and how one should say it, that coaches should learn and practice if they are to be more charming with their colleagues, employees and friends. To become better skilled at charming and positively influencing others, existing and aspiring coaches can study and observe people like Brian Tracy and Ron Arden and benefit from their writings. Charming is about the ability to develop a connection with and influence over others. Be charming.

## Personal Power: Forms and Sources

Chris Argyris (as cited by Hersey and Campbell, 2004) believed that bureaucratic and pyramidal values still dominate most organizations, which has produced many problems in today's society. Perhaps this is due to the fact that many managers are still trying to hold to their powers using inappropriate techniques. Argyris' Immaturity-Maturity Theory explained that people need to undergo seven personality changes in order to become a fully mature individual. These changes included: moving from a passive state to a state of increasing activity, dependency to independence, few ways of behavior to many ways of behavior, shallow interests to deep interests, short term views to long term perspectives, subordinate to superordinate, and lack of awareness to becoming fully aware. Argyris theorized that companies keep employees from realizing their full maturity and potential by failing to give them the ability to move from immaturity to maturity at work. A hierarchical organization usually does not allow for much empowerment, thus people remain immature. In such a work environment, many people are given minimal control over their job responsibilities and are encouraged to be passive and dependent upon others. People are not encouraged to think for themselves and are expected to rely on managers to make decisions. Subordinates focus on tasks and report to their supervisors. Those supervisors report to their supervisors and so on. The span of control becomes larger at the top, but is narrow and finite at the bottom. Workers at the bottom perform repetitive and routine tasks. They often become bored and fail to make decisions on their own or take greater responsibility. Decisions are made by managers and often restrict creativity. The hierarchical structure usually keeps subordinates dependent on managers. Subordinates infrequently achieve any self-confidence and do not wish to move up in the organization. Although some flat organizations with few hierarchical levels tend to move beyond Argyris' theory, it is believed that his theory is alive and well in corporate America. This is why organizational leaders need to change their perspective and develop effective coaches. Furthermore, each employee should take personal responsibility for increasing his/her power and influence in the organization.

No matter where you are within an organization you should be trying to influence people in just and fair manner toward better performance. If you are a manager you can, for example, use your position and personal power to influence the people who report directly to you (this is known as managing down). If you are trying to influence your supervisor, senior executives, and associates you must depend on personal power (this is known as selling-up). It is through trust and confidence that an effective relationship can be built. In coaching and influencing others either up or down, professionals are likely to "sell up" and manage "down." According to Dr. Paul Hersey, an individual should "sell up" in order to influence the followers' behavior, and therefore could rely on personal power to develop rapport and cohesiveness between him/herself and the follower. On the other hand, one manages "down" because in order to influence one has to use position power; which is using authority to delegate down, such as using rewards and punishment and personal power; to develop commitment and respect from followers. Hence, both personal and position power has to be used to effectively manage down. According to experts, there is not one best type of power for influencing others in all cases and situation; results have proven that leaders may need various power bases depending on the situation. Each base of power has its own importance; for example, expert and legitimate power is believed to be the reason for compliance, while referent power is associated with follower performance and satisfaction measures.

*Power*, according to Drs. Paul Hersey and Ron Campbell, is defined as a leader's potential for influencing others; as opposed to the definition of leadership which is a leader's attempt to influence others. Power is an important topic in leadership because power has the potential to influence; it is the "horsepower" of making leadership work. According to Hersey and Campbell (2004) and other experts in the behavioral sciences fields, as previously mentioned, there are many types of power including the following:

1. *Referent power* uses high levels of communication and support and is based on good personal relations with the follower.
2. *Legitimate power* allows the leader to induce compliance and influence behavior by virtue of the leader's position within the organization.
3. *Position power* is the extent to which managers are willing to delegate authority to subordinates, and this power must be earned on a day-to-day basis. Because managers already have legitimate power, that power tends to flow down in an organization once confidence and trust has been established by a subordinate, and that subordinate is ready to take on additional responsibility.
4. *Coercive power* can be helpful in dealing with people of very low job readiness. This power base reminds people of the consequences of failing to progress.
5. *Expert power* is associated with individuals at high levels of readiness. Because these people are both willing and able to do their jobs without close supervision, they will award a manager power for having high levels of skill and knowledge.
6. *Reward power* can increase the effectiveness of the leadership. The willingness of subordinates with low to moderate levels of readiness may be enhanced by the leader's access to rewards for desired behavior.
7. *Personal power* is the extent to which followers are committed to their leader. Personal power flows up in an organization from followers, as it is not inherent. In order for one to establish confidence and trust in their managers, they must sell up and influence managers by using personal power.
8. *Information power* means the leader has pertinent data that can provide information to maintain and improve performance of the follower. The leader can clarify and explain issues and the follower will have their questions answered, thus improving confidence levels for independent decision making. Information power is where the leader has access to information and is able to provide this knowledge to improve the follower's performance.
9. *Connection power* comes into play as the subordinate begins to develop readiness, but is still concentrating on avoiding punishment. If a person perceives the manager as having strong connections, the person may respond out of a desire to solidify a connection to the manager for personal gain.

The definition of a leader is a person who attempts to influence the behavior of people or a group. Power is the leader's actual potential to influence others. The most desirable situation is to have both personal power and position power. Personal power stems from the followers and flows up the organizational hierarchy. It is not an innate quality and can vary day-by-day. It is the way the followers feel about the leader and their willingness to follow that leader. On the other hand, position power is delegated by the leader's supervisors and flows down the organizational chart. Leaders receive the authority to distribute sanctions, punishments and rewards. Both sources of power can be taken away, with position power removed by supervisors and personal power removed by followers. When effectively managing down, leaders must influence direct reports and staff members with both personal power and position power. Many experts see personal power as enabling commitment and loyalty, whereas position power commands respect and compliance. Overall, personal power is more valuable toward maintaining better interpersonal relationships. In fact, personal power is used to accomplish the act of influencing followers through managing down as well as the act of influencing supervisors through selling up. When trying to influence executives and supervisors, the leader relies only upon his or her personal power. This is especially useful when the leader has little or no position power. He or she must establish a good rapport with his or her associates and develop mutual trust and confidence. The amount of personal power gained will impact how much position power is granted. Broken down further into as many as seven bases (coercive, connection, reward, legitimate, information, referent, and expert) by Hersey and Campbell (2004), there is no single best type. Effective leaders must diagnose the situation; reviewing the task and evaluating the employee's readiness level. Next, the leader selects and applies the appropriate leadership style along with the correct power base to influence behavior. A comprehensive model can be used to determine appropriate power and style per the follower's readiness levels. Studies have shown that referent and expert power strongly influences employee performance and satisfaction, while legitimate and expert power induces employee compliance. Many variables affect the leader's selection of a power base, so he or she must become familiar with the situational use of power.

Subordinates must prove to their managers that they have the requisite skills necessary for them to receive power and authority. Although there is no best type of power, the most favorable situation for leaders is when they have both personal and position power, which constitutes an interaction-influence system. Additionally, expert and legitimate power is most important for compliance, but expert and referent power are strongly related to follower performance and satisfaction. One thing is for sure, power is perception and in order to influence followers, one must use their power or risk losing it.

To increase their internal power, coaches also need to continuously develop their own information and level of confidence through intrapersonal communication and believing that they can succeed. Dr. Marshal Goldsmith, an executive coach, believes that coaches need to internalize the following four concepts (Personal Communication on July 2005 in Escondido, California; Hersey and Campbell, 2004): I choose to succeed, I will succeed, I have succeeded, and I can succeed.

"*I choose to succeed*" is a belief successful people tend to have. Many successful people do not like to be manipulated or controlled. By taking matters into their own hands and deciding to succeed, the person is in control of his/her own destiny. Thus, people will have a deeper commitment to becoming successful and pleasing themselves. When people have personal commitments in their own success, they take ownership, and work hard towards achieving their goals. Each person must make his or her own magic and success. One must make a personal commitment to oneself and not necessarily always rely on outside sources for achievement. Once one owns the decision to succeed, one will not give up in the face of adversity and work even harder to achieve goals.

"*I will succeed*" is an unflappable sense of optimism that many successful people personify. This type of self-talk increases confidence in overall ability, and this confidence is contagious. Many successful people believe the people around them can be successful too, just by virtue of affinity. Successful people tend to be very busy and face the danger of over-commitment. If one believes it can be done, and one sets his or her mind to it, anything is possible. Success is contagious and once you achieve something, the feeling permeates, and makes you want to achieve over and over again.

"*I have succeeded.*" Successful coaches often have a positive impression of their past performance. High achievers not only believe that they have achieved results; they tend to believe that they were instrumental in helping the results get achieved. This tends to be true even if the positive outcomes were caused by external events that they did not control.

"*I can succeed.*" Successful managers and leaders tend to believe that they have the internal capacity to make desirable things happen for themselves and their people. They see opportunities where others see threats. This comfort with ambiguity leads people with high self-efficacy to take greater risks and achieve great returns. In addition, they do not feel like victims of fate. They believe that they have the motivation and ability to change their world; this is why they will find external control and manipulation very distasteful.

For example, with regard to a college degree and academic success, one can say the following: I completed the college program because I chose to be successful in my career and as a personal goal. I know I can succeed because I have stuck with it regardless of the obstacles I have experienced throughout the process. I know I will succeed because I have not given myself any other option. I know I have succeeded because I know I will not give up and continuous effort will eventually lead to my success. I must see success and live it in order to experience it. Every effective researcher, manager and coach must say "I believe I am successful, I act successful and I leave no room for anything else. Success is inevitable." Some wise people tend to say that if you believe you are a good person, then you will be. So, be one, even if you have to fake it at first, eventually it will be a part of you.

According to Drs. Marshal Goldsmith, Paul Hersey, and Ron Campbell, successful coaches and managers can do many things to become even more productive. The following are some of their suggestions (Hersey and Campbell, 2004): Most successful people's positive view of their performance can make it hard to hear disconfirming information from others about themselves and their performance. Successful people should receive input on important self-selected behaviors as perceived by important, self-selected raters who are highly respected. After receiving input from respected peers, select one or two important areas for behavioral improvement in the coming months and year. To increase commitment, involve respected colleagues in the behavior change process by asking them to observe the change, provide feedback on the progress and help with the behavior change.

Successful people can become more productive by seeing the connection between their behavior change goals and their personal goals. In moving closer to doing this, successful people need to let go of the past and focus on the future, while envisioning a positive future that will enable them to achieve their goals. They should learn to be a supportive coach not a cynic, critic or a judge. This will allow them to move beyond setbacks and encourage them to participate in the process of change. Finally, successful people need to develop a follow-up process that provides an opportunity for ongoing dialogue with colleagues. This is important so the executive does not fall back into the same behavior pattern. Additionally, successful people should regularly seek "feed-forward" feedback. The "feed-forward" feedback exercise with one's colleagues and other coaches can provide suggestions for the future which is where success lies. To summarize, Dr. Marshal Goldsmith's thoughts and the recommendations of Drs. Hersey and Campbell, to become even more productive, successful leaders and managers (coaches) can:

- Get ongoing executive coaching and mentoring.
- Be a supportive coach, not a cynic, critic or judge.
- Develop a follow-up process that provides an opportunity for ongoing discussion on some of their selected behaviors with selected colleagues.
- Give and receive feedback that focuses on the future from those around you in all levels.
- Be open to a learning and growing environment and let go of the past when it doesn't apply or work in new situations.
- Keep an eye on "over-committing" themselves.
- Work on a few behaviors that can make a real difference.

## Coaching and Influencing Styles of a Leader

Similar to effective leadership and management, coaching is about bringing about change in behavior and, ultimately, outcomes. Since the main objective or purpose of coaching is to help coachees change, success is achieved when there is observable shift or higher performance in the ultimate outcome. Essentially, since change requires a better vision of the future, coaching is a major component of effective leadership. There are many academicians and practitioners that study, write about, and conduct research on the topic of leadership to discover the "best" traits and styles of leading others. Experts agree that while there is no one best style of leadership, successful leaders are those who can adapt their behavior to meet the demands of each unique situation. The experienced leader can use many complex and subtle means to exercise his/her influence and stimulate those he/she leads to creative and productive efforts. Leadership is not about winning a popularity contest, as is often the case with politics, but rather leadership is about doing what is right in each situation.

*Leadership* can be defined as the process of influencing an individual or a group of individuals while providing an environment where personal, professional, or organizational objectives can successfully be achieved. Leadership, as a performance management vehicle, is the process by which one person exerts influence over one or more individuals and inspires, motivates, and directs their behaviors toward the achievement of individual, group and/or organizational objectives. The individual or person who exerts any form of influence that guides behavior toward a predetermined objective is considered to be a leader. Effectiveness, in the context of leadership, is doing the right things for the right reasons at the right times. Effective leadership can greatly enhance and increase the ability of the individual, the group and the organization to successfully meet both its current and prospective challenges as well as opportunities in the areas of gaining a competitive advantage, fostering ethical behavior, providing a motivational work environment, and recruiting and retaining a diverse workforce. A person's leadership style is formed by the specific ways in which he or she chooses to influence other individuals. A person's leadership style shapes the way that this individual approaches the various functions of management, which are planning, organizing, leading, and controlling. All individuals working in professional organizations have their own personal leadership styles that determine how they lead others and how they perform the concomitant management functions.

Coaching requires diverse skills since people are diverse and each person may prefer to be coached differently for different tasks. For example, some people want to be told what to do, when to do it and how do it. On the other side, some individuals prefer or would like development, guidance and direction from a coach. Bacon and Spear (2003, p. 88) call these two extremes as directive (telling others the what, when and how aspects) and nondirective (providing development, guidance and advice as needed); and claim that most coaches tend to use more directive approaches, regardless of whether or not this approach is preferred by the coachee. One problem with always using directive coaching might be that these coaches tend to influence and lead others mostly from their own perspective. Of course, as mentioned by Bacon and Spear (p. 89), directive coaching is an appropriate way to coach in some circumstances…but not with everyone at all times as it can hinder their development and progress. Bacon and Spear (2003, p. 90) write that "nondirective coaches have learned to help others by helping them to help themselves," which is perhaps similar to a servant style of leadership. Bacon and Spear further explain that "Nondirective coaches don't have the glamour associated with directive coaches; in fact, by design they choose to work with subtlety and near invisibility as their influence fades into the choices they help their clients make" (2003, p.90).

In the behavioral perspective of leadership, there are two clusters of leadership behaviors discussed that focus on the people or tasks. First, people-oriented behaviors include showing mutual concern, trust and respect for subordinates. People-oriented leadership tends to result in higher job satisfaction among subordinates, as well as lower absenteeism, grievances, and turnover compared to using task-oriented style. Also, job performance tends to be lower than for employees with task-oriented leaders. Second, task-oriented leadership styles generally include behaviors that define and structure work roles to ensure that everyone follows company rules in order to reach performance capacity and meet the established standards. Task-oriented leadership can result in lower job satisfaction as well as higher absenteeism and turnover among subordinates. Behavioral leadership scholars conclude that some people are high or low on both styles, others are high on one style and low on the other, and most individuals are somewhere in between in the continuum.

Situational Leadership Theory (SLT), developed by Drs. Paul Hersey and Ken Blanchard, states that effective leaders vary their style with the "readiness" of followers, and match the "readiness" of the follower to one of the four leadership styles, which include telling, selling, participating, and delegating. So, the leader's effectiveness is highly dependant on whether the person's leadership style is appropriately matched to the situation and the readiness of the follower. It must be acknowledged that some situations have leadership substitutes which identify contingencies that either limit the leader's ability to influence subordinates or make that particular leadership style unnecessary. Effective leaders adapt their styles to fit a broad range of individuals and variables impacting their situations. Dr. Paul Hersey claims that "leadership is any attempt to influence the behavior of another person or persons," and effective leadership is adapting one's behavior to the performance needs of the person or persons. Effective leaders diagnose, adapt, and communicate based on the readiness of their followers in the workforce and other situational variables. Dr. Hersey defined a person's *readiness* level as their ability and willingness to perform the task at hand and this definition considers two types of readiness: job and psychological. Knowing a person's (follower's) readiness level and effectively adapting one's leadership style to match the readiness level is an important element of making sure the job gets done successfully. As such, Situational Leadership applies to professionals in business, government, the community, volunteers, religious leaders, as well as to parents, and others who have a need to influence the effort of others.

Situational Leadership Theory, according to Hersey and Blanchard, proposes that individuals can change their leadership style (behavior) depending on the situation and the readiness of the follower. Drs. Hersey and Blanchard are of the mindset that leaders can and do change their styles depending on with whom they are working. The situational leadership concept is based on the interactive interplay among direction (task behavior) provided by the leader, socio-emotional support (relationship behavior) provided by the leader and the readiness of the follower on the specific task that needs performing. According to the model, there are four readiness levels:

1. R1- followers are unable and unwilling to perform the task.
2. R2- followers are unable but willing to perform the task.
3. R3- followers are able but unwilling to perform the task.
4. R4- followers are able and willing to perform the task.

The situational leadership concept attempts to keep a balance between high tech (task behaviors) and high touch (relationship behavior). Once the followers' readiness is determined, a manager or a leader can choose from the four leadership styles suggested by Hersey and Blanchard's model that focus to some extent either on task behavior or relationship behavior. *Task behavior* is the extent to which leaders engage in top-down communication by explaining what the follower is to do, as well as when, where, and how each function is to be accomplished. *Relationship behavior* is the extent to which leaders engage in joint communication with followers while providing socio-emotional support. The four corresponding leadership styles (telling, selling, participating, and delegating) that match these readiness (R) levels are as follows:

1. *R1- matches best with "Telling," high task-low relationship.* The manager or the leader defines the roles needed to the do the job and tells followers what, where, how, and when to do the tasks.

2. *R2- matches best with "Selling," high task-high relationship*. The manager or leader provides step-by-step and disciplined guidelines to get the job done while being supportive.
3. *R3- matches best with "Participating," low task-high relationship*. The managers, or the leader, along with followers (employees and/or colleagues) jointly decide how to get the job done with the required quality standards.
4. *R4- matches best with "Delegating," low task-low relationship*. The manager or leader provides little directions and little support to the followers since they know how to get the job done and they are very willing to do it independently.

Of course, there are perhaps thousands of situations that could use many different leadership styles. The situational leadership model has four leadership styles to keep it simple and easy to understand, so it can be applied by individuals of different skill levels and competencies. In each situation, the model encourages managers to match the style with the followers' level of readiness thus providing the most appropriate amount of task behavior and relationship behavior for the specific task on hand. Dr. Hersey (Personal Communication at NSU, 2006) provides the following recommendations for each of the four leadership styles:

- Style one or *telling* is best when attempting to influence low levels of readiness. Alternative words that describe the telling style are guiding, directing, and establishing.
- Style two or *selling* is best when attempting to influence low to moderate levels of readiness. The leader attempts to get the follower to buy into doing the task psychologically. Alternative words that describe the selling style are explaining, clarifying and persuading.
- Style three or *participating* is best when attempting to influence moderate to high levels of readiness. The key is to encourage the follower to participate and get involved. Alternative words that describe the participating style are encouraging, collaborating and committing.
- Style four or *delegating* is best when attempting to influence high levels of readiness. This is where the follower has almost all of the decisions for both decision-making and implementation of the activities to get the job done. Alternative words that describe the delegating style are observing, monitoring and fulfilling.

As the readiness of the follower (person performing the specific task) increases in terms of performance, the leader should adapt by reducing task behavior and increasing relationship behaviors. As the follower becomes totally ready by showing successful performance, the leader should reduce both task and relationship behaviors to the lowest level possible. Overall, coaches and managers apply this model similar to medical practitioners who deal with patients that complain about a pain in parts of their bodies. The medical doctor must first diagnose the cause of the problem and then prescribe the right medication to alleviate the problem or pain. Dr. Hersey says that a prescription without diagnosis can basically amount to malpractice. Similarly, a manager or a leader must first diagnose the follower's level of readiness with each person in his/her team, which can include many personalities, and then act with an appropriate leadership style. Diagnosis, or assessing ability and willingness of the follower to see what leadership style is needed, should be followed by matching an appropriate leadership behavior and then implementation of the leadership style to make sure the job gets done with the required quality in the allotted timeframe.

### Leadership Philosophy and Lessons from the Military[13]

The 2007 Jossey-Bass book entitled *Leadership Lessons form West Point*, edited by Doug Crandall and foreword by Jim Collins, emphasizes that the mark of a great leader is the art of balance. *Leadership Lessons from West Point* draws richly on the tenets espoused by Sun Tzu's *Art of War*; these include trust, benevolence, strictness, self-discipline, credibility, wisdom, unconcern with fame, and having the ability to put the followers first. Crandall (2007) addresses the difficulties, contradictions and balance needed for great leadership, a quality that is vital to business. He draws on the reflections and experience of twenty contributors whose combined expertise in sociology, psychology, group dynamics, organizational psychology, social psychology, and business leadership, to outline the art of leadership in the modern world. Crandall and the contributors explore the many facets of leadership, drawing liberally on their experience as military leaders who have served both as professors at West Point and field commanders in both peacetime and war.

Crandall presents a compelling picture of leadership in the military as it exists today. Crandall and his contributors outline their varied personal leadership transformation and spend time explaining pertinent changes like self awareness, moral philosophy, charisma, objective diagnosis of failure, and learning the core duality of leaders as followers. They then map out the development of leadership values which include the hardest lessons of learning from failure, delegating responsibilities and the need to be a great follower – having faith in those you are trusted to lead. Only after internalization of the fact that everyone is a leader and the hard work it takes to achieve effectiveness and understand the fallibility of our very humanity, can one truly lead. Crandall and the contributors then delineate the various leadership styles that have worked in a variety of situations with the disclaimer that there is no one magic prescription for the right leadership style. Crandall and the contributors details the various leadership options available when having to lead organizations including managing expectations, cultural diversity, change, and commitment, going on to explore alternative views such as socialization of leaders, duality of the leadership roles, real and perceived authenticity of the leader, self confidence, and trust in delegation.

Crandall's purpose in *Leadership Lessons from West Point* is to provide a guide for the leader. The approach is not one of soapbox lecturing as is the case with most books of this nature; instead it is one of careful reflection tempered with research, along with examples of the age-old compromise required on the part of the leader. Crandall and the contributors go on to map out the pros and cons associated

---

[13] Contributed by Reccia N. Charles, St. George's University. Book reviewed for the *Journal of Applied Management and Entrepreneurship.*

with different leadership styles along with the morality and ethics involved. This is done by outlining the fundamental core values that is required of an effective leader and the role the leader plays in an organization. The main strength of the book rests on Crandall's ability to harness the expertise and experience of twenty other experts who have demonstrated leadership in a variety of circumstances. Remarkably, Major Crandall and the contributors also includes comprehensive examples from their experiences and research including observation of others who have inspired them; which can prove invaluable to the leader that resides in all of us. Moreover, time is dedicated to the art of balancing the various roles of the leader, even giving the reader gentle reminders that some of the greatest leaders have experienced failures and are merely human.

*Leadership Lessons from West Point* will prove to be very useful to the aspiring entrepreneur, coach, manager, and business leader. Crandall and the contributors do not tackle business leadership directly, they tackle the essence of leadership and the correlation to business can easily be inferred. Accordingly, the businessperson may read this book and not find in it a step by step guide to becoming an effective leader in his/her business environment. However, the book is one of lessons and reflections about effective leadership. This book is handy for the business practitioner, who is interested in effective coaching and leadership strategies that can be applied to change management, strategic management, organizational commitment development, diversity management, and organizational strategy. In fact, it is an excellent read for anyone who needs to learn or develop leadership skills. The book provides varied mental insight and operational frameworks necessary for leader/follower success. Experience has always proven to be the best teacher; however, given the complexity of the business world, other people's experiences can serve as a good proxy.

### Summary

Coaching is about helping employees and colleagues strategically perform at their highest capacity. In other words, coaching is about managing performance and helping people become successful in what they are doing and what they plan to do. According to Dr. Randolph Pohlman, "Often people argue about what is the most important process or technique for success in the workplace; when it comes to leadership and management, the answer is clear—it is people, since they create all of the rest" (Personal Communication, April 2, 2007). As a coach and a manager, if you take care of your people in a timely manner with respect, sensitivity and professionalism as perceived by them, all the other "mumbo jumbo" stuff will fall into place; and yes, according to some views, other than people, all the rest is "mumbo jumbo." Of course, an important aspect of leadership, management and coaching is to effectively influence others.

Influencing is basically working with other people to get the results you want, but without destroying the relationship, and it is almost always necessary when dealing with people over whom you have little or no control. Influencing is all about the relationship and communication with the other person or group; it is about identifying the specifics of the situation on hand, determining both parties' goals, using the correct behavior that relates to push, pull and push/pull energies, and attuning to their communication style. Somewhat different from coaching, influencing involves the consideration of several foundational factors. The goal of the influencer and the goal of the influencee must be considered. The influencer must determine who it is that he/she needs to influence to achieve the goal. This step should be taken carefully since, frequently, the person who first comes to mind may not be the person who can assist in achieving the goal. Once the influencee is identified, the goal is determined and stated in a positive manner. The goals and mindset of the influencee must also be considered. The influencer should use empathy and consider how it would feel to be in the influencee's shoes. What is the influencee's history with the situation? How has this person reacted to influencing in the past? What types of proposals have won the other person's approvals historically? In organizations, the role of influencing is critical to the health of the organization. Influencing gives the edge needed to get what we want and guides more productive business relationships, even when we have the so-called authority to enforce rather than cultivate compliance. In many ways, influencing is the way business gets done. One may do something to help a fellow worker out, not because one is obliged due to a chain of command but because of their relationship.

According to experts, successful leaders and managers, if they are to become even more productive, they can let go of the past and focus on the future; they can be a supportive coach, not a cynic, critic or judge; they can develop a follow-up process that provides an opportunity for ongoing dialogue on selected behaviors with selected colleagues; and they can practice receiving feedback from respected colleagues about their performance and in order to get suggestions for the future.

### Discussion Questions

1. What is "coaching"? What role can it play in organizations? Give an example. How does coaching and coaching skills relate to leadership and leadership skills? What are some of the common sets of skills that are used by both leaders and coaches? Can a person be an effective leader without being a good coach? Discuss your thoughts and examples.

2. What is "influencing"? What role can it play in organizations? Give an example. Influencing, which considers the development of trust and relationship as defined in this book, requires understanding one's own goals as well as the other party's. Why is it important to consider both of these factors when influencing others?

3. What is a "push" strategy and how does it differ from "pull" strategy? Discuss using an example for each.

4. What are two important ingredients for effective coaching and why? Give an example of each.

5. What is the role of influence in situational leadership styles? Discuss an example for each of the four styles.

6. What are some best means of increasing one's level of influence with colleagues and employees? List five strategies that might work with both groups.

# CHAPTER 4

## The Coaching Process and Steps

It is more important than ever today for everyone in the organization to perform at his/her highest capacity. Organizations are faced with increased competition, new markets, competitors from global environments, new and updated technologies, demanding and knowledgeable customers, and at times fewer skilled workers. These variables of skill building and performance enhancement are valid in any industry in the twenty-first century. Coaches work with their employees to achieve more with less, solve attitude problems, and are able to work with and inspire difficult associates to be productive. They are able to do all this by communicating with their employees, listening to them and getting their feedback, developing trust with others, documenting their performance goals, following up on promises and agreements, and by being caring and compassionate.

In a coaching process to build an employee's skills and enhancing performance standards, coaches tend to clearly state the performance problem or their expectation, get the employee's agreement on the problem, create practical solutions to the problem, agree on a specific action plan to solve the problem, and follow up as agreed upon. Effective leaders, managers and coaches understand that developing people for peak performance provides the much needed competitive edge, since the human asset in many cases is the most difficult asset to be imitated by competitors. However, due to the day-to-day pressures of getting more things done faster, some managers may only focus on current production and fail to develop the skills and competencies of their most important asset, their associates. The objectives of this chapter are to understand the vital role of effective coaching and how coaching skills can be used to keep the organization and people competitive. Furthermore, managers and leaders should be able to utilize effective coaching techniques and apply the steps to coaching when working with employees to reinforce and guide everyone toward high performance. Managers and leaders need to also gain an understanding of managing the differences of employees and how to coach them on an individual basis. Once managers and leaders understand the concept of being an effective coach, then they can formulate a development plan for their employees' coaching needs in the workplace.

Whether this information is new to you or not, it is essential that there is a sense of comfort and consistency throughout the company with respect to the value of coaching. Coaching can enhance the working relationship between managers and employees. Coaching topics tend to discuss the strategies involved in the leadership process in order to cultivate an environment conducive to growth and development. By becoming an effective coach, you will be able to develop the people who serve your customers, promote your products, and manage your systems; and those whom you effectively coach will be on the road to peak performance. The following are some of the compelling coaching thoughts:

1) The primary benefits of coaching are improved individual performance; bottom line results including profit, client service, and competitiveness.

2) Before exploding or writing the worker up on a formalized warning, try one-on-one coaching.

3) Employees need to know that you appreciate their positive efforts on every day performed tasks and not just major accomplishments.

4) Organizational coaching seeks to improve performance, productivity, and/or teamwork and views the coach as the expert who motivates and gives advice.

**Coaching Benefits and Situations**

Due to the changing demographics of the business world such as more competition and the introduction of new technologies, organizations are discovering that traditional tactics of management are no longer enough to remain competitive. As such, coaching is becoming recognized and practiced as an effective tool to increase morale, performance and the "bottom line" through the success of each individual associate. For example, studies have shown that most employees who received coaching in their jobs say that it improved their job performance and professional success. In some organizations where coaching is effectively practiced as a management style, the bottom line performance is two to three times better than the traditional "command-and-control" type of organizations. Furthermore, it has been proven that employee commitment increases when there is a strong, positive relationship between the manager and his/her employees. These types of relationships are developed best as a result of effective coaching. Bacon and Spear (2003, p. xv) mention that coaching provides a solution for many of today's challenges and the following are some of them:

- Real time learning by the coach and coachee.
- Personalized learning for each associate.
- Integrated learning to help associates balance the demands of their jobs with those of their personal priorities.
- Sustained attention to growth and development geared toward behavior changes.
- Accelerated on-the-job learning to better meet the demands of the changing workplace.
- A changed role for managers of learning organizations.

Bacon and Spear (2003) mention that about 53% of employees say that they would like more coaching; 60% say that they want better coaching than they are receiving in their workplaces, and 56% say that the coaching they receive is not helpful or developmental. While employees want more, and better, coaching in their jobs, managers need to develop their own personal skills if they are to glean the benefits of a highly productive workforce. Managers need to become better coaches and develop a focused and developmental relationship with each employee. Effective relationship-oriented coaching creates more knowledgeable and competent employees, reduces errors and rework, and it greatly assists in bringing new changes to the culture. Both effective and ineffective managers tend to know what makes a good coach. The difference lies in being able to transfer this knowledge into successful actions with employees to increase their performance and success. Effective coaching skills:

- Make your job as a manager easier as it enables greater delegation leaving you time to take on bigger projects.
- Build your reputation as a developer of people while increasing the productivity of people since they will know the expectations and the fact that what they do matters.
- Develop trust and a good relationship between you and your people.
- Increase creativity, innovation, morale, and teamwork since everyone will feel safe working in an inclusive environment.

Simply stated, coaching is about developing a trusting relationship with your people so you can jointly clarify expectations and departmental goals thereby leading to specific action plans for their achievement. As such, there are many situations where coaching skills will be very effective and the following list presents some of them.

1) Reinforcing good performance.
2) Motivating employees to new heights and peak performance levels.
3) Orienting a new employee into the department or organization.
4) Providing new knowledge to individuals about changes and tactics.
5) Training a new skill for a new task that needs performing.
6) Following up on competencies passed on during a training session.
7) Explaining the current or new standards and how they can be achieved.
8) Setting priorities for effective time management with those employees who need it.
9) Inculcating someone into the cliques and groups which may exist within the political circles.
10) Clarifying expectations and correcting poor performance.
11) Increasing the self confidence of an employee about the task or new responsibilities and challenges.
12) Conducting a performance review.

Everyone has benefited, to some extent, from the guidance, assistance and leadership of effective coaches during one's socialization in the society at an early age, at school, at one's initial job, during advancement opportunities, during challenging times, during changes, and during happy times. Effective coaches can be personal or professional at any stage in one's life. When managers think of their past experiences related to effective coaches and other such leadership experiences, most people tend to remember their coaches from ten, twenty and thirty years ago because they made such a positive impact on them. Those who look up to you for guidance and direction (such as your children, employees, students, and colleagues) are likely to have similar positive memories if you use effective coaching techniques with them. Most professional people who look up to you are likely to fall into one of the following three groups with regard to their performance on a specific task:

1) *Below standard performers.* People in this category are not performing at the desired level and need to add new competencies. People in this group might be new in their roles or they might be veterans whose skills are below standard. *Clarify and set the standard for them.*

2) *Satisfactory performers needing new skills.* People in this group have to unlearn old behaviors and learn new skills. Typically, they are performing well today, but their skills will be obsolete or insufficient as priorities evolve and new challenges become a reality. Changes in work demands, organizational strategies, or competitive forces might precipitate the need for a new direction. *Set new direction and expect the development of new competencies.*

3) *"Going beyond the limit" performers.* In this group, you help people reach their full potential. They need to stretch their limits and find fresh applications for their skills so that they do not become stale or restless. You might not notice these developmental needs if people are content within their comfort zone and they are meeting organizational needs. Sometimes you need to stir people up and expose them to new possibilities to get maximum yield from their talents. *Set free and challenge them to new heights.*

## Coaching Roles

Effective coaching, as mentioned before, is a continuous process of conversational collaborations and interactions aimed at assisting others unlock and realize their full potential one task or one skill at a time and at a pace appropriate for the person being coached. The essence of coaching is unlocking people's potential, through stimulating questions, so they can maximize their own performance. Effective coaches keep in mind that imposing their way of accomplishing tasks is not their objective because that is not part of coaching but rather dictating. Effective coaches accept the challenge knowing that the growth and development journey is a continuous process, and that learning how to learn and develop are the real goals for both individuals (coach and the coachee). Effective coaches FOCUS on being (Plum International, 2003):

- *Fair.* Coaches earn respect by being fair and equitable to all of their associates.

- *Objective.* Successful coaching requires measurable criteria for observation and thoughtful analysis. They observe, analyze and discuss relevant issues with their associates for developmental purposes.

- *Collaborative.* Effective coaches acknowledge that the responsibility for improving performance and increased knowledge rests with the individual where the coach only offers assistance and guidance to the right direction. They lead, support, encourage, and synergize together with the individual.

- *Useful.* Impactful coaching produces value-added action plans that are doable given the time frames as well as the individual's level of competence and skills. The execution makes a difference.
- *Sincere.* Coaches must genuinely believe that employees and associates are the most important asset for the organization. They speak and act from the heart.

Effective coaches play the roles of *communicators* (encourage, inform, praise, raise awareness, and collaborate), *performance leaders* (set clear expectations, serve as role models, empower, help, and challenge), and *catalysts* (vehicles for change, remove barriers, and enable others to reach their full potential). *The Practical Coach* video offers many insights and suggestions on coaching for all leaders. The following are some highlights from this video: Coaching can be the single most important thing you do as a leader or manager; never let good or poor performance go unnoticed; when you see good performance, say it and praise it; don't let poor performance go unnoticed, make it private and positive, and or real personal issues and poor personal habits: first, prepare the teammate/associate, and second, be gentle and to the point. *The Practical Coach* video offers a concept, called the "*Two Minute Challenge,*" that coaches can use with their employees using the following steps:

- First, state what you observed.
- Second, wait for a response.
- Third, remind the person of the goal.
- Fourth, ask for a specific solution.
- Fifth, jointly agree on the solution and its implementation.

Overall, it is important managers follow-up and not let good or poor performance go unnoticed. Perhaps, some of these steps from the *Practical Coach* video can apply to your department or life. Which ones are you able to apply in your workplace or your personal life as a coach? Document them and plan on using them immediately to help improve performance while following the coaching guidelines.

## Coaching Guidelines

Coaching is not an innate skill but rather it is learned. It occurs through one's life personally and professionally. Effective coaching is the process of letting people know that what they do matters to you and to the organization. Furthermore, it is about letting them know that you are there to help them be the best they can be as their success is important. It is also about being sincere, specific and to the point about both good and poor performance so they can take personal responsibility for their achievements. From this perspective, coaching is and it can be one of the most important functions managers perform because it communicates performance levels, expectations, importance of the tasks and responsibilities, and a caring attitude. The following list summarizes some of the main elements involved in coaching.

1. Before beginning the coaching session, be sure to plan exactly what you want to achieve, and the potential benefits for the other person.

2.  Start on a positive note and establish a common ground by having a supportive environment.
3.  Communicate clearly, listen effectively, show that you care, and do not "beat around the bush." Clearly and caringly state the challenge, opportunity, and/or expectations.
4.  Be respectful of the other person's feelings, honor and dignity. Create a non-threatening environment for the interaction, dialogue and discussion.
5.  Be culturally sensitive by getting to know the other person's background, culture, values, and anticipate his/her reactions.
6.  Avoid value judgments, stereotyping and labeling the behavior of others.
7.  Use empathic listening skills to clarify your understanding and the other person's perspective.
8.  Stay with the point and do not get side tracked with other issues. Restate the purpose of the session and ask what specific things can be done to increase or improve performance. You can offer assistance but avoid providing solutions – let the individual come up with the solutions. Your job is to lead them in the right direction.
9.  Document and clarify the specific plan suggested by the employee, the expected level of performance and how the plan will improve performance. Seek agreement and summarize the conversation.
10. End on a positive note and thank the person for coming up with the specific plan.

As an effective leader, managers need to recognize the value in coaching associates to premier performance. Good coaches plan the work and communicate tasks clearly to their people. Earlier, it was discussed that effective coaches FOCUS on being fair, objective, collaborative, useful, and sincere. Now, we can discuss it a bit differently from Dr. Ken Blanchard's perspective by saying that an effective COACH is:

- *Committed* - good coaches have the desire and motivation to coach their associates. They genuinely want their associates to learn and develop.
- *Open Minded* - effective coaches have minds that are like sponges. They are open to and welcome new ideas, they listen to what associates have to say, and they use associate's suggestions when appropriate.
- *Adaptable* - good coaches do not worry about circumstances beyond their control. They handle change on the spur-of-the-moment and are able to bend with the wind. Effective coaches understand that the world is changing from a melting pot (everyone like me) to a salad bowl (accepting individual differences).
- *Consistent* - effective coaches respond predictably to their associate's job performance. They consistently praise good behavior and confront poor performance.
- *Honorable* - good coaches stand for high integrity. They create an environment where trust exists.

## Coaching Procedures and Steps with Associates

Coaching requires that managers or coaches describe the performance gap (problem or expectation) to the employee/coachee, get the coachee's (employee's) agreement on the problem or performance gap, brainstorm on possible solutions to the problem or performance gap, agree on a specific action plan to solve the problem or performance challenge, and follow up as agreed upon. In other words, coaches should pursue the following procedures when coaching an employee:

1. *State the problem.* Clearly state the problem, challenge, performance gap, and future expectations.
2. *Agree on the problem.* Both the coach and employee must agree on the performance problem or expected standards. The consequences of status quo should also be discussed.
3. *Develop alternatives to solve the problem.* It is important that the employee comes up with possible solutions. Of course, the coach can ask open-ended questions or provide hints or possible suggestions to guide the employee.
4. *Select an action plan to solve the problem.* The employee and coach should jointly agree on a solution that enhances performance or eliminates the problem. Specific timelines, actions, and standards must be clarified as part of this action plan.
5. *Follow up to make sure the problem has been eliminated.* As agreed upon in the action plan, the coach and employee should jointly assess the outcome and proceed accordingly.

Now that the basics of coaching along with its principles, roles and responsibilities have been discussed, we can discuss the basic steps involved in a comprehensive coaching process. There are five specific steps in the coaching process as you oversee the work done with and through your colleagues and associates. As such, effective coaching requires:

- Planning,
- Supporting others for good performance,
- Communicating and/or setting a time to increase performance,
- Leading others to higher performance, and
- Following up and confirming effective achievement of objectives and expectations.

These five key steps will help you become more effective in getting the work done with and/or through your associates or colleagues. While the steps apply to all people you want to influence or help toward better performance, the following sections will discuss them with regard to one's direct reports (employees) and colleagues.

### *Planning for Coaching*

A very important part of coaching is proper planning. One of the things we all learn as we get older is the importance of good planning before starting anything. Think of a gathering or the largest party or social event you have helped with and how much planning was required. Consider your most recent vacation trip and the planning of all events. Did you need to do any planning or did you delegate all tasks? Of course you did some planning, even if it was to follow someone else. We can all probably also think of occasions when we didn't plan properly and paid the "price" as a result.

With regard to planning, it is best to analyze, prioritize and schedule important tasks such as coaching individuals to higher performance. When we analyze the work or challenges ahead, we think about when each task needs to be completed, as well as how long each task is going to take. One also needs to think about why the coaching task needs to be done for one's associates. The planning stage is when you are supposed to spend the time to make sure that you understand as completely as possible the tasks you are assigning when coaching an associate. Taking the time to fully understand this responsibility during the planning stage will save time-consuming, and possibly, expensive, rework later.

### Supporting Associates

Support is the encouragement, the praise, the "thank you," and the sincere appreciations you give associates or colleagues as they work on their assigned tasks. Support makes people feel good about themselves, what they do, the organization, the profession, and about their jobs at your department. Associates commit to doing their best when you provide appropriate encouragement to them. Support is an important element of following-up on the assigned tasks and expectations.

Every manager must take about fifteen minutes each day to go around and catch people doing the right things. As such, you will encounter your associates performing many tasks effectively each day. This gives you the opportunity to observe your associates and provide specific comments on their performance. Don't say *great* job as you hurry past an associate. Instead, stop and say, "You're doing (mention observed task) very well (name) and I am very pleased with it." Personalized, sincere, and specific praise is the most effective form of support for your associates. It tells them that you're aware of what they're doing and that you value their work efforts. It tells them that what they do matters.

So, do you remember the last time you gave encouragement and support to your associates? Remember, you will achieve better results with sugar than with vinegar. Make sure your associates know how much you care about them and appreciate the work they do for you and their company each day.

### Communicating with Associates

As discussed above, enhancing performance requires that coaches open their mouths and communicate by describing the performance problem or expectation, getting the employee's agreement on the problem, creating possible solutions to the problem, agreeing on a specific action plan to solve the problem, and following up as agreed upon. Therefore, effective communication and listening skills are critical for coaches. Associates have the right to know how they are performing and you must clearly convey their progress to them on a regular basis. You should give continuous feedback to associates through effective coaching. You should provide effective feedback to your associates, based on the thoughts generated from your observation and analysis of their performance. Keep in mind that effective feedback is clear, specific, timely, practical, and sincere.

It is best to make individualized feedback regarding performance private, positive and performance oriented. Effective communicators prepare the individual for the occasions where the performance is an issue, by letting them know, that "we need to discuss your performance because it is important." During the session, effective coaches do not beat around the bush and they get right to the point. They do not get side tracked, but stay focused on the performance issue until they get a specific commitment and plan from the individual to improve it. The coach can end the session by summarizing the performance issue/challenge, repeat the expectations, review the specific plan which the employee created, and wish the individual success with it. Of course, the coach needs to follow up to make sure the expectations are met.

Since performance discussion can be emotional, it is best to master the skill of empathic listening. It is important that coaches are caring, gentle and understanding in such situations without losing focus of the performance issue. Coaches use effective listening skills (such as empathic listening steps) which can be done by:

- Repeating the message.
- Summarizing the content of the message.
- Reflecting on the feelings of the message.
- Restating both the content and feelings of the message in your own words. And,
- Using good judgment with regard to determining which of the above steps are appropriate for each situation.

### Leading Associates

When associates do not perform to job standards or expectations, managers and coaches must provide some direction to lead them in enhancing their performance. When you lead associates to higher performance by asking effective questions, you help them solve problems with their assigned responsibilities or tasks. The key is to lead them to the right solution so they maintain ownership for the problem, its solution and the successful execution of steps needed for improving it.

### Following Up on Plans

Following up and evaluating your associates' work is essential to ensure satisfactory task completion. Your associates realize what standards you're holding them to by your participation in evaluating their performance. After you've finished leading associates in the right direction, you need to follow up and analyze their performance. Based on observing the final performance, you can confirm expectations or lack thereof by communicating and supporting the associate through quality interaction and feedback. Confirming task completion and the achievement of expectations at specific quality levels allow you to show your interest in your associates and their work. Whether feedback is positive or negative, it serves to encourage higher performance and involvement. Giving effective feedback also helps associates make the necessary adjustments to improve the quality of their work.

## Intelligence and Coaching Styles[14]

Social and interpersonal skills are important elements of a coach's success. All managers should understand emotional intelligence and work on increasing their emotional and social intelligence quotient (EQ/IQ). Emotional intelligence is basically the capacity to know oneself and to know others. Emotional intelligence is about being able to effectively work and get along with others. It has been said that IQ contributes about 10% to a person's success in life, wisdom and knowledge contributes about 25%, and emotional intelligence contributes about 65% to one's personal and professional accomplishments. Through internal reflections and values clarification, one can further understand one's goals. Also, by learning various social and interpersonal skills, one can become skilled at winning and influencing more friends.

A coach can increase his or her emotional intelligence through self-awareness, managing emotions and having self-control, motivating others, showing empathy, and handling relationships. *Self-awareness* means observing oneself, learning and gaining relevant values and behaviors. *Managing emotions* mean handling feelings correctly so that they are appropriate for the situation and people involved. *Motivating* oneself requires channeling emotions in the service of a goal; motivating oneself requires having emotional self control. *Empathy* requires showing sensitivity to other's feelings and concerns and their perspective; it also means appreciating the differences in how people feel about things. Finally, *handling relationships* effectively means managing emotions in others; as well as gaining social competence and social skills on a continuous basis. Emotional intelligence is basically a type of social intelligence that requires the ability to monitor one's own feelings as well other's emotions, while using factual information and other situational variables to guide one's thinking and decisions. These characteristics associated with emotional intelligence are the essence of effective leadership and coaching.

### Intelligence and Its Multiple Forms

In 1983, and after extensive research, Gardner published his book *Frames of Mind* with its radically new conception of intelligences. Previous views of intelligence had entailed a single, yet multi-faceted, factor of intelligence labeled "g." Also, the claim that some individuals possessed more intelligence than others was an accepted fact. Moreover, intelligence was viewed as stable, capable of being measured even early in life (Gardner, 1983). In contrast to the prevailing view, Gardner (1999) later suggested the existence of multiple intelligences, each of unique yet equal significance, present in every normal individual. Strengthening one's intelligence, he claimed, was the whole purpose of education, training and

---

[14] This section is coauthored with Stefanie D. Wilson, University of Hawaii; and Belqis Majboor, University of Florida.

development. Gardner situated intelligences in culture and in context, which proved them useful; he argued against the appropriateness of pencil and paper tests for assessing intelligence. Although these tests conceivably measure "g," Gardner challenged their validity as predictors' of the ability to solve problems and succeed in real-world situations. For Gardner, this concept of intelligence seemed to pass by many strikingly talented individuals, and a focus on "g" appeared biased and clearly unproductive. While there are many forms of intelligences that researchers study and focus on, performance managers and coaches should at least be familiar with a few of them, especially the practical, social and emotional forms.

*Practical intelligence* is commonly known as common sense and it makes up that aspect of successful intelligence that is relevant to timely adaptation, shaping, and decisions in everyday life using tacit knowledge. Experts have suggested that demonstrating practical intelligence by only using tacit knowledge is not sufficient for effective leadership; however, it is an important aspect of leadership effectiveness as any workplace is likely to need workers with tacit or practical intelligence skills. Furthermore, tacit intelligence is inclined to be more closely related to a particular situation and experience. Perhaps the use of tacit knowledge by workers may provide for a greater understanding of intelligent behavior in real world settings, as well as foretell success in such settings.

*Social intelligence* was introduced by Thorndike, who defined it as the ability to understand others and demonstrate good judgment or get along in relation to others (Sternberg et al., 2000). According to researchers, "What sets apart the newer conceptualizations of intelligence from the older intelligence as a stable trait approach is the view of intelligence as a process of adaptation" (Riggio et al., 2002, p. 148). Studies indicate that there is a multidimensional aspect of social intelligence that includes understanding and dealing with people coupled with social adaptability. It has been said that "Cognitive skills and knowledge interact with environmental demands in a mutual shaping that enhances the adaptive fit of the individual to the environment" (Riggio, et al., p. 149). The intelligent person handles this situation accordingly. "The intelligent person musters current knowledge and ability to relate to the problem environment in a flexible way that allows for the acquisition of new skills and knowledge helping individuals to develop solutions necessary for goal attainment" (Riggio et al., p. 149). The socially intelligent person is believed to have a generous degree of cognitive abilities such as openness with others, and behavioral elements such as interpersonal warmth. Also, "The socially intelligent person is adept at reading the characteristics of the situation for cues and clues that define the nature of the interpersonal context and the appropriate behaviors for the context" (Riggio et al., 2002, p. 150). The socially intelligent person demonstrates leadership effectiveness. Furthermore, "The effective leader knows when a situation requires formal authority and presentation or a more informal and intimate setting; social knowledge is a requisite for appearing as a credible leadership figure" (Riggio et al., p. 150).

*Emotional intelligence* is about self-awareness and self-management. The history of emotional intelligence research has been a little over a decade and has invoked much interest on the topic. Riggio et al. write that "The most recent explosion of interest in intelligence and leadership has been fueled by the success of Daniel Goleman's Emotional Intelligence" (2002, p. 3). In 1995, Goleman was instrumental in bringing popularity to the concept of emotional intelligence. Goleman, a psychologist, argued that factors other than IQ contribute greatly to success and happiness. Goleman said such factors include patience, persistence, and the ability to empathize with and respond well to the emotions of others" (Post Gazette Publishing Company, 1996, p. 2).

Salovey and Mayer coined the term emotional intelligence and introduced the ability and mixed models as views of emotional intelligence (Sternberg et al., 2000). Emotional Intelligence (EI) evolved from studies and research conducted by such theorists as Gardner, Williams, and Sternberg who proposed broader approaches to understanding intelligence. Like other theorists, Goleman believed that IQ testing misses the mark in determining who will be successful in life. Kaschub writes that "The essence of Goleman's theory of emotional intelligence can be reduced to the following statement: Success results from an awareness of one's own emotional state and an awareness of another's emotional state that lead to productive action" (2002, p. 10). Productive action is the ability to use emotions to reason and solve problems resulting from effectively implementing the emotional intelligence components. Riggio et al., (2002) cited the following components of emotional intelligence:

- The ability to recognize your own emotions or your own feelings as they happen and handle these emotions.
- The ability to engage in self-control to motivate oneself.
- The ability to recognize the emotions of others.
- The ability to handle relationships (p. 174).

Riggio discussed the Goleman's ideas on emotional intelligence that were expanded to include 25 competencies grouped into five basic categories, which include:

- *Self-awareness*: Emotional awareness, accurate self-assessment, and self-confidence.
- *Self-regulation*: Self-control, trustworthiness, conscientiousness, adaptability, and innovation.
- *Motivation*: Achievement, commitment, initiative, and optimism.
- *Empathy*: Understanding of others, developing others, service orientation, diversity, and political awareness.
- *Social skills*: Influence, communication, conflict management, leadership, change catalyst, building bonds, collaboration/co-operation, and team capabilities (p. 60).

Effective coaches and leaders influence others to take action. According to Goleman, "The most effective leaders are alike in one crucial way: they have a high degree of what has come to be known as emotional intelligence; recent research clearly shows that emotional intelligence is the sine qua non of leadership" (1998, p. 92). Emotional intelligence skills can assist in various leadership functions, but the successful leader will require more than just emotional intelligence to be successful. While being aware of one's emotions and the emotions of others certainly influences managerial performance, it is also necessary for effective coaches to use, understand, and manage emotions to achieve leadership success. Leaders and coaches should be in touch with their emotions and use their emotions to be effective. It is paramount that effective leaders and coaches have the ability to understand emotions and the ability to recognize relationships between emotions, the meaning emotions convey, and how emotions change from one state to another. Managing emotions allows leaders and coaches to handle the stress of organizational life and the multi-faceted opportunities it presents. Effective leaders and coaches demonstrate the ability to focus on the appropriate coping strategies versus the emotion itself, while staying focused on creating and enhancing long-term interpersonal relationships.

### *Raising Your Social IQ*

Some scientists believe that "people smarts" are wired into each person's brain system. Daniel Goleman, in his 2006 article entitled *"Can you raise your social IQ?"* states that "Ideas about intelligence are being frantically revised as science discovers brain systems that make us smart in ways that have little or nothing to do with traditional IQ." Goleman states that empathy and social skills are two of the main ingredients for social intelligence. Empathy and social skills are inclusive of being able to make an effective first impression and getting a good sense of people's feelings and intentions. According to Goleman (2006), the "Social brain" engages when people are interacting, thereby creating a back-and-forth communication that keeps our encounters on track and makes emotions contagious. For example, the brain-to-brain connection between two individuals coordinate the timing of laughter among them as it does the speed of a romantic kiss between two people who are physically and emotionally attracted to each other.

While it is true that people are intrinsically born with certain predetermined social IQ, Goleman (2006) says, everyone is able to improve on it. For example, Goleman recommends the following essential elements for developing better listening skills which are important for having empathy:

- *Commit yourself to real change.* Think about how effective listening could enhance your relationship with others in the community, family and work environments.
- *Get feedback from people who know you well and those that you admire or respect.* How do they think you can listen more effectively is one question that you can ask them. Model after great performers and great listeners in your life.
- *Be watchful.* When you are most likely to trigger a habit that you are trying to change, consciously break the habit by responding as you have already changed the behavior.
- *Use failures as opportunities.* Each time you revert to an old habit, think about how you could handle that same situation differently the next time.
- *Keep practicing.* All of life can be a laboratory for practice and experience. Learning as much as you can with each experience and don't be afraid to try new approaches and new motivations.

According to researchers, "The road to success will always include enough general intelligence to do the job; but, in the future, being a star will require a hefty dose of the social variety as well" (Goleman, 2006). Despite the differences in acquired or hereditary intelligence, and to become socially competent individuals, all professionals should continuously learn the skills of social intelligence as recommended by experts. The book entitled *"Social Intelligence: the New Science of Success,"* written by Karl Albrecht in 2006, discusses some basic tenets of human relations that should be practiced by each professional and manager in the workplace. Albrecht's goal is to help professionals, managers and leaders see the beauty in human behaviors and at the same time to let people understand those behaviors that differentiate effective leaders from ineffective ones. Effective leaders, according to Albrecht, are those leaders who exhibit nurturing behaviors: behaviors that make people feel valued, capable, loved, respected, and appreciated. The book recognizes other forms of intelligence such as abstract intelligence, practical intelligence, emotional intelligence, aesthetic intelligence, and kinesthetic intelligence. Albrecht defines emotional intelligence as self-awareness and self-management, while social intelligence is defined as the way to deal with people. The idea is that one has to know the self first before one can improve the situation of others. The interesting and powerful thought about Albrecht's book, is that it does not focus on teaching about different human traits or personalities, rather, and more practically, it focuses on the natural principles or fundamentals that partly lead to, or form those individual traits and behaviors that are readily observable on either routine or continuous basis in various contexts. Another interesting observation of social intelligence is that at some level the concept ties into the theory of ethical behavior and leadership, which also advocates methods of dealing with individuals, groups, and organizational activities on a fair, consistent, and sound basis.

The implication of social intelligence, as presented by Albrecht, using the acronym "S.P.A.C.E." is that executives and employees may be socially smarter about how their actions and behaviors shape their immediate and future life and work situations, as well as the immediate and future life and work situations of their work subordinates and loved ones. The "S" factor represents *situational awareness* or the individual's situational radar and ability to understand and empathize with people in different situations. Situational awareness, similar to situational leadership skills, could be tied to a manager's ability to sense people's readiness to successfully complete a task as well as their feelings and intentions. Situational awareness includes the leader's belief in multiple ways to solve problems, as well as the leader's belief that he or she is not self-centered. A self-centered individual will find cooperation by others difficult to accept; he or she will find it difficult to get people to accept him/her or share themselves with him/her. "P" stands for *presence*, or the way the leader affects others through his or her physical appearance, mood and demeanor, body language, and approachability. Albrecht states that leaders' behaviors must communicate a sense of confidence, professionalism, kindness, and friendliness to the followers. As a leader, one must pay special attention to the sense of presence he or she is communicating to others in order to be accepted and taken seriously. "A" stands for *authenticity*, which measures how honest and sincere a leader is both to him or herself and to the followers. Authenticity means a solid, trustworthy person with a positive attitude and an upstanding character. Finally, the "C" in S.P.A.C.E. means *clarity*. Clarity is the leader's ability to make him or herself known and clear to his or her followers. Clarity measures your ability to express your thoughts, opinions, ideas, and intentions clearly to your audience or listeners. To influence other people with our ideas and thoughts, leaders must present the information in a way that makes it easy and fast for people to understand. Finally, "E" stands for *empathy*, which addresses how considerate the leader is to people's feelings. The leader must be able to show people that he or she can identify with and appreciate them for who they are. It is this sense of connectedness that establishes a condition of rapport between two people and inspires followers to cooperate with their leaders.

Effective interpersonal relationships are an important tool for quality leadership and productive organizations. Furthermore, developing a positive relationship with a diverse workforce could come from a corporate culture that institutes better corporate behaviors through education and training in the area of workforce diversity management.

### *Staying Focused on a Balanced Coaching Perspective*

Since coaching is not necessarily about winning, effective coaches and leaders keep the idea of winning in proper perspective. For example, striving to win is important in sport, but not necessarily the sole purpose of it. However, it must also be acknowledged that the goal of winning for athletes can bring out the best in them with regards to better performance, attitude and approach to life. Coaches must not lose sight of the long-term objectives, which is helping athletes to develop and improve sports skills, have fun, and do well in sport competition (Coaching Guide, 2007). Effective coaches understand that winning or striving to win is not more important than the athlete's well-being as a human being. The same is true for coaches and leaders in the workplace as they must put their employees' health and well-being first; in other words, people must come first. Therefore, coaches should keep "winning," the bottom-line, and high performance in its proper perspective if they are to make work and teamwork enjoyable for everyone.

As an individual leader, one should decide on a coaching philosophy, paradigm or perspective. According to the Coaching Guide (2007), your coaching philosophy, paradigm or perspective will determine:

- How you decide to teach skills and strategies.
- How you organize your practice and competition methods.
- How you discipline others.
- What role you give each person in making decisions.

Coaches lean toward the philosophy, paradigm or perspective of being authoritarian, casual, or cooperative (Coaching Guide, 2007). Historically, coaches have been expected to be authoritarian as their role models probably practiced this style of coaching. Today, employees and coachees are encouraged to think for themselves and ask "why something needs to be done?" Asking why is good because it allows people to be co-creators in their professional experience. Table 4.1 compares the three primary coaching styles (Coaching Guide, 2007).

Each leader must ask, "What kind of coach do I want to be?" Then, he/she must strive to become that type of a coach through a balance of learning and practice.

As a coach, one should want to find a balance in the styles that will allow him or her to be firm when needed, while letting employees have fun and also letting them have a voice in their training and development experiences (Coaching Guide, 2007). Coaches provide the right direction and instruction as needed and allow employees to make decisions and assume responsibility as per their timing and level of readiness.

Coaches should be developing a good picture of their coaching styles and some of the most important characteristics in developing a coaching style seems to be knowledge of one's profession, motivational skills, and showing empathy or concern for others. Of course, there is no substitute for knowing the rules, techniques and strategies in coaching. Coachees will value you, your expertise and the experience when they gain from it. This respect also gives you credibility that you can use in teaching coachees how to enhance their performance and reach for higher standards. As a leader or coach, you can have all of the skills and knowledge, however this means very little if you are not able to pass it on to your coachees and motivate them to better performance. Empathy is the ability to readily understand others by being aware of their feelings, thoughts and emotions and how they impact performance. Effective coaches make the effort to understand their people's strengths, weaknesses, joys, frustrations, anxiety, and anger. One important key to effective coaching is to know yourself and to continually assess how your coaching experiences impact your ability to enhance everyone's performance.

Table 4.1 – Influencing Perspectives (Coaching Guide, 2007)

|  | *Authoritarian* | *Cooperative* | *Casual* |
|---|---|---|---|
| *Philosophy* | Win centered | Employee centered | No emphasis |
| *Objectives* | Task objectives | Social & task objectives | No objectives |
| *Decision Making* | Coach makes all decisions | Decisions are guided by coach, but shared | Employees make decisions |
| *Communication Style* | Telling | Telling, asking, listening | Listening |
| *Communication Development* | Little or none | High | None |
| *What is Winning* | Judged by coach | Judged by employee and coach | Not defined |
| *Athlete Development* | Little or no trust in the employee | Trust in the athlete | Trust not shown |
| *Motivation* | Sometimes motivates | Motivates all | No motivation |
| *Training Structures* | Inflexible | Flexible | None |

### *What is Your Coaching Style?*

A person's socialization and background, as well as his or her personality characteristics are likely to heavily influence and determine his or her style of coaching. As stated by Herman Aguinis (2007, p. 201) in his *Performance Management* book, coaching styles can be categorized into four categories or quadrants: driver, persuader (expresser), amiable, and analyzer.

*Driver*. The driving style coach tells the employee what to do, how to do the task, and when to do it. Driver coaches tend to be assertive, task-oriented, and get right to the point. Drivers tend to:

- Focus on results.
- Take charge.
- Make quick decisions.
- Like challenges.

*Persuader (Expresser)*. In the persuading style of coaching, managers try to "sell" the employee on what needs to be done so the person would want to do it because of its benefits. They are expressive and assertive. Persuaders tend to also use more body language and stay focused on the beneficial consequences of completing the task successfully and building relationships. Persuaders tend to:

- Create excitement and involvement.
- Share ideas, dreams, and enthusiasm.
- Motivate, inspire, and persuade.

*Amiable*. Coaches using the amiable style work on getting everyone to be happy. They rely more on their feelings and what the right thing to do might be based on situational factors, rather than always relying on "cold" facts. Amiable coaches tend to:

- Cooperate to gain agreement.
- Provide support.
- Communicate trust and confidence.

*Analyzer*. Analyzers tend to assess the results and outcomes, while following the established rules and procedures as a consequence for the next step. They coach employees based on the rules and policies that are established in the training guide or a manual. Analyzers are not always assertive, but they are task-oriented and do stay focused on facts rather than feelings. An analyzer coach tends to:

- Focus on facts and logic.
- Act when payoff is clear.
- Be careful not to commit too quickly.

As a coach, it is best to be adaptable and use a relevant style as per the needs of the coachee and other situational variables. To determine your coaching styles, complete the Coaching Style Questionnaire at the end of this chapter. What is your dominant coaching style? Which coaching style would be the best one for you? Which coaching style is likely to be the most effective in your department or industry? Of course, as per the assessment of coaching experts and researchers, there is not one best coaching style. Effective coaches do what needs to be done as per the needs of their employees and organizations. Effective coaches learn about their employees' needs and work with them on setting new and relevant development goals. In achieving the stated goals, effective coaches may provide direction or tell employees what they need to do, coaches may sell employees on an idea, at times coaches might be the cheerleaders by empathizing with their employees, and, at other times, coaches might want to simply stick to the facts, rules and established procedures. In other words, effective coaches use a style that best matches the needs of the situation, the organization, and the employee at a given time. According to Herman Aguinis, "Ineffective coaches stick to one style only and cannot adapt to use any of the other styles" (2007, p. 201). Coaches that can adapt their styles to the needs of the employee and the situation tend to be most effective. In other words, effective coaches are likely to use a style that best matches with the concept of situational leadership styles. Sometimes, a coach might need to be assertive and, in other times, he or she might need to simply be responsive to an employee's situational needs. The process of adjusting assertiveness as a coach or one's style of responsiveness to the needs of employees, requires both willingness and ability on the part of the coach to successfully adjust his/her behavior to accommodate people whose readiness levels, concerns and expectations are different.

Effective coaches need versatility which is defined as adapting one's behavior to meet the concerns and expectations of others. Versatility requires understanding, appreciating, and adapting to other styles and needs. Versatility can improve work communications and ultimately the productivity of one's employees. Managers and leaders adjust their styles and use various skills to accommodate the needs of their employees. For example, to become more versatile, amiables can take the initiative and express a sense of urgency when appropriate; and they can assert firmness and self-assurance about their ideas on issues. Analyticals can take risk, or be willing to take shortcuts through procedures; they can also make decisions on the basis of intuition when appropriate. Drivers can show patience when others try to express the merits of their ideas and engage in a thorough analysis of situations. Expressives and persuaders can pay attention to details supplied by others and keep their emotions open, but under control. While all people are versatile to some degree in their communication, some individuals are more versatile than others. However, all of us can improve our versatility. Effective coaches, as suggested by experts and trainers, can use the ASAP and STAR models with employees and customers who are upset or dissatisfied. The ASAP model requires that coaches:

- *A*ttend their feelings/emotions by listening without judging.
- *S*hare their understanding and empathy for each employee's concerns.
- *A*nswer their concerns by presenting ideas/solutions.
- *P*lan action after recognizing the problem.

The STAR model requires that coaches provide:

- *S*upport by encouraging employees to take action and asking questions.
- *T*ime for employees to think about the issue or to discuss it later.

- *A*ssurance or the feeling that one understands the employee's perspective.
- *R*educed risk by discussing solutions and how they can help.

As a coach, to increase your assertiveness by *telling* employees what to and how to do something, do the following:
- Demonstrate a willingness to get to the point.
- Volunteer the information you have to others.
- Be willing to express points of disagreement.
- Summarize the positions you feel others are suggesting.

As a coach, to increase your assertiveness by *asking* questions and gaining employees' approval, do the following:
- Be open to others' opinions, concerns and feelings.
- Acknowledge the value you place on other people's time.
- Demonstrate a willingness to follow the lead of others.
- Ask for cooperation, but do not demand it.

As a coach, to increase your responsiveness by focusing on the *task*, do the following:
- Acknowledge the ideas and points that others make.
- Articulate expected results of taking action.
- Talk about the task; reference facts as well as feelings.
- Try to organize your thoughts in a logical pattern when communicating.

As a coach, to increase your responsiveness by focusing on the *people*, do the following:
- Take the time to establish rapport with your coworkers.
- Reinforce other people when they express good ideas.
- Share your feelings or personal information.
- Allow yourself and others to break the routine while problem solving.

Regardless of the style or styles coaches use, if they are to build trust with their people, they need to consistently show patience, honesty, compassion, and courage. Consistency, in this regards, is the effort and intent to accommodate others' concerns while still being themselves. Coaches should be flexible, adaptable and consistent when it comes to caring for people and organizational outcomes.

## Coaching by Asking Questions

Asking good questions is important for one's own personal development as well as for leading and guiding coachees in the right direction. Robert S. Kaplan (2007) states that "There comes a point in your career when the best way to figure out how you're doing is to step back and ask yourself a few questions...Having all the answers is less important than knowing what to ask" (p. 86). During the early stages of one's progress in climbing the ladder of management hierarchy and leadership people are likely to receive plenty of guidance, direction, support, and encouragement. However, much of this guidance, support and encouragements tend to disappear as one climbs this ladder of management or leadership success to a higher level. Kaplan states that as a manager, "You were closely monitored, coached, and mentored...but as you moved up the ladder, the sources of honest and useful feedback became fewer, and after a certain point, you were pretty much on your own" (2007, p. 86). Once a person has been a manager or a coach for a number of years, then he or she is likely to receive very little to no feedback on his or her day-to-day responsibilities from upper echelons. Of course, if and when a mistake is made, it is usually too late to do anything about it. The reality is that even successful coaches and leaders are likely to continue making mistakes in their careers all the way until retirement. Sometimes, coaches and leaders develop certain habits that make them successful, but such actions and behaviors might no longer work as effectively as they used to in the early stages of their careers. As such, asking the right questions from oneself becomes important for improvement purposes. Furthermore, a manager or leader's priorities are likely to change, and determining and working on the most important objectives is critical...since focusing on too many priorities are often no better than having none at all. Kaplan mentions that "I have learned that a key characteristic of highly successful leaders is not that they figure out how to always stay on course, but that they develop techniques to help them recognize a deteriorating situation and get back on track as quickly as possible" (2007, p. 88). Successful leaders and coaches, according to Kaplan, reflect upon their vision and priorities, manage their time effectively, provide regular and direct feedback to their associates, have a list of successors for key positions, evaluate the alignment of the company's structure with their stated mission and vision, are able to lead under pressure, and stay true to themselves. In his article, Kaplan outlines seven types of questions that leaders and coaches can ask themselves on a period basis to test themselves for reflection and personal improvement purposes (p. 90):

1. *Vision and priorities.* How often do I communicate a vision for my business? Have I identified and communicated three to five key priorities to achieve that vision? If asked, would my employees be able to articulate the vision and priorities?

2. *Managing time.* How am I spending my time? Does it match my key priorities? How are my subordinates spending their time? Does that match the key priorities for the business?

3. *Feedback.* Do I give people timely and direct feedback that they can act on to enhance performance? Do I have five of six junior subordinates who will tell me things I may not want to hear but need to hear?

4. *Succession planning.* Have I, at least in my own mind, picked one or more potential successors? Am I coaching them and giving them challenging assignments? Am I delegating sufficiently? Have I become a decision-making bottleneck?

5. *Evaluation and alignment.* Is the design of my company still aligned with the key success factors for the business? If I had to design my business with a clean sheet of paper, how would I design it? How would it differ from the current design? Should I create a task force of subordinates to answer these questions and make recommendations to me?

6.   *Leading under pressure.* What types of events create pressure for me? How do I behave under pressure? What signals am I sending my subordinates? Are these signals helpful, or are they undermining the success of the business?

7.   *Staying true to yourself.* Is my leadership style comfortable? Does it reflect who I truly am? Do I assert myself sufficiently, or have I become tentative? Am I too politically correct? Does worry about my next promotion or bonus cause me to pull punches or hesitate to express my views?

By effectively reflecting upon one's vision and priorities, managing one's time, providing regular and direct feedback to associates, having successors for key positions and tasks, evaluating the alignment of the company's structure with the mission and vision, leading under pressure, and staying true to themselves coaches can improve their performance and that of their organizations' each year. Successful coaches and leaders "periodically struggle during stretches of their careers...to get back on track, they must devise techniques for stepping back, getting perspective, and developing a new game plan" (Kaplan, 2007, p. 95). Such a self-analysis process through effective questioning and reflections on one's current status on a regular basis can help coaches work through complacency and other leadership challenges that might come up in their careers. While intrapersonal reflections and self-analysis questions are important for self improvement purposes, effective coaches must also be able to ask developmental and leading questions from their associates and followers as well.

Good coaches will always give support to associates, but when associates are not performing up to the standard for the job, it is necessary to provide effective coaching by asking leading questions to assist them in the thinking and solution generation process. When coaching associates, you help them solve problems they are having with the tasks they have been assigned. Every associate will have difficulties with some task at one time or another. That is why the coach's support is so vital. You will be able to spot an associate who is having trouble and coach them to a solution for the problem.

There are at least two main reasons why people do not like to ask for help. *First*, some people cannot admit, even to themselves, when they cannot do a job. *Second*, others can admit it, but they are afraid to ask for help because they do not want to appear incompetent. These two reasons are very similar, but the reactions when you ask if there are any problems, are very different. Some individuals who cannot admit they need help will answer "No problems here" or something similar. Associates who are afraid to ask for help will be relieved if you phrase your question in a non-threatening way.

When supporting and leading associates, it is important to focus on the work results and not on the person. If the results are not what you expected, ask the following questions: What happened? Why did it happen? What can be done to prevent it from happening again? Never assume that the associate is incapable of doing the work. If you have concerns about an associate's overall performance, talk to your coach and/or mentor when needed, and privately to the associate in a very empathic manner.

Instead of just telling associates the solution to a problem (assuming you have a solution), try asking questions that will help them discover the solution. This method has the benefit of making the associate feel that he or she was part of the solution and, additionally, associates will tend to remember the solution much better, since they reasoned it out for themselves.

There are many common questions that one might ask during a coaching session. What are some questions you can think of that would help in coaching your associates? You might want to think of coaching situations other than work that one may experience. For example, teaching a child a new skill or coaching an athletic team requires coaching skills. Using questions as a coaching tool is particularly valuable when it is necessary to suggest alternate resources to associates who are having difficulties. The resource may include another piece of equipment, a different type of tool or product, and another associate who is skilled in the task.

The one habit that you, as a coach, must guard against is helping an associate who is having difficulties by doing the task yourself. Of course, there will be emergency situations where a coach may do this, but in general, it is not a good idea because it can hinder the employee's development. There are many reasons why coaches should not do associates' jobs and the following are some of them:

- It is not your job.
- The associate will not learn to do the task independently.
- If you consistently do tasks yourself, instead of coaching others, you are not doing your job.
- It is much more time-consuming if you do tasks yourself, rather than coaching associates to better performance.
- Allowing your associates to take responsibility for task completion helps them develop their skills.
- You are responsible for "running" the department and not the other way around. So, don't let the department "run" you!

### *Coaching Challenge and "The Practical Coach"*

Effective coaches encourage, inform, praise, raise awareness, collaborate, set clear expectations, serve as role models, empower, help, challenge, serve as vehicles for change, remove barriers, and enable others to reach their full potential. One should remember that coaching others to higher performance can be the single most important thing one does as a leader or manager. Also, skilled managers and coaches never let good or poor performance go unnoticed. When effective coaches and managers see good performance, they say it and praise it. One should not let poor performance go unnoticed by saying it privately to the employee and making it positively anchored toward future performance. For real personal issues and poor personal habits: first, prepare the teammate/associate; and second, be gentle and to the point in stating the problem that needs fixing. *The Practical Coach* video, as previously mentioned, offers many insights and suggestions on coaching for all leaders. The video offers the "*Two Minute Challenge*" with the following steps: First, state what you observed; second, wait for a response; third, remind the person of the goal; fourth, ask for a specific solution; and fifth, jointly agree on the solution and its implementation.

Perhaps, some of these steps from the *Practical Coach* can apply to disciplining employees without punishment in order to effectively fix problems and enhance performance. A manager's responsibility, as a coach and as a leader, is best fulfilled when he or she maximizes long-term value for his or her department, organization, and the society through the use of available resources and effective discipline management approaches. Effective managers jointly and collaboratively work with their employees to increase each worker's commitment to the job, enhance his or her performance on each task, and maximize each associate's long-term value to the organization.

### Coaching Reflections

Every person has needed coaching as a baby growing up. The same is true when we grow up as professionals in our fields. "None of us has gotten where we are solely by pulling ourselves up from our own bootstraps. We got here because somebody bent down and helped us," said Thurgood Marshall, U. S. Supreme Court Justice. For coaching to be effective, choose an appropriate time for coaching, interaction and two-way feedback. Use focused and planned questions to guide others to their own awareness and solutions. Provide feedback about behavior that others can use to maintain and improve their own performance. Listen to understand the message behind the words, the feelings and the thoughts behind them. Develop a high level of trust with your people by forging a partnership with them. You can use various surveys to find out how your employees, bosses, and colleagues feel about you. You can determine how they feel about you or how they see you as a leader by asking them to confidentially fill out *"The Way We See Me Questionnaire"* (included in the Exercises section of this book) or a survey similar to it. Based upon this feedback, you can develop a plan to increase the level of trust between you and your people, and you can make sure you are seen the way you want to be seen as a leader by behaving as such. Finally, develop, revise and update your personal plan periodically for increasing your coaching skills and effectiveness.

At first, one may experience some challenges when coaching through questioning because the tendency is to give associates the answer. Learn to ask the right questions and practice effective listening as you coach others. Your associates will feel better about themselves, and the company, when they are allowed to participate with you in the problem solving or performance enhancing process.

As associates are working on their tasks, you need to encourage them to seek help when needed. You must let associates know you are available for any questions or problems arising from the completion of their tasks. If they are uncomfortable coming to you, then advise them to seek help from other, skilled individuals.

### Summary

Coaching is about specific goal-oriented collaborations and communication to influence others toward successfully achieving their personal and professional goals. Just like any other skill, coaching requires knowledge, patience, and practice. Coaching and enhancing employee performance requires that managers and coaches open their mouths and communicate by describing the performance problem or expectation, getting the employee's agreement on the problem, creating possible solutions to the problem, agreeing on a specific action plan to solve the problem, and following up as agreed upon.

According to a coaching expert and coaching workshop facilitator, Susan Klein, "Coaching is an advanced form of communication, that when used properly, can increase performance, improve motivation and retention, reduce stress, and create better working relationships." Ms. Klein is the founder and president of an international coaching firm that creates immediate impact and sustained results with coaching services. For over fifteen years, Ms. Klein has worked with executives, managers and business owners through coaching, training and executive development workshops. Klein facilitates the popular workshop entitled "*Coaching Skills for Managers*," which is a one-day practical workshop that gives executives, managers, and business owners the basic skills they need to be effective coaches in their organizations. Klein claims that "Growing and developing their staff and managing change are some of the most important tasks for a manager," and effective coaches are skilled at both. Some of the topics covered by Susan Klein in the *Coaching Skills for Managers* program include:

- The coaching model communication: listening and sensitivity to hear what is really going on.
- Language - powerful dialogue and strong messages to lead.
- Effective questions - asking the right questions allows for natural wisdom.
- Requesting action - steps to effective action and accountability.
- Motivation - keeping oneself and others motivated.

Experts, such as Susan Klein, emphasize that although the awareness of the coaching keys is essential, practicing is paramount to developing an effective coach. In coaching workshops, attendees often begin to practice real-world coaching scenarios in a simulated environment. Such exercises are usually accomplished through lively, experiential and practical team and one-on-one activities.

### Discussion Questions

1. What is coaching and how does it apply to twenty-first century managers and leaders? When and where can leaders or managers coach? Can coaching be used in any industry? Discuss how and where. How is coaching different from telling people what to do? Does one need to be a manager to be an effective coach? What kinds of skills are needed for effective coaching?
2. Is there a relationship between coaching and productivity/performance?
3. How can the questioning method be used by coaches to understand their people and enhance performance?
4. Discuss the characteristics of effective coaches. What are some best practices in becoming the type of leader or coach one wishes to be?

5. Is there a relationship between trust and effective coaching? How can coaches increase trust between themselves and their employees and colleagues?
6. How can mentors assist managers and leaders to become effective coaches?

### Coaching Style Questionnaire[15]

The coaching style questionnaire, taken from the *Coaching Guide for Special Olympics: Principles of Coaching*, provides a framework for determining one's most dominant coaching preferences and styles.

*Directions*: Table 4.2 has 15 rows of four words (across). From each row (across), select two words out of the four that best describe the way you see yourself. If all four words sound like you, select the two that are most like you. If none of the four sounds like you, select the two that are closest to the way you are.

Table 4.2 - Coaching Style Questionnaire (Coaching Guide, 2007)

| A | B | C | D |
|---|---|---|---|
| All business | Bold | Personable | Deliberate |
| Organized listening | Telling | Courteous | Listening |
| Industrious | Independent | Companionable | Cooperative |
| No-nonsense | Decisive | Talkative | Reflective |
| Serious | Determined | Warm | Careful |
| To-the-point | Risk Taker | Amiable | Moderate |
| Practical | Aggressive | Empathetic | Nonassertive |
| Self-controlled | Authoritative | Show Emotions | Thorough |
| Goal Directed | Assertive | Friendly | Patient |
| Methodical | Unhesitating | Sincere | Prudent |
| Businesslike | Definite | Sociable | Precise |
| Diligent | Firm | Demonstrative | Particular |
| Systematic | Strong-minded | Sense of Humor | Thinking |
| Formal | Confident | Expressive | Hesitative |
| Persevering | Forceful | Trusting | Restrained |
| _____ | _____ | _____ | _____ |

On Table 4.2, total the number of words circled under each respective column. Plot those numbers on their respective axes of the grid in Table 4.3. For example, if you circled six words in column A, mark the A axis next to the 6. Complete the same procedures for columns B, C and D. Then extend the marks into each respective quadrant to create a rectangle. Table 4.4 shows a completed rectangle.

---

[15] The Coaching Style Questionnaire and its examples were retrieved on January 25, 2007 from, and it is available on, the Special Olympics website under the Coaching Guide for Special Olympics: http://www.specialolympics.org/.

## Table 4.3 – Plotting Grid for Coaching Styles

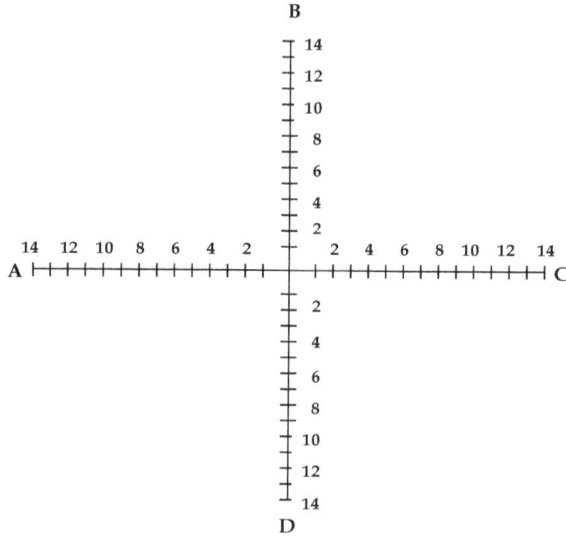

**B**

```
        14
        12
        10
         8
         6
         4
         2
14 12 10 8 6 4 2    2 4 6 8 10 12 14
A ├─────────────────┼─────────────────┤ C
         2
         4
         6
         8
        10
        12
        14
```
**D**

## Table 4.4 – Completed Coaching Style Grid Example

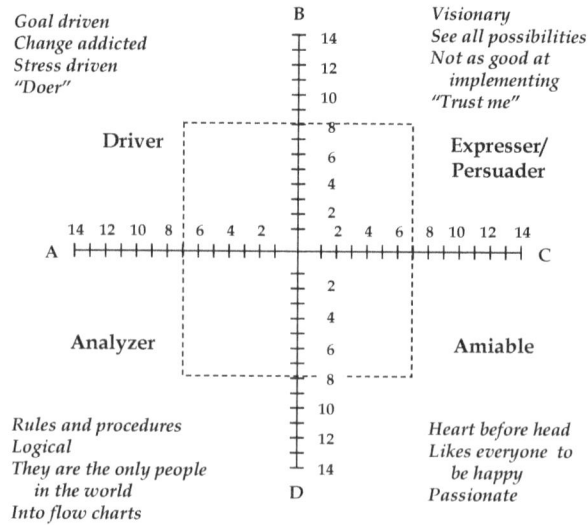

*Goal driven*
*Change addicted*
*Stress driven*
*"Doer"*

**B**

*Visionary*
*See all possibilities*
*Not as good at*
*    implementing*
*"Trust me"*

**Driver**

**Expresser/**
**Persuader**

```
14 12 10 8 | 6 4 2    2 4 6 | 8 10 12 14
A ├──────────────┼──────────────┤ C
```

**Analyzer**

**Amiable**

*Rules and procedures*
*Logical*
*They are the only people*
*    in the world*
*Into flow charts*

*Heart before head*
*Likes everyone to*
*    be happy*
*Passionate*

**D**

# CHAPTER 5

## Coaching for Work-Life Balance[16]

Ambition, enthusiasm, dedication, drive—all characteristics of a high performing individual. However, without the proper balance, even individuals who possess all of these traits and others that are characteristic of success, risk burnout, growing job dissatisfaction, and slipping performance. Given that coaching is a method for "creating more effective conversations, for assessing and reformulating values and goals, and reaching solutions," it is an ideal methodology for assisting top performers in their quest for excellence and struggle for balance (Zeus & Skiffington, 2002, p. 2). This section reviews the "burnout" phenomenon prevalent in today's society, and coaching strategies that can be applied to restore work-life balance. The specific case that will be addressed by the coaching plan is that of an overcommitted (but well intentioned) physician who is acquiring formal education in business and is approaching burnout herself. The goal with this coaching situation is to preserve the performance, longevity and satisfaction of this overcommitted "top performer."

### Work/Life Imbalance & Burnout

The problem of work-life imbalance is prevalent and costly in today's society. According to Julia Chang, "In a recent poll by online career site Monster.com, 81% of workers said they were not happy with their work/life balance. Companies that ignore their employees' need for better balance risk burnout and high turnover" (Chang, 2005). Turnover is expensive for organizations and "A general approach to calculate employee turnover cost is to use 50% to 200% of an employee's annual salary" (Zahorsky, 2006). Burnout is costly to individuals in a variety of ways including, "psychological problems such as depression, irritability, helplessness, anxiety, reduced organizational commitment, and job satisfaction...decreased job performance,...and stress related health effects" (Siegall & McDonald, 2004). The cost of burnout can be measured by organizations in, "increased health benefit costs, increased absenteeism, increased employee assistance program usage and increasing employee disengagement" (Allen, 2004). Increasing work pressures come from a variety of sources but include external sources such as "restructuring and consolidations, longer work hours, increasing demands to focus on bottom line

---

[16] Contributed by Patricia M. Hagan (M.D.), Nova Southeastern University. The example used for application of coaching is hypothetical.

results, the quickening pace of technological and market changes, and shorter product cycles" (Wah, 2000). Alternatively, individuals may self-impose pressure for continual accomplishments as "Some people feel pressure from our achievement-driven culture to accomplish more – and to do it faster – than their peers" (Waldroop & Butler, 2000). Individuals who recognize the diminishing returns of their time investments, may turn to coaching to help restore a healthy work/life balance and achieve a greater professional and personal satisfaction. This is the motivation for personal coaching in the real-world, hypothetical example highlighted in this section.

**Personal Coaching**

The personal coaching of high achievers is a niche area of the field of coaching. Experts state that "Today life skills or personal coaching is widespread and focuses primarily on personal growth and development issues outside of an organizational context...The life coach works with individuals who want to change and grow, to restructure or improve their lives, to work through transitions and to find fulfillment and balance" (Zeus & Skiffington, p. 18). Simply stated, these high achievers seek out coaches when they "want to change their lives for the better" (Ramsey, 2000). According to Ramsey, individuals "use coaches to inspire them and bring out their best in all facets of daily living." Individuals may consult a coach for a host of different reasons with the principle understanding that coaching is for anyone who wants to excel and achieve their goals.

*The Coaching Process*

Fundamentals of personal coaching include a process that is, "a collaborative, client-centered relationship." Coaching is "both coactive and proactive," and "The role of the coach is to question, listen, probe, push or do whatever it takes to provide clarity, focus and support for achieving life and work goals" (Ramsey, 2000). According to Zeus and Skiffington, the process of coaching generally follows four phases: 1) establishing a coaching partnership; 2) action planning; 3) the coaching cycle; and 4) evaluation and follow-up (2002, p. 60). The timing and content of each phase is determined by the situation being coached and the individuals in the coaching relationship. According to Zeus and Skiffington, "Personal change is an individualized process. There is no one model of change that fits all coachees. It is not a linear process and usually occurs in stages" (2002, p. 31).

While having certain similarities, coaching and therapy are substantively different from one another. According to Bluckert, "the intention is different, with coaching strongly grounded in work effectiveness and performance rather than wider life issues...Therapy issues often focus around...how to improve skills in making (personal) contact and building and maintaining satisfying relationships. Coaching issues tend to revolve around people management, strategic planning...and personal development" (Bluckert, 2005).

## The Coachee

Certain characteristics of the coachee contribute to a greater or more diminished likelihood of success with regards to the coaching process. The characteristics described by Michael Frisch are: "1) significant personal or familial problems, upheaval or upset (negative); 2) risk tolerance: the willingness to try new approaches and tolerate discomfort, awkwardness, and vulnerability (positive); confidence and self-efficacy (positive); 3) emotional resilience: the ability to accept feedback, depersonalize setbacks, and stay motivated (positive); 4) psychological curiosity and insight (positive); and 5) the classic motivation to change (positive)" (Frisch, 2005). The interplay among these and other factors can dramatically affect an individual's coaching process.

It is important to recognize that while some individuals may want to change, they may have a resistance to change. "Resistance to change is natural in organizations, individual clients and yes, even consultants...Part of any successful project is to navigate through this resistance and emerge with insight into new behavior choices" (Goldberg, 2005). Certain personality types may have a more natural resistance to change. "Alpha" types who have risen through the corporate ranks present a unique group to coach" since they (Alpha males and females) may be resistant to change as they, "can be defensive and resistant to criticism" (Ludeman & Erlandson, 2004). With effective coaching, this resistance can be managed and change can be accomplished for their benefit and to the benefit of their organizations.

## Work/Life Balance Solutions

Through coaching, individuals can put into place certain strategies that contribute to better work/life balance. Described by Buckner and Sandholtz, these strategies include alternating, outsourcing, bundling, tech-flexing, and simplifying (Buckner and Sandholtz, 2003). According to research, individuals "realized that they wouldn't achieve balance by running faster, working harder, and cramming more into their lives...They accept that the three elements of balance – meaningful work, satisfying relationships, and personal rejuvenation...rarely come together in a tidy, stress free package. So, they use a variety of methods to rebalance their lives into a more satisfying, sustainable pattern" (Buckner & Sandholtz, 2003). Alternating describes individuals who "want it all, but not at once...They throw themselves into their careers with abandon, then cut back or quit work altogether and focus intensely on their families or outside interests" (Buckner & Sandholtz, 2003). Through outsourcing, individuals focus on those areas that are most important in their lives as "Outsourcers achieve work-life balance by off-loading responsibilities-usually in their personal lives-to free up time and energy for the tasks they care the most about" (Buckner & Sandholtz, 2003). According to Buckner and Sandholtz, "bundling should not be confused with juggling, rather bundling succeeds in "giving separate tasks greater meaning by putting them together." Through bundling, individuals choose fewer activities that provide for them greater meaning. Through tech-flexing, individuals create a more flexible schedule and more efficient use of their time as "techflexers don't use technology to increase the work hours in a day...Rather, they use it to liberate those work hours from the rigid 9-to-5 structure" (Buckner &

Sandholtz, 2003). Finally, simplifying allows individuals to "reduce the time and energy devoted to non-essential activities, whether at work or at home" (Buckner & Sandholtz, 2003). These strategies figure prominently in a coaching relationship directed at achieving work-life balance.

### *Alignment Coaching*

Before implementing strategies for work-life balance, a coachee must be familiar with his or her value system and specific priorities. Coaching can then "make sense of one's life and fundamental values and meaning that get expressed through choice and action" (Lazar & Bergquist, 2004). This defines alignment coaching. Using coaching to help individuals look at their own fundamental values and meaning and how to best express those through choice and action would likely help decrease the work-life dichotomy. Understanding one's spiritual, philosophical, ethical, and life/career thoughts makes for a better platform for decisions that are in alignment between life and work and pay appropriate respect to both. Alignment coaching can be very helpful as a foundation for overcoming work-life imbalance, resulting in improved satisfaction in both areas.

### Coaching Phases and Explanation

The coachee, Paula Hulk[17] is a "Type A" overachiever. Like many other high achieving individuals, she struggles with work-life balance. Let us say that Paula is a 35 year-old accomplished physician, a single parent to a gifted 10 year-old boy, avid runner, and full time student studying business. The constant flurry of activity was always energizing to Paula, but lately she has found herself consistently fatigued, increasingly cynical about work, and annoyingly "inefficient" as per her perceptions. She is aware that she is approaching burnout as based on the Maslach Burnout Inventory as per "high scores on exhaustion and cynicism, and low scores on professional efficacy, are indicative of burnout" (Schaufeli & Bakker, 2004). Paula's current state has her looking for a new job, contemplating leaving school and having abandoned exercise altogether given her overall low energy level and general distress. She is seeking a professional personal coach to help her regain her work-life balance, combat burnout and regain her satisfaction with her work and her life.

Paula's situation has developed over time. Her busy clinical practice has been short staffed for three out of the past five years including the entire past year. With increased clinical time, there is less time for professional growth opportunities, family time or restorative time that previously was spent on exercise. Simultaneously, the administrative and managerial responsibilities of the job have dramatically increased, requiring significantly more time. The formal course work in business was designed to provide the education that she would need to be most effective in her expanded managerial role, but it requires a significant investment in time to complete. In addition, she has always prided herself in academic excellence and has compounded her time depleted situation with the additional commitment to put forth an "A" effort in all of her course work. According to the work of Siegall and

---

[17] This is a practical, yet hypothetical example, used to demonstrate a coaching plan.

McDonald, this situation is ripe for burnout as "People have limited resources (e. g. time, energy) with which to run their lives…burnout results when a person does not have the sufficient/appropriate set of resources to meet the set of job demands/requirements" (Siegall & McDonald, 2004). Paula has responded to the stress of imbalance between resources and demands according to the "Conservation of Resources" theory where "In response to situations of stress, people attempt to cope by rebalancing their resources and demands…a reasonable response to experiencing burnout could be to shift resources from where they are not being productive into areas that promise a better payoff" (Siegall & McDonald, 2004). She has found herself withdrawing from situations and individuals associated with work. She has become very interested in other work opportunities and is at risk of leaving her job. By exploring the services of a personal coach, Paula is looking at the most efficient use of her resources for the greatest gains in her life, personally and professionally. She is seeking to be fully engaged in her work and personal lives at a much reduced stress level. The four phases of coaching will now be applied in Paula's case.

### *Phase 1: Establishing the Coaching Partnership*

The coaching plan begins with establishing a coaching partnership. Paula is looking for a personal coach skilled in alignment coaching, specifically life and career coaching. She will screen candidates for the coaching role based on credentials, recommendations and experience. Once she selects a coach, both parties will begin establishing the relationship. In this situation, the coach will delve far into Paula's past allowing him or her to "examine broad and enduring life and career patterns" (Lazar & Bergquist, 2004). This will require excellent listening skills and close attention to detail on the part of the coach. The coach will carefully interview Paula to gather enough information for a comprehensive needs assessment. During the assessment he/she will learn about her values which include: hard work, striving towards excellence, helping others, remaining intellectually and physically active, promoting good health and including fun in things whenever possible. During this phase the coach and coachee will clarify expectations of each other. This enables the development of a coaching contract and the initiation of coaching sessions. In this situation the coaching, "often involves inventories, specific sets of interview questions, and planning exercises…The coach may play the role of catalyst, cheerleader, or even goad, encouraging a colleague to take specific steps that will move him or her towards specific goals and personal aspirations in both life and career" (Lazar & Bergquist, 2004). The establishment of those goals is central to the next phase of the coaching plan, the action planning.

### *Phase 2: Action Planning*

Once Paula has established a relationship with a personal coach who has taken a detailed inventory of her background and situation, the stage is set for action planning. "The life coaching approach provides an opportunity to recognize and identify the full range of life domains and their concerns, then ensure that work was appreciated within that context, rather than vice versa" (Lazar & Bergquist, 2004). During this phase values, vision and goals are established. According to Zeus and Skiffington, "The coach and coachee discuss the coachee's strengths and challenges, the coachee's vision of the future and the overall objectives of the coaching relationship...The coach and coachee now move from the general to the specific and work on establishing specific personal (or organizational) goals" (Zeus & Skiffington, p. 76-77).

In Paula's case, the coach could help her use Chuc Barnes' book, *Get Your Ducks In A Row*. He or she would guide her through the third chapter, "Know Where You're Going," where it is essential to pick a professional, personal, and "outrageous" priority/goal and then learn how to "chunk" it down to a series of manageable steps. In working through this, Paula would identify that she most wants to be remembered at work as a physician who most positively impacted patient care; that her greatest personal goal is to be the best mother possible to her son; and that her most "outrageous" dream goal is to be able to complete a 26.1 mile marathon quickly enough to qualify for the Boston Marathon! The coach will then help her realize her goals by creating "SMART" goals from her priorities, namely goals that are: Specific, Measurable, Attainable, Results-Oriented, and Time-bounded.

In looking at her most important professional goal, positively impacting patient care through her role as a highly competent physician, the coach would have her "chunk" down that goal. She would have to say that over the next year she would like to work with nursing, the other physicians and administrators to establish a quality improvement program. She would like to systematize three areas of patient care that are already informally reviewed by the nurses and apply readily available tools to the process. She will enlist the help of the nurses already involved to collect the data. At the end of the year the entire team will sit down and review the projects and decide on how to build upon their experiences for the next year. Given that this is her primary goal, Paula can then see that attendance at certain other meetings or completing administrative paperwork does not contribute towards the completion of this goal. Part of Paula's coaching may then be directed at exploring the different balancing strategies available as they relate to her most important goals and all of the other activities in which she engages. Those strategies include alternating, outsourcing, bundling, tech-flexing, and simplifying (Buckner and Sandholtz, 2003). The coaching plan, as it relates to her professional role, would then include the need to "outsource" or delegate attendance at some of those other meetings or completion of administrative duties that do not contribute to the most important goal, the creation of a quality improvement program. This process, of taking the general and making SMART goals, would then be repeated for the main personal and extracurricular goals.

In the personal realm, Paula would have to decide exactly what it means to be the best mother possible for her son. She would be forced to pick a specific goal, like being able to review Daniel's homework and schedule with him each day. She would then protect as much time as possible either at the end or beginning of each day to insure that she can accomplish this review. On days that she had to work, Paula could use cell phone technology to "check in" with Daniel. Providing consistent contact surrounding school work and schedule allows Paula to be an involved parent, and helps her structure her day and other commitments. Other activities, like getting Daniel to extracurricular activities, can be delegated to others without affecting the primary goal. Paula then can conserve energy for the most important priorities in three main realms: professional, personal and extracurricular.

In the extracurricular realm, Paula has a clearly definable goal, to complete a marathon in a prescribed amount of time to qualify for the Boston Marathon. In this situation, the personal coach would work with her to establish a reasonable exercise routine and a doable time goal for the race. Having completed the action planning phase for each of the important realms of Paula's life, the coaching plan would then move to the coaching cycle phase.

### Phase 3: The Coaching Cycle

The coaching cycle is the actual progress phase of the coaching relationship. "Once the coach and the coachee have established the goals and strategies of the alliance, most of the remaining sessions are devoted to reviewing the coachee's progress and addressing any obstacles or difficulties that may arise" (Zeus & Skiffington, P. 77). Paula and her coach would meet weekly at first as the process to attain the really important goals while implementing appropriate balancing strategies is launched. The coach would have to be attuned to dealing with any resistance towards coaching by Paula. Once there is progress in goal attainment and resolution of Paula's "burnout" the interval between sessions can be lengthened. Once Paula is certain that she has attained the skills that she needs to set appropriate goals and maintain work-life balance, it would be time for the final phase of the coaching plan, the evaluation and follow-up.

### Phase 4: Evaluation and Follow Up

Given that the coaching process has been dynamic between Paula and her coach, both parties have a good understanding of the successes and challenges of the coaching program. This final stage "provides an opportunity for the coach to offer a summary of results of the coaching interventions, his or her evaluation, and recommendations for follow-up coaching" (Zeus & Skiffington, p. 79). The coach would be able to conclude how successfully Paula followed the SMART goals that she created. He or she could comment on how Paula had used her success in these areas to problem solve and avoid situations that would have otherwise contributed to burnout. The coach could show Paula how her actions following the coaching reflected her core values and goals and helped her maintain a work/life balance. Critical to this phase is preventing slippage; so "The coach and coachee must develop strategies to ensure the coachee maintains his or her gains and skills and that slippage does not occur" (Zeus & Skiffington, p. 79). Focusing Paula on her deepest priorities, rather than her need for achievement would help prevent slippage and maintain the hard won work-life balance that the coaching plan helped her achieve.

**Focus on Strengths to Increase Productivity**

The traits of great leadership are commonly described by such words as vision, communication, trust, discipline, credibility, wisdom, expertise, and concern for others. While such traits may very well describe effective leaders, what is a common truth is that successful individuals are always able to continuously put their strengths to work for them. In other words, successful leaders and coaches tend to be involved in more of what they enjoy doing and, as a result, they often do it very well. Great leaders, managers and coaches are able to recognize and capitalize on their own strengths as well as those of others. Decades ago in the twentieth century, the late Peter Drucker during 1966, mentioned that effective leaders and managers should build on their own strengths as well as the strengths of their employees, colleagues, and superiors to make their organizations more productive and competitive. Furthermore, experts have historically encouraged leaders and managers to stay focused on what works for their organizations, rather than spending too much time and resources on issues that have not produced any positive results.

For most individuals in this world, the mythical world of being one's own boss, driving a different Ferrari or Porsche each day of the week, living in the hills and owning a ranch, playing golf every other afternoon, earning more money than one can possibly spend in a life time, and having a job that one loves near the ranch is not a reality. While thinking of the dream world can certainly be pleasing, as momentary as it may be, most individuals simply want to have sufficient opportunities to do more of what they like to do in their existing departments, organizations and industries. So, instead of looking for a "pot of gold" or the perfect dream job in a new organization or industry that may or may not exist, individuals and their managers can learn how to reshape existing jobs around their likes and desires to make it more pleasing. The key in increasing performance and productivity in the workplace, is in making sure that one is prepared and empowered to do more of what he or she likes doing and consistently engaging one's strengths.

The book entitled *"Go Put Your Strengths to Work: Six Powerful Steps to Achieve Outstanding Performance"* provides a clear vehicle for discovering personal and professional success through efficiency, effectiveness and productivity in the workplace. Instead of theorizing and lecturing, Buckingham (2007) provides a number of great reasons for putting one's strengths to work with practical examples and step by step guidelines in the book along with an internet component for surveys and videos to support the concepts of helping people become more productive, creative and focused on their goals. Besides capitalizing on one's strengths, people are also given encouragement and support to also stop their weaknesses or actions that weaken them. Buckingham and his colleagues have designed the Strengths Engagement Track (SET), which is available to those who own a copy of the book at www.SimplyStrengths.com, to help track the reader's progress toward using his or her strengths and to pinpoint how engaged his or her strengths might be in the workplace. The interactive web survey can reveal how engaged a person's strengths are now and how engaged they will in the future. It is the continuous and focused engagement of a person's strengths that can create personal and professional success. The survey asks questions about one's mind-set and typical behaviors and, as a result, provides some conclusions. The Strengths Engagement Track survey provides a score, known as the *Present dial*, which reveals how engaged one's strengths are currently in comparison to a national representative population from the United States' workforce. This score is a measure of how well one is doing at living up to his or her potential. The *Future dial* score, representing a trend line, reveals how engaged one's strengths are going to be in the future. Besides individuals, teams can also take the survey and have a team score that can be compared in the future periods or years for progress. High performing individuals and teams tend to score high on both the Present and Future dials. High performing individuals have their strengths engaged, and they know why and how to sustain these levels of engagement regardless of the circumstances surrounding them.

Marcus Buckingham points out that most employees do not even come close to making full use of their personal expertise, knowledge, and assets in their places of work. According to the data provided by Buckingham, about 17% of workers believe that they use all of their strengths on the job. So, focusing on employees' personal assets or strengths and empowering them to do so is important for enhancing productivity in the workplace. As seen from the plethora of books, training videos and coaching consultants on the topic of motivation and recognition of one's strengths or core competencies, one can certainly see that such issues will be a topic of conversation in most employee development workshops and training programs in the coming decades. Of course, this is not another fad of the month, year, or decade because the focus of the strength movement is in helping leaders and coaches find success at work from inside out. In other words, leaders and managers are able to achieve success by understanding themselves and using their strengths toward organizational objectives both individually and with others on the team. Buckingham (2007, p. 9) states that organizations which promote the idea that "People are their greatest asset," actually mean "People's strengths are their greatest asset." Most organizations in today's knowledge and service economy understand that the value of their human resources asset lies in their ability to be creative, innovative, critical thinkers, and effective decision-makers. According to Buckingham, the leaders of such firms as Intel, Best Buy, Accenture, and Wells Fargo have committed themselves to becoming and building strengths-based organizations. The Major League Soccer organization provides a Strengths-Based Coaching course for aspiring soccer coaches. In this workshop, instead of issuing the traditional yellow and red cards to punish players for misbehaving, coaches are encouraged to give out "green cards" in order to draw a player's attention to a good play that needs to be repeated or one that shows teamwork in the field. Leaders and coaches should focus on people's strengths, not necessarily to make them happier, but, to help them become more productive performers in the department or organization. Buckingham states that:

> Today the strengths movement is everywhere: the corporate work, the worlds of public service, of economics, of education, of faith, of charity—it has affected them all. It has its detractors, of course, but an appeal as universal as this begs the question "Why?" Why do so many people from so many different worlds see such power in the strengths-based perspective? …Because it works better than any other perspective (Buckingham, 2007, p. 5).

Employees that do have the opportunity to work to their strengths every day as professionals in their organizations are likely to be on teams that have lower employee turnover and high customer satisfaction. Furthermore, organizations that empower their employees to fully play to their strengths are likely to see increases in employee and departmental productivity, the retention of their employees, and the loyalty of their customers. While selecting the right employees based on their talents, setting clear goals, praising employees for a job well done, and staying focused on the team's mission can be great tools for enhancing productivity, according to Buckingham (2007, p. 9), the best tool for getting each person to be highly productive is getting him or her to play to his or her strengths.

In *Go Put Your Strengths to Work,* Marcus Buckingham discusses the following concepts and offers practical tools to understand them:

- Using telltale signs to identify one's strengths.
- Taking specific steps each week to create one's desired job by shaping current tasks toward the activities that strengthen a person's potential and eliminating those that do not assist one in this direction.
- Doing certain tasks persuasively enough to make colleagues and bosses want to help put one's strengths to work.
- Behaving consistently and creating habits in life to stay focused on the strengths path regardless of the personal or professional changes that may impact one on a day-to-day basis.
- "Pushing" employees to be more productive by guiding them to their personal and professional strengths.

*Go Put Your Strengths to Work* is about exercising and identifying what is best and most effective for each person and applying these strengths in the workplace. Buckingham (2007, p. 17) encourages leader, managers, employee, and coaches to do away with the traditional "pull" behaviors and replace them with "push" discipline. With the "pull" approach, managers tell employees what is expected and what goals need to be achieved. On the other side, the "push" discipline is initiated by the employee taking personal responsibility for identifying his or her own strengths as well as weaknesses. Once these strengths are identified, one can take a stand for them, clarify and communicate them to one's colleagues, and seek support from everyone in the department toward them. In other words, the employee must take personal responsibility for pushing his or her strengths in the workplace and seeking more opportunities to use them in worthwhile projects and tasks. One must consistently speak out about one's personal values and strengths in order to create a high performing team or organization. As discussed by Buckingham (p. 19), the six-step discipline for putting one's strengths to work are: busting the myth that fixing weaknesses is a good way to achieve high performance; getting clear about one's personal strengths and goals; freeing one's strengths and making work fun by getting involved in enjoyable tasks; stopping one's weaknesses from weakening one's opportunities; speaking up in regard to one's personal strengths to get more opportunities for doing what one enjoys doing; and building strong habits of being in control, feeling authentic, fulfilled, and valued by constantly staying focused and playing on one's strengths and staying away from activities that can drag one down the pessimistic path. Buckingham states that:

To build your life around your strengths, you don't need to wait for the perfect job, the perfect boss, or the perfect situation. Besides, these things may never come. Instead learn how to take stock of your strengths, how to take control of your time, and how to make the two gradually, inexorably, and deliberately converge. Start with your own life, and to paraphrase Mahatma Gandhi, be the change you want to see in your team (Buckingham, 2007, p. 32).

Buckingham's book will be a useful read for business leaders, managers, new employees, and their coaches. Most readers will find this book to be a step-by-step guide that can assist one become more productive in the workplace. The book is a step by step guide for recognizing one's strengths and capitalizing on them. *Go Put Your Strengths to Work* is appropriate for business and management students studying leadership strategies that can be applied to enhance one's coaching influence and productivity in the organization. Overall, *Go Put Your Strengths to Work* is a recommended reading for anyone who wants to develop his or her coaching and leadership skills.

### *Be Positive and Believe!*

Putting one's strengths to work requires knowing what they are, being positive about them, and deeply believing in them. Many individuals, during their childhood years, believe that through their power and influence they can live a long life, fly, talk telepathically with others, and discover new leading cures and technologies. These same adult individuals, once passed their youth, tend to be conditioned through socialization in the family, education system, peers in the workplace, and media to believe there are boundless limitations to the possibilities they used to believe as children. Such thinking and socialization can lead to seeing the weaknesses rather than possibilities or their own personal strengths. Consequently, for example, people may not believe that they have the qualifications for jobs that they should be fully capable of performing without much training. People who see themselves as limited in this world are likely to see their careers, relationships, physical health, and other aspects of life as incomplete in one way or another since what they want will always appear out of reach for them. These types of thinking need to be replaced with a truer and more positive perspective. It is through the paradigm shift of replacing self-limiting perspectives with an empowering view that one can truly believe that his or her dreams are within reach or the realm of reality. Change best happens when one changes his or her beliefs about his or her capabilities. Everyone should realize that the world is flexible, changeable, and the boundaries are not set in stone or concrete walls. Each person can change his or her realities of the world by changing his or her perspectives about what is possible and doable. Some of this change may require a little push in the right direction, as demonstrated in the words of Poet Christopher Logue:

> Come to the edge.
> We might fall.

Come to the edge.
It's too high!
Come to the edge!
And they came,
And we pushed,
And they flew.

A change in perspective, sometimes, requires that one experience the environment beyond the boundaries of his or her comfort zone. It means that one should take calculated risks to experience the new realities and possibilities by "jumping in with both feet." Of course, such possibilities can better lead to success through a positive attitude, preparation, planning, and a true belief that it can happen. It is very true that positive thinking is better than having a negative attitude or perspective as the positive mindset can certainly lead to better results, attract more friends, and make life less stressful. As many experts and philosophers would recommend, one should definitely be positive and compassionate; however, what is even more powerful is what one actually and truly believes mentally, spiritually, and psychologically through his or her heart. It is the deep feelings from one's heart that can impact a person's head and habits. A person's heart controls the feelings which can lead to what he or she thinks about in his or her head that eventually leads to certain behaviors and habits. So, by controlling the heart (feelings), one can also influence his or her head (thoughts) and habits (behaviors) in order to move beyond most obstacles and self-limiting beliefs. Experts, such as Gregg Braden who is the author of "*The Spontaneous Healing of Belief: Shattering the Paradigm of False Limits*," tell us that people can heal their ill feelings and bring miraculous transformation in themselves when they actually go "beyond their minds." One can best move from his or her head to the heart by discovering who he or she actually is, and doing what he/she truly believes in intrinsically to live a joyful and healthy life.

### *Summary*

With an effective personal coaching plan, Paula Hulk can avoid/remedy burnout by restoring and then maintaining work-life balance. The coaching plan specifically involves the identification of core values and goals and then the establishment of priorities based on those underlying goals. Once the priorities have been established, Paula can focus on creating SMART goals for each of the priorities. Work and personal responsibilities that do not contribute to accomplishing the SMART goals and thus do not fit with the top priorities need to be managed away whenever possible using the most appropriate balance strategy, either alternating, outsourcing, bundling, tech-flexing, and simplifying. Paula can then seek self-gratification and personal development in the areas that are most important to her rather than ineffectively through tasks that are assigned to her by others. In finding those areas of values congruence between her priorities and those of her work establishment, Paula is taking an important step in reducing future likelihood of burnout as "value congruence between the worker and the organization is predictive of job satisfaction" (Siegall & McDonald, 2004). This coaching plan allows Paula to measure achievement based on completion of her top goals and priorities rather than external measures of success. In this situation, by focusing and achieving rather than juggling, Paula, her patients, her family and her medical practice all benefit in the end. The goal of preserving Paula's performance, restoring her satisfaction and promoting longevity in her current position could all be accomplished after a successful personal coaching program.

### Discussion Questions

1. What is work-life balance and why is it important?
2. Is there a link between work-life balance and productivity? Discuss.
3. What are some possible consequences of work-life imbalance?
4. What can personal coaches do to help coachees stay in balance?
5. List five things that one can do to maintain a work-life balance.
6. Why should people be doing what they are good at doing?
7. What can managers and employees do to recognize their own strengths?
8. What are the benefits of engaging one's strengths?

# CHAPTER 6

## Coaching Disruptive Behavior[18]

The dilemma of disruptive behavior by physicians in clinical or business settings unfortunately remains a common occurrence. These behaviors often have destructive impacts on many facets of affected organizations, and can even influence both the quality of healthcare received by patients and the relationships enjoyed with clinical and business constituencies. To complicate matters further, these episodes are frequently carried out by bright (often brilliant) physicians whose medical practice and clinical judgment are considered superb by colleagues and co-workers. These individuals also tend to be highly productive. The paradox created, then, is one of unacceptable behavior coupled with a valued physician resource. As a consequence, healthcare organizations are faced with the need to manage this paradox in order to sustain valued relationships with external partners (hospitals, payers, referring physicians and patients), while simultaneously retaining both those clinical resources that are the recipients of these behaviors and managing to optimize the performance of the perpetrators of them as well.

Current organizational approaches to physicians with behavioral problems tend to focus upon management of the physician and the signaling event once the episode has occurred. Management, in general, focuses upon a situational evaluation including risk and legal analysis, and upon interventions such as mediation, coaching, disciplining or counseling (Keogh & Martin, 2004). This, perhaps, is in part an explanation for the ubiquitous nature of this problem (Pfifferling, 1999) as this approach manages, but does not address, factors causing the troublesome behavior in the first place and, therefore, cannot serve to mitigate its frequency or severity. While there are no studies which convincingly prove that targeted coaching reduces the incidence of disruptive physician behavior, it does make intuitive sense that specifically designed and proactive coaching programs may result in its reduction.

The intent of this section is to review the literature as it relates to the scope and impact of this problem, and describe a coaching approach to self-awareness with the goal of reducing disruptive behavior in physicians. The coaching philosophy will not focus on coaching style or technique, because they are often related to the personality and skill of the coach and the needs of the coachee. It will address approaches to evaluating the coachee's needs with specific attention given to dealing with emotions, leadership styles, and communication styles and influencing skills.

---

[18] Contributed by Keith S. Meredith (M.D.), Nova Southeastern University.

## Coaching Disruptive Behavior

"Managing disruptive behavior is one of the most stressful and challenging tasks that any executive faces, but the rewards of directly addressing this behavior when it first occurs reaps many dividends for patients, for staff and for fellow physicians" (Keogh & Martin, 2004, p. 22). This comment highlights the combined problem of frequency and emotional intensity attributable to this problem, as more than 95% of physician executives responding to a survey reported regularly encountering physicians exhibiting these problem behaviors (Weber, 2004). The nature of these behaviors are varied and range from angry outbursts (like throwing surgical instruments or browbeating nurses) to breaching sexual boundaries and substance abuse. In the survey results published by Weber (2004), about 38.9% of executive respondents acknowledged that when it came to behavioral problems financially productive physicians were treated more leniently than their less productive colleagues. This favoritism further compromises leadership effectiveness and undermines the potential for long term positive behavioral change.

## American College of Physician Executives Survey Report

Weber (2004), in his report of an extensive survey of physician executives, documented both the frequency and nature of disruptive physician behaviors. Sponsored by the American College of Physician Executives, this comprehensive survey of 1,600 physician leaders described the extent of behavioral problems in otherwise high-functioning physicians. Like the report from Delbecq (2001), Weber noted a high percentage (>95%) of leaders who have dealt with disruptive behavior during their leadership terms. He also noted that over 35% reported the need to address problem physician behavior on at least a monthly basis. Over half (57%) replied that the inappropriate behavior was directed toward clinical subordinates like nursing, pharmacy and respiratory care staff. Twenty-nine percent of these exchanges were noted to occur with other physicians or members of the administrative staff, and in only 20% of circumstances did staff feel "safe from reprisal" if they reported wrongful physician behavior. A disappointing 82% of all events were described as simply disrespectful.

The nature of these outbursts and their repetition sheds additional light on the problem. Fifty-one percent of the disruptive behavior was noted to be the result of physician refusal to embrace teamwork or feelings of frustration and vulnerability due to organizational changes; conflicts between other physicians and staff accounted for another 36%; and "turf" battles among physicians another 4%. Finally, over 70% of survey respondents reported that physician behavior problems were perpetrated by the same individuals over and over again. When one takes these findings in the context of deferential treatment given to high producing doctors, a recipe for failed rehabilitation and continued poor behavior is the clear result. Only 34% of executives responding to this survey said that physicians were treated similarly or more harshly than other employees when issues of behavior arose.

Approaches taken to manage these behaviors varied. When evaluated, the survey showed that in the two years prior respondents noted their institutions had acted in the following ways to address problems with physician behavior: 1) discussed problem with physician – 95%, 2) delivered written warnings to a doctor – 68%, 3) ordered counseling – 53%, 4) terminated the physician – 36%, and 5) did nothing – 31%. These tactics met with varying success. The survey showed that attempts to intervene and correct physician behavior were successful 75-100% of the time in only 14%. Indeed, respondents reported that failure occurred half or more of the time in over 60% of their organizations.

This potential combination of executive incapacity and emotional management cost, with the added burden of damaging behavior frequency can be crippling to organizational leadership; and this without accounting for the additional negative impact on employee retention, patient outcome, patient safety, and external client relationships. There is an opportunity to mitigate adverse behaviors and their impacts with a specific coaching approach intended to develop both physician leaders and staff physicians alike.

**Coaching Physicians**

Coaching physicians is increasingly recognized as a valuable adjunct to the development of current and future physician leaders (Thilo, 2004). Many of the skills that make excellent physicians, like rapid and independent decision making, are the antithesis of those required for leading successful healthcare systems; and they may in fact contribute to the dissonance experienced by non-leader physicians functioning in systems led by physician leaders who are influenced by current managerial thought. This collective dissonance adds to physician frustration and contributes to the notion that doctors that have transitioned to management have gone over to the "dark side" (Kibort, 2005, p. 52). These frustrations and those mentioned above, are often played out in emotional outbursts or other disruptive behaviors that are projected upon other members of the healthcare team. To anticipate these frustrations and assuage fears of "administrative physicians" a coaching philosophy, made integral to physician development, may allow for the accumulation of the tools needed so that individual physicians can anticipate and alter their own behavior. This can be accomplished by an increased understanding of how to improve communications with others, how to work with peers as effective members of the team, by obtaining a better understanding of their impact on others, and by developing an awareness of new ways to approach demanding situations (Thilo, 2004). In addition, the acquisition of the skills of self-management, self-awareness and empathy not only prepare the coachee for leadership, they prepare him/her for the navigation of life (Goleman, 1995). Coaching is a relationship, between the coach and the coachee, which influences the coachee to make behavioral changes that optimize personal performance and growth through continuous learning and self-reflection. Coaching, therefore, can be a journey to acquire emotional intelligence, develop attuned leadership styles (Arond-Thomas, 2004), and improve situation appropriate communication and influence techniques (Marvel, Gunn, & Brezinski, 2004; Ludeman & Erlandson, 2004).

**Emotion and the Workplace**

Goleman (1995), in his classic work on emotional intelligence, discusses this combination of cognition and emotion that comprises an intelligence that is not entirely rational, nor is it entirely emotional. Yet it is a level of comprehension that is entirely human as it explores the natural and holistic relationship that exists between knowing and feeling. From an epistemological perspective, it addresses the true meaning of knowledge. Based upon data from several researchers, the clear implication is that successful leaders exhibit these attributes more abundantly than their not so successful counterparts. In fact, multiple studies over the last 20-30 years suggest that 80-90% of differences between superior and average performers can be attributed to differences in emotional intelligence (Arond-Thomas, 2004). Physicians are trained in rational decision making. This is reinforced by the concrete nature of statistical analysis and differential diagnosis which are by intent and design devoid of emotion or bias. As a result, many of the core competencies needed by the physician to matriculate the complex emotional landscape of modern healthcare are unavailable to him/her. As Arond-Thomas (2004) describes in her work on emotional intelligence and physician behavioral problems, "Disruptive behavior is a non-specific marker for concerns that can range from a lack of intra- and interpersonal effectiveness skills to deeper problems such as chronic stress, burnout, depression or other mood disorders and substance abuse." This contribution of incomplete resource development for physicians in the realm of emotional intelligence (self-awareness and self-management in particular) appears to, in part, explain the transference of uncomfortable emotions to disruptive behavior. But do emotions play a significant role in the understanding of organizational behavior?

Recent work in organization studies does suggest a growing understanding of the role of emotions in workplace behaviors. In the view of Sturdy (2003), "Emotion, like gender before it, is coming to be recognized as a central feature of organizations. Indeed it has been claimed that we are on the brink of relocating feelings as a focal point for organizational studies." Further, studies in clinical environments clearly suggest that emotional climate, defined by Brown and Brooks (2002) "as the set, or sets, of emotions or feelings, shared by groups of individuals implicated in common social structures and processes, and significant in the formation and maintenance of political and social entities and collective behavior, is the atmosphere that employees perceive as created in their organization by practices, procedures, and rewards." This emotional climate then sets the foundation for group behaviors and varies significantly, as groups evaluate their value and collective contributions to organization and unit goals. In fact, the now classic Hawthorne studies of Elton Mayo and his colleagues, which showed that feelings like affiliation, competence and achievement were more potent as motivators than were environmental changes designed to promote efficiency, effectively demonstrated the importance of modifications of emotional climate on worker productivity (Hersey & Campbell, 2004).

The complexity of dealing with emotion in the coaching context must not be taken for granted. Zeus and Skiffington (2002) offer several key coaching suggestions to assist with the dynamic and fluctuating nature of emotions. They offer that when approaching the coachee, the coach should internalize the importance of separating what one feels from what one does (taking responsibility for emotions);

understanding the clear relevance of one's choices and actions; acknowledging that emotions alone have no intrinsic moral value; accepting that emotions by themselves are not functional or harmful and that they can be contradictory in nature; and that cultural and gender differences in emotional expression exist. To assist with engaging physicians in the discovery of their intrinsic and life experience influenced personality characteristics and situational responses, some authors suggest the use of behavioral tools with expert interpretation as a cost-effective option (Wintermeyer, 2005). The authors suggest assessments like the Myers-Briggs Type Indicator, the Thomas-Kilmann Conflict Mode Instrument, the Stress Resiliency Profile, and the 16 Personality Factor Questionnaire for use through a formal process. The choice(s) of instrument should match desired outcome to the intention of the instrument. The results obtained should allow the coach to formulate a more personalized coaching plan that incorporates assessment findings. Further, as the importance and specific relevance of individual and group emotions and emotional climates become clearer, focused strategies designed to incorporate them into targeted and personalized coaching plans need to be developed and evaluated for efficacy.

## Leadership

Most medical professionals are skilled in only a few leadership styles. These leadership styles have evolved in good part because of the cognitive skills and scientific acumen acquired to successfully practice medicine. In general, they are consistent with the heroic behavior model and have been described as "commanding" and "pacesetting" styles by some authors (Arond-Thomas, 2004). Since the leadership skills that have been acquired by most physicians are the direct result of the technical skills gained during medical professional training, they have little to do with follower task or readiness considerations and, therefore, have no intrinsic flexibility. This inflexibility can interfere with team cohesion and productivity. Studies suggest that organizational climate accounts for 20-30 percent of performance and that 50-70 percent of employee perception of organizational climate comes from their view of leadership (Arond-Thomas, 2004). An example of the leadership's positive influence on organizational climate, and therefore, team performance can be found in the work by Edmondson (2004). In her evaluation of organizational climate factors that could influence nurse medication error detection and reporting to minimize preventable adverse drug events she found that nurse manager coaching, nurse manager direction setting, unit performance outcomes, and the quality of unit relationships (this included relationships with attending physicians) all positively correlated with the desired group behavior (i.e. improved patient safety) with correlation coefficients >0.70 and two-tailed $p<0.03$. This work clearly relates the importance of nurse manager and, to a lesser extent physician, leadership behavior on group (i.e. nursing unit), rather than individual performance. She concludes that, "It appears that nurse manager behaviors are an important influence on unit members' beliefs about the consequences and discussability of mistakes" (Edmondson, 2004, pp. 85-86). Interestingly, Edmondson also makes a connection between the leadership behaviors of the nurse manager and emotional responses of the group. These emotional responses are played out in avoidance and correction of errors, unit performance, and quality of unit relationships. This supports Sturdy (2003) and

Brown and Brooks' (2002) theories that emotion, and emotional climate, play a significant role in organizational performance and complements the contention that leadership behaviors have a direct impact on emotions.

The development of an array of leadership styles, that is responsive to followers (healthcare team, patients, administrators, etc.), will limit the negative consequences of inappropriate behavior by expanding the leadership skill set and mitigating frustration and unwanted emotional responses. Studies by behavioral scientists (Hersey and Campbell, 2004) clearly support the importance of this approach to flexible (situational) leadership. An additional leadership concept has been described by Lipman-Blumen as Connective Leadership (Lipman-Blumen, 2002). In this work she proposes six essential strengths that add to the connective leader's attributes of negotiation, persuasion and integration. They are: 1) ethical political savvy; 2) authenticity and accountability; 3) a politics of commonalities; 4) thinking long-term, acting short-term; 5) leadership through expectation; and 6) a quest for meaning. These attributes, if mastered, would create a rich leadership fabric to address the relationship dominant leadership environment that defines twenty-first century healthcare. These and other leadership theories and models will help prepare the physician for the ever changing dynamics of the modern healthcare arena. Thus, leadership readiness is fundamental to follower accomplishment; this creates a superb opportunity for a coaching approach to physician growth to excel.

**Communication and Influence**

In addition to honing an array of leadership styles, improving approaches to communication and understanding the value of influencing techniques will also improve team results and limit leader and staff frustrations. However, many physicians fit the description by Ludeman and Erlandson (2004) of the "Alpha Male" (or female). The males are characterized as self-confident and opinionated, highly intelligent, action oriented, having high performance expectations for themselves and others, preferring a direct communication style, highly disciplined, and perceiving themselves as unemotional. There are obvious advantages to these characteristics in the tense and potentially emotionally charged environment of patient care scenarios (especially critical care situations). But these attributes, which are considered by the Alpha Male as strengths, can also be significant weaknesses. Self-confidence can also convey intimidation and arrogance; high levels of intelligence can result in intolerance of less intelligent colleagues; action orientation can create impatience; direct communication styles may engender fear and a failure driven culture; a disciplined persona sets standards that others may not reach; and an unemotional presence can convey disinterest and therefore stymie inspiration and *esprit de corps* (Ludeman & Erlandson, 2004).

In contrast to the Alpha Male, Ludeman and Erlandson relate that the Alpha Female places more value on interpersonal relationships and acknowledges the feelings of those around her. They also do not seek as often to be dominant, choosing instead diplomacy. They tend to understand the importance of positive motivation and, therefore, avoid engendering fear and generally avoid conflict. Their weakness is that their more validating style can send the false impressions that "all is well when it is not" (Ludeman & Erlandson, 2004, p. 61).

These characteristics create the circumstance described earlier by Weber (2004) where favoritism influenced management of behavioral problems because of the high performing nature of these personalities. In addition, Alphas appear to be "surprisingly oblivious to the effect they have on others" (Ludeman & Erlandson, 2004, p. 60). This creates an interesting challenge to coaching professionals who must tailor their communication and influencing style to "reach" this population who tend to be keenly analytical and unconcerned with significant detail. So while approaching the topic of communication styles, the coach will need to use a direct and commanding method so as to not bore the coachee. Once so engaged, the importance of adjusting communication styles to mirror that of the influence object in order to meet desired objectives has a better chance of incorporation into the Alpha's repertoire because of its result orientation. In addition to developing this range of communication styles, approaches to influencing others by understanding the nature of communication energy can also impact desired communication results.

A study designed to understand inter-physician expressions of differences of opinion in meetings showed interesting results. In this work by Marvel et al. (2004), the authors analyzed audiotapes of meetings involving physicians, clinical staff, nurses, and administrators. They identified two discussion categories, push statements and pull statements, characterized the relative frequency per meeting of each and determined the impact of both on the outcome of each meeting, i.e. the meeting objective was satisfied. They found that "a higher frequency of pull statements was associated with group consensus outcome whereas push statements were associated with outcomes based upon one person's opinion" (Marvel et al., 2004, p. 44). In addition, they noted that the gender of participants had no impact on the frequency of push or pull statements.

To analyze these meetings, these authors identified a difference of opinion in each meeting by first noting acknowledgement of conflict (a statement showing recognition of a difference of opinion) within the meeting context. They were able to then characterize the interpersonal processes and decisions expressed during meetings as follows: 1. Advocacy (expressing or explaining one's opinion); 2. Inquiry (an attempt to understand another person's perspective); 3. Affirmation (validation of another's opinion); 4. Self-disclosure (sharing one's feelings); 5. Summarizing (offering a summary of the discussion); 6. Interruption (a comment that cuts off another person); and 7. Humor (a remark followed by laughter) (Marvel et al., 2004, p. 45). Of the forty-five meetings with an identified conflict, 41% of confliction resolution occurred with an individual solution, 19% by group consensus, 7% by vote, 19% were tabled, and 14% resulted in no decision. The most common discussions processes noted were advocacy (5.7 times per meeting) and interruption (4.8 times per meeting). Advocacy was noted in 100% of the meetings and interruption in 79%. Further, when comparing meeting outcomes by type, i.e. individual solution or group consensus, they found nearly equal amounts of mean "push" statements (4.2 vs. 5.5). On the other hand, there was an almost three fold increase in mean "pull" statements (1.0 vs. 2.8) favoring the group consensus process. As a result, the authors hypothesized that an increase in inquiry and group consensus will occur if "group leaders minimize interruptions during meetings" (Marvel et al., 2004, p. 46).

Developing within the coachee a range of communication styles and strategic communication energy, as suggested by Vengel (2000), will support developing leadership and emotional competencies by giving voice to their expression. Because communication is the method by which one expresses emotions and implements attuned leadership styles, the incorporation of targeted approaches to both communication styles and communication energies can only enhance leadership effectiveness and limit frustration. This in combination with the self-awareness, self-management and relationship management qualities of emotional intelligence should serve to give the physician leader the tools to both coach physician staff to minimize disruptive behavior and manage its occurrence.

## Opportunities for Management: Scope of the Problem

Reports published by Delbecq (2001) and Weber (2004) both describe the alarming frequency with which destructive behavior has been witnessed by queried executives. In the former paper, 88% of the senior executives responding replied having experienced a personality they loosely described as "evil" during one of their management tenures. "Most of these executives also believed that they intuitively recognized this aberrant personality sooner than they had facts to support it; reacted too late to their presence; and felt poorly equipped to deal with them because traditional policies and procedures were inadequate" (Meredith, 2006). To add to this, "The evil individual sucks the life juices from the organizational group by unusually destructive behavior, crippling the group in such a way that positive spirit is lost" Delbecq (2001, p. 222).

### Organizational Impact

Healthcare organizations, whose core competency is the provision of specialized care, rely on their human clinical resource to accomplish their mission, vision, and goals. Thus, these resources are mission critical and circumstances and events that negatively impact work environments risk job dissatisfaction and resultant employee/resource turnover. This turnover is made more complex not only by the expensive nature of employee turnover itself, but by the current shortage of potential replacements. The very healthcare marketplace dynamics which fuel the stressors contributing to disruptive physician behaviors are also reducing the number of potential candidates by both attrition among existing clinicians and lack of interest in healthcare careers among youth (Silverstein & Kornacki, 2000). Pfifferling (1999, p. 58) summarized that "the disruptive physician or professional undermines practice morale, heightens turnover in the organization, steals from productive activities, increases the risk for ineffective or substandard practice, and causes distress among colleagues." The climate that attends these individuals creates a swath of chaos that must negatively influence productivity and team job satisfaction and reflects some of the weaknesses of classical medical education.

Traditional medical training favors physician autonomy and independent decision making (Keogh & Martin, 2004). This, unfortunately, does not prepare physicians for the demands of current medical practice. Today's healthcare climate of larger physician groups, decreasing physician reimbursement, rising professional liability and general overhead costs, and increasing patient expectations all contribute to the need for doing more with less while simultaneously doing it better. Common solutions to these challenges include enhanced teamwork and the development of clinical practice guidelines. Both are intended to distribute workloads across the healthcare clinical spectra and to improve standardization among and between clinical groups. The Institute of Medicine, in their report entitled *Crossing the Quality Chasm* (2001), developed six specific aims intended to address these issues. In their view, healthcare should be safe, effective, patient-centered, timely, efficient, and equitable. To accomplish these aims, they believe that the development of high-performance teams and organizational supports to direct and manage change is crucial to the successful delivery of quality care (Institute of Medicine, 2001b). Disruptive behavior, by its nature, interferes with change processes and limits team cohesion and growth potential.

### *Recommendations: Coaching*

The call for bringing targeted coaching approaches to physician development has been made by several authors referenced in this chapter. Most suggest that coaching should be made available to physician leaders which may reflect mostly the bias of the authors. Other, more recent work, has offered that coaching may positively influence decisions by physicians to achieve important professional transitions by helping them align their personal values and goals with those of their professional life (Manion, 2005). There is an indirect suggestion within the literature reviewed above that coaching techniques may have a positive effect on physician behavior, which is otherwise pre-programmed to create conflict in the current team-oriented and increasingly non-hierarchical healthcare environment. The negative organizational impact created by this training/actual conflict and subsequent disruptive physician behavior begs a meaningful and sustainable solution and coaching appears to address these issues.

To date, there exist no data which confirm or refute a casual relationship between a targeted and personalized coaching program and a reduction in the frequency and/or severity of disruptive physician behavior. If one accepts the premise that the current cost of this phenomenon is staggering and endangers an already limited and valuable resource, efforts should be taken to evaluate approaches to finding meaningful solutions. Historical or randomized controlled trials of coached and un-coached physicians could answer this important question. Studies of this type are needed to clearly delineate which coaching variables of style and content have the desired behavioral impact and which do not.

### *Summary*

This chapter has been focused on the development of an argument for the use of targeted (addressing issues of emotional management, leadership styles, and communication/influencing skills) and personalized (acknowledging variations in personality type and life experience) coaching to reduce the frequency and severity of disruptive behavior among otherwise highly-functioning physicians and professionals. There is clearly demonstrated need to begin mitigation efforts and to not accept after-the-fact management alone. This is supported by the documented ineffectiveness of management approaches and the real tendency of leaders to participate in favoritism for those most likely to be offenders. The coaching of both physician leaders and staff physicians would appear to be the most productive, with the goal of preparing the former to manage disruptive events and assist the latter with acquiring the self-awareness skills and intervention tools to modify potentially destructive behaviors before they occur. The value to healthcare organizations can be measured in the reduction of costs to recruit and maintain clinical and non-clinical staff. The value to healthcare can be measured in improvements in patient outcomes with reductions in the resources required to achieve them. Currently, no supporting data exists which confirm a potential causal relationship between this approach and a reduction in disruptive behavior. Organizations with vested interests may have significant incentives to consider answering the questions posed in this chapter.

### *Discussion Questions*

1.  What is disruptive behavior? Discuss at least three examples from two different industries or jobs.
2.  What are some possible causes of disruptive behavior?
3.  Are women associates likely to cause more disruptions in the workplace or men employees? Discuss your thoughts, logic, reasons, and observations.
4.  What role does emotion play in the workplace?
5.  Is there a link between emotional intelligence and disruptive behavior? Discuss.
6.  What can leaders do to positively influence disruptive behavior? Discuss and list five specific recommendations.
7.  If a professional like a employee (such as a physician) consistently demonstrates disruptive behaviors, what might be the possible consequences to the people involved? Discuss.

# CHAPTER 7

## Evaluating, Influencing and Coaching Performance

Coaching and influencing can take place every day with any person in one's life activities. However, in the workplace, coaching and influencing with employees is often geared toward the achievement of organizational and departmental goals through the strategic alignment of tasks, behaviors, and activities. Today's managers and leaders face many challenges and changes in the management of their departments and organization, including ethical challenges, morale concerns, theft, stealing, malpractices, low quality products or services, as well as the need for ethical marketing strategies and proper life-work balance. Dealing with such changes and dilemmas require them to monitor the performance of their employees, observe their behaviors, and evaluate whether or not they are aligned with the desired expectation. After an appropriate assessment, managers and coaches can begin the influence and coaching plan.

"Coaching," "influencing" and "engaging" techniques are necessary to help everyone in the department successfully go through the necessary changes to achieve the desired goals. This chapter reflects upon the evaluation or assessment of performance as well as the coaching and influencing of employees to the desired performance.

### Evaluating Employee Performance

One of the responsibilities of managers, leaders and business owners are to inspire their employees to do what is right, perform their tasks at a high level, and create an overall competitive work environment in the organization. To inspire employees, leaders and managers must demonstrate by their actions and attitudes that they honestly and sincerely support them to be successful. Every manager should attempt to inspire his or her people to be the best that they can be by being a good example. Furthermore, two other main responsibilities of managers, leaders and entrepreneurs are to regularly assess and evaluate the performance of their employees and through effective communication, coach, discipline and help them grow. While these responsibilities may appear to be easy as people are paid to do their work and they should do them, assessment and evaluation of performance are more complex. Great leaders, managers and entrepreneurs should be able to assess and evaluate their employees' abilities and capitalize on each person's strengths while helping them grow. As stated by most performance management writers and experts, successful management is about regularly identifying, growing and promoting high-performing employees, while targeting underperformers for relevant coaching, training and improvement purposes. New leaders, managers and entrepreneurs should learn the skills needed to monitor the day-to-day performance of their employees and department, assess and evaluate performance, conduct effective performance reviews, coach and develop employees for high performance, reward and reinforce good performance, and discipline or terminate poor performers.

Today's leaders and managers should understand and execute an effective performance management system or program as part of their performance improvement process. Performance management can be seen as an ongoing interaction process between managers and employees about their goals and objectives that need to be achieved if they are to be successful personally, professionally, individually, and as a team. According to Barry Silverstein, "Performance management is a process-oriented approach to evaluating and supporting employees," which ideally "takes place from the moment the employee is hired to fill a position at a company to the moment the individual leaves the organization" (2007, p. 4). Silverstein states that a successful performance management system involves four basic components: 1) a clear organizational definition of performance, 2) a training and development program focused on performance improvement, 3) an objective evaluation system for employee performance reviews, and 4) a strategy or method for recognizing and rewarding good performance (2007, p. 108). The steps to an effective performance management program can include establishing performance goals, regularly monitoring performance, developing skills through training or coaching, formally evaluating and documenting performance during the designated review dates, and recognizing and rewarding good performance (Silverstein, p. 111). An effective and comprehensive performance management program can help organizations develop a competent and motivated employee base, increase their productivity standards, produce quality products and services, and achieve their corporate goals. Organizations that have a comprehensive performance management system, then naturally performance evaluation or continual performance appraisals will be one major element of that program. There is a slight difference between performance evaluation and performance appraisals as practiced in most companies. While a performance evaluation process is a continual process of informally and formally assessing the work of associates on a weekly, monthly and quarterly basis, performance appraisals are typically conducted once a year. Instead of waiting till the end of a year or the designated performance appraisal period, managers should monitor, observe and assess the performance of their employees and departments on a regular basis. When they see positive results and good performance, managers should immediately communicate such findings to the employees producing them as to acknowledge and appreciate their work. Furthermore, regular acknowledgement and appreciation of good work reinforces such behavior and performance. Similarly, instead of waiting until the end of the week or the performance appraisal period, managers must also communicate their expectations and the desired results when they see poor performance through effective coaching. This communication and feedback must be immediate, timely, sincere, and goal-oriented using proper coaching skills.

Periodic employee evaluation and communication about performance can increase productivity, enhance job satisfaction, develop employees, achieve organizational objectives, and allow for timely rewards and promotions.

In *"Evaluating Performance: How to Appraise, Promote, and Fire,"* by distilling the wisdom of industry experts, author Barry Silverstein (2007) discusses performance management systems, promoting employees, dealing with underperformers, evaluating team performance, and effectively implementing performance management in today's work environment. The goal of this book is to help managers and entrepreneurs effectively evaluate employees and manage their work for high performance. Silverstein states that "most companies will hire younger employees with fewer years on the job—individuals who need well-defined goals, on-the-job training and continual supervision" (2007, p. 4). Silverstein continues to say, "There are no shortcuts to employee evaluation, but there are processes, strategies, and techniques that help managers evaluate employees more effectively." As part of a comprehensive performance management program, the first for managers is to begin hiring the right individuals for their organizational cultures and departments. Of course, hiring the right person begins by having the right job description for the specific job and its responsibilities. According to Silverstein, a job description is a hiring blueprint and if it "clearly states job requirements—skills, initiative, and interactions with coworkers and other departments—it not only ensures that candidates will be qualified, it also becomes the managers guide for managing and evaluating employee performance" (2007, p. 10). Once the right employee is hired, one should keep employees engaged with the departmental and organizational objectives. Helping employees align their personal goals and objectives with those of the organization's can help them see how what they do links with the firm. In other words, by being involved in the achievement of the organization's goals employees see their contributions and will stay motivated.

Silverstein offers five steps that managers and leaders can use to effectively manage the performance of their employees in the organization (2007, p. 13):

1. Strategically plan the right tasks, involve the employee performing them, and set high expectations.
2. Monitor, observe, assess, and evaluate each employee's performance on a regular basis.
3. Provide relevant training and development opportunities for each employee so they can perform their jobs successfully and be ready for advancement.
4. Review the performance of employees using a standardized and fair rating scale for objective measurement.
5. Reward good performance with positive reinforcements and correct poor performance through goal setting and coaching skills.

The most difficult aspect of employee evaluation for most experienced and new managers seem to be the communication of poor performance. Of course, once a manager identifies an underperformer, it is the manager's responsibility to either correct the situation through effective coaching or terminate the employee (Silverstein, p. 54). Noticeable signs of performance problems with employees can be observed from a major change in attitude, minimal effort on the job, inability to concentrate, and becoming a loner. It is the manager's duty and responsibility to expect the desired performance or quality of service from each employee. When a personal problem is preventing the employee from performing at the desired level, the manager should communicate the expectation and stay focused on the desired performance level. Of course, when employees face personal challenges, managers should listen and empathize. While managers cannot and should not solve their employees' personal problems, they should continue to expect the same standards from everyone at all times. While confronting poor performance is not always a pleasant situation, a manager's first objective "should be to improve the employee's behavior," (Silverstein, 2007, p. 59) instead of simply allowing the employee to be fired or terminated. If the situation does not improve, then the manager or coach can pursue a progressive discipline process in a respectful and professional manner. Silverstein provides the following "Dos and Don'ts" for terminating employees who do not improve their performance to the desired level in a timely and agreed upon manner (2007, p. 74):

1.  Conduct regular evaluations and provide feedback to enhance performance, and prevent a possible termination.
2.  Consider demotions and transfers if other jobs seem to be a better fit for the person.
3.  Stay calm and cool during an employee termination and dismissal process. Be respectful of the employee and his or her ego. If and when possible, continue to have a functional and personal relationship with the employee.
4.  When terminating an employee, meet with the person privately and, if needed, have a human resource professional present. Prepare a termination letter which clearly states the reasons for the dismissal.
5.  Don't terminate an employee if you have not helped him or her improve or fully documented the reasons for the dismissal.
6.  Don't become angry or emotional during the process as that is not helpful for you, the organization or the employee.
7.  Don't make negative statements about the dismissed employee to his or her colleagues in the department.
8.  Don't allow senior employees to leave without getting an agreement or release about such issues as not taking the organization's customers to a competitor, etc.

These suggestions are helpful for both new and experienced managers and business owners. New leaders, managers and entrepreneurs should get the needed tools for the assessment and evaluation of performance if they are to be successful individuals. The tools and insight can help them build rapport and camaraderie among staff and various teams. Reading such books as "*Evaluating Performance: How to Appraise, Promote, and Fire*" can help one learn invaluable concepts, techniques, and skills for effective communication, conflict management, and performance evaluations.

One should keep in mind that there really isn't much value in recruiting and hiring employees, investing in their training, orienting them to the organization over several days or weeks, and then letting them "sink or swim" to see if they can be successful or not in this new culture or work environment. Instead of having a hands-off style of management, managers must take personal responsibility for the success and failure of their employees by leading them in the right direction through effective coaching, and praising their good work as soon as they see it. What is even more interesting to remember and emphasize to new managers and leaders is that by occasionally offering sincere praises about good performance and positive reinforcements, even new managers can motivate their employees, increase departmental morale, and improve performance. According to Silverstein, "If you provide informal feedback regularly, and formally evaluate performance at least quarterly, the annual performance appraisal will be easier for both you and the employee to manage—and far less intimidating" (2007, p. 33). The goal for any performance evaluation and review at its conclusion should be for the employees to walk away with a clear understanding of what they are doing right as well as what they need to improve in order for them and their organizations to be successful in the coming months and year(s). Standardized performance management and evaluation programs can lead to the promotion of employees who demonstrate leadership ability, sustained high performance, initiative, diplomacy and interpersonal skills, ability to set and achieve strategic goals, and positive attitude.

Silverstein's *"Evaluating Performance: How to Appraise, Promote, and Fire"* book is a useful read for business owners and managers that want to strategically coach and influence their employees, suppliers and customers toward organizational objectives. Most readers will find this book to be a quick, step-by-step guide that can assist one become more effective in the assessment and evaluation of performance in the workplace.

## The Concepts of Coaching and Influencing[19]

Today's real world dilemmas present managers and leaders the opportunity to coach and influence employees through a cultural change and/or behavior modification in order to achieve organizational goals. When changes are presented conflicts are revealed and different emotions may be manifested by those being affected. The conflicts presented need to be solved in order to proceed towards goal achievement, and emotions have to be dealt with in order to alleviate group or team tension and prevent further conflicts on the way.

To solve the conflicts encountered in a given situation and deal with the emotions that could emerge in the process, effective communication skills are unequivocally necessary. These skills are essential in helping those affected by the changes introduced to become self-aware of the need for those changes, and to take responsibility for their required participation in the success of common goals achievement. In other words, a strategy is necessary to help the individuals to stay aligned and focused with the common values and goals by providing them with tools that facilitate effective communication, self-awareness, clarification of goals, responsibility and commitment, change adaptation, and to find better ways to reach solutions to their daily challenges and perhaps conflicts. This strategy is basically what is recognized as "coaching." Actually, coaching can bring to the situation presented the following recognized benefits: "improved teamwork, improved relationships with peers, improved job satisfaction, and reduced conflict" (Zeus &

---

[19] Contributed by Rafael Gonzalez (M.D.), Nova Southeastern University.

Skiffington, 2002, p. 3). Key for successful coaching in assisting to achieve positive changes in the relationships that contribute toward the goals attainment is getting to know who the stakeholders are, determining the behaviors that need to be changed or modified within the team, and involving the stakeholders in the process (Goldsmith, 2004).

The task of getting individuals, over whom poor or little control exist, involved and committed toward goals that may be in conflict with their own is another responsibility of coaches and managers. The process of doing that, without destroying the relationship, is best known as "influencing" and involves certain behaviors that require "push," "pull," or "push/pull" energies as described by Vengel (2000). *Push energy* is required when "an effort is necessary to impress upon others the necessity or urgency to do something" (Vengel, p. 31); it is being direct and persuasive through the "offering of specific suggestions" (Vengel, p. 32). *Pull energy* is showing understanding of other's ideas or thoughts and requires open conversation by asking open and/or focused questions, and effective listening (Vengel, p. 34). *Push/pull energy* is basically a combination of the previous forces.

Vengel described "five key behaviors" that are used with each of the influencing energies: with push energy, *assert* (when there is the need to be direct and to be seen in charge), and *suggest* (when the other person is open for it and a softer approach is needed); with pull energy, *ask open and focused questions* (when more information is needed, when seeking for alternatives, or when looking for closing), and *summarize* (when the other person needs confirmation that has been listen to or is showing anger, and when multiple issues are at play); and for push/pull energy, *offer incentives* (when the other person needs to know the benefits, and an agreement to solve a conflict is needed) (Vengel, p. 82-83).

### Communication Skills

The processes of coaching and influencing require effective communication skills in order for one to be successful. Effective communication skills require an open dialogue and attentive listening between the coach and the coachee, with the intention of creating the healthy environment to understand each other, to explore ideas or alternatives, and to establish trust and rapport. Coaching is based on conversations with the intention of exploring a topic to obtain better understanding of the "ideas, feeling, opportunities, obstacles and solutions" each of the parties can bring in (Zeus & Skiffington, p. 159).

When establishing an open dialogue, honesty and trust must be a central part of the conversation, by clarifying the real intentions and what is desired, by being self-aware of how things are said, and by establishing active and effective listening. Two modes of dialogue have been described in coaching: transactional and transformational (Zeus & Skiffington, p. 160). The first one, *transactional*, relates to the dialogue in which ideas and information are shared; the second one, the *transformational* dialogue, relates to the conversation that is aimed for a change.

The process of dialogue described by Zeus and Skiffington (2002) includes five stages: *Stage 1*-where rapport is created through promoting discussion and trust; *Stage 2*-where the needs, values, emotions, beliefs, conflicts, and choices are explored; *Stage 3*-in which goal identification is facilitated, and the obstacles and their solutions are reviewed; *Stage 4*-where strategies are developed as well as the means for feedback and monitoring; and, *Stage 5*-maintenance of new behaviors is ensured.

During the dialogue process several communication barriers or interferences can be encountered. Among them one can find selective perception, information overload, distrust, anxiety, hidden agendas, and false expectations (Zeus & Skiffington, p. 162). Zeus and Skiffington (2002) describe techniques to overcome these interferences: *effective listening skills* (relax communication, seek understanding, focus on the context of what is being said, paraphrase and reflect, clarify, and summarize), *questioning* (how, what, when, where type of questions, clarifying, elaborating, challenging, and confronting questions), and *reframing* (exploring and challenging a statement and giving it another meaning).

Guttman (2005) talked about developing a "third ear" in the process of listening, which involves detecting messages from the way people dress, where they sit, their gestures, how they stand or sit, and who avoids eye contact. To develop the third ear the coach needs to take a "bird's-eye view" of the situation and the group, to focus on the person and not on the problem, watch the interactions, be more of an observer, watch people's reactions, and pretend to be a reporter to sum up the interaction.

Sometimes during the process of communication the situation calls for confrontation. When it happens, the coach risks losing some of the trust already developed in the relationship with the coachee. Ways to deal with this are presenting the facts without judgment, formulating the comments while avoiding value judgment, and by asking the coachee to confirm or refute the comments (Guttman, 2005).

The art of communicating also takes into consideration the communication style of the person being coached or influenced. Four communication styles have been described: *the authoritarian* prefers to be in control, fast paced, and prefers brief communication; *the analyzer* prefers to deal with facts, slow paced, and do not decide without having all the information; *the visionary* prefers to deal with the big picture, fast paced, wants to be in the spotlight, and share the vision with others; and, *the supporter* prefers to deal with people, makes decisions in the context of relationships, is cautious before taking action, wants input from all involved parties, and wants to be in the loop (Vengel, 2000, p. 51-60). The coach or the influencer must adjust or be attuned to the coachee's communication style to facilitate engagement, develop trust, and build rapport.

When the leaders are the ones playing the role of coach, the conversations that take place in the communication with their followers could be more time pressured and goal emphatic. Getting the things done without altering the relationships with their followers, leaders must have prudence, must show enthusiasm and positivism, and lots of clarity. According to Booher (2005), there are six keys to get the things done: be plain-spoken, be specific, be positive whenever possible, be persuasive, be prompt to answer, and avoid polarizing people. In other words, the leader must be clear and involving, persuasive and engaging. Honesty above all should set the tone of the conversations.

### Dealing With Conflicts and Emotions

As part of the process of coaching and influencing in a given situation, conflicts that are encountered must be solved by exploring opportunities and alternatives for solutions, and emotions must be dealt with by exploring and understanding their origins. In the process of solving an encountered problem the leader must be a role model in managing the differences in view points, must encourage a healthy debate, avoid impulsive decisions, and support rational confrontations (Guttman, 2004).

According to Guttman (2004), the best way leaders deal with conflict is by holding people accountable for the issues and working toward the solutions from the team's perspective. When a conflict emerges the issue must be surfaced and dealt with as quickly as possible. Conflicts many times arise from misinterpretations, poor goal clarification, and from lack of engagement in teamwork. Therefore, the leaders must focus on being sensitive, defining where the responsibility relies upon and what are the critical components of the issue, and to look for ways of relieving the pressure without suppressing disagreement.

Coaching through conflict resolution involves recognizing the behavioral patterns of those in conflict, who may adopt one of four patterns: *playing the victim-*say nothing and act powerless, *leave-*physically retreats from the situation, *changes position* or *confront-*addresses the issue openly. Also, the leader must facilitate confrontation as "it carries the greatest benefit at the least cost" (Guttman, 2004), and must establish the rules of engagement, which dictate no third party intervention, no outside supporters, no accusation in absentia, no personalization of the issue, and aiming to solve the issue or let it go.

Another way to facilitate the solution of a conflict or problem is the use of the *force-field analysis* based on the Kurt Lewin's field theory (Zeus & Skiffington, p. 259-261). In this analysis the positive forces that help effecting a change are called the *driving forces*, and the negative or opposing forces that keep from effecting a change are called the *restraining forces*. In this exercise the forces are charted at opposite extremes and, by visualizing the description of the forces discussion, brainstorming, collaboration and clarification are facilitated.

Through the process of any change individuals respond with emotions, which may be classified as positive or negative. Common positive emotions are joy, happiness and surprise, but in many of the changes that occur in organizations the emotions elicited are negative ones, such as anger, fear, sadness, shame, denial, and jealousy (Zeus & Skiffington, 2002, p. 199). Coaching can help the coachee deal with the inherent emotions of a particular event or situation by using the appropriate skills and techniques. In particular, organizations that have as their primary product the delivery of services based on human resources are composed of people that have to deal with their emotions on a daily basis, and is precisely through emotions that they relate to others in the organization. It is from these emotions that people develop feelings about other people, their jobs, the workplace, finally having an impact on their performance (Zeus & Skiffington, p. 195-196).

When coaching, negative emotions must be paid attention to and the opportunity for positive ones must be grabbed. Helping and influencing others work toward the common goals requires free expression of emotions through a genuine and honest communication. Emotions define "a particular affective state with a determined value to the individual, implying a tendency to a particular action or reaction" (Zeus & Skiffington, p. 198). How much value a specific situation has for the individual and what expectations the individual has about the situation, based on personal thoughts and convictions, are the two major components of an emotional response.

Some of the accepted purposes and elements of emotions include helping to deal with major survival issues presented by our physical and social environment; emotions can make one change from non-adaptive behavior; they alert us by showing the relevance of our concern to the event-we feel fear if threatened by it; and, they are involved in and control the management of our goals (Zeus & Skiffington, p. 201).

As described by Zeus and Skiffington (2002) there are some general principles one must follow when coaching through emotions: be responsible for one's emotions (do not let the emotions control your acts); be responsible for the reaction; emotions do not have an intrinsic moral value; emotions are neither functional or harmful; emotions can be contradictory and ambivalent; and, there are cultural and gender differences in the expression of emotions. When helping in dealing with emotions the coach can use *self-disclosure* (relate to his/her own experience only when it had a good outcome), *exploration of the coachee's emotions* (recognizing the extent of the emotion and how it may impact the coach-coachee relationship and the coachee's life and work), and *reflecting on the emotions* (basically rephrasing the coachees' statements, which reassures the coachees that they are being heard).

During the process of exploring emotions the coach must do the following: be clear on what is the objective of the exercise; identify the emotion with the highest intensity; pay attention to the coachee's non-verbal language; and, use different styles when reflecting on the emotions (use synonyms, relate to personal experience, and use empathy rather than sympathy statements) (Zeus & Skiffington, p. 202-207).

Dealing with the emotions that emerge from the individuals in a work group or team is an inevitable task for the leader, and sometimes professionals with expertise in the field may be a necessary resource to help the team-members deal with their emotions. As conflicts must not be suppressed, emotions must not be restrained. Allowing this to happen may corrode the team efforts toward goals accomplishment; it will have an impact on the leader's efforts for follower's engagement, performance and productivity, and it will put obstacles in the way for culture and in its readiness for change.

### *Leading Toward Engagement*

It has been proven that employee commitment increases when there is a strong, positive relationship between the manager and the employees. Leading toward engagement demands from the leader to build rapport, develop trust, and sustain ongoing open communication with all the team members. According to experts, the following are some elements that the leader can use while coaching the followers: reinforcing good performance, motivation to new performance levels, orientation of new employees, teaching about new changes, training new skills, following up, explaining the standards, setting priorities, clarifying expectations, increasing self-confidence, and conducting performance review.

Leaders also require several skills to be successful in achieving results through others. The following traits or skills have been described as necessary in this process: *collaborative*-working together with the people; *inventive*-alert, creative, and quick thinker; *skilled*-this reinforces credibility; *visionary*-share a vision with others; and, *mindful*-be self-aware of how their behavior is impacting the followers (Daniels, 2005). Daniels also describes six basic principles the leader must follow in order to allow for committed employees: focus on the situation not on the person, maintain self confidence and self-esteem of others, maintain constructive relationships, take initiative to make things better, lead by example, and think beyond the moment. The latter is of particular importance as it maintains the leader in alert for short and long-term consequences of the group's actions.

Branham (2005) reported that only 25 percent of workers are fully engaged, 55 percent are not, and 15 percent are actually disengaged (working against team interests), with the latter group adding a heavy monetary cost to the organization. Working toward engagement requires knowing the reasons or causes for disengagement so one can get to identify what can help in the process of engaging people. The main reasons for disengagement are not due to salary or monetary compensation, but due to poor job motivation, perception that there are poor chances for growth and development, not enough challenges, undocumented job descriptions, feeling undervalued or unrecognized, feeling stressed, and loss of trust and confidence in the leaders. Branham recommends several engagement practices to minimize the problem: give realistic job expectations; take more time in hiring the right people; provide managers training in performance management and coaching; provide self-assessment workshops; acknowledge all improvements and contributions; maintain reasonable workload; and, gain and maintain trust and confidence of employees by conveying a clear and inspiring vision and by "walking the talk" with them.

A great deal of persuasion energy is many times necessary to influence and engage people. The process of influencing strives from the leader's ability to understand the follower's expectations, concerns and feelings, and to frame communications in order to connect with them and their interests (Conger, 2002). The communication framing process is defined by Conger as building the leader's position around the goals and rewards shared by the followers, incorporating values and beliefs that are regarded as important to them, and paying attention to the verbal and non-verbal language used.

In any new organization change or transformation the leaders must help their followers to engage and commit toward the new or remodeled goals that will require influencing and coaching skills, which include honest and open communication, and dealing with the solution of conflicts and emotions that may emerge thorough the process. All these elements are oriented toward the maximization of the working relationships, and therefore, toward the accomplishment of the desired goals.

### Coaching, Influencing and Engaging

*Coaching employees.* One main purpose of coaching underperforming or disruptive employees is to clarify with them the goals, help them become self-aware of unwanted behaviors, to help them acknowledge the responsibility for their actions, and to get them ready for change adaptation. The goals of the coaching process can be to improve teamwork and interpersonal relationships with colleagues, suppliers, customers, and bosses, as well as to reduce the conflicts that their previous behaviors have elicited.

This coaching exercise may need to be done individually and with the group as a whole. Having a coaching session with each one of them will allow the individual to come up with specific solutions that may be hindered by the group pressure. At the same time, having the coaching session with the whole group will provide information about their interrelationships and definition of each person's role in the group. Getting to know this information will help to identify how their feelings coalesce or collide.

Throughout these coaching sessions an open and honest dialogue should be what sets the tone of the interaction. The intention of the conversation must be clarified, and in this particular case should be to explore their ideas and feelings about how the service can be improved or modified to help achieve the desired goals. One must not forget that the conversations should be in essence transformational as the aim is to inflict a change in the individual or group's behavior.

These conversations may take more than one or two sessions and should have the purposes of first creating rapport with each of the individuals in the group as the first stage; then, as a second stage (which could be in the same first session) clear the way for expression of their emotions, their beliefs, and for the identification of possible conflicts. During these first two stages of the conversation several barriers can be encountered as the individuals may manifest anxiety, distrust, and false expectations. Particular attention must be paid to their non-verbal language and their interactions.

It is then important to clarify during the process, as many times as necessary, what the desired goals are, to talk in a relax manner and to confirm that they understand what is being said perhaps through questioning and reframing their statements. Questions like: "How do you feel about the goals shared between you and the organization?", "What changes do you think can be made in order to achieve those goals?" And reframing statements like: "We have been running this service for many years and the customers we serve trust us" with, "I understand from what you are saying that the service can benefit from your presence as there has been no complaints about the services provided before." The latter could be confrontational, but confronting or challenging statements may be necessary to help increase self-awareness of the individual. For this part of the process a questionnaire with open and focused questions could facilitate the discovery of obstacles and self-awareness. In the third stage of the dialogue the obstacles toward goal achievement are to be identified and solutions to them must be explored. It is during this stage that confrontational issues may be encountered and thorough clarification and solution elaboration must be promoted. For this stage, a force field analysis chart could help explore these issues and the solutions to them.

The fourth stage of the conversation process, not necessarily in the same session, the strategies for teamwork should be discussed. For example, establishing how the work schedule will be divided among the employees, how the customers will be contacted, and developing a training program for all associates. Also, performance review and quality control monitoring processes should be explained during this stage, and space for feedback should be provided. The last and fifth stage of dialogue would be an ongoing process of communication geared toward reinforcing and the maintenance of desired behaviors.

*Influencing employees.* Influencing a situation calls for all the effective use of the three energies described by Alan Vengel. A genuine effort has to be made to influence all employees to work toward the accomplishment of the desired goals established. The key behaviors described for push, pull and push/pull energies should be considered and the appropriate sequence of their use is to be established.

The sequence of key behaviors planned for this group's influencing exercise could be as follows:

- "Assert" (push behavior): As it is often the perception of some associates that the part-time employees are not always actively self-aware of the behaviors that have caused some dissatisfaction with some of the customers, during the influencing exercise the managers and leaders will need to be direct and clear about the desired goals and convey the message to everyone (part-time and full-time associates) that their work will be closely monitored and evaluated.

- As the first behavior used may evoke anger and multiple issues may be discovered, the second behavior to be used is to "summarize" (pull behavior); the intention of this behavior is to let employees know that their emotions and perspective are understood and acknowledged, and to clarify any confusion they may have. Other issues or hidden agendas could be explored during this part of the exercise.

- The discovery of hidden issues will then call for the third behavior, to "ask open and focused questions" (pull behavior); the intention with this behavior is to explore and acquire as much information as possible from them in relation to the way they used to work before, and alternatives they may recommend for service improvement.

- After the above is completed, "summarizing" may need to be used again to clarify what has been said and to see if what has been recommended fits into the plan structure to achieve the desired goals.

- As the changes to be implemented in the way they used to work are discussed, they may feel threatened or unmotivated; at this point push/pull behavior may be in order. "Offering incentives" may help solve some of the issues, and help reach an agreement.

*Engaging employees.* The best and only way to get employees to align their goals with those of the organization is to get them engaged and committed. In order to facilitate their engagement the common goals must be clarified thorough an honest and open communication.

"Walking the talk" is a necessary task for the organization's leaders. This implies active participation in their work, setting the example, nurturing the relationships with all personnel, suppliers and vendors. The main purpose is to develop rapport and build trust. Another important aspect related to this is to become available for any need or difficulty they may have.

Continuous evaluation of their performance through peer review and quality control analysis will reassure them that their work is not only monitored, but that their actions toward goal accomplishment will get noticed. If that is the case, recognition opportunities must be implemented to motivate them to stay in the right track.

### Improving Workplace Performance

To be successful as a coach or leader in today's workplace, managers must go beyond acquiring knowledge, they must be able to successfully and strategically apply their learning and achieve measurable results. Roger Chevalier's 2007 book, entitled *"A Manager's Guide to Improving Workplace Performance,"* is a guide to not just knowledge acquisition but also to actionable steps that managers can take for the creation of measurable outcomes in the performance of their people and departments. Chevalier emphasizes that the key to workplace performance is in identifying problems before they become major barriers, finding solutions, and evaluating results. In the mean time, to achieve high performance, managers and coaches must also work on developing and motivating their people while removing any obstacles that may prevent them from performing their responsibilities at the highest possible levels. Chevalier writes that "you have exactly the employees you deserve. If you have coached your people properly, you should have been able to build a high-performing team within a year" (2007, p. 7).

The author of *A Manager's Guide to Improving Workplace Performance* speaks from experience as he has personally "done it and been there." Roger Chevalier has about thirty years of work experience in employee performance and training. He has also served as the Director of Certification for the International Society for Performance Improvement (ISPI). As stated by Chevalier based on his years of experience and observations, there are countless number of managers and supervisors who know how to identify flaws in their employees' overall performance; however, only the best managers and supervisor seem to know what it takes to fix the problem so their people can be high performers. Through a performance-coaching process, managers are encouraged to work with their employees and peers in the preparation, coaching, and review of performance improvement. Chevalier emphatically states that "If you have not clearly communicated your expectations to employees regarding both their key activities and the desired results; if you haven't taken the time to observe your employees and provide timely, behaviorally specific feedback; if you haven't kept records of your employees' performance throughout the appraisal period; if you haven't gotten their input and held a constructive counseling session; then you haven't earned the right to write their evaluation" (2007, p. 11). It is the manager's job and duty to begin the appraisal and improvement process by reviewing the plans for each individual and what he or she must do to be successful in a given quarter or year.

Managers should keep in mind that poor performers often need more specific feedback regarding activities that they need to do in order to be successful; and high performing employees need to know the expected or desired outcomes because they can often figure out the needed activities by themselves. Of course, during the performance of their jobs and the achievement process, managers should observe and provide both motivational and corrective feedback as needed. The feedback to employees needs to be balanced, and this can be done through a sandwich style by providing four positive complements to reinforce good behavior with every constructive or corrective statement. In the performance-coaching model and the performance-appraisal process, Chevalier (2007, p.17) encourages managers and coaches to perform specific tasks at the beginning, during, and ending processes. At the beginning, managers need to review workgroup plans, identify goals, focus on key activities, and develop a game plan; during process, managers need to observe performance, provide timely feedback, adjust goals and activities, and keep a good record of performance; and finally, at the end process, managers need to get the employee's input, review performance, counsel as needed, and prepare the official performance appraisal form.

According to Chevalier (2007), for managers and coaches, there really isn't a greater or better contribution that they can make to the long-term success of the organization than that of developing capable and motivated individuals that are able to quickly and successfully respond to the changing demands of their jobs and today's competitive global work environment. In his book, Chevalier uses real-world dilemmas and scenarios to demonstrate to managers how to take their employees from good to great by:

- Coaching them through a standardized and strategic performance appraisal process during each given year.
- Developing them to use effective leadership styles for each employee and each new task or responsibility.
- Counseling them to strategically improve performance.
- Identifying performance challenges.
- Describing poor performance standards in a measurable manner.
- Preparing viable alternatives, assessing them and selecting one for implementation.
- Executing the plan, following up, and adjusting as needed.
- Evaluating the outcomes of training and changes implemented, while assessing its impact on the organization.

Marshall Goldsmith writes that "At the end of the day, a manager's job is simple—improving workplace performance. If managers are not improving workplace performance, why are they wasting the organization's valuable resources?" (p. vii, Foreword in Chevalier's 2007 book). Both Goldsmith and Chevalier encourage managers to involve their employees and peers in the planning, coaching and leadership process. Goldsmith's research with over 86,000 respondents from major corporations shows that "Managers who involved their people back on the job and actually applied the concepts they were taught were seen as becoming far more effective leaders—not by themselves, but their coworkers. Managers who didn't apply what was learned didn't get any better" (p. viii, Foreword in Chevalier's 2007 book). Through their positional and personal power as well as coaching, mentoring, counseling, and leadership skills, managers should create a work environment where employees can excel at their jobs. The coaching and work improvement skills suggested in this book or by other experts such as Goldsmith, Chevalier, Covey, Peters, Senge, Drucker, Hersey, Blanchard, and other respected professionals only work if they are studied, understood, and successfully applied. If current and aspiring managers actually learn these concepts, practice them, involve their people in the learning and application processes, and follow up or adjust as needed, they will achieve improvement and high performance in their departments and organizations. Chevalier provides the following tips for performance coaching (2007, p. 19):

- Begin each coaching session with a review of the main organizational goals.
- Link the organizational goals to the coachee's job description and his or her contribution.
- Allow the coachee to present his or her input on what tasks and activities are important in the achievement of the organizational goals.
- Observe performance during the performance appraisal process and provide timely feedback frequently.
- Develop employees in every interaction.
- Confront poor performance as it happens and take corrective action.
- Ask "what happened" and how can it be done differently to achieve better results.
- Let employees present their perspective, and use their input as much as possible.
- Keep good records for all employees and their performance records.
- Hold a performance review session before writing the formal performance appraisal form.
- Provide positive reinforcement when you catch people doing things right.
- Praise the person for a job well done, and constructively criticize poor performance appropriately.

Through a thorough assessment process, managers and coaches could perform a gap analysis to determine where an employee's performance is and where it should be. Once a gap analysis has been performed, the next step is for the coach and coachee to jointly set realistic goals and determine how to best achieve them. The performance-coaching process presented by Chevalier complements most comprehensive performance systems, as it provides a structure or framework for the way managers and coaches interact with their employees before, during, and at the end of a performance appraisal and improvement process. Just like most other models, this process begins with proper planning, communicating performance expectations and standards to employees, developing an implementation or execution plan, and following up to make sure the employee is on target. In the mean time, managers and coaches should reinforce positive outcomes and take corrective actions as needed. In other words, managers and coaches should never let good or poor performance go unnoticed. Managers and coaches should never lose track of the fact that they create a work environment for their people where employees can either excel or flounder (Chevalier, 2007, p. 199). Managers and coaches must make sure their employees are able to excel and should strategically help them be successful.

Overall, today's coaches and managers need to be effective and efficient: they must do the right jobs right. Doing the right things right requires the skills of creating a healthy work environment, while leading and coaching people to continuously improve their performance.

## Coaching, Counseling and Mentoring to Boost Performance

Being successful and gaining respect in an industry requires that organizations develop and nourish their human resources for high performance. Competitive and successful organizations tend to not only have employees that meet their individual goals in the firm, but many of them will also need to exceed industry expectations. The best way to meet company goals and exceed industry expectations is to have managers and leaders who can develop the organization's employees to be creative, innovative, and professional experts. Florence M. Stone mentions that "With escalating time pressures and constant change, upper management has their eye out for managers who can recruit capable employees, develop the skills they need to today's jobs, and prepare them to handle tomorrow's jobs; who can recognize their obligation to confront poor performers and who will work with these people to find a solution or make the tough decisions to terminate those who are dragging down the rest of the team; and who can keep their superstars shining even when there is little opportunity for advancement or dollars for increased performance" (2007, p. 1).

Stone's 2007 book, entitled *"Coaching, Counseling & Mentoring: How to Choose and Use the right Technique to Boost Employee Performance,"* discusses important competencies for all managers and leaders. Research, experience and observations have shown that effective coaching, counseling, and mentoring can greatly improve employee productivity, morale, commitment, and satisfaction. This book provides best practices and a complete guide for managers to encourage employees to do their jobs well by coaching them, prevent and fix poor performance through timely counseling, and helping extraordinary performers excel through a formal or informal mentoring process. Poor performance and people problems should not be ignored since avoidance often leads to worsening of the situation. People problems that are ignored can eventually have a negative impact on the assessment of the employee, his or her colleagues, as well as the manager and organization. Since coaching, counseling and mentoring skills are not always taught or practiced in business schools or by employees before they become managers, they are likely to not understand how to perform each function effectively. *Coaching, Counseling and Mentoring* provides self-assessments tools and practical dilemmas and scenarios along with useful techniques for improving performance.

In the second edition of *Coaching, Counseling and Mentoring,* Stone provides updated and practical scripts for effectively speaking with employees about sensitive issues. This updated edition also includes useful information on working with off-site employees, how to approach a counseling session when an employee denies that a problem exists, distinguishing between mentoring and supervisory roles, and what to do when coaching, counseling and mentoring efforts do not produce the desired results. *Coaching, Counseling and Mentoring* is a must have toolbox for current, incoming and aspiring managers if they are to effectively build their confidence and skills along with the performance of their employees and colleagues. Readers of *Coaching, Counseling and Mentoring* will learn how to improve their own productivity as well as the performance of their employees and colleagues by:

1. Orienting new employees to the expectations and providing them the needed skills.
2. Assessing training and development needs of all workers.
3. Encouraging problem solving and brainstorming techniques.

4. Building open and clear communication lines.
5. Being an effective active listener.
6. Conducting productive counseling with employees who are not performing as planned.
7. Being a good mentor.
8. Helping ordinary performers become higher performers.
9. Helping new employees have high performing role models.

Stone also differentiates and provides clear definitions for coaching, counseling, and mentoring. Besides clarifying the terms, Stone has written this book to help managers and coaches perfect these required skills if they are to lead a high performing team, department and organization.

*Coaching* is defined as continuously providing timely feedback and encouragement to help employees perform their jobs well. For managers, coaching involves recruiting the right candidates, assessing each employee's development needs, and providing them avenues to achieve the needed capacity. Coaches who are able to motivate employees to meet personal and departmental objectives, and those who are able to correct poor performance via developmental and proper counseling skills will also be known as great managers and leaders.

*Counseling* is defined as proactively being involved with employees to improve sub-par or poor performance. Counseling is really about making sure the performance targets are being met; and when performance falls short of the desired objective, managers and employees must take corrective action. Poor performance can negatively impact the employee, the team and others in the department. Other negative impacts of poor performance can include lost productivity, business, time, talent, and self-esteem. As such, poor performance should be dealt with appropriately through effective counseling skills. Effectively counseling means working to remedy the poor performance and not to demean the employee. Counseling should be an honest collaboration and feedback session about performance and outcome clarification. The counseling session should also seek agreement from the employee on a solution that meets the expected or desired performance quality level. Coaches can counsel or discipline employees by communicating honestly and openly, listening actively, and asking probing questions. A typical discipline process might include issuing a verbal warning, documenting a written warning, providing a reprimand if poor performance is not improved, suspension of the poor performer, and termination. The objective of counseling for the coach is to get the employee's agreement that there is a problem (or opportunity for improvement), determine the cause(s) of the problem, agree on a solution or action plan to correct the issue or performance gap, follow up to make sure the problem is corrected and to reinforce good performance.

*Mentoring* is defined as establishing a relationship with mentees to help top performers excel in their careers and industry. Mentoring is different than coaching as mentors go beyond correcting performance and achieving job-specific objectives. The objective of mentoring is to share relevant wisdom and experience that can enable high performers to become recognized for bigger and better achievements in the company or industry. When coaching and counseling is not needed, a manager can become a role model, a facilitator, or an advocate for their outstanding performers (especially when there are limited immediate growth or promotional opportunities) in order to keep them motivated and sustain their productivity.

Overall, coaches can help employees do well, please their superiors, and achieve development and promotional opportunities. Through their abilities and effective coaching, counseling and mentoring skills, managers can take ordinary individuals and convert them to extraordinary performers in the industry. The five abilities or principles of coaching mentioned by Florence M. Stone (2007, p. 14) are as follows:

1. Ability to gather the needed information in a timely manner.
2. Ability to listen effectively and attentively to others.
3. Ability to be aware of one's surroundings and what is happening in the environment.
4. Ability to instruct employees and provide direction.
5. Ability to provide feedback in a sensitive manner.

Gaining the above mentioned abilities can help coaches better perform their jobs and responsibilities which may include: hiring the best employees, having clearly-defined expectations from each department and employee, providing regular and timely feedback, having a standardized and strategic performance appraisal process, providing relevant training and development, creating a motivational work environment, being a role model, and consistently reinforcing good performance and behaviors. Managers who have strong people skills or the competencies of coaching, counseling and mentoring will be able to strategically build high-performing teams and organizations that go beyond what is expected. Stone states that successful organizations and leaders want and reward managers who are skilled at the competencies of coaching, counseling, and mentoring. Successful managers and coaches empower their employees for success and high performance by doing the following elements (Stone, 2007, p. 41):

1. Training and preparing employees for opportunities.
2. Believing in the employee's abilities.
3. Being clear about expectations and performance standards.
4. Building on employees' strong points or strengths.
5. Sharing information with employees.
6. Encouraging employees to believe in their potential and capabilities.
7. Recognizing and rewarding each employee's accomplishments.

Effective coaches and managers are able to create a pleasant work environment for all employees so they can remain motivated toward high quality and top performance. Of course, the success of each employee in his or her job also means success for the manager and organization. Stone (2007, p. 223) mentions that "Aside from the personal pride you will take in building and then overseeing a highly productive workgroup, you will have the knowledge that your team's successful track record is reflecting well on you." *Coaching, Counseling and Mentoring* book is a useful guide for managing departments and leading people toward high performance.

## *Summary*

Ramon Venero, a practitioner and senior manager in the field of human resources, summarized some pertinent material from the presentation of Professor Edward E Lawler, from his session on *"Good Jobs and Effective Organizations: What it Takes to Create Them In America."* Lawler's current book, on which his presentation was based, is *The New American Workplace* which he co-authored with James O'Toole, DPhil. Dr. Lawler delivered his presentation at the SHRM's Annual Conference in Washington D.C. in June 2006. Their book examines the change in the American workplace over the last 30 years and makes some predictions about the future as well as commentary on the present. According to Venero (Personal Communication, July 2006), reflected in the research is a literature review of some 2,000 research articles resulting in 16 chapters of the book. The survey work, funded by SHRM, included an inquest of the Fortune 1000, historical data, archival data and new data. Dr. Lawler's presentation covered many areas, including work/life balance, performance pressure, and compensation. Dr. Lawler stated that "Fifteen percent of the population have a 24/7 work-life because of better connectivity. These people are better educated and command a better income. Some corporations are helping their employees cope with this new life style" (Ramon Venero, Personal Communication, July 2006). Furthermore, there is more performance pressure today than before due to a much more competitive economy and it is both functional and dysfunctional. If both employers and employees can respond adequately to it through effective coaching and performance management techniques (functional), then the pressure can be a positive force. Last but not least, the current compensation ratio between the highest paid employee and the lowest paid employee in corporate America is now 600 to 1. This surpasses the ratio of the 1920s which was the previous high water mark. The pay of the low skilled or low educated people is poor and worst than ever before and they are being left behind. Overall, Lawler says that many large companies want to *buy* rather than *build* competencies. A global company can buy competencies anywhere. The future suggests that training and development will be employee self-directed and self-financed. For Lawler, there are definite "winners and losers." At the top of the winners' list are corporate executives who are the "rock stars" of business. They are paid and treated like rock stars and they are becoming as important as the companies they lead. On the other side of the equation, the relatively unskilled and relatively uneducated as a group have gotten worst and worst with no solution in sight. The United States is, wants to be and should be, according to Lawler, the leader of the global economy. In order to maintain its position of leadership, the U.S. needs constant reinvention and the role of managers and coaches are critical in energizing their employees to high performance. The best managers, leaders, coaches, and organizations are going to be those that require high involvement from all of their people if they are to be globally competitive.

According to Barbara Alston, practitioner and researcher, "Leadership is an integral part of our everyday existence and positive results continue to emerge from the literature on all three aspects of leadership paradigm; transformational, transactional and laissez-faire" (Personal Communication, March 28, 2007). Today's coaches and managers need to be transformational leaders as they assess performance and lead employees to higher levels of achievement so their companies can become globally competitive. Alston believes that technical experience and intellectual quotient (IQ) are no longer the only two measures of managerial or leadership success in the modern workplace. Alston claims that interpersonal skills have become an essential component to effective leadership and coaching if employees are to perform at their best. For this reason, understanding the effects of proper employee evaluations on performance deserves more attention from researchers and academicians.

Traditionally, the evaluation of performance in most firms has focused on the past; this is not productive. Instead, a comprehensive performance management and evaluation program should be ongoing, developmental and future-oriented. According to the Manager of Employee Relations—Maria M. Pinto, at Nova Southeastern University, "Performance management is the process of managing performance all year long to support high performing employees" (Personal Communication, March 28, 2007). In other words, performance management or performance evaluation is not a one-time event, but rather a process of reviewing achievements, strategically planning for future performance, and ongoing coaching. Similarly, employee evaluation and performance management, according to the Compensation Director at Nova Southeastern University—Kim Greenfest, should be ongoing, include continual feedback between the employee and manager, be focused on the future, have a long-term orientation, include setting goals and objectives, and be rewarding of incremental achievements (Personal Communication, March 28, 2007). Both Maria and Kim, facilitators of *"Performance Management and Goal Setting"* workshop, feel that managers should take a sufficient amount of time to properly plan and execute effective performance evaluations and appraisals since the time spent in strategically engaging the employee is basically an investment in the future success of the employee as well as the organization.

Evaluating, coaching, influencing, and engaging employees in a strategic manner toward the achievement of organizational objectives is a major responsibility of all managers. As such, managers should practice effective coaching and performance management skills. When dealing with performance challenges, experts encourage managers to go through the following steps when coaching employees in a face-to-face discussion: get the employee's agreement that there is a problem, jointly discuss possible alternatives, mutually agree on the actions that need to be taken by the employee to solve the performance gap between what is expected and desired, follow up to make sure the employee is progressing as agreed upon, and positively reinforce any progress or achievement (Fournies, 2000, pp. 156-187). Fournies mentions the following suggestions and requirements for managers and coaches if they are to be successful at eliminating low performance in the workplace (2000, pp. 216-221):

1.  Accurately assess and identify the behavior change that you want.
2.  Make sure the employee's behavior affects the results.
3.  Get maximum involvement from the employee during the face-to-face interaction and solution generation processes.
4.  Provide specific feedback to the employee about the behaviors or activities that are causing the actual performance challenge or gap.
5.  Identify both the necessity and need for change.
6.  Clarify to the employee that he or she is responsible for his or her behavior and expected standards.

7. Make sure the employee understands and believes that your true objective is the employee's best interest as well as that of the organization.
8. Role model the expectations of high performance and top quality to all employees.
9. Praise progress and employee achievements.
10. Be prepared for the next step.

Fournies mentions that "Your ability as a manager is measured by what your employees do, not by what you do; therefore, the facts of life dictate that, as a manager, you don't get paid for what you do, you get paid for what your employees do (2000, p. 9). So, make sure to help your employees be the best that they can be and positively influence their performance.

A manager's job is to assess an employee's performance, praise him or her for a job well done through effective recognition programs, and capitalize on his or her strengths. As a highly productive salesperson and manager, Eleanor Marschke has experienced the glow that comes from recognition many times; personal experiences of such magnitude have provided her the motivation to view recognition from a different perspective (Personal Communication, June 2006). The term "employment engagement," according to Marschke, is no longer just a "catchy" phrase. Human resource management must recognize that people truly are the most important financial asset to the corporation. Marschke believes that companies with higher employee engagement tend to have higher returns on length of employee tenure than their competitors, and higher return on investment as well as on operating margins.

Overall, recognition increases the ability of a corporation to achieve its business goals. For example, employees who receive proper recognition will spot new business opportunities quicker, take initiative in their jobs and be more loyal. Numerous companies have some form of recognition programs; but, in order to reach a more effective level, companies have to implement them into their core values, mission and vision statement. The overall objective in recognition is to enhance the communication process. According to Marschke, a human resource professional, manager, or a coach has an opportunity to contribute to this process by doing the following:

- Thank employees frequently.
- Direct praise to the appropriate individual.
- Remember the best and forget the rest.
- Make employees feel valuable.
- Create a strategy of recognition.
- Reward results that are measurable.

Based on the suggestions for coaching and influencing described thus far, the following are some strategies or considerations intended to help managers and employees reach the desired results and solutions to the challenges they encounter.

- Both the manager and employee must be clear about their goals, duties and rules.
- Managers can and should meet regularly with underperforming individuals and/or the entire team, as appropriate, to eliminate performance problems.

- Individual and team meeting can be implemented with the objectives of:
  - Exploring ideas, recommendations and alternatives to promote a collaborative environment to improve the service.
  - Helping discover potential conflicts and explore their solutions. This will include discussing and finding answers to complaints that customers may have against the service.
  - Discussing the findings obtained from the ongoing peer review and quality control monitoring. The intention of these measuring tools is to improve the quality of service.

Besides the formal coaching and influencing sessions geared toward disciplining disruptive or underperforming employees, the recommended strategies are intended to facilitate goals achievement, and the engagement of all employees in the organization. Engaging people is not an easy task, particularly when they feel threatened. If the organization's interest is to keep them working in the team the efforts must be directed toward building rapport and trust. Reinforcing the change of behaviors by recognizing even the small achievements, and allowing employees to actively participate in the decision making for the development and growth of the service, the feelings of threat may be minimized and engagement facilitated.

### Discussion Questions

1. What is performance evaluation?
2. What are some best ways to assess, appraise, and evaluate an employee's performance?
3. What is employee engagement?
4. Why should managers and coaches attempt to engage their employees in the objectives and goals of the department? What are some ways of engaging employees in the department or organization? Discuss.
5. What is a pull strategy and when is it used?
6. What is a push strategy and when is it used?
7. What is the purpose of involving and engaging people in the performance improvement process? Discuss.
8. What is influence? Does it differ from manipulation? If so, how? Discuss.
9. What can coaches do to effectively influence others in the direction of higher performance? Discuss.

# CHAPTER 8

## Alternative Work Arrangements[20]

Alternative work arrangements offer organizations flexibility in conducting their respective operations and providing employees a balance in their work and personal lives. Employees face challenges of being caregivers for elderly parents, two-earner families with children, single parents, etc. At the same time, work itself and the workplace has changed just over the past several years, resulting in the need for alternative work arrangements. This chapter researches arrangements specifically focusing on varied flexible employee schedules and telecommuting, with the resultant impact on worker productivity.

Productivity, of course, is considered by many economists to be a critical measure of economic well-being. The chapter finds that some of these arrangements may not be feasible in all organizations, departments or for certain positions within a department. When such arrangements are feasible, management must take into account seasonal or cyclical changes in workloads, the nature of an employee's responsibilities and myriad other factors before considering such an implementation. Employee retention and increased satisfaction can be benefits that result from constructing sound alternative work arrangement options. Finally, managers should monitor closely these types of schedule changes and must ensure that any kind of alternative work arrangements will not result in loss of teamwork, productivity or cohesiveness within their departments. Hence, this provides management to rectify problems that negatively impact productivity or adversely affecting a level of productive output with a given level of input or worked hours.

### A Productivity Focus on Flexible Schedules and Telecommuting

In any discussion of employee coaching and performance management, alternative work arrangements should be discussed. The authors suspect that when employers consider implementing any type of alternative work arrangement, a corporation or other entity should consider all options available, the workload, type of work and especially, an employee's past performance. Clearly, any kind of alternative work arrangements require initially working things out, and a reasonable scheduling commitment from both the employee and the respective manager. There will be staffing needs, work responsibilities, work duties, organizational needs,

---

[20] Contributed by Richard J. Conwell, Nova Southeastern University.

previous employee performance, budget needs, equipment needs, privacy, and security concerns. These aspects are reviewed in this chapter along with additional areas and/or other variables to consider when implementing any type of alternative work arrangement. This chapter also reviews the implications of alternative work arrangements and the resultant impact on employee productivity. Economists generally view productivity – output per hour of work – as the most important determinant of economic well being (Schmitt & Baker, 2004). As reflected in Table 8.1, we have seen employed individuals in the United States over the past two decades grow to 143.7 million with an associated unemployment rate dropping to 4.7 percent.

Table 8.1 - Employment Trends (U. S. Department of Labor)

EMPLOYMENT AND UNEMPLOYMENT IN THE UNITED STATES

CALENDAR YEARS 1985 – 2005 (IN THOUSANDS)

| YEAR | EMPLOYED | UNEMPLOYED | UNEMPLOYMENT RATE |
|------|----------|------------|-------------------|
| 1985 | 107,150 | 8,312 | 7.8% |
| 1986 | 109,597 | 8,237 | 7.5% |
| 1987 | 112,440 | 7,425 | 6.6% |
| 1988 | 114,968 | 6,701 | 5.8% |
| 1989 | 117,342 | 6,528 | 5.6% |
| 1990 | 118,793 | 7,047 | 5.9% |
| 1991 | 117,718 | 8,628 | 7.3% |
| 1992 | 118,492 | 9,613 | 8.1% |
| 1993 | 120,259 | 8,940 | 7.4% |
| 1994 | 123,060 | 7,996 | 6.5% |
| 1995 | 124,900 | 7,404 | 5.9% |
| 1996 | 126,708 | 7,236 | 5.7% |
| 1997 | 129,558 | 6,739 | 5.2% |
| 1998 | 131,463 | 6,210 | 4.7% |
| 1999 | 133,488 | 5,880 | 4.4% |
| 2000 | 136,891 | 5,692 | 4.2% |
| 2001 | 136,933 | 6,801 | 5.0% |
| 2002 | 136,485 | 8,378 | 6.1% |
| 2003 | 137,736 | 8,774 | 6.4% |
| 2004 | 139,252 | 8,149 | 5.9% |
| 2005 | 143,730 | 6,754 | 4.7% |

With this kind of data, this chapter begins by reviewing appropriate definitions, available evidence on the trends with these type arrangements, advantages and disadvantages, considerations and how such arrangements are best implemented in the workplace. This chapter will be developed based on a collection and analysis of primary data along with any specific experiential knowledge of organizations that have implemented alternative work arrangements. Finally, a search of any other relevant articles and/or tabular, statistical, data that has been recently published are selected to include in this chapter as well.

**Definitions/Work Arrangements**

A full-time employee is often one who works a fixed 40 hours per week on a regular basis, and a part-time employee is an employee who works about 20 or fewer hours per week. An auxiliary employee works a fixed number of hours per week between 20 and 40 hours on a regular basis. These employees can be either exempt or non-exempt. Exempt employees are those that hold a position that is exempt from any overtime pay set forth by requirements of the Fair Labor Standards Act of 1938, as amended. These positions are generally executive, administrative, professional or external sales positions as covered in this Act. The positions must also meet the minimum salary requirements of the Act and be paid on a salaried basis. Non-exempt employees are employees that hold a position that is entitled to overtime pay under the provisions of the aforementioned Fair Labor Standards Act, and are paid hourly. The following details varied definitions and/or work arrangements that are referred to throughout this chapter:

*Compressed Workweek Schedule*: One option for employees in alternative work schedule arrangements includes the compressed workweek schedule in that the employee works fewer than five working days during a workweek. This single week option, or compressed workweek, involves a full-time employee being approved to work four days, e. g. 10 hours per day and then has the fifth day off. Some companies may exclude both Mondays and Fridays as possible off days. Compressed work schedules – longer hours, but for fewer days – may build loyalty by giving employees more days to handle personal duties (Pierce & Dunham, 1992).

*Nine-One Option*: Another definition that deserves discussion are the nine-one option, which encompasses a compressed workweek in which an employee works approximately 8.88 hours per day, excluding lunchtime, for nine days and has the tenth day off. This idea simply involves condensing full-time hours into fewer than ten business days or two workweeks. Like the one-week scenario, this type of compressed work schedule can improve coverage and even allow space and equipment to be used more effectively and efficiently. Based on the authors' experience within the service industry, when this option is used on a voluntary basis, it has shown to improve employee morale, gives employees a greater degree of satisfaction, reducing stress in their work and personal lives, and favorably impacts overall workplace productivity.

*Flex Schedule*: Still another option would be the flex schedule where an employee gets prior approval to start their workday earlier or later than the company's normal or established starting time for the shift in which the employee is assigned. A flex window is adhered to in which a supervisor-approved window of time permits an employee to arrive for work as early as, e. g. 6:00 a.m. and as late as e.g. 9:00 a.m. Some workers prefer to arrive at work late and leave later, while others may wish to arrive early and leave earlier. Again, the respective manager and employee agree on the schedule, which revolves around a set of core hours when the majority of employees are, indeed, at work. This alternative work option would appeal to parents of children who can be home in time to greet them arriving from school, or handle afternoon automobile repair shop or personal banking tasks, etc. For the company, a flex schedule can often mean better coverage and, again, it is a cost efficient method to improve employee morale. Finally, it can simply be a way to resolve work/personal scheduling conflicts and sharply reduce lateness and absenteeism.

*Telecommuting:* Telecommuting is still another way that permits eligible employees to do some of their work at home or another work location away from the main office. It enables companies to hire employees with disabilities who otherwise could not commute to the main office. It serves to cut back on occupancy and real estate expenses and can improve productivity with usually fewer distractions.

*Job Sharing:* One last option to be discussed is job sharing. Here the responsibilities of one full-time equivalent employee (FTE) are shared between two part-time people. Usually, the two employees maintain close communication through telephone or e-mail, and cooperate on their job functions. They can even rotate time spent with a three-day week for one and a two-day week for the other. The next week, the situation may reverse itself for the other employee.

## Overview

Increasingly, many companies are offering and maintaining alternative work arrangements for employees. They are subject to management approval and are approved generally on a case-by-case basis. The main reason for this kind of approval process is that some of these arrangements may not be feasible in all departments or for certain positions within a department, or may be available only during certain times of the year. Generally, when such arrangements are determined to work, management must take into account the ability to maintain appropriate production and service levels, the nature of the employee's responsibilities, the department's capacity to manage varying schedule requests, the employee's performance, age, gender, disciplinary record, reliability, and ability to meet deadlines. One can see in Table 8.2 that age, in a non-discriminatory way, may be an important consideration because historically the percentage of men over age 65 in the U. S. labor force has generally decreased over the past hundred years, although in the past five years it has increased slightly to 19.0 percent in 2004. Elderly women, too, in the workforce have also recently increased to 11.1 percent for the same period.

Hence, alternative work schedules may continue to be more desirable if offered in their regard. Table 8.3 concerns gender-related statistics, and over the past few years one can see that employed female participation in the labor force has only experienced a slight decrease to 46.5 percent, while males approximated 53.5 percent in 2004.

Also important is the employee's willingness and ability to depart from their approved alternative work arrangement to accommodate business needs. Finally, seasonal or cyclical changes in workloads must be addressed to ensure a high degree of productivity is maintained or strived for. Only when the aforementioned situations appear positive for alternative work arrangements, can flex schedules, telecommuting, compressed workweek options, occasional work from home and other flexible arrangements be implemented.

Table 8.2 - Elderly Worker (U. S. Department of Commerce)

| ELDERLY IN U. S. LABOR FORCE | | |
|---|---|---|
| 1890 - 2004 (%) | | |
| YEAR | MEN | WOMEN |
| 1890 | 68. 3% | 7.6% |
| 1900 | 63. 1% | 8.3% |
| 1920 | 55. 6% | 7.3% |
| 1930 | 54. 0% | 7.3% |
| 1940 | 41. 8% | 6.1% |
| 1950 | 45. 8% | 9.7% |
| 1960 | 33. 1% | 10.8% |
| 1970 | 26. 8% | 9.7% |
| 1980 | 19. 0% | 8.1% |
| 1990 | 16. 3% | 8.6% |
| 2000 | 17. 7% | 9.4% |
| 2004 | 19. 0% | 11.1% |

Companies must be cognizant of the fact that the Fair Labor Standards Act does not permit the averaging of hours over two or more weeks. And, full-time non-exempt employees must receive overtime pay for hours worked in excess of the standard workweek. Again, in any kind of workable alternative scheduling arrangement, the supervisor or manager has the right to cancel, suspend, or modify an employee's work arrangement privileges at any time for a business or performance-related reason. Also, except in emergencies or for discipline-related problems, an employee's immediate superior should provide an employee with advance notice of a management imposed change in an employee's flexible working arrangement privileges.

Table 8.3 – Employment Gender (U. S. Department of Labor)

| EMPLOYED PERSONS BY GENDER (IN THOUSANDS) | | | | | |
|---|---|---|---|---|---|
| YEAR | MALE | FEMALE | TOTAL | % MALE | % FEMALE |
| 2003 | 73,332 | 64,404 | 137,736 | 53.2% | 46.8% |
| 2004 | 74,524 | 64,728 | 139,252 | 53.5% | 46.5% |

*Advantages*: Some of the advantages that can be garnered with alternative work arrangements, telecommuting, etc. include increased morale and productivity. Employees value flexibility when it comes to managing their work and personal lives.

Employees also understand the sense of trust placed in them that goes along with alternative work arrangements. Therefore, it has been the authors' experience that these types of arrangements can often generate a renewed sense of appreciation and increased morale and productivity. Studies have shown that productivity among telecommuters often declines for a short period initially, and then increases after a period of adjustment. Productivity gains of 15% to 25% have been typical among telecommuters (Gordon, 1988). Telecommuters also tend to work harder and longer than do their office-bound counterparts, putting in additional hours beyond their daily stipulated quota or converting their commuting time saved by telecommuting to work. Productivity can also increase because of reduced absenteeism, increased morale, and higher efficiency due to working at one's more productive hours (Sing, 1996). In still another study, six out of nine companies found that telecommuters consistently met or were ahead of their deadlines for deliverables and were then able to take on additional work (Olson, 1983). Another benefit is that of lower rates of absenteeism and possible turnover. Employees that can arrange their own schedules to meet personal needs, while still meeting the expectations of their job, are less likely to miss work. As Griffeth and Hom (2001) discussed, turnover costs can be quite high when one factors in replacement costs, training costs and separation costs of an employee. Alternative work arrangement offerings may serve to mitigate voluntary, dysfunctional turnover situations and retain effective employees who cannot be easily replaced. Another advantage is that of reducing commuting stress, thus allowing employees to avoid the typical rush hour, thus making the daily commute more tolerable during less busy times of the day. There can, too, be a savings in commuting costs either with telecommuting or a reduction in reporting for work one less day a week or bi-week. Alternative work arrangements can also increase retention of employees who are offered flexibility, and may be more likely to stay with an organization, therefore reducing termination and hiring costs. Many of today's top performing employees are looking to join organizations that offer alternative work arrangements and focus on balancing work and personal life. By offering these types of schedules, a company may increase their ability to attract stellar performers and talent in today's competitive job market. Two final apparent advantages would include the possibility of reduced overtime with flexible schedules, enabling an organization to manage peak times more efficiently while reducing the need for overtime, and offering expanded hours of operation. Offering employees greater flexibility may result in employees being available during non-traditional hours or peak hours. Also, since employees are not starting and stopping at the same time in a specific shift, lunch breaks can be more easily staggered, waiting times reduced, etc. Finally, cost reduction is a big advantage. Since 1991, AT&T has freed up some $550 million in cash flow – a 30% improvement – by eliminating offices people do not need, consolidating others, and reducing overhead costs (Apgar, 1998).

*Disadvantages*: These would include some obvious, but workable situations. One disadvantage would be the occasional lack of supervision that is possible. However, this does not have to occur because managers' in co-located or proximal areas can ensure that supervision is always available. In the case of employees who work outside the department or telecommute, supervision is just a telephone call or e-mail away. Still another possible disadvantage is that of scheduled meetings. This, too, is workable in that it may be necessary for employees to adjust their schedules accordingly on the day of an important meeting. Also, they can utilize conference calls to ensure that meetings occur without any delays. Another possible down side to alternative work arrangements is the possible loss of cohesiveness in that a manager may be concerned that this could result in loss of teamwork and cohesiveness within a department. Of course, managers may be forced to now "think out of the box." Management and employee personnel can have regularly scheduled one-on-one meetings in person or by the telephone, off-site meetings with employees, etc. Finally, there could be administrative issues in that, initially, a manager would have to spend more time dealing with scheduling issues and concerns. However, like any schedule, an alternative work arrangement should work itself out once the schedules are implemented. This extra time spent up front could be far outweighed by the other aforementioned advantages.

## Alternative Work Arrangement Examples

There have been findings from the Workplace Flexibility Effectiveness Demonstration Project, sponsored by the Alfred P. Sloan Foundation, that there are measurable and direct links between flexible work arrangements, improved performance and increased productivity. The authors have surveyed in the literature several corporations and gathered data on corporations that have experienced positive results from the implementation of alternative work arrangements. These include the following examples:

*AstraZeneca Pharmaceuticals, Inc:* This corporation found that "flexibility is highly correlated to the ability to manage the pressures of work." Also, "individuals who take advantage of flex schedules have less burnout." AstraZeneca Pharmaceuticals, Inc also found that its employees had a higher level of commitment compared to employees from other companies. According to AstraZeneca's new hires, 84 percent said that flexibility was an important factor in their decision to join the company, and 73 percent rated the importance of flexibility as very important in their intention to stay at AstraZeneca Pharmaceuticals, Inc with another 23 percent rating it as somewhat important (Lyman, 2004).

*Bristol-Myers Squibb:* This is an example of a global pharmaceutical and related healthcare products company whose mission is to extend and enhance human life. They found that flexible work arrangements help with retention of employees. A survey conducted by the firm in 2004 found that of employees hired in the last three years, 20 percent said that the Bristol-Myers Squibb flex program influenced their decision to join the company. This survey detailed that 91 percent reported that their schedules have a positive effect on their productivity, 67 percent have informal flexibility, 71 percent labeled informal flex time very important in terms of their intention to stay, 71 percent said they have the flexibility they need in their work schedules, and 29 percent claim they would leave the company were it not for formal flex work options. Bristol-Myers Squibb (2005) is recognized as one of the 10 Best Companies for Working Mothers. This is the eighth consecutive year that the company has been listed in the ranking of the 100 Best Companies, and the fifth year in a row Bristol-Myers Squibb has been named a Top 10 company (Working Mother Magazine, 2005).

*Pitney Bowes, Inc*: This company is the world's leader in mailstream and document management solutions, and it used its Postage-by-Phone Spokane, Washington primary call center to implement flexible work schedules. Its team developed flexible work arrangements, expanding hours during peak days at the beginning of each week. It reported reduced overtime costs by as much as 80 percent in April and May 2005 compared to the previous two months. Pitney Bowes, Inc. now plans to expand its workplace flexibility pilot project to other call centers (Society for Human Resource Management, 2005).

*Frito Lay*: Frito Lay, which is a PepsiCo subsidiary, piloted flexible work arrangements with its district sales personnel in several nationwide offices. It saw overall sick days for those employees in the Gulf Coast zone reduced from 104 days to 12 days, an approximate 88 percent reduction. The number of days spent handling delivery routes for absent employees decreased from 18.7 days to 6.8 days, an almost 64 percent decrease. PepsiCo is considering adapting the concept to other divisions within their corporation, both in Frito Lay and other subsidiary holdings (Society for Human Resource Management, 2005).

*Chubb, Inc*: Chubb, Inc is a leading property and casualty insurer, and they piloted flexible schedules for 90 days with two casualty claims processing teams and one internal support team at its Western Claims Service Center. All three teams, which involved a total of 17 employees and 3 supervisors, met or exceeded the goals they set for an overall 5 percent improvement in performance. The company reported a 50 percent reduction in unscheduled time off each month and a 40 percent decrease in overtime hours per employee during its 90 day initiative. Employees were offered some control over their hours in return for taking responsibility for getting their teams' work done well. Most opted for compressed workweeks or flexible lunch hours and starting and quitting times. Chubb, Inc. has since extended the process to other company teams (Shellenbarger, 2005).

Finally, a Society for Human Resource Management survey of 450 employers completed in 2004, found that 57 percent offer flex time, 34 percent offer a compressed workweek, and 19 percent offer telecommuting on a full time basis (SHRM, 2004). From 1974 to 1995, productivity grew at around 1.4 percent a year. Productivity growth in the United States accelerated to about 2.5 percent a year from 1995 to 2000. Growth in output per hour in the third quarter of 2005 alone was a striking 5.4 percent. In fact, output per hour has grown at an average annual rate of nearly 3.5 percent over the last three years (Varian, 2006). Table 8.4 reflects this output per hour in private business for both male and female from Calendar Years 1987 to 2004, with the 2004 index indicating 115.0 or 15 percent over Calendar Year 2000 data.

Varian goes on to speculate that much of this increase is due to information technology improvements which, of course, are necessary, essential and enables most alternative work arrangement accommodations, e.g. telecommuting, e-mail, sophisticated staffing and scheduling systems, etc. It is believed that these positive productivity changes have also been concurrent with greater numbers of alternative work arrangements in the United States being introduced, which also accounts also for this realized improvement overall in work output or worker productivity.

Table 8.4 – Output in Private Business (Bureau of Labor Statistics)

| OUTPUT PER HOUR IN PRIVATE BUSINESS | |
| --- | --- |
| ALL PERSONS (1987 - 2004) | |
| (INDEX: YEAR 2000 = 1.00 | |
| YEAR | INDEX |
| 1987 | 77.5 |
| 1988 | 78.7 |
| 1989 | 79.5 |
| 1990 | 81.1 |
| 1991 | 82.5 |
| 1992 | 86.0 |
| 1993 | 86.4 |
| 1994 | 87.3 |
| 1995 | 87.5 |
| 1996 | 90.1 |
| 1997 | 91.8 |
| 1998 | 94.4 |
| 1999 | 97.2 |
| 2000 | 100.0 |
| 2001 | 102.8 |
| 2002 | 107.0 |
| 2003 | 111.2 |
| 2004 | 115.0 |

## Implementation Considerations

When a company considers implementing any type of alternative work arrangements, they should consider the options available, the workload, and type of work as well as the employee's past performance. Alternative work arrangements require collaboration and commitment from both the employee and the manager. The following considerations must be factored in to the pre-planning of alternative work arrangements:

*Staffing Needs*: Managers should always consider staffing needs, productivity expectations, and the resultant constraints in the work process. They have to think about the need for coverage during peak work times or during breaks. Can these times still be served using an alternative work arrangement? Is it important to have someone from the department available in person at all times? Managers must assess which employees conduct similar work and assess whether they can rotate time away from the office in order to maintain adequate coverage levels. Is it possible for these employees to gain some flexibility while still meeting expectations? How will the department manage the various schedules? Is it important for employees to know when other employees in the department are scheduled to work? If so, is there a way to communicate this information? How often will schedules change?

*Business Needs*: The implementation of alternative work arrangements can have both organizational and employee benefits. However, it is important that the business needs drive the availability of alternative work arrangements. This does not mean that the status quo is necessarily the only way to achieve current business needs. It is important that managers question the current way work is being completed in order to see the true potential of implementing alternative work arrangements. A manager must think about the primary purpose of their department, and how the department fulfills that purpose. The questions must be answered in that can employees conduct their work using an alternative work arrangement and still meet expectations?

*Work Duties*: Once it has been determined that there is a mutual benefit, the type of work must be considered. The employee's primary responsibilities and duties must be suitable for an alternative work arrangement. Corporate decision makers with management input must focus on the types of tasks within a function. It would be important to review the position description, and determine if certain tasks can be performed during any hours of the day? What resources are necessary to complete these tasks? Will there be any delays in progress if an employee is working an alternative work arrangement? Managers must be aware that it is not absolutely necessary for all the work to match perfectly to an alternative work arrangement. Managers must demonstrate flexibility in their decision-making. If they find one or two tasks that do not allow for an alternative work arrangement, build in some reasonableness so those tasks are still completed, while allowing for some secondary flexibility.

*Budget and Equipment Needs*: Some alternative work arrangements may and will require special equipment or access to specific systems or databases. It is critical that these concerns along with their impact on the budget be considered. A manager working in concert with the employee can make a list of equipment needed or system access and review each item to determine the impact of the budget and the availability of access. Again, these costs must be weighed against the benefits of the alternative work arrangement.

*Previous Performance*: A manager must review the employee's previous performance history. Is the employee's performance currently meeting job expectations? Does the employee show self-motivation and strong work habits that may be necessary when working an alternative work arrangement? Does the employee have a good understanding of their work responsibilities and expectations? Has the employee shown good time management skills and self-discipline?

*Privacy and Security Concerns*: Depending upon the business and the company's unique situation, there may be concerns related to the protection of certain types of information and even personal security for employees after "normal" working hours.

Finally, a manager must take into consideration what hours do customers actually expect service? What are the peak hours and what are the trough hours? Will it be necessary to budget for additional equipment so that systems can be accessed remotely? What method will be used to track the various schedules? Can resources and assets in the workplace be used more efficiently by approving requests for alternative work arrangements? For example, can a manager eliminate floor space or existing cubicles by approving more work-at-home or telecommuting arrangements? Again, all these situations are many and varied, and demand that these and other questions be considered and understood clearly between all concerned.

## Implementing Alternative Work Arrangements

The implementation of adopting alternative work arrangements in a company or corporation should generally encompass the following processes:

*Discussions with Management*: Before reviewing an alternative work arrangement plan with employees, management should review among themselves any possible constraints or upcoming changes that may impact the feasibility of implementing the program in any department. Are there any other strategic initiatives or work changes, cross-departmental or corporate-wide concerns that may affect a department? It would be important for all management personnel involved to discuss both the benefits and perceived barriers to implementing alternative work arrangements. Hopefully, the benefits of such an arrangement will outweigh the costs. Everyone must be open-minded and think outside the typical day shift work schedule, e. g. 9:00 a.m. to 5:00 p.m. The goal here is to result in a situation with a content, more productive, and engaged workforce.

*Discussions with Employees*: Once management has a good understanding of company business needs and possible constraints, supervisors and management should assess the employee interest in alternative work arrangements. This can be done in individual meetings or a staff meeting, or simply by utilizing a survey tool completed by employees. It would be important for supervisors to stress to employees that it may not be feasible to implement everyone's wish list when it comes to alternative work arrangements. Employees should be queried on how flexible they may be and what would work best for them and the department. Also, impress upon employees that business needs ultimately drive the availability of alternative work arrangements. Stress, also, that this process may take time to implement, and it may even be tried on a trial basis to determine if it would be suitable for a full implementation.

*Determine what will Work*: A manager should be pragmatic, now that all employees involved have a reasonably good understanding how things will essentially work. They should be acutely aware of situations involving their respective critical business demands for the department that may not be able to be altered or situations involving a specific staffing level, coverage, etc. Again, internal and external customer needs should be of paramount concern. A manager should then categorize the different alternative work schedules requested or suggested by employees, and eliminate any apparent or requested arrangements that will not meet the business needs or are not suitable based on the employee's past performance. It is critical that all involved are open to interacting with others during odd shifts, and perhaps performing work differently. Just because coverage is needed five days a week does not automatically eliminate the alternative work schedule idea. Rather, it may still be possible to meet the business needs of a department and still offer this kind of employee work schedule flexibility. A manager should continue to review plans over several days before implementation, because it is better up front to consider alternative options and implement a survey tool, rather than put something in place that will simply not work.

*Review Available Options*: Once finalized with a plan that appears will work, a manager should meet with employees on an individual basis. Employees are generally more open to discuss their individual requests if held one-on-one. The manager simply outlines the details related to the alternative work arrangement including scheduling constraints, business needs, work times, days, reasons why the arrangement may need to be adjusted, and finally expectations related to performance. As in most situations, time spent up front with any major change can reduce problems and confusion later on down the road. Both the employee and manager should then execute some type of written understanding on expectations, deliverables, etc.

*Final Implementation and Ongoing Review*: Once everything is in place, the employee can begin the new work arrangement. Depending on business needs, it would probably be a good idea to stagger implementation across a department or corporation. This can serve to reduce service or production interruptions until everyone is used to the new arrangements or schedules. Going forward, managers should discuss any concerns related to alternative work arrangements with their employees. This is where productivity measurement is critical to compare output per work hour in the new alternative work arrangement with a previously established baseline output per worked hour. Productivity advances or that ability to produce more with the same or less input, are a significant source of increased potential national income. The U.S. economy has been able to produce more goods and services over time, not by requiring a proportional increase of labor time, but by making production more efficient. Clearly, feedback will be important throughout the process in order to make changes where necessary and forge ahead.

### Summary

From the authors' experience, as well as through interviews with both corporate and student contacts, flexible scheduling through alternative work arrangements invariably ranks number one in requests by employees. Indeed, employers have been responding by gradually expanding alternative setups as one can see throughout this chapter. A 2005 study of 1,092 employers by the Families and Work Institute in New York found employers are significantly more likely to offer compressed workweeks and flextime than they were in 1998 (Shellenbarger et al., 2005). Of course, communication between the employee and manager is critical in establishing an initial alternative work arrangement. These discussions should cover backup plans when an employee is not available, and when a customer or other employee needs something fast. The right flexible work arrangement will serve both employee and management needs if designed correctly. Clearly, it is important for senior management to envision the workplace that includes alternative work arrangements, with a concurrent strategy in place to design and promote this kind of flexibility.

Firms are moving from vertically integrated organizations to more specialized ones that outsource non-core functions and to more decentralized forms of internal organization. One can expect a shift away from more permanent, lifetime jobs toward less permanent, even non-standard employment relationships and work arrangements. These arrangements may be particularly attractive to workers trying to balance work and family obligations or to the people who would benefit most from alternative arrangements. Retention, of course, can be the primary resultant benefit in a sound alternative work arrangement within a corporation. In the final analysis, alternative work arrangements are being increasingly implemented by employers to improve productivity, and save myriad costs involved with traditional, full-time employment relationships. Employers and employees are entering into part-time, flexible hours, telecommuting, etc. to accommodate employee needs and to increase retention and morale. It is one of the most familiar clichés in the business world: "No one ever says on their deathbed that they wish they had spent more time at the office." But it wouldn't be a cliché if the words did not have some measure of truth – and the truth is, "it's often easier to spout platitudes about working smarter, not harder, than actually leaving the office before the sun sets" (Mitchell, 2003).

### *Discussion Questions*

1. What is an alternative work plan?
2. Why should employers and coaches offer flexible work hours for their employees?
3. How can employers put more retirees and others interested in part-time work into their workforce?
4. What is telecommuting? Who benefits from it? Discuss examples.

# CHAPTER 9

## Coaching Females in the Workplace

Women throughout the world tend to face certain biases, stereotypes, and the glass ceiling in the workplace as they attempt to reach higher in the hierarchy of management. This chapter discusses gender differences as well as some of the obstacles and possible means of combating various challenges that women face in the workplace. The chapter focuses on coaching as one solution for women, minorities, and underachievers of all backgrounds. It is hypothesized that small successes lead to huge results, and underachievers can eventually have the self-confidence to achieve high level organizational goals, as well as significant personal achievements through effective coaching and fair development and promotion opportunities.

Coaching is a process that takes time, practice, planning, and collaboration with employees. Regardless of their gender, effective coaches build rapport, create a supportive work environment, speak honestly, act courageously, provide timely feedback, listen attentively, provide a better vision of the desired future, ask relevant questions, plan for growth and development, and follow-up on action plans.

### Understanding Common Gender Differences

Individuals at all levels of the organization are expected to deal with gender differences and solve problems generated by lack of understanding these differences. These gaps are often created by societal conditionings, lack of awareness, a not caring attitude, and the changing environment in the workforce. While problems are often perceived as being negative, they can give rise to opportunities for restructuring or new methods of doing things better, faster, and more competitively.

Society starts treating boys and girls differently from the time they are born. We dress them in different styles of clothes and in different color outfits; we sing different songs to them; we encourage them to take on different hobbies; and we treat them differently because of their gender. Therefore, they respond differently in their business dealings. Aristotle said it first over thousands of years ago, and the same principle and concept still holds true today:

> You get a good adult by habituating a good child to doing the right thing. Praise for truth-telling and sanctions for fibbing well, in time, make him or her "naturally" honest. Abstract knowledge of right and wrong no more

contributes to character than knowledge of physics contributes to cycling (Michael Levine, NY Times, 1989).

The same habitual approach applies to adults as well as children, because learning and moral development do not stop at adolescence but continue throughout one's life regardless of gender. Formal as well as informal education and training in coaching diverse individuals, therefore, are critical in the business sector; and can make a difference in creating an awareness of sensitive ethical dilemmas and solutions which lead to and reflect moral behavior.

Males learn to compete (through competition in sports, their domineering personalities, etc.), which is related to conflict and one best method of doing things or one final winner. Whereas females learn to be compassionate and caring as they grow. Boys spend 50% of their time moving from one thing to another; they do something, learn from it and move on to something else. Boys do what they are told and when the coach asks to "go to the right," boys do not say "oh coach, I was thinking about going straight, what are your thoughts about it?" Girls want to be involved in the entire decision-making process.

Men, as boys, learn how far to push people to get the job done before pushing becomes destructive. Boys learn to take risk which is often the best way to become successful. Boys learn not to cry and let their feelings get in the way. Boys learn that when the game is over, it really is over and after the game they go out celebrating and sometimes even with the members of the opposing team. While, for most women the end of the game is not really the end; the argument of the games can last a life time. While boys are goal focused, girls are process focused. Males assume that the president of a company needs to act like a president otherwise he or she will not be treated as one, while females may feel bad/guilty driving a brand new Mercedes when the rest of the employees are driving Hondas and Tercels. Men behave according to the hierarchy while women behave according to a flat structure.

Girls learn not to take risk and be careful. They learn to avoid conflict and be nice. They learn to develop relationships. While women will talk to ten other people about a friend that they are not happy with because they did something wrong or unproductive; but they do not mention it to the person/friend which caused it because females, during their childhood years, have learned to develop relationships and not destroy it. Boys will usually confront the person and get it over with regardless of future consequences to the person or the relationship. Generally, girls attempt to negotiate a win/win situation, while men attempt to get a win/lose situation.

Males, sometimes, think that females waste a lot of time talking to people about irrelevant stuff; to most males this "small talk" is unproductive. While males think that small talk is a waste, females value and cherish this because it builds relationships. On the negative side, when female bosses chit chat with male employees, the employees may not see the job as being important or requiring immediate attention.

Males answer with one word statements (yes, no, had a meeting, the day went fine, good, etc.), while females want to talk about what happened throughout the day, in detail which at times may sound very boring to males. Females come home wanting to discuss every detailed activity that happened in their day, while males want to hear only the results. Females do not want to hear advice from men at all times; as matter of fact, most often females just want a listening ear. It has been said that men have the gift of advice, while women have the gift of understanding. As males, we do not hear people all the way through before we start giving advice. We make assumptions, because we think we know what others want, and we want to be helpful by jumping into conclusions and giving advice which is usually wrong if it is not based on accurate understanding. This is how males are conditioned, as goal oriented individuals, whereas women are more process oriented. Both genders attempt to do their best, but they do so by different rules which may not seem right to the opposite gender because it may not be the usual way of doing things for them.

Males and females approach situations and solve problems based on what they are conditioned to throughout their lives. Males are authority and rank oriented, while females are process or involvement oriented. These approaches are right in some areas while not the best method or approach in others. But, since we are used to doing them according to only one approach, we keep doing them automatically and similarly in all situations thinking it is the best method. Just like time management, if you are used to doing things that are deadline driven, then you always do those deadline-driven things because they appear important and procrastinate on proactively preparing for things ahead of time.

Males and females define "being a team player" differently. Being a team player to males mean doing what it takes to do the job and following order in any given situation. To males, being a team player means knowing your rank and being disciplined enough to obey authority. To females, this may sound mindless because one person gives order and everybody else automatically follows without challenging the orders or having a discussion about it. Being a team player to a female means being involved, caring for one another, and helping each other. To some males this is not the most efficient manner of working in a team and may appear to be somewhat manipulative.

Males have friendliness while females have friends. To males, friendliness come and go as the situation fits, but to females, friends are friends unless they get into a major fight or disagreement about something. So, friendliness is very situational and temporary to males and not necessarily to females. In meetings, males of powerful behaviors (characters) attempt to dominate the conversation around their own ideas (dogmatic style), while females, in general, want to share everyone's thoughts because they were conditioned to the word "share" as they were growing up. Research shows that females in general do not speak much in meetings, and this is because they do not want to dominate the meeting; their general work ethic is to share and everyone should have their opportunity and turn to speak. Women tend to put their statements in the form of a question, while males make statements of how it should be or what they should do. Males resist being influenced especially when others are present; while women smile and accept the facts as they come about or surface during the meeting. Males interrupt and females wait their turn to speak. To males the meetings take place outside the meeting (networking and politics), while females talk about things together in the meeting. Decisions, for males, are often made in the coffee room and hallways and the meeting is a ceremony or symbol to formalize the decision.

Women have a tendency to start essays with "I hope to accomplish...," while men have a tendency to start their letters or essays with "I will accomplish..." To most people, the males will accomplish it because they are positive and determined; while the female statements may appear somewhat weak and not very strong. We write and speak differently in regards to our genders.

Males like to keep their emotions buried, while females like show their sad faces. If a female has a sad face, it is best to ask her what is wrong; otherwise she may think that you are ignoring her and are not interested in her disagreement or discontent. Females like to talk to others while facing them; on other hand males like to talk to each other standing side by side because facing each other represents conflict and competition. If you are not facing a female while she is talking, she may feel as though you do not care about what she has to say and are not interested. However, males interpret the face-to-face conversations as aggressive and competitive behavior.

The integration and understanding of female leadership traits can improve the ethical climate of a firm by bringing more sensitivity, caring treatment of customers, more creative approaches to problem solving, more effective relationship-building skills, creating greater trust in interpersonal affairs, and being supportive and understanding of supervisory style. Women in the workforce are often wrongly and stereotypically viewed as less decisive, slower to make decisions, or even naive at times. The best approach might be to combine the best traits of each sex at various levels of management in the organization to have a balance of both sides. This will enable individuals to help each other by developing strong solutions to their daily challenges; and they could learn from each other in the process.

### Gender Differences and Perceptions in the Military[21]

A 2007 article entitled "*A Long-Term Study of Sex Differences in Attitudes towards Women's Roles in the Military and in Combat*" coauthored by professors Edward F. Murphy, Jr., Regina A. Greenwood, Jaime A. Ruiz-Gutierrez, Terrell G. Manyak, Bahaudin G. Mujtaba, and Arnel Onesimo O. Uy studied the results for attitudes towards women's roles in the military and in combat occupations and found that both males and females agreed that female officers had the same chances at promotion as males did, and women would be just as good as general officers as men. Both sexes felt that women should be treated equally in normal societal roles in the military. Murphy et al. concluded that the negative attitudes towards women's roles in the military emerged when discussing attitudes towards women in command and combat occupations. Males expressed the view that females should not be allowed to enter combat occupations; that women would not be as good as men in command positions; that women would not perform as well as commanders as men did; and that women received equal treatment in high performance ratings. Females on the other hand, expressed the view that they should be allowed into all combat occupations; that they should be allowed to serve as commanders; that they would be just as good

---

[21] The complete article was prepared and published at NAMS, 2007, by E. F. Murphy, Jr., R. A. Greenwood, J. A. Ruiz-Gutierrez, T. G. Manyak, B. G. Mujtaba, and A. O. Uy.

as men as commanders, and that they did not receive equal treatment in performance ratings.

All of these attitudes are related to the legally mandated discrimination that prohibits women from serving in combat occupations. Women are not allowed by military rules and regulations and Congressional oversight laws to enter all combat occupations and women have rarely been given senior command and general office positions, except as tokens. Women believe that, since they are not allowed into all combat occupations, their chances at getting high performance ratings are diminished; consequently, they have less opportunity for getting command positions, and less opportunity for being promoted to senior leadership positions (the ranks of colonel to general officer). The military's combat exclusion laws discriminate against women, and they do not allow the military to fully utilize the outstanding skills and abilities of military women.

The results of this research study in 2007 by Murphy and his colleagues confirm that male and female attitudes towards sex roles are changing and have become more equalitarian over the past ten years. The findings indicate that over 90 percent of all attitudes towards women in society have become more equalitarian for men and women, although women were significantly more equalitarian than men. The attitudes towards women in the military and in combat occupations show that males and females believe that women should be assimilated into the military, but when the question comes to women entering combat occupations, men do not want women to be in combat occupations; women believe they should be. Overall, men in the military still have negative attitudes towards women entering combat occupations, while 80 percent of military females felt combat exclusion regulations should be eliminated so women can be fully assimilated into the military's organizational culture.

Other studies have indicated that women were less likely to reach senior officer ranks above the grade of major (0-4), because less than 30 percent of the eligible females decided to remain in the military to compete for the higher level promotions. During focused interviews women explained that they left the service because of limited combat occupational roles, sexual harassment, and work family conflict. Female officers are often concentrated in occupations perceived to offer more limited long-term career opportunities. Female officers seem to believe that their traditional non-combat roles provide limited opportunities to advance to senior ranks.

This study showed that both sexes felt that women should be treated equally in normal societal roles in the military, but men responded that females should not be allowed to be in combat occupations or in command positions, that women would not perform as well as commanders, and that women received equal treatment in high performance ratings. Females believed that they should be allowed to serve as commanders, would be just as good as men as commanders, should be allowed into all combat occupations, and they believed they did not receive equal treatment in high performance ratings.

The implications for decision makers in all organizations, not only military organizations, are broad. First, women expect to be treated equally on the job and they expect to be given the same opportunities for advancement as men. Minimum standards and physical strength requirements should be set for occupations, like combat occupations, and both males and females should be allowed to enter those occupations if they meet those standards and/or physical strength requirements. This research focused specifically on the military where traditional stereotypes have changed, but some stereotypes still exist, and these stereotypes are still marginalizing the value of women in the military. Women are still not fully assimilated into the military's organizational and power structure.

Research results indicate that the greatest hindrance to full assimilation of women into the military, are the rules and regulations that prohibit women from entering all combat occupations, and the requirement that the military services notify Congress before opening any new combat occupations to women. Similar findings are not only limited to the military. Numerous studies of the civilian sector have shown that the limited opportunities for promotion of women into top corporate leadership positions lead women to their departure to form their own small companies. Consequently, managers and coaches must do a better job of encouraging, influencing and supporting women to achieve their goals without searching for advancement opportunities elsewhere.

## Coaching the Underachieving Female[22]

This section presents a framework for motivating the Hispanic female underachiever in an organization. A real coaching situation is presented along with a plan of action. We shall address the organizational and individual concerns of the underachiever and examine ways to motivate and overcome resistance. The section further explores coaching techniques and useful tools geared towards breakthroughs. Finally, it explores a coaching plan solution to affect positive change and achievement.

By and large, people want to feel good about their contribution to society, their reason for being, and how they interact with others. For many, satisfaction can be derived at work in the form of good interpersonal relationships, challenging work, and pride in job performance. Fredrick Hertzberg opined the most effective tool to motivate employees is by creating conditions that foster intrinsic drive such as promoting feelings of competence and providing recognition (Bartol and Srivastava, 2002), but what happens when this idea does not appeal to certain individuals?

Anita has worked with the organization for approximately 15 years, and has remained in variations of the same position since her hire date. She is of Puerto Rican descent and now squarely in her 50s. Every once in a while, Anita applies for higher level positions, but rescinds her application when she is required to undergo skills testing. A high school graduate hailing from a New York borough, Anita has not seen the inside of a classroom for sometime and by all accounts, her lackluster educational experience was demoralizing. Thus, she becomes frustrated and seems to believe that seniority, rather than skill will get her to the next level. Anita has been comfortable in the same routine for many years, and it will be a challenge to break her out of this repetitive daily exercise. She is bright enough to take on new tasks, but hesitates in doing so. She lacks motivation, but becomes disappointed when passed over for

---

[22] Contributed by Gina H. Harris, Nova Southeastern University.

promotion. Anita is an underachiever, who is set in her ways, slightly older than her counterparts, and does as little as possible to maintain her position.

Anita's situation as the underachiever is a common problem despite race, creed or color; however, underachievers have the power to undermine an organization if unattended. This section explores vehicles to motivate Anita (and her ilk), address the cultural problems she may have with achievement, and provide ideas to move her from an underachieving employee to a performer.

## *Creating a Performance Culture*

Most organizations want to create a performance culture by utilizing their employees' talents and energy, but how does a company inspire these feeling in the underachiever? In many cases, "cause is the absence of a performance culture" as people need to understand what they are working towards and why, in an effort to motivate (Reid and Hubbell, 2005, p. 1). In order to achieve high performance with the underachiever, an environment of trust and candor is required (Reid and Hubbell, 2005). This setting reduces defensiveness when questions are asked and this derives greater value from employee talents and spurs them on to contribute. Having a trusting environment encourages a free exchange of information where punishment is not a factor. According to Reid and Hubbell, when conflicts are addressed and unfulfilled commitments exposed, people can speak their minds without retribution, leading to resolution of issues. Moving beyond "safe talk" allows for creativity (Reid and Hubbell, 2005).

When coaching the underachiever, simplicity and focus needs to be achieved. The coach will also want to play up the coachee's strengths and determine how to best utilize these in the organizational setting (Reid and Hubbell, 2005). Using the SWOT (Strength, Weaknesses, Opportunities, and Threats) analysis is one way to isolate strengths and build on them. The coachee must also be accountable for his or her performance expectations, both in the coaching process and within the organization. Role clarity and priorities are a factor in both processes, as well.

The underachiever may lack self-confidence due to inadequate education and believe he/she may not have the capacity to do well in a performance culture, and therefore, may not even try. Many years ago, Socrates challenged society by wagering he could teach a slave, with no formal education, the Pythagorean Theorem just by asking the right questions and listening carefully to the meaning behind the answers. It worked because Socrates understood the "power of questions and listening" (Reid and Hubbell, p. 4). In coaching, one can learn much by asking open-ended questions and really listening to the answers given by the coachee.

Other ingredients to coaching are setting expectations, ongoing feedback, and measuring progress with recognition and rewards (Reid and Hubbell, 2005). With the underachiever, the reward of pride with contribution should be a great motivator. Research reveals most people want an opportunity to express their talents and competence, and when given the chance, they usually deliver and surprise.

Overall, performance of the underachiever is a function of accountability, feedback, motivation, self-confidence, communication, and collaboration. With good performance, rewards will come and the combination of all of these factors should move the underachiever to a high performer (Reid and Hubbell, 2005).

## Changing the Behavior of Underachievers

One would assume organizations would not allow their underachievers to get away with poor performance; however, this is not always the case. Many managers avoid challenging their underachieving employees because it supposedly takes time and attention away from other, more important tasks (Jones, 2005). Many underachievers simply engage in repetitive, non-productive behaviors because nobody wants to put forth the effort in helping them improve. Thus, expectations for underachievers are lower and differ from the rest of the organization. Underachievers are not likely to understand the higher organization expectations either; however, using valuative coaching may motivate underachievers to raise the bar (Jones, 2005).

Valuative coaching outlines where coachees stand and what they need to do to change (Jones, 2005). Using non-threatening communication, coaches emphasize how that underachiever adds to the organization and pinpoints situations where the coachee's productivity did not meet expectations. The goal is to understand the coachee's point of view and find the disconnect between the organizational expectations and the employee's actions. The purpose of valuative coaching is not to solve problems, but simply assess and convey value, often by using high-achieving employees. By reinforcing desired expectations, it is theorized the underachiever will make an effort to do better.

## In Search of Mediocrity

Spend time in any bookstore and you will find stacks of books regarding management excellence. Many are best-sellers that promote achievement, greatness, and stories of charismatic leaders who have overcome adversity in the face of daunting circumstances. It would be a wonderful world of workers if all our co-workers and employees shared the burning desire to be the best that they can be…but this is not reality. Many of our co-workers and employees are satisfied just to be. Not to be good, great, or even promising, just to be…mediocre. Nobody writes best-selling books about the mediocre employee because it is not an exciting topic. However, this topic is ripe for further investigation to determine why some people choose to be average.

For purposes of this material, mediocrity is defined as ordinariness, and considered an unacceptable ambition for people in the workforce (Marren, 2004). Of course, mediocrity is judged by the performance of others. It must be distinguished from incompetence or stupidity, and does not usually result in discharge from an organization (Marren, 2004). Mediocre employees "will never achieve the heights of excellence, but it will often outlast the exceptional, and will always manage to beat out the truly bad" (Marren, p. 5). In other words, mediocre or average employees have the potential to be better employees; they simply need guidance and coaching to do it.

It is suspected that mediocre employees have a sense of self-hatred because they are often compared unfavorably against high achievers. They believe promotions are in reach, but their inability to receive one due to lack of motivation results in a personal morass that feeds upon itself (Marren, 2004). They may also view management as more worthy and ranked by achievement. Since the underachiever has no standing, power or authority, their negative self-talk will never take them to higher positions in the organization.

In essence, mediocrity is the child of negativity, self-victimization, and a dearth of confidence. It seems as if the coaching process was tailor-made for these types of individuals, and coaches need to use various techniques to draw out the emotional baggage and negativity these people possess.

### *Coaching for Results*

If we fold the mediocre employee into the coaching process, we will want to see results. Coaching is about achieving results and developing capabilities (Tangri, 2001). It requires a significant investment from both the coach and the coachee, that results in the ability to have the coachee guide him/herself and make the right decisions later.

The first step in coaching is goal setting. The coach needs to set specific, measurable goals targeting what needs to be accomplished. Keeping this in mind, the coachee needs to have the ability, authority and resources to accomplish these tasks. In the coaching process, you cannot force the employee to improve, they have to want it! One of the ways to figure out what motivates the employee is determining what is important to them (Tangri, 2001). If you are able to provide the employee with meaningful rewards, he/she will produce and the coach will reap the benefits of success.

Oftentimes, employees may say they do not have time to perform the task. However, "If you don't have the time to do it right, why do you have the time to do it over?" (Tangri, p. 3).

One basic dilemma with underachievers is they do not know what they want to do, and may not be in the right position to realize their goals. Although this is not the optimal situation, it is an opportunity for underachievers to take another position where their passion may shine through. However, if the coach can determine what drives the underachiever and what will make them happy, the coach, coachee and organization will meet their objectives.

### *If They Don't Care, Don't Waste Your Time*

Generally, people want to help others, but what if people don't want help? This is a valuable lesson in the coaching process and can save the coach a lot of time, effort, and energy. There are going to be some coachees who are beyond coaching. Some just do not want the help, and coaches must be accepting of that fact, rather than beat themselves up believing they have failed.

Marshall Goldsmith, a leader in the coaching field, has experienced this for himself. As a high achiever, the notion that somebody would not want to improve themselves was foreign to him. He believed "other people would get better solely because of my presence," but this was not the case (Goldsmith, 2004, p. 1). Goldsmith learned people have to want to change, and the best coaching in the world will not make a difference if the coachee is not committed to the process (Personal Communication, July 2004; Center for Leadership, Escondido, California). Some underachievers are happy to be right where they are, and coaching is not the answer. When this case presents itself, the coach must know how much effort to give before moving on. The amount of effort is a professional decision to be made by the experienced coach.

### Helping Successful People Get Even Better

We have now come to the point where our underachiever has made great strides and breakthroughs with coaching. Now that things are going well, they may feel no reason to change, but there is always room for improvement. Research has shown that very successful people have four underlying beliefs that differ from their peers, they are: I choose to succeed; I can succeed; I will succeed; and I have succeeded (Goldsmith, 2003). This positive self-talk could be the difference between slight improvement and self-actualization.

When people choose to succeed they are committed to achievement and feel a sense of ownership. Having these traits, people are much more likely to reach their goals. Knowing people can succeed is the "definition of self-efficacy" and the belief that drives a person to achievement (Goldsmith, 2003, p. 7). Many people with this belief have a need for self-determination and an internal locus of control that affects decision-making abilities. Knowing that they are in control of their own destinies makes success reachable.

Positive self-talk affects one's beliefs and guides them along the path of success. Highly successful people understand that they will succeed and this concept is preordained in their minds. Their "whatever it takes" mentality shows them the way. Lastly, once people have reached their goal, they become even more confident and egotistical in their abilities.

Achievement is an ongoing process as is improvement. Goldsmith suggests people should focus on two areas for improvement after every successful endeavor, and feedback is imperative. Highly successful people will get better based on their own efforts, and with a guiding coach, coachees can achieve even higher levels of performance.

### Problem/Issue/Explanation

At the outset of any coaching situation, the coachee is often plagued by myriad emotions that may hinder the process. Anita may experience anger, fear, sadness, shame and/or jealousy which are the most common types of emotions that rear their ugly heads in the arena of change (Zeus and Skiffington, 2003). Many are coping mechanisms that assist people in dealing with new situations, and tend to represent management of goals. There are a number of approaches to help Anita overcome her emotional turmoil and move forward towards goal achievement. These approaches, among others, will be addressed in the Coaching Solutions portion of this composition.

Next, the coach faces numerous hurdles in trying to influence Anita. First, Anita has been comfortable in the same routine for many years, and it will be a challenge to break her out of this repetitive daily exercise. Next, she lacks confidence to do the job because of her skill level. Her age is a factor, because she has not attended any educational facility in over 30 years, and her collectivist culture and orientation may be hindering her progress. Finally, and probably most important, Anita lacks support from her direct supervisor who is content to keep Anita right where she is, and knows if Anita moves to another position, the supervisor will have the headache of interviewing, training, and working with someone new.

Before moving forward with the coaching process, let us reflect on Anita's situation. In the 1970s and 80s, there was a high demand for clerical workers and many women joined the workforce to increase family incomes, often to offset high unemployment rates for male workers. This movement coined "pink collar" brought average educated women of all races and backgrounds into the labor force accepting jobs offering low pay, low prestige and limited opportunities for advancement (Gilbert & Kahl, 1993, p. 74). Many of these women remain in low paying occupations due to their inability to move in and out of the workforce because of family obligations and self-imposed limited work hours. Many women with high school education are not confident enough to make the leap to managerial jobs, and women with soft skills and family responsibilities do not always make time to get reeducated. Anita may have fallen into this category.

Research has shown that some Hispanic groups in the United States have a large school dropout rate when compared to other ethnic groups (Padilla, 2002). Because education is not a strong value for some individuals and often undervalued by some parents, it is not surprising that achievement at any level is poor. Additionally, educational achievement is not rewarded by parents in some Hispanic homes, thus motivation to seek new skills is not viewed as adaptive which diminishes viable impulses (Padilla, 2002). Families have great influence over children and shape emotions, ambitions and future success. If Anita's family was not interested in achievement, this concept would likely spill onto her inner drive to succeed, hindering high productivity. Lastly, life experiences shape people's perceptions regardless of age, gender or race (Arthur Patterson, Personal Communication, March 21, 2006). As members of a minority, females and Hispanics in the United States have probably experienced some sort of discrimination, which affects perceptions and willingness to integrate (Padilla, 2002). Alienated people often feel powerless, victimized, and sometimes employed beneath their education and experience level, which is also known as being underemployed (Art Patterson, Personal Communication, March 21, 2006). As a Hispanic woman, Anita's cultural foundation and her perceptions of the world, greatly impact the ability to move forward in the organization and learn new skills. Anita's external locus of control, self-fulfilling prophecy bias, and lack of confidence must be overcome to aid Anita's growth process.

"As we all know, facing up to certain facts about ourselves can be uncomfortable, even upsetting. The coachee also has to recognize that he or she is adopting a learning role, and appreciate that this is not an inherent criticism of current abilities but rather an opportunity for growth and personal development" (Zeus & Skiffington, p. 130). Anita's knee-jerk reaction to coaching will probably be one of defensiveness, and as a coach, one must make sure Anita does not view the coach as a threat to her self-esteem, but just the opposite. She needs to understand that coaching would improve and support her rather than accentuate her shortcomings.

Without question, stimulating an underachiever like Anita will be challenging, but a thorough coaching plan, and exercises to address emotional blocks and other types of resistance should move Anita in the right direction.

### The Coaching Plan

According to Zeus and Skiffington (2002, p. 80), "Coaching is a personal relationship-a genuine connection which develops between two parties over time" and requires a good "fit" in order to be a successful endeavor. The Ivey Business Journal cites openness, trust and candor as elements that contribute to a successful coaching relationship. There must be a "willingness to speak the unspeakable" which can only be effective if a strong relationship has been established (Reid and Hubbell, 2005, p. 2). Positive human performance requires high level interpersonal communication and trust is the first building block (CMOE, 2005). In coaching, trust and interpersonal communication is a two-way street. Not only must the coachee be open to the coach's guidance, but the coach must trust that the coachee will execute. If the coachee fails to adhere to the suggested plan due to a lack of trust, the coaching process will be an exercise in futility.

Understanding that trust and frankness are building blocks for the coaching relationship, the first step would be to collaborate with Anita on a coaching plan to outline goals and expectations. It is important for Anita to know what she can anticipate during her coaching sessions, how she will be assessed, how many sessions she will require, and how long each session will take. She will want to know if the sessions are confidential and if any written documentation will go into her personnel file. These are appropriate questions that should be answered in order to establish rapport, trust, and dispel some of the mystery during this process.

During the first true coaching session with Anita, the coach would clarify roles and ask how coaching might assist Anita. Ironically, most people do not know what they want or where they need improvement, which is why coaching can accelerate performance (Tangri, 2005). The goal in the first session is to give Anita a roadmap to coaching and form a collaborative partnership where Anita's welfare is paramount. However, Anita also needs to be committed to the process and want to improve herself by exploring new ways of learning and examining her emotions. If Anita can do this, she is ready to move forward.

The second coaching session would focus on setting influence goals and understanding Anita's non-conforming blocking devices. How does she view promotions in her organization, and is she willing to take on greater responsibility at her office? To begin, the coach would list the times organizational performance expectations were higher than hers and emphasize how her talent adds to the organization (Jones, 2005). "Differing productivity expectations are a major source of dysfunction in the workplace" and focusing on the differences can resolve unmet expectations (Jones, p. 1). The coach should avoid being critical or finding fault with her current performance and resist telling her how to improve. More importantly, the coach requires Anita's perspective on why she applies for positions, and then changes her mind. Is it about confidence, laziness, fear, or does she not want to change? To draw Anita out, ask open-ended question and utilize push/pull energy.

Push/pull energy is best used when one must be assertive and persuasive, while being inspirational, collaborative, and concerned about the other person's views. It is a unique dichotomy applied to produce breakthroughs and meaningful exchanges by using a combination of hard and soft influence tactics (Vengel, 2000). Hard tactics are usually used by people in positions of authority, while soft tactics rely upon personal power and when collaboration is needed (Thacker, 1995). Push/pull energy tends to make people feel useful. When offered by a trustworthy and respected source, pull energy produces "buy in" and awakens the passion needed to perform. When decisions are based on pride, people tend to perform at higher levels (Cherney, 2005). Further, taking pleasure in one's own competence and talent, adds value to the situation. The coach should pull Anita in with open-ended questions encouraging feedback and dialogue. It is important to appeal to her passion, and in turn, offer her the rewards she desires such as money, position and pride. Anita needs to feel important on both a personal and professional level, and push/pull behavior leads to long standing effects and potential breakthroughs.

In order to acquire more insight into Anita's personality, the coach could ask her to complete a values profile. It is suspected Anita is not aware or has not thought about her purpose or values in the organization, and this may open her eyes to future goals.

Another tool for Anita to utilize is the SWOT analysis. The SWOT analysis is an acronym for strengths, weaknesses, options/opportunities, and threats; and is considered a useful tool for decision-making in particular situations. The SWOT analysis allows for proactive thinking by subjectively assessing data in a logical order, or grid (Chapman, 2005). By having Anita categorize her strengths, weaknesses, options, and threats, she will better understand her strengths, improve on her weaknesses, uncover opportunities, and manage or eliminate threats, thereby making the decision process more effective (Mindtools, 2005).

In subsequent coaching sessions with Anita, the coach will dialogue, problem-solve, and review self-limiting beliefs and habitual patterns. It is important to explore potential obstacles and get a feel for how Anita is advancing and what feelings are generated by these actions. It is the coach's responsibility to guide and help Anita along in this process, and allow her to arrive at the answers for execution of goal achievement. One day, the coach will be gone and Anita will have to make her own logical decisions. Therefore, it is incumbent upon the coach to equip Anita with the tools necessary to continue the process after the formal coaching session ends.

### Coaching Solutions

As discussed, Anita may experience emotional turmoil as a result of the coaching process. She may be plagued by fear, self-limiting beliefs, bad habits, and anger. Anita may lack confidence, education, and support to do her job more efficiently and be perfectly satisfied with her mediocre routine. Thus, Anita may be completely resistant to coaching and display defensive behaviors. All of these reactions are normal coping mechanisms that coaches often encounter, and the coach has numerous tools to help the coachee move past these behaviors and onto goal achievement.

First and foremost, Anita is an emotional person and will be deeply affected by the notion that somebody is interested in her welfare. Unfortunately, the reaction might not be positive. It is assumed that Anita's primary reaction will be one of defensiveness and a good coach knows, "...facing up to certain facts about ourselves can be uncomfortable, even upsetting. The coachee also has to recognize that he or she is adopting a learning role, and appreciate that this is not an inherent criticism of current abilities but rather an opportunity for growth and personal development" (Zeus and Skiffington, p. 130). In order to be truly accepting of the coaching process and the feelings associated with it, Anita must own and accept her emotions in order to move past them. Just because she is angry, does not mean she has to act upon that anger. If Anita does happen to act out her emotions, she must take responsibility for that behavior. Once emotions are identified, a coach can work with them, and one of the ways a coach can relate to a coachee is by relaying a personal experience that has been mastered. The coach must maintain an objective attitude at all times and determine which emotions to explore, their depth and not impose his/her own emotional language which could damage the coaching process (Zeus and Skiffington, 2003). Once emotions have been recognized and accepted, Anita's coping style and resistance should be explored. Understanding what triggers the emotion and the defense mechanism used to digest the information can result in extinguishing reflexive outbursts and bad behavior. It can also allow the coach to determine what is holding this underachiever back from true performance. In Anita's case, using a formal method to redefine the problems and emotions that keep her performance at a sub-standard level would be helpful.

The formal coaching process would encourage Anita to explore the reasons for her underachievement. Then, she would be asked to describe the actual state of the problem and the desired state. Next, Anita would need to verbalize the advantages and disadvantages of the actual state of her problem, and then the desired state. The coach would ask Anita open ended questions designed to elicit her feelings and emotions that prevent her from reaching the desired state. Together they would redefine the problem and preventative emotions until a strategy is determined to address the underlying issue. The purpose of a formal coaching process is to assist the coachee in overcoming her hesitation to reach the goal. Given Anita's clear boundaries, this would be a productive exercise for both coach and coachee.

What is holding Anita back? If Anita wants to change, and the problem lies with her fear, that concept must be addressed. Is she fearful that change may spotlight her deficiencies and make her position obsolete? Is she fearful of failing because she is unwilling to commit to learning new skills? Maybe she is fearful of success and undermining her relationship with her supervisor? Maybe her heritage or social foundation is getting in the way? Self-limiting beliefs need to be taken into consideration when looking for the personal brick wall holding Anita back from achieving more.

Self-limiting beliefs require the coach to challenge behavior and allow the coachee to explore discrepancies, contradictions and irrational ideas that may be the cause of goal blocking (Zeus and Skiffington, 2003). Anita needs to address her feelings about fear and describe the worst case scenario. Quite possibly, her response may change the way she views fear and allow her to move on in the process. Maybe her lack of self-confidence hinders her achievement and she needs to explain what hinders better performance. Facing one's fears is a daunting task and most individuals tend to ignore them because it is easier than facing them. However, owning and accepting one's fear, just like owning one's behavior and emotions is the only way to make inroads to achievement.

Let us say Anita shows up to coaching sessions, but continues to oppose change. She manages to address emotions and self-limiting beliefs on a superficial level and the true roadblock has not yet been uncovered. Additionally, Anita's work ethic has not improved and even declined. How would the coach deal with this resistance?

Resistance has been called "a defiance against anxiety" and is a major challenge facing all coaches (Zeus and Skiffington, p. 225). A technique entitled DxVxF>R can assist a coach in uncovering the coachee's dissatisfaction with a situation, explore vision, and help the coachee take action (Zeus and Skiffington, 2003). Ultimately, it will explain why the coachee is resistant to change. Anita should write down reasons regarding her current dissatisfaction with the situation. Next, she needs to visualize future possibilities and assess how the situation could be changed. Anita would need to delineate the actions she needs to take in order to make the vision come to fruition and overcome resistant factors (Zeus and Skiffington, 2003).

When coaching Anita, it is important to observe non-verbal cues like adaptors and affect that can reveal subconscious information about feelings and attitudes (Gibson, et al., 2006). Adaptors are "expressions used to adjust psychologically to the interpersonal climate of a particular situation" (Gibson et al., p. 431). These include drumming fingers on a table, twirling hair, and tapping a foot, which are considered stress relievers. Affect displays directly communicate emotions, and are often manifested in facial expressions and body positioning. Zeus and Skiffington (2002) propose certain techniques for working with non-verbal signals including pacing, mirroring, and leading. They also suggest asking if the coachee is uncomfortable and having them explain why. Freud stated "the unconscious mind of one human being can react upon that of another without passing through the conscious mind" which is how we arrive at body language (Zeus and Skiffington, p. 232). Conversely, if body language is interpreted incorrectly or relied upon too heavily, the coaching relationship can suffer. As such, Anita must never feel she is being manipulated or mimicked as this can break the bonds of trust and communication already achieved.

In this coaching relationship, both Anita and her coach will have a lot of work ahead of them. However, if they are committed to the process, and can overcome obstacles by using a multitude of techniques, Anita should no longer be an underachiever but a highly productive member of her organization.

## Coaching and Value Creation[23]

While all forms of diversity are important and coaches must understand each of their employees, the overall objective is the long-term creation of value for everyone involved and their organizations. A good read for the creation and

---

[23] Contributed by Les Carter, St. Edward's University. Book reviewed for the *Journal of Applied Management and Entrepreneurship*, 2008.

communication of value through an effective coaching and leadership philosophy is the concepts discussed by Lynda Gratton. Professor Gratton, in her 2007 book entitled *Hot Spots*, completes her trilogy of work focused on understanding why and how energy is created and dissipated in the workplace. Her analysis of the capacity and importance of human capital and its relevance in generating a positive, creative work environment reveals that relationships are the driving force. Through these relationships with fellow employees, value is created for the organization. *Hot Spots*, according to Gratton, are events where value is created through the consistent and passionate exploration of what is known and what is unknown. "Hot spots" are events, places and times where cooperation flourishes, creating great energy, innovation, excitement, and productivity in the department or organization. "Hot spots" can be teams, departments, organizations, conferences, cafeterias, production floors, hallways, and other places where associates are jointly working as a team in creative and collaborative manners. "Hot spots" cannot and should not be mandated, but they can be nourished, encouraged and supported in today's workplaces by all coaches, managers and leaders.

Gratton's research leads to insights that can benefit companies. Hot Spots evolve through four elements: cooperation, boundary stretching, an igniting purpose, and productive capacity. Gratton is a professor of management at London Business School leading the executive education program in Human Resources Strategy in Transforming Organizations. Her research efforts concentrate on linking academics and executives, including observing and recording activities in companies such as BP, Goldman/Sachs, Nokia, and OgilvyOne. Through this research she formulated her observations into the theory of how Hot Spots emerge. From these initial observations, Gratton formulated a research project that included 17 companies targeting more than 500 employees in 42 work teams in the United States, Europe, and Asia. While the goal of the book is to aid managers in their efforts to maximize value, the heavy research focus and discussion make it more suitable for coaching or executive education programs.

The author explains the four basic elements for Hot Spots, and concludes the book with the leader's role. In addition, there are several appendices that concentrate on research methodology and resources. The chapters develop and explain Gratton's components of Hot Spots: *Cooperative Mindset, Boundary Spanning, Igniting Purpose, and Productive Capacity*. Gratton created a formula for Hot Spots to indicate that the elements are not only synergistic, but multiplicative:

$$\text{Hot Spot} = (\textit{Cooperative Mindset} \times \textit{Boundary Spanning} \times \textit{Igniting Purpose}) \times \textit{Productive Capacity}$$

Gratton further explains the formula by stating that if any of the three elements inside the parentheses are lacking, then the potential energy for a Hot Spot is significantly reduced. The capacity of this potential energy to be converted into productive energy resulting in value creation is dependent on the productive capacity of the personnel within the Hot Spot.

In *The First Element: A Cooperative Mindset,* Gratton describes the importance of relationships in the workplace. For relationships to emerge as Hot Spots, the individuals must be willing to freely give their human capital – intellectual, emotional, and social – to others. They will do it willingly and not because they are directed to do so. Companies will have to focus on supporting and developing the individual needs and on the network of relationships that exist in the workplace to promote that willingness. Toward that goal, companies can encourage a mindset of cooperation by supporting practices that: encourage selection of cooperative employees, reward team performance, develop leadership practices that model cooperation, support mentoring and coaching, and foster informal activities that encourage a sense of mutuality.

*The Second Element: Boundary Spanning* proposes that when the exploration and combinations of knowledge of individuals in a Hot Spot reach across boundaries, then novel insights are generated that benefit the company. Value creation emerges when the strong relationship ties within Hot Spots exploit the knowledge of the individuals and cross boundaries to members of other teams. Methods to encourage this behavior can be through the promotion of cross functional tasks and project teams, development of practices that encourage cross boundary participation, informal socialization practices that create connections across boundaries, succession planning practices that involve lateral job moves, and selection and training about boundary spanning.

When the individuals in a team discover an interesting and exciting purpose, they are ignited and the energy created by their boundary spanning cooperation propels them to action. In *The Third Element: Igniting Purpose,* Gratton states that there are three ways to ignite the team – a question, a vision, or a task. A question sparks debate and activity. A vision creates a future state with clarity that requires energy and action. A task is meaningful, ambiguous, and developmental. At the center of these three ignition methods is conversation among peers. Leaders must ensure that the spark is ignited by using conversation, supported with insightful data, emphasizing values, and time and space for reflection.

For Hot Spots to become productive there are five practices that must be followed. Because the complexity of a Hot Spot as assessed by the extent of distance between members, the degree of difference between members, and the percentage of strangers, the emphasis on productive practices becomes greater for the company to benefit from the Hot Spot. The productive processes required include: appreciating the talents of individuals, making public commitments, quickly resolving conflicts, synchronizing times when people work in different time zones, and establishing a pace that allows for reflection and timeliness. Participants – leaders and team members – must make and keep public, voluntary, and explicit commitments.

For Hot Spots to evolve in companies, leaders must influence the practice and development of the process. By acting as Socrates, leaders will encourage teams to develop difficult questions by giving them confidence. The individuals will try to address problems with new vision and use discipline to resolve the issues. The leader must stimulate the creation of new friendships for personal networks to develop that will cross boundaries. Values and visions for the company come from leaders. Executives can design processes for the emergence of Hot Spots through five phases: locating Hot Spots, mapping the system, linking them to business goals, identifying leverage points, and taking action.

Gratton summarizes her research by stating that Hot Spots cannot be summoned forth or controlled, rather they must emerge by building relationships.

These relationships must contain the four elements of the Hot Spot (*Cooperative Mindset, Boundary Spanning, Igniting Purpose, and Productive Capacity)* and be supported within the company. Hot Spots are events where value is created by exploiting what is known and exploring what is unknown. Gratton's research leads to insights that can benefit companies. The concepts discussed in Hot Spots make for an excellent read and a great coaching tool for executive education seminars or programs.

*Summary*

Women, like most other minorities in the United States as well as many other countries, continue to face many biases, stereotypes, and the glass ceiling in the workplace. This chapter discussed some of the challenges and possible means of combating these types of challenges. The chapter discussed coaching as one solution for women and minorities. Coaching is more than a job; it is a relationship between two committed people dedicated to the same goals of growth and development. Whether female, Hispanic or from "outer space," the foundation of the coaching process is established with trust, collaboration, and high levels of interpersonal communication. Bacon and Spear (2003, p. 264) offer several principles to effectively coach females and other minorities in the workplace, and the following are some of their suggestions:

- Know the recent research regarding differences for women, people of color, socioeconomic disparities, and among groups of people from diverse sexual orientations.
- Ensure empathy for those who are different and are seen as "different."
- Recognize how stereotypes and other biases could be impacting you (the coach) and others who deal with a female or minority employee.
- Help coaches verbalize their personal experiences in the workplace.
- Recognize and discuss with the coachee the energy required to "fit in" or to "stand out."
- Use culturally sensitive coaching techniques to explore and plan for desired behavioral changes as needed.
- Provide networking opportunities for those who experience the isolation of being different.
- Be aware that coaching is about the coachee as well as the system. So, make sure the system is set up to help the coachee grow and develop.

Using a variation of processes and techniques, coaches can help minorities and underachievers determine what is important to them and what emotions and cultural norms may be holding them back from progress. It is not a process that occurs overnight, but one that takes time and commitment. Small successes lead to huge results, and underachievers can eventually have the self-confidence to achieve high level organizational goals, as well as significant personal achievements through coaching.

## Discussion Questions

1. Are there management and leadership differences in styles based on one's gender?
2. How are men different from women in terms of how they approach teamwork?
3. Men and women are different. What do men need to know about women? What do women need to know about men?
4. What is coaching and how can it be used to develop employees in the workplace?
5. What are some signs of employees who are not living up to their full potential?
6. What can managers do to provide employees with opportunities so they can reach their full potential?
7. What are some other suggestions, besides coaching underachievers, for getting employees to live up to their full potential?
8. Can men and women reach the top ranks of management using similar strategies? Discuss your thoughts, suggestions, and explanations.

# *CHAPTER 10*

## Communication: The Art of Listening

Communication takes place whether it is intended or not. Communication is the process of exchanging information in ways that ensure a mutual understanding of content and feelings; this includes being heard and understood. Effective communication can also be defined as the transfer of information from one person to another, without the meaning being changed. Often, communication takes the form of speaking and listening. While speaking is done for the purpose of being understood, listening is the real tool for understanding, learning and growing. Being a good listener sets you apart and helps you become a much better communicator while speaking. Have you ever had someone describe you as "a very good listener?" If so, it is a compliment that says quite a bit about you. Remember, people are like fruit; therefore, human beings are either green and growing (learning and thriving), or ripe and rotting (suffering mental stagnation and atrophy). Living a life of continuous learning pays a wealth of dividends, if people listen and use their learning effectively.

Every person without a hearing disability has been listening to what is said since before he or she was born. Yet, it is one of the most difficult skills of human interaction. Listening is not natural, which means that people have to work at it; and furthermore, not listening, like communication, is irreversible. What you don't hear is gone and you may not get the opportunity to listen again.

### Training and Development in Interpersonal Skills[24]

Today's national and multinational organizations are made up of diverse human beings from around the globe; these unique and diverse individuals tend to best operate within a group or team environment and need effective interpersonal communication skills in order to successfully achieve their stated organizational objectives with their peers. This implies interdependent roles and relationships that are unified in the actions of individuals who make up the organization; therein lies the challenge for management to effectively communicate with their people. An effective manager is one who possesses the right skills and personality for a given position within the organization. However, almost all experts agree that successful coaches will need effective communication and interpersonal skills in order for them to achieve their personal and professional goals. As such, understanding and acquiring effective interpersonal skills become very important for all managers if they are to

---

[24] Contributed by Lisa M. Mujtaba, University of Central Florida.

successfully achieve their goals and compete in today's global economy. Today's workplace is full of many challenges and managing people through effective communication is one of them. Another one of these challenges is how individuals relate to one another in the workplace through meaningful discussions and dialogue. The population of many countries and industries, today, seems to be very diverse, and this diversity presents a challenge, especially in the area of communication for the workplace. Interpersonal communication requires specific skills that leaders and coaches can master in order to effectively communicate with their employees, colleagues, suppliers, and superiors. However, before one can relate to another person, he or she would need to know him- or herself. Getting to know oneself can be time-consuming and difficult at times. We do not always realize the consequences of our choices or decisions, and for managers this is a very important aspect of everyday work life.

Stephen P. Robbins and Phillip L. Hunsaker's 2006 book, entitled *Training in Interpersonal Skills: Tips for Managing People at Work,* is an excellent tool for improving and helping individuals as coaches, leaders and managers to relate to their co-workers, staff, vendors, and other stakeholders. The beginning six chapters focus on one's inner-self. Chapters one through three discuss a person's self-awareness and self-management. The style that each person uses as a manager affects all of the people around him or her. It is important to know oneself and one's strengths and weaknesses as a manager. Chapters four through six are about various forms of communication, such as verbal, non-verbal and written communication. All these forms are a vital part of any organization. Communication is something every manager should strive to improve. In a diverse work environment, things that are said or written can more often be misinterpreted between individuals and people working in various departments within a large organization. Sometimes, this miscommunication can affect people outside of the organization such as media, vendors, and suppliers. Some of such miscommunications can be very costly to the organization and its stakeholders. Therefore, it is important for leaders and managers to master the skills of effective interpersonal communication.

One of the ways that managers make a difference to the company is if they have the correct skills to motivate their co-workers. Chapters seven through nine focus on motivation, coaching, counseling, mentoring, goal setting, and empowerment skills. Managers must realize that it is very difficult for themselves and their employees to be motivated without a specific goal to achieve. As such, the setting of specific goals and its timely communication to all relevant personnel become extremely critical. The next section of the book is about leading people. Leadership style, managing change politicking, and persuading skills are discussed so managers and leaders can effectively use them as they deem appropriate with their people in the organization.

Throughout *Training in Interpersonal Skills: Tips for Managing People at Work,* there are either self-examination questions or exercises that can be completed individually and in a group setting. The group exercises can be a great source for thought-provoking discussions and for managers to realize that there may be more than one way to deal with a situation. These group exercises are scattered throughout the book. However, they are even more emphasized in chapters 14 through 20 which focus on working with teams, running meetings, diversity, ethical decision making, creative problem solving, resolving conflict, and negotiations.

*Training in Interpersonal Skills* is an excellent resource book for a current or a new manager or coach that is attempting to enhance his or her influence and communication skills. The content of the book is very relevant to today's diverse and global workforce. A manager's self-awareness, knowing how he or she affects his or her company and actual communication skills could create a success for the department or it could lead to failure and costly misunderstandings. This book is recommended for managers, upcoming managers, coaches, business students, management scholars, leadership specialists, and others who are interested in effective interpersonal communication skills. Readers can learn and apply effective interpersonal skills with their team members in the workplace.

## Communication and the Art of Connecting with Others[25]

Communicating effectively is an essential element of success in today's world where the multiple factors for misunderstandings have converged in one familiar globally competitive and diverse social and cultural environment. The art of effective communication becomes an indispensable tool at all levels as we master connecting with people and businesses from varied social, cultural, linguistic, philosophical, and economic-political backgrounds. In a complex environment where survival becomes evermore difficult, we must seek and create opportunities by learning how to overcome differences, build rapport, and communicate effectively with anyone.

In *The Art of Connecting* (2006), Raines and Ewing contend that professionals can overcome differences, build rapport and communicate effectively by recognizing that (a) there is always a bridge as people do have more in common than they really think, especially in today's global business and social environments; (b) curiosity is the key since curious people direct attention outward, toward others, rather than focusing on themselves, hence creating avenues for initiating and maintaining good communication; (c) what you assume is what you get; there will always be an inability to connect if there is no rapport and if individuals perpetuate differences; (d) every individual is a culture; understanding that a person's identity is the sum of his or her unique experiences, both professional and personal; and (e) there are no strings attached; master communicators recognize that relationships form over time and communication requires development of rapport along the lines of meeting individual expectations where possible.

According to Raines and Ewing, the effective communicator brings individuals together through appreciating individual differences and building sound platforms and pathways to connection. The authors believe that great connections start with what we feel and think about people who are different from us, and they give us five paths to making good a connection: (a) clarifying your attention; knowing what you want to accomplish in the communication ahead of time in order to create focus and guide your interaction with the other party in a constructive direction; (b) noticing your own reactions; avoiding labeling or stereotyping because

---

[25] Book review provided by Donovan A. McFarlane, St. Thomas University.

of emotions, self-limiting beliefs and attitudes; (c) searching for familiarities; looking for common grounds with other individuals as common grounds help to build rapport and bring us together; (d) using cues; the effective communicator must use his or her eyes and ears and carefully watch for subtle and non-subtle signals others send; and finally, (e) experimenting and adjusting; great connections according to Raines and Ewing depend on continually trying something new, noticing the response, and adjusting based on feedback obtained.

According to Raines and Ewing, in communicating one needs to clarify and be constantly mindful of his or her intentions, which might be for example: to establish rapport, communicate respect for the person or his or her experience, increase openness between parties, transform an adversarial atmosphere into a cooperative one, deliver value, learn from the differences between parties, overcome hesitation, provide reassurance, obtain information, etc. In addition, it is important for the communicator to notice his or her reactions to the other parties in communication. These reactions might include fear and anxiety, defensiveness, self-righteousness, anger and impatience, judgmental reactions, apathy and boredom or even disgust or disappointment, etc. Searching for and finding similarities between the communicator and the party or parties communicating is also essential for connection. Oftentimes people will share things in common such as geographic connections, recalling learning experience, food, and a variety of things which can develop rapport and overcome any existing differences. Certain cues about people can indicate values or possible preferences, and these can be useful to the observant communicator. For example, cues such as hairstyle, clothing and jewelry, grooming, meeting place and environment, eye contact, energy level, and posture can help the effective communicator to discern things about his audience.

According to Raines and Ewing, the success of the communicator and being an effective communicator involves developing a point of view that balances "me", "you" and "they" perspectives, that is, first-person point of view, second-person point of view, and the third-person point of view. Raines and Ewing contend that effective communicators connect with others by "changing perspective" and "mentally stepping out of their own experiences to observe the interaction as if they were outside observers." They believe that changing perspective can improve the quality of our interactions. Also, the effective communicator learns how to work with differences in groups by learning about the audience, establishing rapport and obtaining feedback; these are keys to connecting in groups. In addition, Raines and Ewing teach us how to overcome differences, build rapport and communicate and connect effectively with others by using learning activities and feedback assessment.

Raines and Ewing's book present numerous examples of effective communicators to demonstrate how we can develop the mastery skills of communicating in diverse environments, accepting diverse perspectives; me, you and they; first, second and third person as we attempt to convey information, feelings or ideas. The book will help coaches and leaders to better develop rapport with employees and business partners, as well as in communicating their goals and vision.

## Effective Communication

Synergistic teams have members that share information with each other in a clear manner while building effective relationships by speaking with each other and listening well. In other words, all the members tend to communicate well with each other. *Communication* is simply exchanging information. *Effective Communication* is sharing information with others in such a way that they understand what you are saying. The goal of effective communication is mutual understanding. In a team environment, the goal of effective communication is to make sure each team member is clear, concise, and credible in what s/he says to others. Getting one's point across and getting the results one wants requires that one build credibility, use logic and radiate positive emotional power. Using the power of asking effective questions is a good strategy for building credibility as an effective team member or leader in a diverse work environment. In order to build trust and credibility, managers can ask the following questions and make sure that they can be answered with a positive or yes answer:

- Do people know what to expect from you? Test whether your employees and colleagues know what to expect from you.
- Do people believe you do what you say? Audit your consistency in living up to your word.
- Do people believe you pay attention to their interests? Evaluate how well you show people you are representing their interests.
- Do people believe you are competent to carry out what you say? Test whether your competence might be in question.

Building trust and credibility takes time and, just like a strong character, they can be chiseled over time by consistently showing courage, honesty, and compassion in dealing with others.

One should always consider the basic elements of communication when encoding messages. The basic elements of communication includes the message, the sender, the receiver, the medium for communication, the language of the sender and receiver, the environment, and perceptual filters of all individuals involved. With regard to the basics of communication, one can consider and discuss the following questions and variables:

- Who will communicate: the appropriate addressor?
- Whom: the appropriate person or persons to whom the message should be communicated – the addressee/s or audience.
- What: appropriate content of the message.
- How: appropriate language, medium, and style, for communicating the message.
- When: appropriate time for communicating the message.
- Where: appropriate location for communicating the message.
- Why: appropriate reasons for communicating the message through the chosen medium.
- Perceptual filters: what is the receiver's cultural background and how has he or she been socialized?

Effective communication and listening skills are critical for managers of a culturally-diverse workforce. Associates have the right to know how they are performing and managers must clearly convey their progress to them on regular basis.

Managers and team leaders should give continuous feedback to associates through effective coaching. Managers and team leaders should provide effective feedback to associates, based on the thoughts generated from factual observations and analysis of their performance. One should remember that effective feedback is clear, specific, timely, practical, and sincere. It is best to make individualized feedback regarding performance private, positive and performance oriented.

Effective communicators prepare the individual for the occasion where the performance is an issue, by letting them know, that "we need to discuss your performance because it is important." During the session, effective managers and leaders do not "beat around the bush" and they get right to the point. They do not get "side tracked" and stay focused on the performance issue until they get a specific commitment and plan from the individual to improve it. The leader / manager can end the session by summarizing the performance issue/challenge, repeating the expectations, reviewing the specific plan which the employee created, and wishing the individual success with it. Of course, the leader / manager needs to follow-up to make sure the expectations are met.

### Miscommunication through the Hierarchy

We can communicate vertically or horizontally in our organizations, communities, and families. However, there are some mishaps that can happen when communicating through letters and the chain of command. Effective coaches must avoid such mishaps and misunderstanding. The following is an example of what happened while communicating through the hierarchy (presented by Carole M. Howard, 1998 in *Excellence in Management Conference, Chicago*).

*From city manager to assistant manager*: Next Thursday at 10:00 am, Halley's Comet will appear over this area. This is an event which occurs only once every 75 years. Call the department heads and have them assemble their staffs on the city hall lawn and explain this phenomenon to them. If it rains, then cancel the day's observation and have the employees meet in the council chambers to see a film about the comet.

*From assistant manager to department heads*: By order of the city manager, next Thursday at 10:00 am, Halley's Comet will appear over your city hall. If it rains, then cancel the day's operation and report to the council chambers with your staffs where you will show films, a phenomenal event which occurs every 75 years.

*From department heads to supervisors*: By order to the phenomenal city manager at 10:30 next Thursday, Halley's Comet will appear in the council chambers. In case of rain over the city hall, the manager will give another order, something which occurs only every 75 years.

*Notice on the bulletin board*: Next Thursday at 10:30 the city manager will appear in our council chambers with Halley's Comet, something which occurs every 75 years. If it rains, the manager will cancel the comet and order us all out of our city hall.

*From employees to friends*: When it rains next Thursday at 10:30 over the city hall, the phenomenal 75 year old city manager will cancel all work and appear before the whole staff in the council chambers accompanied by Bill Halley and the Comets.

### Listening and Management Communication

While many individuals in the workplace believe they are effective listeners, very few actually are listening well. Much of the time people think they are listening depending on the human ear to absorb what is being said. This type of thinking might be analogous to reasoning that because one has eyes s/he is automatically able to read and comprehend what is being read. Of course, this type of logic is false and not necessarily true. Inadvertent bad habits such as interruptions, allowing distractions, jumping to conclusions, daydreaming or giving in to boredom are barriers that prevent people from becoming attentive listeners. Some individuals are usually ignoring speakers, pretending they are listening, or they are selectively listening to the person who is talking instead of being active participants in the listening process. For a quick test and reflection, write *"T"* for true or *"F"* for false next to each of the statements in Table 10.1 about listening in order to check your present awareness of this important communication skill.

Table 10.1 – Listening Awareness Inventory

\_\_\_ 1. People who get the facts right are always good listeners.
\_\_\_ 2. Listening involves more than using your ears.
\_\_\_ 3. Hearing is the same as listening.
\_\_\_ 4. Good listening comes naturally when one pays attention.
\_\_\_ 5. You can listen well and do other things at the same time.
\_\_\_ 6. Posture affects listening.
\_\_\_ 7. Most listening distractions can be controlled.
\_\_\_ 8. If you cannot remember something, you were not really listening.
\_\_\_ 9. Listening is a passive activity.
\_\_\_ 10. Good listeners never interrupt.

Knowledge of the facts and listening are not necessarily the same since one can get the facts without being a good listener. As stated in the second statement of Table 10.1, listening does require more than just one's ears as it is an active process of hearing, processing and matching what is heard with the sender's nonverbals and tone of voice. So, the second, sixth and seventh statements in Table 10.1 are true and the remainder are false.

In order to become aware of the active listening process, at the basic level, managers should understand that hearing, listening, and effective listening are different terms and concepts since their definitions vary. For example:

- *Hearing* is the process of receiving sound waves through the ear and brain. Hearing does not equal listening because listening is more than just hearing.
- *Listening* is the active process of mentally interpreting sound waves in the brain. People focus their hearing upon stimuli they wish to attend to and must interpret them into meaning and action.
- *Effective listening* is purposefully paying attention to and desiring to understand the other person's point of view. Effective listening requires giving and receiving feedback. *Feedback* is verbal or nonverbal response to

an object, a message, behavior, or performance that often affects the receiver either positively or negatively.

Managers must go beyond simply hearing and listening to effectively understand others. The best way for one to progress toward effective listening is to make some conscious changes to become better. According to experts, to listen with concentration requires that one become more aware of the degree of communication, both its verbal and nonverbal elements. To listen effectively one must hear and select information from the speaker, give it meaning, determine how one should feel about it, and, if appropriate, respond in a matter of seconds. The speakers' purpose must be understood as it influences the way one listens and how it is perceived. The speaker and the listener must have the same purpose if communication is to be effective. Many decades ago, the research of Dr. Albert Mehrabian showed that 7% of communication tends to be through the words (what one speaks), 38% is the vocal (how one speaks), and 55% is through nonverbal.

There are varying types of listening such as casual, attentive and empathetic, each increasing in level of concentration. *Casual listening* uses minimal attention, as with television or radio. *Attentive listening*, for instance, requires analysis of information, remembering content, and questioning the speaker; while in *empathetic listening*, there is full understanding of the speaker's views, values, attitudes, emotions, and feelings.

Listening style reflects the attitude and behavior of the listener and can be a barrier to good communication. Evaluation, interaction of an individual listener, the circumstances, and other persons in the process can all be barriers to effective listening. Anxiety and a chain reaction or trains of associations are psychological processes that can interfere with listening. Anxiety makes the mind wander from the current communication situation that maybe related to the immediate circumstance or unrelated to the specific encounter and becomes the preoccupation that prevents listening. The chain reaction or train of associations occur more frequently the less interested the listener is in the topic as the mind begins to follow its own train of associations rather than that of the other speaker.

The speaker's style, verbal and non-verbal expressions, clothes, mannerisms or age can also have a negative or positive impact on listeners. Speakers who use rhetorical questions may create inattention on the part of listeners as the listener may have begun to answer the question differently, now following a different train of thought to its logical conclusion rather than the speaker's train of thought.

The listening aspect of managerial communication has implications throughout the organization. For the managers, not listening means a significant loss in reduced contact with workplace reality, while for the employees a manager not listening or lack of attention means loss of morale at not being heard and understood. Managers must want to listen; they must also show employees that they want to listen, and allocate time for listening. To listen effectively is to reach clarity of understanding, and to understand clearly is to respond appropriately. In order for one to respond appropriately communication has to be enhanced, which is through support cooperation. To support cooperation is to improve morale that can lead to increased job commitment. To increase job commitment is to focus on productivity.

Good listening is a key to success in any business environment. Listening effectively can increase income, improve company's profits, keep one aware of what is going on in the organization, make an individual more promote-able, increase job satisfaction and improve the ability to solve problems. Poor listening is one of the most significant problems facing businesses today. Business relies on clear communication, when communication breaks down, costly mistakes are made. Organizations pay for mistakes caused by poor listening with lower profits, and consumers pay for the same mistakes with higher prices.

### Listening Basics

Listening is a gift which does not cost anything; yet lack of it will. Listening is a skill that anyone can learn and develop. Listening is about caring and acknowledging the other person; so we should do it often and with sincere and honest intentions. Most people listen at about up to 25% of their capacity. So, we have a tendency to ignore, forget, distort or incorrectly interpret 75% of what we hear. Today's business environment has an abundance of information that cross one's ears and most of it is blocked by the subconscious mind because they add little to no value to the current work process. This process, through the perceptual filers, conditions the mind to constantly block information that is not valuable at the present moment. The negative side of this is that we lose much valuable information because of the tendency to block things and not overload ourselves. Therefore, making an effort to clearly communicate is important in today's society, in personal events and in business settings. Miscommunication can be very costly in both one's personal and professional lives. In general, an average person is likely to daydream about 50% of the time. If you wander at least once per minute, it is too much. You would need to force yourself to listen harder and concentrate by improving your listening skills. Not listening effectively can cause many costly mistakes and hurt feelings. For example, a dispatcher routed a fleet of drivers to deliver building material to the wrong state due to miscommunication. The dispatcher heard the city (Portland) but not the state (Maine). So, eight trucks full of building material went to Portland, Oregon which is about 3,000 miles off course. This mistake cost the company over $100,000 and perhaps created many disappointed customers who did not get the materials on time. Listening is about caring and motivating. People normally do their best when they know someone is listening (caring) or paying attention to them. This was proven in the Hawthorn studies where worker productivity went up when the amount of lighting was increased or decreased. In other words, employees appreciated the fact that they were being given attention and consultants talked with them about their views, thoughts, and work environment.

The Christopher's in *Prayer to be a Better Listener* wrote that "We do not really listen to each other, at least not all the time. Instead of true dialogue, we carry on two parallel monologues. I talk. My companion talks. But, what we are really concentrating on is how to sound good, how to make our points strongly, how to outshine the person with whom we are talking." The tendency to speak and make our points might be one of the major causes of not listening effectively. Because of this tendency, we listen in different ways and use various levels of listening at different situations. The following are the five identified levels of listening which are discussed in most communication courses.

- *Ignoring.* Not paying any attention, sleeping, talking, etc. Not caring. You don't receive messages at this level. You don't concentrate on listening.
- *Pretending.* Giving the appearance of listening, occasional nod or a response. You give the appearance of listening. You give an occasional head nod or similar form of body language to make the sender think that you're listening, but you're really not.
- *Selecting.* Grasping certain key words here or there but not listening. You select parts of the message that you feel are important. You don't hear or you instantly lose other parts of the message.
- *Attending or active listening.* Listening intently, grasping the content and perhaps even repeating back what you heard--also called "Active listening," listening with ears for the facts. You're focusing on the message being communicated. You're listening for content and asking questions for clarification.
- *Empathic.* The highest level of listening. Listening with the eyes and the heart for feelings and emotions. It is seeing how the sender sees the situation. You're now seeking to understand the emotions and feelings of the sender, as well as understand the content of the message being communicated. This is the highest level of listening.

Studies show that the first three of the five levels of listening are the levels people most commonly use. It is at the fourth and fifth levels of listening where effective listening takes place.

### *Autobiographical responses*

When one communicates with others, he or she tends to listen only enough to be able to respond. We often do not listen to understand or empathize. Since we listen in this way, the responses are likely to be "autobiographical." That is, our responses come out of our own experiences and perceptual filters. Stephen Covey (1989), author of *The Seven Habits of Highly Effective People*, grouped autobiographical responses into four categories: advise, probe, interpret, and evaluate. The acronym for these responses is "A PIE." We have a tendency to use these autobiographical responses when we are in conversation with others. A major barrier to effective communication can be autobiographical responses. *Autobiographical responses* are the statements or judgments that you make about others based on your experiences. Autobiographical responses aren't always bad, but they are inappropriate when you use them before you've reached understanding. We all tend to diagnose a problem before having enough information and this can lead to miscommunication. As an effective communicator, your goal should be to first understand the other person and then have the other person understand you. These autobiographical barriers are being discussed to help you recognize and eliminate them.

- *Advise*: Telling others what they should do based on our (biased) perspective. We advise when we make recommendations or suggestions based on our own past experiences.
- *Probe*: Asking questions to direct the conversation toward things that come from our frame of reference. We probe when we question the speaker to find similarities with our past experiences.
- *Interpret*: Explaining why they are acting the way they do based on our experiences. When we interpret we are explaining others' behaviors and actions' based on our own past actions.
- *Evaluate*: Judging (agreeing or disagreeing with) the situation, which could be verbal, facial, or through body posture, based on one's opinion. We are evaluating when we judge by either agreeing or disagreeing based on our own values.

None of these autobiographical responses meet the needs of the person with whom we are trying to communicate. The one thing the four autobiographical responses have in common is the assumptions we make about others based on our own experiences, which can become a barrier to effective listening and overall communication. The main connection between multicultural communication competency and autobiographical responses is our "mental tapes or perceptual filters." If, in a multicultural conversation, we are using autobiographical responses, we may very well be operating on "automatic pilot." Of-course, being on "automatic pilot," or responding based on past conditioning, is never effective when communicating with people and making decisions regarding others.

### *Listening without Judgment*

Listening is an active process rather than a passive one. However, most often, individuals think about what they are going to say next instead of actually listening. Furthermore, instead of trying to understand, individuals are often conditioned to advice, probe, interpret, and evaluate (APIE) what the other person is saying. The key to effective listening is to avoid pre-judging the other person or what he or she is saying, and consciously focus on understanding before trying to present one's own perspective.

At least half of all communication time is spent listening. Studies show that we listen more than we perform any other activity except breathing. Yet we often take listening for granted, never realizing that it is a skill that can be learned. Listening is:

- Receiving information through your ears (and eyes).
- Giving meaning to that information.
- Deciding what one thinks (or feels) about that information. And
- Responding to what one hears and sees.

We listen at about 25% of our potential, which means we ignore, forget, distort, or misunderstand 75% of what we hear. Poor listening is a significant problem in business today because business relies on clear communication. When communication breaks down, costly mistakes occur. The good news is that you can always assess your listening skills and improve upon them. For example, to get a numerical score about your listening ability you can rate yourself on the listening behaviors using the Listening Scale Survey (LSS – located at the end of this chapter).

Listening requires paying attention. Hearing is non-selective and involuntary. However, when you choose to listen, it is on purpose. From the constant noise around us, we select what we want to listen to because the information is determined to be useful. This information moves from short-term memory to long-term memory. Short-term memory is a "holding pen" for incoming signals from the senses. In order to protect us from too much stimulation short-term memory has a limited capacity and is easily disrupted.

For instance, a mail clerk would not likely retain much information from a technical discussion about data transport protocols because he or she would have no use for the message. The information would probably be held in short-term memory for 1 to 30 seconds and then dismissed. If the information we hear is not recognized and selected for processing, it is dismissed from short-term memory and not remembered. In order for information to move to long-term memory, one must *choose* to listen.

Paying attention means not interrupting others and not being driven by emotions. Words, issues, situations and/or personalities trigger people emotionally. When these issues trigger one's emotional "hot buttons," verbal messages become distorted, either positively or negatively. When issues are emotional they can become or create barriers to effective listening. When hot buttons are activated, one tends to tune out, distort, or prejudge these emotionally charged messages. This can cause one to interrupt the speaker. Both listeners and speakers have mental filters (such as biases, attitudes, perceptions, memories, etc.), which help or hinder the interpreting process of listening.

Questions are a listener's most powerful tool. With the right questions, you can manage a conversation, clarify what you are hearing and elicit more information. Use open-ended questions to probe for more information. Open-ended questions encourage the speaker to explain, expand, describe, explore, or elaborate. Use open-ended questions when:

◊ The speaker is uncommunicative or reluctant.
◊ You need to bring out the other person's concerns, ideas, or feelings.
◊ You need to understand the big picture.
◊ You're not certain exactly what information you need, or you need to clarify some points.
◊ You're trying to build involvement, trust, or rapport. And
◊ You want to promote self-discovery.

Watch someone who listens attentively. This individual probably makes eye contact and/or focuses on the other person while actively listening. Effective communicators listen with their eyes as well as their ears. They acknowledge the person by nodding and making attentive noises from time-to-time. When acknowledging what you hear and, as appropriate, make sure you:

◊ Express your point of view.
◊ Present your evidence without backing the other person into a corner.

◊   Explain why.
◊   Acknowledge other people's feelings.
◊   Try to see the other person's point of view.
◊   Agree where you can.

Managers, leaders, teammates, and employees can listen actively to their team members and colleagues by practicing the skills of empathic listening as emphasized by Dr. Carl Rogers and Dr. Stephen R. Covey. The best forms of listening are active and empathic listening as they can lead to learning, understanding, and higher levels of trust among people. One can use the active listening process to understand what is being said in a professional work environment. However, when emotions are involved, when the listener does not feel understood, and when the speaker is not clear about what is being said then it is best to use the empathic listening process.


**Listening Empathically**

Empathic listening has been at the forefront of communication research since the 1960s. It was first discussed by Carl Rogers. It has also been known as the Rogerian communication exercise. Dr. William James of Harvard University says, "The deepest need of every human being is to be understood." We often fail to take the steps necessary to really understand our family members, associates, peers, and customers. We have a tendency to resolve the situation before making an accurate identification of the problem. If you have a tendency to solve problems before knowing the problem or its cause, then you're not alone. Sometimes our cultures condition us to listen, not with the intent to understand, but with the intent to respond. Therefore, it is best to fully explore emphatic listening process and skills to help you reach a higher level of understanding so that you may respond effectively and appropriately when interacting with others.

Empathy means compassion, commiseration, understanding, and emotional identification. While listening empathically you simply reflect the other person's feeling and sayings. *Reflect* means to think seriously about or contemplate something. *Empathic listening* is the process of listening to both the content and the feelings of a message. You reflect on the meaning and emotions of the message and then restate your understanding to the sender. The process of empathic listening gives you the opportunity to reach true understanding in communication. Empathic listening can be very effective in achieving mutual understanding among two or more parties. However, empathic listening is not a panacea for major problems or personality concerns. It is simply a process that can lead to better understanding of what is being communicated. There are many examples of empathic listening leads or phrases you may use when you are applying the process of reflective listening. Some of the listening leads can include the following:

• As I hear it, you feel as if. . .
• To me, it's as if you're saying you want. . .
• What it sounds like you're saying is, you need. . .
• If I'm hearing you correctly, you feel that. . .

- I'm not sure, but it seems as though you desire. . .

As you can see, empathic listening responses seek to understand the feelings and emotions of the sender along with the content meaning. Empathic listening process is especially useful when there are emotional topics being discussed.

Overall, *empathic listening* is the process of discovering the sender's perspective, thoughts, and feelings by encouraging the sender to self-disclose through active listening and/or empathy. Empathic listening involves listening with the eyes and heart for feelings and listening with the ears for facts, thoughts and views. Since performance discussions between colleagues, managers and employees can be emotional, it is best to master the skill of empathic listening. It is important that listeners are caring, gentle and understanding in such situations without losing focus of the performance issue. Effective listeners use the empathic listening skills which can be done by:

- Repeating the message.
- Summarizing the content of the message.
- Expressing or reflecting on the feelings of the message.
- Restating both the content and feelings of the message in your own words.
- Using good judgment with regard to determining which of the above steps are appropriate for each situation.

### Benefits of Listening

Effective listening is not a passive activity nor easy. As a matter-of-fact, it is hard work, mentally draining and requires 100% of one's attention. The following are some of the reasons one should commit to this hard work called *listening*.

1. *You can learn by listening.* You can learn about the subject being discussed and the person speaking if you consider his/her emotions, expressions, temperament, personality, word choice, reactions, pace, non-verbal, and so on.
2. *You can gain more friends by listening.* The speaker will appreciate you more for letting him/her talk and for listening actively or empathically to him/her while s/he expresses him/herself.
3. *Listening can reduce tension.* Giving the other person a chance to get his/her problem or viewpoint off his/her chest may help to "clear the air" of tension and hostility.
4. *Listening helps solve mutual problems and resolve disagreements.* You cannot agree or disagree intelligently with the other person until you understand his/her point of view. Remember, understanding the problem is often half of the solution.
5. *Listening leads to better work and cooperation from others.* When a person feels that you are really interested in him/her and his/her problems, thoughts and opinions, s/he respects you and is inspired to cooperate with you.
6. *Listening helps you make better decisions.* Through listening you can draw upon the experience of people who also work in the same area, thus helping you develop better judgment as well as to uncover additional facts.

7. *Listening can help you do a better job.* Try asking the people you work with, work for, or work alongside for suggestions as to how you can do a better job, and then listen. You may be surprised at the good ideas you can pick up by applying this suggestion.

8. *Listening can prevent major problems and catastrophes.* When we talk before we listen to the other person in a discussion, we stick our necks out, make decisions we later wish we could withdraw, state criticisms we later regret, or commit ourselves to actions we can not or will not carry out. So, listen, understand, confirm and then speak if necessary.

9. *Listening can build self-esteem and self-confidence.* If you listen to and understand the opponent's arguments, you can be confident of accurate rebuttal. If you listen, you can spot "loopholes" in the other person's argument, and gain confidence in your own case.

10. *Listening can give you time to think.* The average person speaks about 150 to 250 words per minute and your capacity to listen is probably about 400 to 600 words per minute. You can use this extra time not only to improve your understanding of what is being said, but to think up answers, make decisions, and plan prospective actions, when appropriate.

### *Summary*

More and more organizations are recognizing employees as their most important asset. It is, therefore, incumbent on management to factor mutual understanding among employees as a source of motivation and teamwork. When it comes to true empowerment and its effective communication to the workforce, leaders should recognize the significance of employee input to the employee, the team, and the organization. It is interesting to note that the principle of mutual understanding impacts society at all levels.

Human beings have communicated for thousands of years; yet miscommunications seem to happen despite so much experience with it. Most people agree that communication skills are extremely important, especially for a culturally diverse workforce and their effective management. The chapter stated that effective communication is the process of exchanging information in ways that ensure a mutual understanding of content and feelings; this includes being heard and understood. This chapter described the various levels of listening, barriers to effective listening, and detailed out the skill of empathic listening for effective communication and negotiation with one's family members, friends, as well as one's colleagues in a the workforce.

### *Discussion Questions*

1. What is effective communication? How is "effective communication" different from "communication"?

2. Can one effectively be listening, thinking and talking with someone at the same time? Discuss.

3. How is listening different from hearing?

4. What are some common barriers to listening? How can one overcome such barriers in order to listening effectively?
5. What are autobiographical responses and how do they impact listening?
6. What are three benefits of listening? Provide personal examples of how you have benefited from listening.
7. What is active listening?
8. What is emphatic listening?
9. Try the skill of emphatic listening with four friends and colleagues and document your results. Try this technique with people that you do not know and document the results.
10. Is empathic listening easy, difficult, natural, or does it require conscious focus? Describe your thoughts as per your experience with your colleagues, family members, people you meet for the first time, and professionals in the community.

## Listening Scale Survey

You can rate yourself on the listening behaviors using the Listening Scale Survey (LSS) and the following guidelines:

4= Almost always
3= Most of the time
2= Some of the time
1= Almost never

Place a check mark in the appropriate box. Multiply the rating number at the top of the columns by the number of check marks in that rating area and record the results in the sub-total columns. Add the sub-totals and place the results in the area marked "Total Overall."

| | When listening I do the following: | 4 | 3 | 2 | 1 |
|---|---|---|---|---|---|
| 1. | I pay attention, even though the subject may bore me | | | | |
| 2. | I refrain from finishing the other person's sentences | | | | |
| 3. | I wait for the speaker to finish before evaluating the message | | | | |
| 4. | I maintain eye contact | | | | |
| 5. | I listen for feelings as well as subject matter | | | | |
| 6. | I show nonverbal responses to demonstrate I'm listening: nodding, smiling, leaning forward | | | | |
| 7. | I give brief verbal responses: "Uh-hum, M-m-m, Oh" | | | | |
| 8. | I stop myself from interrupting the one speaking to me | | | | |
| 9. | I seek to reduce or eliminate distractions | | | | |
| 10. | I ask questions only to clarify something said | | | | |
| 11. | I demonstrate I have an open mind and do not respond negatively to the other's ideas or feelings | | | | |
| 12. | I often paraphrase what I hear to make sure I have heard it correctly | | | | |
| 13. | I work to make myself really want to listen | | | | |
| 14. | I listen carefully to understand the main message | | | | |
| 15. | I maintain emotional control, no matter what is said | | | | |
| | *Sub-totals* | | | | |
| | *Total Overall* | | | | |

Now, after totaling the scores see next page for the results.

## *Listening Scale Survey Results*

Now that you have determined your overall total from the Listening Scale Survey (LSS), you can use the following ranges of numbers to determine your listening score area:

| | |
|---|---|
| 50-60 | Congratulations! You are an excellent listener. Keep listening intently with everyone. |
| 40-49 | Good going! You are a good listener, and you could be even better. |
| 30-39 | Keep working on it. Listening skills will help you solve problems. Practice the skills of active and empathic listening when you can. |
| 15-29 | You really should get serious about learning to listen. Take classes and learn active listening skills. Try to consciously focus on hearing others and what they are trying to communicate both verbally and non-verbally. Once you have mastered active listening techniques, then, focus on using empathic listening skills when emotions are involved, when you don't understand the speaker, and when the other person does not feel understood. |

# CHAPTER 11

## Conflict and Negotiation Management

Effectively resolving employee and interpersonal conflicts are an important and mission-critical aspect of a manager's responsibilities. Effective coaches and managers are always focused with a balance of concern for people and production. As such, besides resolving conflicts through negotiation practices, effective managers are performance-focused and developmental in their leadership and management styles as they are first and foremost concerned about the well-being and success of their employees. Besides appropriate training and employee development practices, managers work toward coaching employees in the "right" direction to meet acceptable professional and performance standards in the workplace. Furthermore, coaches and managers need to understand conflict, and their own conflict management and negotiation styles, in order to develop an effective high performing team in the department.

### Self Awareness and Conflict Management[26]

Howard M. Guttman, the principal of *Guttman Development Strategies Inc.*, specializes in building high-performance teams, executive coaching, and strategic and developmental alignment. Guttman's (2004) article, "Conflict Management," relates to the key roles leaders must play when managing differences in a group and when attempting conflict solving. Not only must the leader play role model, but he or she must also have the ability to help others deal with conflict by "making them accountable for confronting issues and working toward solutions" (Guttman, 2004). The conflicting issues must be brought up to the open as soon as possible for quicker resolution, taking into consideration how it is presented to the involved individuals or group, the words and body language used when surfacing the problem on hand, and by avoiding the exclusion of other key players.

The leader must encourage self-awareness in the group in relation to their performance by asking themselves: how clear the team sees its goals, how effectively is the team accomplishing these goals, how the individuals in the team work together, how conflicts or differences are handled, and how individuals in the team feel about their role and accountability on the team. Leaders coaching on conflict situations must focus on becoming sensitive to the issues, in identifying the patterns of

---

[26] Contributed Dr. Rafael Gonzalez (M.D.), Nova Southeastern University.

interaction among the individuals and their behaviors, in helping the individuals in acknowledging responsibility, and in identifying ways of relieving the pressure the situation brings on the team without deviating from confrontation. According to experts such as Guttman, "Confronting the conflict directly carries the greatest benefit, at the least cost."

Guttman identifies four patterns of behavior when dealing with conflict: *plays the victim*-stays quiet and acts powerless; *leaves*-physically disappears; *change oneself*-changes positions or just lets go; and, *confronting*-addresses the issue openly. To better achieve a solution to the conflict, some rules of engagement must be observed: do not bring in a third party rescuer, do not recruit supporters of your point of view, solve the issue or let it go, do not accuse in absentia, and do not take issues personal. Mastering, and being able to transfer these conflict management skills, must be part of the leader's coaching tools. Conflicts arise in every team and work environment every day. Leaders must be able to help manage the particular situations that are being confronted, and mainly address the importance of not suppressing confrontation. By doing this, tensions are relieved and the team can go back to focusing on the goals.

The situation has to do with the integration of a group of physicians, that was already working at a unit recently acquired and whose individuals' goals do not align with those of the organization.

The scenario presents several issues that can be a source of confrontation and conflict with this group of physicians that are to be integrated. In using the coaching skills recommended by Guttman, the issues this case presents must be handled in a very sensitive way. The physicians have been working at the unit for many years and feel threatened when the issues are brought up. So, the approach to the issues on hand must be first directed toward value-sharing and goals alignment. Allowing them to come up with the conflicts as an exercise may help reveal, acknowledge, and become self-aware of issues that they did not see as problems in the past. The individuals in the group must be helped to clarify the goals now in common, to rate their capability to effectively achieve those goals, to think about working together with new members of the team, and to identify and confront the conflicting issues the new working relationship and work structure bring on to them. Different behaviors may be adopted by the different members of the team. In this particular case the four mentioned behavior patterns have been manifested so far, and practically all the "rules of engagement" (Guttman, 2004) have been broken.

Where can one integrate these techniques or skills in the coaching process? In relation to the case presented and following the coaching process phases by Zeus and Skiffington (2002), the techniques depicted by Howard M. Guttman can be integrated during phase two-*Action planning*, and phase three-*The coaching cycle*. The second phase of the coaching process involves the establishment of goals and values as discussed by the coach and the coachees. It is during this phase, that issues concerning feelings and behaviors that can have an impact on the work to be done are explored. This is the part of the process where goals and values are established, and where one can identify who and what can be affected by the planned changes (Zeus & Skiffington, p. 76-77). Value driven behaviors should have a positive impact on the coaching, but goal alignment may be negatively affected by the conflicts that need to be revealed and confronted.

It is during the second and third steps of the fourth phase of the coaching process-*the coaching cycle* (Zeus & Skiffington, p. 78-79)-that conflicting issues should be deeply explored by reviewing obstacles and behavior patterns identification. It is during this phase where effective communication is the gold standard technique, and active listening becomes of great importance as it facilitates the coachees manifest their conflicting issues, and help them become self aware of behavior patterns that they did not perceive as conflicting ones.

## Conflict Management[27]

Conflict is a reality of life, which everyone faces at one time or another. Leaders, managers, and team members thus need to understand the causes and effects of conflicts and how to respond in the best interest of all members concerned. Conflict is often a characteristic of change. Any attempt to adjust the status quo in an organization can result in conflict. If effectively handled, conflict can be a healthy way of airing differences. However, constant conflict can be anxiety-inducing, debilitating, and destructive. Conflict occurs within and between individuals, groups, teams, organizations, and societies. An effective conflict resolution process includes recognition, awareness, and choice.

Individuals react differently to conflict. Some people seem to thrive on conflict while others abhor it; yet, still a few other individuals can remain unruffled by the most conflicting situations. Individuals also deal with conflict in different ways, some people attack, while others tend to defend. However, most people are consistent in their individual responses to conflict, tending to react the same way over time, developing a behavior pattern.

Conflict often is assumed to be a contest, and it is not. Conflict is part of nature; neither positive nor negative, "it just is," said Thomas Crum (1987). People can choose whether to make conflict a contest, a game, which requires that some players become winners and some losers. Winning and losing are generally the goals of games, but not the goal of conflict management. Effective conflict management requires thinking "win-win" with the goals of jointly learning, growing, and cooperating. Thomas Crum states that conflict can be seen as the interference pattern of energies as seen in nature: "Nature uses conflict as its primary motivator for change, creating beautiful beaches, canyons, mountains, and pearls" (1987, p. 49). It is not whether one has a conflict in his or her life, because everyone experiences it; rather it is what one does with the conflict that makes a positive or negative difference. Crum states that in order for human beings to move beyond success in a diverse environment, they need to strive for turning or making their life of work into a work of art. People need to naturally move into a "you and me" mentality where they see the world as abundant and supportive in all aspects of their lives, from their health to their financial well-being (Crum, p. 25). Crum defines "*alchemy*" as one's ability to change the ordinary into the extraordinary. The ability to change the ordinary to the extraordinary in the middle-ages involved changing common metals into gold; but the alchemy of today involves changing ourselves in hopes of achieving true synergy from the diverse workforce. Crum states that "It is the

---

[27] Originally published in "*Privatization and Market-Based Leadership*," by Llumina in 2006.

pressure of conflict, the interference patterns of energies caused by differences, that provides the motivation and opportunity to change" (p. 25). Nature sees conflict in a positive light, and uses it as a primary motivator for bringing about lasting changes. For human beings, the strength, the will, and the needed skills are available, so long as they are willing to let go of tension, fear, stereotypes, biases, and boundaries.

*Conflict* is the struggle that results when two or more individuals perceive a difference or incompatibility in their interests, values, or goals. Conflicts can arise from ambiguous roles and goals, stereotypes, biases, different procedures, distribution of resources, irreconcilable differences, perception of information and personalities, and the structures in place. In a diverse workplace, every interaction has a potential for conflict. Some conflict is good for team performance. Too much conflict causes team leaders to spend much time responding to it. *Conflict management* is the process of dealing with conflict in an effective manner. Positive conflict (conflict that is managed effectively) is great for team performance, and negative conflict can be very hurtful. Managers can manage individual conflict by:

⇒ Increasing awareness of the source of conflict.
⇒ Increasing diversity awareness and management skills.
⇒ Effectively communicating and listening to the different sides.
⇒ Practicing job rotation and temporary assignments.
⇒ Using permanent transfers and dismissals if needed.
⇒ Changing team's structure.

Furthermore, during an interpersonal conflict with a team member or colleague, one can remain focused on facts, feelings, and future expectations, rather than attacking the other person. Managers must "stick to the facts" and have effective conflict management strategies. According to industry literature and best practices over the past few decades, the following are short descriptions of some of the most common conflict management strategies.

- *Avoidance*: Some people do not feel comfortable dealing with conflict situations so they simply ignore it.
- *Smoothing or accommodating*: Other individuals (managers or workers) offer platitudes to cover up conflict similar to what a mother might do with her two small children, saying in effect, "Don't fight with your brother; let's all watch television together."
- *Authoritarianism, winning, or competing*: With this style, the manager or worker simply dictates the answer to the conflict. In this case, the person is forcing his or her solution on others and wants to win at all costs.
- *Expansion of resources*: In the event conflict is about scarce resources, like a new position in the budget, it is sometimes possible and wise to expand resources, e.g., add an additional position to the budget so that both managers can have a new employee. However, this expanding of resources option may not always be an option.
- *Compromise*: In compromise, everyone wins something. There is no winner and no loser; of course, nobody is completely happy either.

- *Mutual problem solving or collaboration*: Teamwork is the best way for long-term conflict resolution; mutual problem-solving method requires all conflicting parties to hear each other out and work on a solution together.

Day-to-day challenges with employees, colleagues, and bosses serve as laboratories for you to develop conflict management skills. It prepares you to serve as effective leaders, managers, and workers in the workplace. Conflict is best resolved within/by the team itself or by individuals causing the conflict. The best way to resolve conflict is to seek cooperation from all parties involved and to create a win-win solution for everyone through collaboration and mutual problem solving. This way you can meet your needs and theirs. There are conflicts that can be ignored or avoided, but others must be dealt with appropriately. In order to determine the best response, one can conduct a conflict analysis by asking the following questions:

⇒ What is the nature of the conflict and what or who is causing it?
⇒ Whose progress is impacted by this conflict?
⇒ What are the relevant facts surrounding the conflict?
⇒ Whose feelings are being hurt by this conflict?
⇒ What do the conflicting parties want and under what conditions?
⇒ What is the consequence of ignoring the conflict?
⇒ What is the consequence of facing the conflict by forcing a solution on all parties?
⇒ What is the best strategy for resolving the conflict and what resources are needed for this approach?

No matter how hard one works to build a productive team, the behavior of some team members or employees can cause breakdowns and block team progress while hindering everyone's performance. Team members, managers, and team leaders need to recognize such behaviors and learn how to resolve conflicts that arise when diverse personalities are dealing with complex performance challenges. Quickly and effectively resolving such conflicts can speed up the team's progress toward achieving its purpose (performance challenge). When dealing with day-to-day conflicts, misconducts, and disagreements, remember to use the 4-F model by emphasizing the facts, feelings, future expectations, and following up.

➢ *Facts*. Stick with the facts and describe the behavior that is creating the problem or conflict. Avoid attacking the other person. Avoid using "you" statements.

➢ *Feelings*. State the impact of the problem or conflict, your feelings, the feelings of team members, and how the problem makes the team suffer. Use "I" statements by mentioning how the above mentioned problem or fact impacts you or your employees and colleagues.

➢ *Future expectations*. Clearly describe future expectations, norms, and rules of conduct.

➢ *Following up*. Managers should follow up with the parties involved to make sure employees are meeting the expected standards as agreed. If they are, then the manager has an opportunity to reinforce this good behavior.

Otherwise, the manager will have another opportunity to start the process again (or take drastic actions as appropriate).

When conflicts exist, all team members must persist on behavior change until it is changed so the team can effectively proceed with its objective. In an article titled *"Managing Conflict across Cultures,"* co-authors Buller, Kohls, and Anderson (2000) examine the conflicts that arise as a result of ethical differences in a multinational organization. The authors emphasize the importance of resolving organizational conflicts that exist in multinational organizations, by citing numerous examples of organizations that have experienced such problems both in developed and developing nations. It is rare for an organization to have members that have identical values. In a multinational organization, the differences in value systems can be significant, and the potential for conflict can be great. Buller, Kohls, and Anderson (2000) suggest that there are six strategies that are effective in resolving these conflicts. These strategies include *avoiding, forcing, education, negotiation, accommodation, and collaboration.* These strategies are very similar to conflict resolution techniques mentioned in most leadership textbooks. However, according to Buller, Kohls, and Anderson (2000), there are three key factors that differentiate ethical conflict resolution from general conflict resolution strategies: (1) moral significance, (2) power, and (3) urgency. The extent to which these factors exist in an ethical conflict determines the strategy used to resolve it. There are many practical implications from the above suggestions. In most organizations, it becomes imperative for managers to address and effectively resolve conflicts. Also, when confronted with an ethical conflict in a culturally diverse organization, it is important for a manager to be capable of recognizing the key factors in order to determine the most appropriate strategy. Often, managers can use the Socratic questioning process to get each party to think of other "sides" to the issue, in order to eventually reach a mutually agreed-upon solution.

Sharing information with others is a fact of life, but sharing misinformation with others is also a reality. The spread of misinformation often can be the root to much conflict and ill feelings among employees. As such, it is necessary that educated individuals not spread misinformation about community members, managers, leaders, politicians, or one's colleagues in the workplace. The Triple Filter Test provides the wisdom of Socrates about why "grapevine," or certain messages, should not be shared with others, especially when the message has not been verified to see if it is true, important or even useful. Perhaps we can use this story to take a stand and hopefully make ourselves or others "stop" and think about "the spoken words" and its impact on the department or persons involved. People often wonder why some people have such great friends and manage to keep them. If one successfully applies the "Triple Filter Test" in one's conversations, the same could work for everyone. The following is the story behind the "Triple Filter Test," coming from Socrates.

In ancient Greece, Socrates was reputed to hold knowledge in high esteem. One day an acquaintance met the great philosopher and said, "Do you know what I just heard about your new friend?" "Hold on a minute," Socrates replied. "Before telling me anything I'd like you to pass a little test. It's called the "Triple Filter Test." "Triple filter?" said the acquaintance. "That's right," Socrates continued. "Before you talk to me about my friend, it might be a good idea to take a moment and filter what you're going to say. That's why I call it the triple filter test."

1. *"The first filter is Truth.* Have you made absolutely sure that what you are about to tell me is true?" "No," the man said, "actually I just heard about it and..." "All right," said Socrates. "So you don't really know if it's true or not."

2. *"The second filter is the filter of Goodness.* Is what you are about to tell me about my friend something good?" "No, on the contrary..." "So," Socrates continued, "you want to tell me something bad about him, but you're not certain it's true. You may still pass the test though, because there's one more filter left."

3. *"The third one is the filter of Usefulness.* Is what you want to tell me about my friend going to be useful to me?" "No, not really."

"Well," concluded Socrates, "if what you want to tell me is neither true, nor good, nor even useful, why tell it to me at all?" This is why Socrates was a great philosopher and held in such high esteem. If we are able to protect our colleagues, employees, friends, and those we love in this manner, we cannot be influenced by outsiders in having bad notions about them. Rumors, which seem to flow often among people in a diverse work environment, should be stopped and corrected instead of being spread when they have no reality. Rumors can damage an individual or the morale in the organization. Socrates certainly understood the idea behind systems thinking paradigm and how one part can impact the whole person, the whole department or organization, the community, and possibly the society over time. So, always remember the "Triple Filter Test" by passing messages through the filters of "*truth,*" "*goodness,*" and "*usefulness.*" It is a moral imperative to always make sure what is said is true, good, and useful before it is passed on to others. Such a questioning process can reduce misinformation and eliminate possible challenges before they become major conflicts.

It is clear that moral leaders must be able to create an environment in the workplace that influences and moves people to work at improving the system. They also need to believe in both compliance-oriented and integrity-oriented strategies. Compliance-oriented strategy is obeying the law or standards set by the company, government, or other outside sources. However adhering to the minimum regulatory standards is not enough. There must be integrity; the *discipline without punishment* concept is an integrity-oriented strategy for solving performance-related challenges in the workplace through moral and transformational leadership. In essence, the moral leader is a transformational leader. The transformational leadership style lends itself well to the creation of an ethical environment through collaborative communication, teamwork, as well as effective listening, and conflict resolution methods. Moral leaders will help to raise employees to a higher level of morality and motivation. This positive objective is the trend now as well as a prevalent method of leadership, which if practiced effectively, can bring about a more productive workforce. People come into a conflict situation with some experience and assumptions based upon their conflicting situations. Some employees and managers who face a conflict tend to "fight" it, while others might choose the "flight" approach. For example, would you choose the fight or flight approach if you were to have a conflict with your employee, a colleague, or your boss? Oftentimes, people tend to fall somewhere in between the continuum of "fight" or "flight." Once one determines what his or her natural approach might be to a conflicting situation with others, then he or she can determine the advantages and disadvantages of this approach, his or her approach's probability of success in various conflicting situations, and the means of adapting different styles to be more successful.

Most people tend to have one of the five conflict resolution approaches in the continuum of being assertive (meeting one's own needs) to being supportive (meeting others' needs): avoiding, accommodating, competing, compromising, and collaborating. To determine what your dominant style is, complete the conflict resolution survey (provided at the end of this chapter) and circle your two dominant style(s) in the diagram presented in Figure 11.1.

Managers are likely to have one or two dominant styles of resolving conflict. However, it is best to know one's natural tendencies and, if needed, improve upon them as desired. While in some cases "avoiding" might be an effective style for dealing with a conflict, other situations might require the use of collaborating or compromising in order to get things done with other team members. The situational variables should determine the best style. While situations do vary, a person should always keep his/her composure because objectivity and rational decision-making is critical for effective conflict resolution. Furthermore, effective conflict resolution process requires the use of excellent listening skills. While listening effectively, managers can use objective and open-ended questions to clarify further areas of interest for all parties involved.

Figure 11.1 – Conflict Management Styles

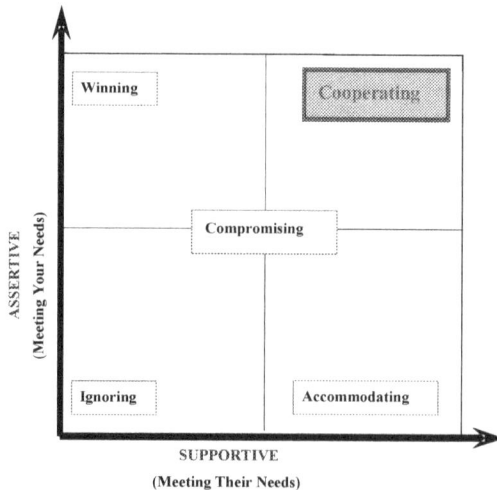

The essence of effective conflict resolution is to work together without offending anyone or being offended. Consequently, one should resolve all differences in a professional manner. It is also beneficial to remember that differences and disagreements can lead to better alternatives, better solutions, new ways of viewing each case, and opportunities for more quality communication. In each obstacle, there can be hidden opportunities. One needs to stay calm, stay "all together" in the face of disagreements, hear each other's differences and views, and then make sure one's views are heard by everyone on the team before agreeing on a final solution. In the case of performance-related conflict with employees, if the conflict resolution process does not resolve the situation, managers then can use a formal employee discipline strategy to correct the process.

### *Positive and Negative Conflict*

One should remember that there is good conflict and there is bad conflict. In *positive conflict*, individuals of different views and personalities tend to show mutual respect for each others' thoughts and feelings in order to develop a strong partnership and eventually synergistic results. However, in *negative conflict*, people view each other as adversaries and are focused on "winning"; thereby, in negative conflict, people attempt to protect themselves, even if such a defense comes at a high cost to others. According to Murphy (1994), whether intentional or not, conflict that is not managed effectively can be a major barrier to one's personal and professional goal achievement. Therefore, managers should commit themselves to mastering an effective conflict management style or process. Murphy (1994) suggests that managers should master and use intellectual, emotional, interpersonal, and managerial skills for resolving conflicts.

1. *Intellectual skills.* These skills and concepts can include such things as being analytical, learning ability, judgment, planning organization, perception, conceptualizing, objectivity, and flexibility.
2. *Emotional skills.* These skills and concepts can include such things as honesty, persistence, ambition, self-discipline, result-orientation, fast pace, initiative, assertiveness, and enthusiasm.
3. *Interpersonal skills.* These skills and concepts can include such things as persuasiveness, sensitivity, gregariousness, listening, communication, and writing.
4. *Managerial skills.* These skills and concepts can include such things as giving guidance, selecting competent people, motivating or creating a motivational work environment, terminating or demoting incompetent employees, delegating, and expecting professional behavior in the workplace.

Conflict management skills and techniques enable managers and leaders to reduce or eliminate those barriers that prevent individuals or a population group from achieving the results desired in the department or in the economy. One can summarize that conflict is simply a by-product of bringing about new developments, growth, innovation, and change toward a better work environment and culture. Just like change, conflict is inevitable. By understanding how to deal with conflict in a positive and performance-focused manner, and actually preventing small issues from becoming major conflicts, market-based leaders' behavior can serve as a model for others in the organization. According to Murphy (1994), leaders and managers can proactively sense and reduce/eliminate conflict by being visionary, giving feedback, getting feedback, defining expectations, and reviewing performance regularly with their employees. The benefits of conflict management can be better relationships with one's employees and colleagues, increased self respect, personal development and growth, increased efficiency and effectiveness, creative and innovative thinking in the department, and synergy or teamwork. Jim Murphy, the author of *Managing Conflict at Work*, mentions that conflict resolution requires time, knowledge, as well as hard work, and suggests a five-step process for all employees and managers to successfully resolve conflicts. According to Murphy (1994), in cases of conflict, one should:

1. Take responsibility for dealing with conflict.
2. Uncover, define, and discuss the real problem.
3. Ask questions and listen.
4. Set goals and create an action plan.
5. Follow up.

Overall, when it comes to day-to-day conflicts, managers have a choice to deal with the conflict, ignore the conflict, or leave the area or department that is causing the conflict. The best choice in many cases, according to experts, would be to proactively deal with the conflict in an effective manner.

*"The Magic of Conflict: Turning a Life of Work into a Work of Art,"* a beautifully written book by Thomas F Crum in 1987, states that conflict is neither good nor bad; conflict just is as "Our lives are not dependent on whether or not we have conflict. It is what we do with conflict that makes the difference" (Crum, 1987, p. 21). Thomas Crum states that, during changing times and major conflicts, "instead of seeing the rug being pulled out from under us, we can learn to dance on the shifting carpet." Thomas Crum quotes Woody Allen who said that "More than at any other time in history mankind faces a crossroad. One path leads to despair and utter hopelessness; the other to total extinction. Let us pray we have the wisdom to choose correctly." The key in managing conflict effectively is to learn how to convert frustration to fascination and disappointing and upsetting thoughts into growth. John Denver, who wrote the foreword for *The Magic of Conflict*, said the following:

> Tom takes us simply, clearly, and profoundly through the nature of conflict and the principles of the Aiki Approach for resolving conflict and moving beyond success, and provides us with real, practical applications of these principles to our daily life. These principles work on an individual level, in the simplest of relationships, and in the most complex, even those between societies and nations which espouse differences in language, heritage, politics, and faith. Transformation takes risk and courage. This is no longer a world of you or me. We must recognize that it is you and me and that together we can create the world, the life that we have dreamed of forever, a world of peace and goodwill among men. A world without hunger. A world without the threat of nuclear disaster and the possible extinction of humanity. Peace is a conscious choice (John Denver, 1987).

Thomas Crum states that discovery is one essential component of effective conflict management because *discovery* is a place that does not know, does not evaluate, and is willing to see what is; *discovery* sees beyond the fight to an open realm of possibilities; *discovery* enables people to let go of the filters of their past and the blinders of their expectations; *discovery* perceives not right and wrong, only inquiry and creativity; and *discovery* turns frustration into fascination and work into play (1987, p. 129). Discovering the right response in each changing moment requires having an open mind as well as an open heart to see new opportunities and the way things are, and then the way they can be. The origin and evolution of every living species have been a lesson of change, as various living species adapt to, and evolve with their changing environments in order to flourish. The same means of adaptation applies to human beings, since change in nature is not an ideological choice but rather one of survival. Change is a choice for learning, creativity, flexibility, and growth; and effective conflict management is the key to bringing about change in an efficient manner. Amid all the change, it is best to remember that flexibility allows one to stretch rather than shrink, and proactively welcoming and embracing change is about choosing a better or pre-determined future. Furthermore, choosing to be synergistic, while involving everyone in the conflict management process, can transform a "personal" vision into a "professional" vision for everyone in the department or the organization.

## Conflict Resolution Options and Techniques

In order to communicate effectively, managers must be cognizant of the different ways in which they can resolve conflicts. Conflict resolution builds stronger and more cohesive organizations and more rewarding relationships. The following are twelve steps for effective conflict resolution, which often are offered by academicians and practitioners.

*1. The win/win approach.* The win/win approach is about changing the conflict from an adversarial attack and defense, to co-operation. It is a powerful shift of attitude that alters the course of communication. One person continually applying a joint problem solving approach can make the difference. Until we give it some thought, we usually are unaware of the way we argue. We often find ourselves with a knee-jerk reaction in difficult situations, based on long established habits, combined with the passing mood of the moment. When challenged we experience loneliness, we feel disconnected from those around us. While people argue over opposing solutions- "Do it my way! No, that is not good! Do it my way!" the conflict is a power struggle. What is needed is to change the agenda in the conversation. The objective should be "I want to win and I want you to win too." It is about thinking "win-win" as explained by Stephen R. Covey in his popular *Seven Habits of Highly Effective People* book, which was originally published in 1989.

*2. Creative response.* The creative response to conflict is about turning problems into possibilities. It is about consciously choosing to see what can be done, rather than existing with how terrible it all is. It is in affirming that you will choose to extract the best from the situation.

*3. Empathy.* It is deemed necessary to develop communication tools to build rapport. Use emphatic listening to clarify understanding. Charles Beck (1999), in his

*Management Communication* book, defines emphatic listening as when one "fully understands the speaker's views, values, attitudes, emotions, and feelings" (p. 63).

*4. Appropriate assertiveness.* It is imperative that managers apply strategies that attack the problem, and not the person. The emphasis of appropriate assertiveness is being able to state your case without arousing the defenses of the other person. The most important factor is saying how it is for you, rather than what they should or should not do. "The way I see it…" attached at the beginning of one's assertive statement, helps. A skilled "I" statement goes even further. When you want to state your point of view helpfully, the "I" statement formula can be useful. An "I" statement says how it is on my side, and how I see it.

*5. Co-operative power.* It is very important to eliminate the "power over" to build "power with" others. When faced with a situation that has the potential to create conflict, ask open questions to reframe resistance. Explore the difficulties and then re-direct discussion to focus on positive possibilities.

*6. Managing emotions.* Express fear, anger, hurt, and frustration wisely to effect change. Additionally, these messages should demonstrate sincerity and trustworthiness matching the intent of the communicators.

*7. Willingness to resolve.* It is important for managers to maintain a willingness to resolve. The more someone inflames, angers or upsets you, the more one realizes the need to learn more about themselves. We must constantly look within ourselves to see whether or not we are projecting, or if there is anything that has interfered with our willingness to resolve. Projection is when we see our thoughts and feelings in the minds and behavior of others and not in ourselves.

*8. Mapping the conflict.* Sometimes issues are simplified when they are written down. A good idea is to define briefly the issue, the problem or conflict in neutral terms that everyone would agree on.

*9. Broadening perspectives.* Everyone should learn to respect and value differences. Just as we are unique and special, so are other people. We all have distinctive viewpoints that may be just as valid from where we stand. Each person's viewpoint makes a contribution to the whole and requires consideration and respect in order to form a complete solution. This wider view can open our eyes to many more possibilities.

*10. Mediation.* The third party mediator should endeavor to be *objective.* He or she should validate both sides, even if the moderator silently prefers one point of view or even when only one party is present. Secondly, the mediator should be *supportive.* He or she should use caring language. Provide a non-threatening learning environment, where people will feel safe to disclose personal issues. Thirdly, the mediator should be *unbiased.* He or she should actively discourage judgments as to who was right and who was wrong. Ask questions such as: What happened? How did you feel? The mediator should endeavor to *encourage participation.* Encourage suggestions from participants. Do not give advice. If your suggestions are really needed, offer them as options not directives. *Strive for a win/win situation* - Turn opponents into problem-solving partners. One can follow the following steps for effective mediation:

◊   *Open* - Introductions and agreements.
◊   *Establish* - Overview: What is the matter? Ask each person to express his or her view of the conflict, the issues, and his or her feelings. Details: What is

involved? Lay out the needs and concerns. Clarify misconceptions. Identify other relevant issues, mirroring if needed.

◊ *Move* - Where are they now? Identify areas of agreement. Encourage willingness to move forward. Negotiation: focus on future action. How would they like it to be? What would that take? Develop options. Trading can build wins for everyone.

◊ *Close* - Completion: contracting. Plans for the future, including appointed time to review agreement. Clarify and offer closing statements.

*11. Designing of options.* It is best to explore all possible options and perhaps break the problem into smaller parts. Furthermore, one should research the situation, gather more information, and establish the constraints involved. When exploring options, always consider the following questions:

◊ Is the option satisfying the win/win approach?
◊ Does the option meet many needs of all parties?
◊ Is it cost effective?
◊ Is it fair?
◊ Does it solve the problem?
◊ Can the problem be settled with only one option?

*12. Negotiation.* The emphasis is on the work relationships among team members. The strategy involves a series of controlled negotiations between participants. One should remember that negotiations involve several principles:

◊ The emphasis should be on the problem, and not on the person.
◊ Focus on the needs, not on positions.
◊ Emphasize common ground.
◊ Be inventive about options.
◊ Make clear agreements.

One always must focus on the issue while maintaining the relationship and trying to resolve the issue. After clarification, members must decide which items they want most and form into pairs to negotiate, usually with a third party to help in the process. Finally, there should be a written role negotiation agreement. The outcome of the negotiation is written down and spells out the agreements and concessions, which each party finds satisfactory.

## Negotiation Process and Techniques[28]

Negotiation is a discussion intended to produce an agreement among different individuals and parties. Cellich and Jain (2004) mention six key factors in order to prepare for any type of negotiation; these are: 1) define the issues; 2) know the other party's position; 3) know the competition; 4) know the negotiations limits; 5) develop strategies and tactics; and 6) plan the negotiation meeting. While there can

---

[28] This material comes from *Cross Cultural Management and Negotiation Practices*, 2007; Ilead Academy Publications.

be many processes to a negotiation model, the main steps to a negotiation can be simplified under four categories which are: (1)-Initiating or pre-planning; (2)-Negotiating; (3)-Closing; and (4)-Maintaining the relationship and renegotiating if necessary. This negotiation model provides a process along with general steps as a guide, and focuses on the future by maintaining a good relationship with all parties involved. It emphasizes a win-win objective with a focus on the creation of a long-term relationship, trust and interdependency.

The emphasis in any negotiation should be on the work relationships among team members. Negotiators, according to experts, can be dodgers, dreamers, hagglers, competitors, or problem solvers. According to Cellich and Jain (2004), the latter style is the best because it leads to a win-win outcome for both parties. The authors also offer a personal assessment inventory that helps the negotiator figure out his or her style as well as the style of the other party. Cellich and Jain suggest that a negotiator should find out which style he or she fits into and adapt to the other party's style. Each negotiation style depends on whether the negotiator in question is task-oriented or relationship-oriented.

Cellich and Jain suggest that the style negotiators should adopt is the problem solving style. In fact, problem solving is most effective in situations where the matter of the negotiation is going to bind both parties to a long-term business relationship. In this case, it is in both parties' interest to engage in a win-win situation. If one of the parties feels that he or she was duped or cheated, future business relations will be jeopardized. The problem solving style is best fit for international negotiation. Every situation calls for a different way of going about a negotiation, depending on the kind of negotiator you are dealing with, and what kind of relation you envision to conduct with your counterpart. If it is a one time deal, the substantive issue is of utmost importance, and trying to establish a relationship based on a fair outcome would be absurd. In this case, being a competitor outweighs the benefits of problem solving. It is difficult to see why a manufacturer, who has a loyal and established client base, and who happens to have excess product to sell in a foreign market, should make any concession on the price of the goods or the terms of the shipment, notably when he or she has no intention to penetrate that foreign market. Concerning international business, there does not seem to be a prevailing negotiation style that applies to all regions and countries. Culture should shape the negotiation style to adapt when faced with parties that share a different cultural background. Indeed, problem solving is the best approach for many cultures. However, some might take the search of common ground, and the attempts of smoothing edges as a sign of weakness, hypocrisy or shiftiness. They expect you to be aggressive and competitive, which is evidence of trustworthiness. Often in third world countries, where business ethics has been eroded by corruption and economical anarchy, the attempt of cooperating and finding joint solutions give the impression that there is a catch, and that the other party cannot be trusted. One cannot be in a ruthless environment where the fate of businesses depends on the good will of a few powerful men, and try to use an approach that can only be interpreted as a weakness and thus remain vulnerable to make for excessive concessions and trade offs. The approach of problem solving applies best to Asian cultures, where the concept of saving face is prominent. In order to cut a deal in an Asian country, the negotiator should take into account the importance of giving the impression to the other party that he or she did not lose by agreeing to his or her counterpart conditions. This happens by giving small concessions, or by finding a joint solution that would avoid a feeling of humiliation and dissatisfaction. This is also the case in countries where the notion of insiders and outsiders is pronounced. In most collectivist countries, foreigners are regarded as being intruders that have to be treated with prudence. Negotiating under these conditions require caution and modesty. The newcomer should be patient about being integrated and adopted as part of the group. Moreover, negotiations in collectivist countries might take a long time discussing and reviewing details of the deal, which are meant to establish a relationship with the other party and to have insights into their intentions.

An interesting negotiating style is the dreamer; this style is evident in linear and collectivist cultures where hierarchy and age seniority is respected. In countries that embrace these values, the task of negotiating with a party that has a higher social status is rather difficult. Dreamers are less likely to be part of the American negotiation style. Being individualists, Americans tend to be less intimidated by higher authority, and negotiate on the same basis with different parties.

Knowing one's personal style is important. Negotiation styles emanate from one's culture and personality, and knowing them would help a person adjust them to meet his/her goals. A person who gets overexcited, loud and pushy during a negotiation might learn that his or her style would offend the Asian counterparts. Whereas, if he or she is reserved and shows no emotions while negotiating with Mediterranean counterparts, the negotiator might be perceived as lacking motivation and interest toward the issue in question and consequently toward the person, which would produce dissatisfaction.

Negotiations are vital to the prosperity of businesses; it is through negotiations that trade, joint venture and growth happens. It is also a sensitive process that can lead to success or loss of important partners, clients or suppliers. Knowing one's negotiation style, and adapting it to different parties' styles and cultures, is the key for a successful outcome.

### *Determine Your Negotiation Styles*

To determine your general style of negotiations, complete the questionnaire (Negotiation Style Assessment and Inventory) provided by Cellich and Jain (2004) by answering the questions based on your opinion and general tendencies when negotiating. The questionnaire is provided at the end of this chapter for you to complete and you will be able to determine your dominant negotiation tendencies which will fall in one or more of the following styles:

- *Dodging (Dodgers)*: Trying to postpone decision-making or finding reasons for not getting involved at all.
- *Dreaming (Dreamers)*: Keeping the major goal in mind; preserving the relationships even at the cost of giving up certain concessions.
- *Haggling (Hagglers)*: Perceiving the negotiation process as a give-and-take game to obtain a good bargain.

- *Competing (Competitors):* Effectively managing conflicts, feeling comfortable with assertive behaviors and being aggressive when appropriate.
- *Problem Solving (Problem Solvers)*: Problem solving requires creativity and flexibility in finding mutually satisfying agreements. It means working toward a win-win solution for the relevant parties.

When negotiating, one can be somewhat assertive (from low to high) or somewhat supportive (from low to high) or both simultaneously. Supportive styles focus on meeting the other party's needs, while assertive styles focus on meeting one's own needs. The key might be to make sure there is a win-win solution for both parties; thereby meeting one's own needs as well their needs. Once you have determined your negotiation scores using the Negotiation Style Assessment and Inventory for the five possible styles, then circle your highest or dominant style.

### *Trump Style Negotiation: Strategies for effective Coaching*[29]

Author George H. Ross, in 2006, wrote a wonderful book entitled *"Trump Style Negotiation: Powerful Strategies and Tactics for Mastering Every Deal"* that deals with helpful strategies for negotiation that coaches can use in their day-to-day dealings. The book's foreword is written by Donald J. Trump, the self-made billionaire in real estate.

In the forward, Mr. Trump states "I like to think of myself as a maverick, someone who's willing to do something that no one else is willing to do." While Mr. Trump provides the vision or big picture he needs an expert advisor, negotiator and real estate attorney to eliminate any roadblocks and finalize the deal. His partner, George H. Ross, who has been co-starring on the popular television show *The Apprentice,* shares tactics and methods developed over 50 years of negotiating experience. According to Mr. Ross, Mr. Trump's vision and organization are the keys to his success. He gained his reputation as a great negotiator because of his insights into human nature. Mr. Ross states that early in his education in the art of negotiating "he was leaving a lot of his boss' money on the table." As a result, he began carefully studying the tactics of the other side in these deals. He learned from "the Donald" *that you negotiate for one thing that exists primarily to serve a different purpose, forms one of the bases of the Trump style of negotiation.* These strategies work for many kinds of deals – buying a car, getting a raise, buying or selling a small investment property or financing a skyscraper.

George H. Ross indicates that negotiation is the ability to persuade the other side into sharing a state of satisfaction with the final outcome. He identifies seven goals to help you succeed in any negotiation. They are the following:

- Goal 1. I want to profit from the negotiation.
- Goal 2. I want to learn as much as I can about the people on the other side.
- Goal 3. I want to find out where the bottom line is.
- Goal 4. I want to understand the constraints surrounding the transaction.
- Goal 5. I want to study the other side.

---

[29] Book review provided by Chris R. Crumley, Trinity University.

- Goal 6. I want to access the people on my side in any negotiation.
- Goal 7. I need to find out what is fair and reasonable.

George H. Ross states that success in any negotiation involves trust, rapport and satisfaction between people. This is the big picture. However, there are eight ways to accomplish these goals. They include finding a common ground with the other side, establishing a good rapport, being a nice person to deal with, finding the appropriate level of communication, understanding the other side and its needs, cementing feelings of trust, learning flexibility and becoming known as a deal maker and not as a deal breaker. Also, the importance of the eight ways to achieve the three goals does not mean a person should act the same way in every negotiation. He suggests that "learn to be a chameleon" by adapting your negotiating style to the environment.

George H. Ross recommends probing to learn what the other side wants. His fundamental rule is "don't accept anything at face value." Also, identify the key people involved in the negotiation and uncover hidden weaknesses and information from the other side. Mr. Ross encourages negotiators to be master salespeople, creating bold solutions to problems, while convincing the other side that they are receiving more than they expected. According to the author, if you build relationships with other people, it makes the deal work. Money is only part of any negotiation, but how to convey your ideas to people on the other side is equally important. Furthermore, you must have tenacity to succeed, and remember that good preparation wins the deal. Another consideration in the Trump Style Negotiation is *Ziff's Principle of Least Effort.* He has concluded that most people will extend the least effort required during a negotiation and that they are primarily interested in the bottom line figures. As a result, intelligent preparation can move the other side from "maybe" to "yes."

George H. Ross wrote that a quick deal is always a mistake. "It might be a good deal, but the speed and pace of the negotiation should be your decision." The reason for a slow negotiation is because it involves satisfying the "ego requirement" of both sides and that takes time. You do not want either side to be unhappy with the outcome. He suggests using timing, deadlines, delays and deadlocks to your advantage. In addition, there are three guiding rules to control the pace of the negotiation. They include not accepting an offer right away, being indecisive, and not making quick negotiations. According to Mr. Ross, human nature determines how deals are made. He discusses "the psychology of negotiating;" people want what they can't have or what somebody else wants, people become overwhelmed with too many decisions, people succumb to the aura of legitimacy, people have a fear of the superiority of others and invoke the power of the simple solution. Mr. Ross distinguishes between actual knowledge and apparent knowledge in gaining information for advantage during negotiation.

George H. Ross proposes to have multiple solutions in mind. Therefore, he maintains that you should review the bottom line, use marketing advantages to improve the bottom line, consider long-term benefits versus short-term negatives, and use flexibility as a strategic tool. In the book, he offers how to prepare for negotiations by digging for information about the other side, presenting guidelines during the negotiations, documentation and the most powerful tool – a *Deal Book*, which is a checklist and organizer that includes points of the deal. Also, a review of every negotiation should be made immediately afterward asking the following questions:

- Was the objective achieved? If not, why not?
- What was good and what was bad?
- How should you revise your original assumptions?
- How should you schedule and time the next meeting?
- What should happen to your notes?

George H. Ross presents power negotiating tactics and countermeasures. These techniques can help you control the tone and pace of the negotiation. He argues the crunch: "you've got to do better than that and that's all I can do." Also, included in his arguments are "nibbling and take it or leave it" strategies. According to Mr. Ross there are three difficult character types in negotiation. First, "Ivan the Intimidator" is usually a person with stature or position who wields a great deal of power and is a bully. Second, the "Know-it-all Charlie" is the most arrogant personality type. Third, the "Waffling Wilma" type never wants to make a decision. The author indicates that these traits are unconscious and the style of negotiating is adjusted to manage people on the other side.

George H. Ross explores ten "get tough strategies" (GTS) and guidelines. This includes set the tone, don't talk, manage concessions properly, aim high, leave as much room as possible, don't succumb to the power of the simple solution, bargain small items for big ones, use deadlines to your advantage, be patient and stingy and be careful in how you request a variation. Also, he lists the "do's" and "don'ts" of skilled negotiators. Among these are trust your instincts, adopt your own style of negotiating, don't talk about your weaknesses, coach your advisors to say as little as possible, don't believe in the "bogey" theory, don't use all the power you possess, and don't forget that there is no right price for the wrong item. The author reveals when to use nonbinding letters of intent and memoranda of understanding. The purpose of these documents is to highlight terms that were not negotiated, and fills the gaps in continuity. Control of the document establishes power by the maker, because the preliminary draft will ultimately be a legal agreement. It acknowledges any hidden negotiators, creates a moral commitment and adds to the time invested in the process. This motivates the parties to close the deal.

The author writes about his most critical negotiations for Mr. Trump as a deal-maker including Trump Tower, the GM Building, 40 Wall Street and the Chrysler Building. He shares with the reader how Trump Style Negotiation developed during the last thirty years in the real estate business, and how you can benefit from the strategic wisdom and tactical skills that made Mr. Trump a wealthy man. The author credits Mr. Trump's understanding of human nature in successful negotiations and how he deals to win. Also, he acknowledges his own role in negotiating the transaction, while Mr. Trump delivers the vision and organization for the deal. The book is enjoyable because of the practical straightforward approach and real life examples. This is a great book for anyone that needs a "streetwise" approach to negotiating contracts. It provides real world business advice based on the experiences of the Trump organization that is not taught in business schools. Furthermore, this reviewer believes this book should be on the supplementary reading list for all managers and coaches that deal with employees, vendors, customers, and suppliers on a regular basis. This book should also be recommended for graduate level scholars in Real Estate. While this book provides a prescription for success in negotiating deals, it is written in a conversational style that opens up "the Donald's" playbook for the price of admission. The book is highly recommended to anybody that wants to become a better negotiator and an effective coach, especially in the real estate industry.

### *Summary*

Managers who are performance-focused and developmental in their management styles characteristically are usually concerned about the well-being and success of their employees. Effective managers attempt to avoid negative conflict through effective leadership and interpersonal skills. Furthermore, these managers understand the realities of conflict in a diverse organization and adapt appropriate conflict management styles in order to develop an effective team in the department. This chapter offered suggestions and steps for coaching and effectively dealing with conflict and negotiation challenges in the work environment.

### *Discussion Questions*

1. What is conflict?
2. What types of conflicts are managers and supervisors likely to face in the workplace? Mention five common interpersonal conflicts.
3. What is the role of a coach in managing conflict? Discuss your suggestions.
4. What are the most common conflict resolution techniques? Which two the most commonly used ones and why?
5. What are the commonly used negotiation techniques? What is your dominant negotiation style? Are there strengths and weaknesses associate with this dominant style? Discuss.

### Conflict Resolution Survey

Effective leadership, management, and communication require an understanding of one's dominant conflict resolution style or one's natural tendencies. To understand your conflict resolution style, use the following scale to describe your typical behavior in conflict.

0 = I never behave this way
1 = I seldom behave this way
2 = I sometimes behave this way
3 = I often behave this way
4 = I very frequently behave this way

Review the following elements and give yourself a score of 0-5, as per the above scale, to determine your natural tendencies. Be honest and candid as you complete this survey.

___1. Insult the other person.
___2. Disregard the existence of a conflict.
___3. Passively comply with the other's demands.
___4. Seek a mutually beneficial solution.
___5. Seek a quick middle ground.
___6. Use threats to intimidate the other person.
___7. Postpone dealing with the issue.
___8. Sacrifice my own wishes for the sake of the other.
___9. Give information so the other can understand my feelings.
___10. Exchange concessions.
___11. Demand to have my way.
___12. Avoid communicating with the other person.
___13. Give in to the other person for the sake of harmony.
___14. Solicit information about the other's thoughts and feelings.
___15. Split the difference with the other person.
___16. Escalate the confrontation.
___17. Sidestep the area of disagreement.
___18. Protect my relationship with the other person rather than win the conflict.
___19. Explore alternative solutions to the problem.
___20. Bargain or trade with the other person.
___21. Punish the other person.
___22. Withdraw from the situation if it becomes threatening.
___23. Yield easily to the other's position.
___24. Attempt to negotiate so that neither person must compromise.
___25. Concede some points in order to win some other points.
___26. Lose my temper.
___27. Change the topic to avoid confrontation.
___28. Let the other person have his/her way.
___29. Cooperate to find areas of agreement.
___30. Compromise.

*Conflict response orientation survey calculation.* To determine your conflict response orientation (CRO), calculate your conflict scores by adding the values marked for the question items in each column. The higher you score the greater your perceived tendency or orientation to utilize that specific communication style (Adapted from Tuttle, Waveland Press, 1985).

| Competing | Avoiding | Accommodating | Collaborating | Compromising |
|-----------|----------|---------------|---------------|--------------|
| 1. | 2. | 3. | 4. | 5. |
| 6. | 7. | 8. | 9. | 10. |
| 11. | 12. | 13. | 14. | 15. |
| 16. | 17. | 18. | 19. | 20. |
| 21. | 22. | 23. | 24. | 25. |
| 26. | 27. | 28. | 29. | 30. |
| Total = | Total = | Total = | Total = | Total = |

### Negotiation Style Assessment and Inventory

The Negotiation Style Assessment and Inventory comes from Cellich and Jain as presented in their 2004 textbook entitled *Global Business Negotiations: A Practical Guide.* It is duplicated in this book with permission from the publisher for educational usage.

*Directions*: To determine your general style of negotiations, complete the following questions based on your opinion and general tendencies when negotiating. For each statement, you can provide an answer ranging from one to five: 1 (strongly disagree), 2 (disagree), 3 (neutral), 4 (agree), or 5 (strongly agree). Once you have answered all the questions then transfer your scores to the table on the next page to interpret your results.

| | Rating (1-5) | Statements |
|---|---|---|
| 1. | | I am not comfortable negotiating. |
| 2. | | I push the other party toward my own positions/interests. |
| 3. | | I avoid hurting people. |
| 4. | | I try to learn the real needs of the other party before making a concession. |
| 5. | | I enjoy making offers and counteroffers. |
| 6. | | I don't like making difficult decisions. |
| 7. | | Before negotiating, I know what results to expect and how to work to obtain them. |
| 8. | | When negotiating, I like to make quick decisions to speed up the discussions. |
| 9. | | I am willing to lower my expectations to save the relationship. |
| 10. | | I encourage the other party to work with me in finding an acceptable solution. |
| 11. | | I avoid getting involved in difficult situations. |
| 12. | | I make sure I have power over the other party, and I use it to my advantage. |
| 13. | | To advance the negotiations, I like to split the difference. |
| 14. | | When negotiating, I make sure the other party feels comfortable. |
| 15. | | I have no problem sharing information with the other party. |
| 16. | | I don't negotiate when I have little chance of winning. |
| 17. | | If necessary, I use threats to reach my goals. |
| 18. | | I like to compromise to expedite the negotiations. |
| 19. | | I make sure the other party explains his or her real needs. |
| 20. | | I like to explore innovative approaches with the other party to achieve maximum outcomes. |
| 21. | | I like taking risks. |
| 22. | | To get what I want, I ask for more than what I am willing to settle for. |
| 23. | | I look for a fair deal. |
| 24. | | To me, personal relationships are vital to constructive discussions. |
| 25. | | I frequently summarize issues we both agreed to. |
| 26. | | I dislike dealing with difficult negotiators. |
| 27. | | I try to create doubts in the mind of the other party. |
| 28. | | To me, negotiating is a game of give and take. |
| 29. | | I do not like to embarrass other people. |
| 30. | | When I negotiate, I take a long-term outlook. |
| 31. | | I avoid getting involved in controversies. |
| 32. | | I do not give away information, but I try to obtain as much information as possible from the other party. |
| 33. | | I look for a middle-of-the-road solution to close negotiations. |
| 34. | | I avoid getting involved in nonessential details. |
| 35. | | I enjoy meeting people. |

**Source**: Cellich, C. and Jain, S. C. (2004). *Global Business Negotiations: A Practical Guide.* Thompson-Southwestern. ISBN: 0538-72658-X. Reprinted with permission.

### Interpreting the Negotiation Style Assessment and Inventory Score

*Directions*:
After completing the survey, transfer your scores from the Negotiation Style Assessment and Inventory questionnaire to the following table and add your responses according to the structure of each column.

| Dodger | | Dreamer | | Haggler | | Competitor | | Problem Solver | |
|---|---|---|---|---|---|---|---|---|---|
| Statement | Rating | S | Rating | S | Rating | S | Rating | S | Rating |
| 1= | | 3= | | 5= | | 2= | | 4= | |
| 6= | | 9= | | 8= | | 7= | | 10= | |
| 11= | | 14= | | 13= | | 12= | | 15= | |
| 16= | | 19= | | 18= | | 17= | | 20= | |
| 21= | | 24= | | 23= | | 22= | | 25= | |
| 26= | | 29= | | 28= | | 27= | | 30= | |
| 31= | | 35= | | 33= | | 32= | | 34= | |
| | | | | | | | | | |
| *Total=* | | Total= | | Total= | | Total= | | Total= | |

*Scoring Example*: If you answered 2 for the first statement on the survey, then you would enter 2 on the Dodger column after Statement 1.

Figure 11.2 – Negotiation Quadrants and Styles

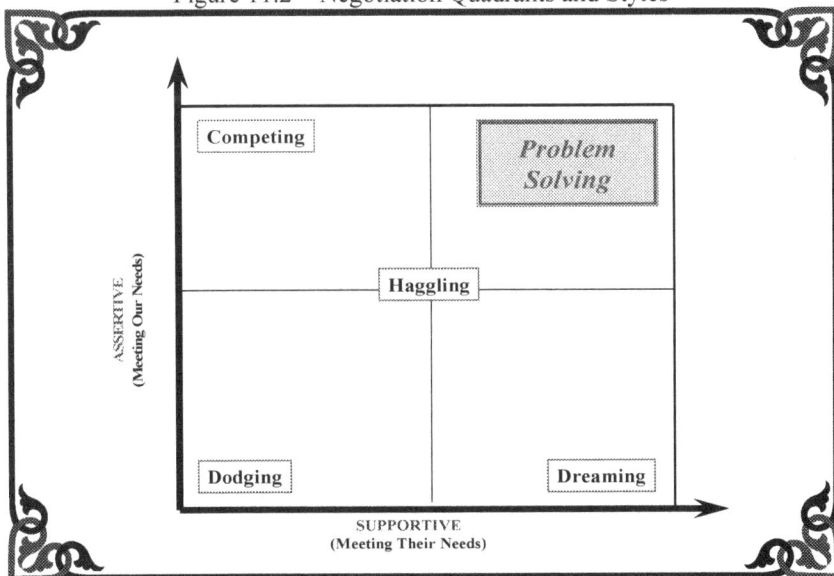

# CHAPTER 12

## Motivation, Discipline and Globalization

The creation of an ethical and a motivational work environment is an important aspect of a coach's responsibility. Such a workplace in today's cross-cultural work environment can result in high morale, greater satisfaction and increased commitment on the part of the employee. Of course, high morale and commitment can lead to better productivity and increased performance. When motivation and positive reinforcement strategies do not work with some individuals, then coaches and managers can use a standardized discipline process to enhance performance.

Employee discipline and terminations are realties and facts of life in today's work environment. However, these events do not have to be negative as they can be objectively used for an employee's developmental needs. Similarly, terminating employees when they are not the right match for the job is a very important element of capacity building as well as a manager's responsibility in the organization. Managers, who are performance-focused and developmental in their leadership and management styles, usually are concerned about the well-being and success of their employees. They attempt to avoid employee termination, discipline, and discharge by recruiting and hiring the right individuals from the outset, while developing and assisting them to achieve the stated objectives through effective leadership styles and appropriate discipline management skills. Accordingly, effective coaches are always concerned about the progressive development of their employees and, thus, resort to a standardized corrective action process when things are not going as expected or according to the plan.

The application of a standardized and consistent discipline process requires one's involvement in understanding human resource management concepts and skills. Besides appropriate interviewing, hiring, and training practices, managers also need to learn effective skills for coaching employee performance, especially when performance is not going in the "right" direction or meeting acceptable thresholds. Effective coaches should develop global skills and must be sensitive to the needs of their diverse employees across different countries and cultures. Since attitude is important for the development of an effective organizational culture, great coaches and managers work on hiring the right individuals from the outset; then, they develop and equip them with the right skills to stay motivated, productive and keep the company competitive. According to Peter Carbonara, senior writer at Money Magazine:

You can't build a great company without great people. But how do you know them when you see them? Over the past few years, a number of companies in a wide range of industries — from airlines to steel, computers to hotels — have asked themselves what separates their winners from their losers, good hires from bad, and they all arrived at the same answer: what people know is less important than who they are. Hiring, they believe, is not about finding people with the right experience; it's about finding people with the right mind-set. These companies hire for attitude and train for skill.

According to Carbonara (1996), there are four principles that define the model for smart hiring: What you know changes, who you are does not; you can't find what you are not looking for; the best way to evaluate people is to watch them work; and you cannot hire people who do not apply.

*1. What You Know Changes, Who You Are Doesn't.* The most common -- and fatal -- hiring mistake is to find someone with the right skills but the wrong mind-set. The best predictor of future behavior is past performance. One's personality is going to be essentially the same throughout his or her life.

*2. You Can't Find What You're Not Looking For.* The best way to select people who'll thrive in your company is to identify the personal characteristics of people who are already thriving and hire people just like them. Companies should work to understand their star performers, identify their target behaviors and attitudes, and then develop interview questions to find people with those attributes.

*3. The Best Way to Evaluate People is to Watch Them Work.* Offer exercises and simulated work dilemmas to see how people work individually and with their colleagues. Also, to promote employees into management and other leadership positions, watch their behavior and recent performance.

*4. You Can't Hire People Who Don't Apply.* Companies that take hiring seriously also take recruiting seriously. Successful companies seldom look for job candidates. Companies that hire in a disciplined and smart manner usually start their recruiting efforts close to home -- with their own people. Most companies with advanced hiring systems encourage family members of standout employees to apply for jobs. The logic is simple: If "who people are" is what matters, who better to hire than people related to your stars?

## Employee Motivation[30]

While employees should be self-motivators and must not wait for anyone to motivate them as this might require a long period and much patience, coaches and managers should do what they can to create a motivational work environment. This requires understanding values and attitudes as they relate to incentive, behavior, job satisfaction and, various motivational variables. Values and attitudes are a basic part of human behavior. *Values* are beliefs about what is right or wrong, good or bad, normal or abnormal. We learn basic values at a very young age from everyone and

---

[30] Originally published in "*Cross Cultural Management and Negotiation Practices,*" 2007 by ILEAD Academy, LLC.

everything around us. By the time we are in our late teens and early adulthood, we have pretty well developed our value system which we will use in relating to the world. During the first few years, children are value programmed mostly by their parents and immediate family members that come into contact with them. Media, especially television, are important value programmers as well. As the child enters school, the latter becomes a major source of values. In the teenage years, parents and family become secondary to peers as the primary source of values. Also, there is a genetic component to values. Regardless of cultural backgrounds, values once established tend to stay relatively stable over time. After the value system has been established, only a truly significant emotional event is likely to cause these values to change. There have been many theories about values. One is the Allport, Vernon, Lindzey "*Study of Values*" which found that there are six types of values: theoretical, economic, aesthetic, social, political, and religious. The combination of these values and their relative strength, they found, could predict one's success in certain occupations. Another very popular value theory is that of Milton Rokeach. The Rokeach Value Survey measures the ranking of certain terminal values (desired goals of life such as happiness or true friendship) and a number of instrumental values (ways of behaving to achieve the end values such as cheerful, helpful, and ambitious). Rokeach's survey has been used in many U.S. based and international studies. Like Allport et al., Rokeach concluded that people attracted to the same occupations tend to show the same value profiles.

While people hold only a limited number of core values, they may have thousands of attitudes. *Attitudes* are how we feel about something or somebody-- either positive or negative. Attitudes, according to experts, have three components: *Cognitive component* - What you believe to be true; for example, I believe continuous education is very important. *Affective component* - what you feel about the belief; example, I disapprove of parents who discourage their children from going to college. *Behavioral component* - what that feeling leads you to do; example, I argue with Mrs. Majboor because she is trying to lead her son to go into the family business instead of going to college. Much of the management literature deals with the attitudes we have about work, especially job satisfaction, job involvement, and organizational commitment.

An important thing to realize about attitudes is that all humans struggle for consistency between their attitudes and behavior. When you are in a situation which demands that you behave against your beliefs and attitudes you suffer from what experts have identified as "cognitive dissonance." *Cognitive dissonance* refers to an uneasy feeling when beliefs and behaviors are in conflict. Individuals will struggle to reorient either their attitudes or behavior in order to bring them back into harmony.

### *Job Satisfaction in the Workplace*

Job satisfaction is one of the four outcome variables that are often studied by management researchers and scholars (the other three variables are employee turnover, absenteeism, and productivity). Job satisfaction is an elusive variable and researchers often measure it using attitude surveys. Some research suggests that productivity leads to job satisfaction. Other research says just the opposite that job satisfaction leads to productivity.

Studies that measure overall job satisfaction among the U.S. workforce show widely varied results. One guess would be that even as the workforce is getting increasingly professional (an item often associated with increased job satisfaction), the overall workforce is less satisfied now than they were in the 1980's and 1990's. The reason for this guess is that this period has been a turbulent time of downsizing and destruction of long-standing cultures like IBM and Enron, leading to increasing anxiety among workers as to the security of their jobs. A feeling of security, as you will soon find out, is a basic tenet of a motivated workforce.

Management authors tell us that job satisfaction is at least partially determined by mentally challenging work, fair rewards, supportive working conditions, and encouraging co-workers. The job-personality fit is also very important. While the relationship between productivity and job satisfaction is not clear, studies show that job satisfaction and absenteeism are at least moderately negatively correlated. In other words, as job satisfaction goes up, absenteeism goes down. There is even a stronger negative correlation between employee satisfaction and turnover. Logically, if we like our job, we are likely to stay there.

### Motivation Theories and Satisfaction

Motivation is one of the most important topics managers and leaders study in the field of human behavior. Everyone wants to know how to motivate their colleagues, bosses, friends, and, of course, employees. The term "motivate" comes from the Latin verb, *movere*, which means to cause movement. Basically, motivation is about causing others, such as employees, to move toward some predetermined objective or goal. Psychologically, motivation deals with others' (employees') needs. Unsatisfied needs cause a tension which leads to a drive to satisfy the needs. The drive leads to search behavior and an examination of alternative ways of potentially satisfying the need. The need is either satisfied or frustrated in which case the search behavior continues.

A good starting point in the study of motivation is an understanding of Theory X and Theory Y popularized by Douglas McGregor. According to the Theory X model, managers believe that people dislike work and are basically lazy. Therefore, they need to be told what to do and how to do it. As such, they need autocratic managers as such a style would best fit with Theory X employees. Theory Y is the contrast to this theory. According to Theory Y, workers enjoy work and especially crave involvement and meaningful work. Workers want responsibility and thus the correct way to lead is through delegation. While Theory Y is widely believed to be the better operation system, it must be noted that not all workers want responsibility and autonomy. This dichotomy between autocratic and participative leadership, however, permeates the motivation and leadership literature.

In general, motivational theories can be grouped under the categories of content and process theories of motivation. *Content theories* of motivation answer the question, "What things motivate people?" Content theories look for external or extrinsic motivators. Process theories of motivation answer the question, "How are people motivated?" *Process theories* look at internal or intrinsic processes of motivation; what is the cognitive process by which people become motivated? Content theories of motivation generally include: Maslow's Hierarchy of Needs,

Herzberg's Two Factor Theory, McClelland's Achievement Theory, and Alderfer's ERG Theory. Process theories of motivation includes: Vroom's Expectancy Theory, Adams' Equity Theory, and Reinforcement Theory.

*Abraham Maslow* was a practicing psychologist who noted through his experience that people have certain categories of needs. In fact, Maslow identified five specific levels of needs that were organized in a hierarchy. The needs are as follows starting from the bottom (physical) and moving up to the top (self actualization): physical, security, social, self-esteem, and self-actualization. Starting with physical needs, initially workers and people in general are motivated by the acquisition of items that assures them of food and shelter. Once these needs are satisfied, the needs of workers "move up" the hierarchy as they become motivated by safety issues. Once satisfied with the security needs, the worker again moves up the hierarchy to the "social needs" level where interpersonal relations are motivational. Many of the social needs to belong and feel needed are played out at work where workers spend so much of their time interacting with others who have similar needs and professional aspirations. When these needs are met, the individual becomes motivated by self-esteem which considers such things as recognition, opportunity for growth and autonomy. Even the keys to the proverbial executive washroom may be an element of self-esteem as they demonstrate recognition. At the top of the hierarchy, often depicted as a pyramid or ladder, is self-actualization. At this level, the individual is free from all mundane concerns and may pursue his or her dreams, become all that s/he can be. Maslow's theory is the most popular motivational theory and most other researchers have used it as a stepping stone. Maslow's theory does provide two important insights that are extremely important to researchers and managers: 1) It states that not all people are motivated by similar things; and 2) It states that the same person is not always motivated by the same thing since his or her needs change over time.

In the early 1950's, *Frederick Herzberg*, another psychologist, studied motivation by asking people to relate critical incidents about when they felt most satisfied and motivated on the job and when they felt most dissatisfied. Herzberg found that these questions received two different types of answers. Thus, the two factor theory was born. One factor, Herzberg called *hygiene factors* (or "dis-satisfiers") which are things that make people unhappy when they are not taken care of but do not motivate them when they are provided. In other words, hygiene factors or maintenance, prevent dissatisfaction but do not lead to motivation. Hygiene factors include a safe working environment, salary, and satisfactory working relationships with peers and superiors. The other factor, Herzberg called *motivators* ("satisfiers") which are the things that, when present, cause motivation, but when absent, cause a lack of motivation (and not dissatisfaction). Motivators are such things as the work itself, autonomy, authority, and responsibility. As can be seen, Herzberg's motivators are equivalent to Maslow's "higher order needs" of self-esteem and self-actualization. Herzberg's hygiene factors are equivalent to Maslow's "lower order needs" of physical, security, and social.

*Clayton Alderfer* essentially modified Maslow's model by condensing the five levels of needs into three categories: E = Existence; R = Relatedness; and G = Growth. *Existence* needs are equivalent to Maslow's physical and safety needs; relatedness equates to Maslow's social needs; *growth* refers to self-esteem and self-actualization. Managers and researchers can compare ERG theory to Herzberg's model of hygiene factors and motivators. *Existence* and *relatedness* equate to Herzberg's hygiene factors and growth relates to Herzberg's motivators. Alderfer sees needs as moving back and forth, not just upward in the hierarchy. Because of the recognition of forward movement, i.e., progression from lower needs (existence) to higher needs (growth), Alderfer's model is called a "need progression" theory. While Maslow's model generally portrays motivation as moving in one direction, which is upward, Alderfer feels that people move back and forth among these three needs of existence, relatedness and growth as situations change. So, according to Alderfer, motivation is situational. As such, it is possible to regress from being motivated by growth needs to being motivated by relatedness.

*David McClelland,* another psychologist, looked at motivation from the perspective that people have either a high need for achievement, affiliation, or power and that this motivation would result in different behaviors in the workplace. Specifically, McClelland felt that high achievers only made up 10-15% of the population, but that these people were the real high producers in organizations. McClelland found that high achievers had the following characteristics: high achievers love moderate challenge; high achievers seek concrete feedback, they want to know how they are doing and they also want to know that the manager knows how they are doing; and, high achievers want to take personal responsibility for the work, they can be productive but they do not necessarily make good managers. McClelland felt that high achievement was largely learned in childhood as people model themselves after high-achieving adults. McClelland also felt that managers could have influence over encouraging high achievement by urging people to have specific goals, face challenges, take risks, and enjoy taking personal responsibility.

*Victor Vroom* looked at the internal, cognitive processes that people go through in order to satisfy needs and thus become motivated. Vroom explains that the behavior workers decide to display depends upon what they expect to achieve from that behavior. According to the Expectancy Theory model, the individual effort one is motivated to exert depends on his or her judgment of how well s/he can perform (first level) and what s/he thinks that performance will earn (second level outcome). According to Victor Vroom and the Expectancy Theory: "*Expectancy*" is the probability that the level of effort workers put in will achieve the desired level of performance; "*Instrumentality*" is the probability that performance (first level) will lead to the desired second level outcome or reward; and "*Valence*" is the value of the reward or how much workers want or do not want the second level outcome.

*John Stacy Adams* says that motivation comes and goes for the individual employee at least in part by his or her perception of equity in the workplace. Thus, the individual compares his or her inputs (skills, experience, time on job, seniority, etc.) and outputs (job title, benefits, salary, responsibility) with the inputs and outputs of a "referent" person. Depending upon that comparison, the individual concludes that his or her own input/output ratio is equitable or inequitable. When inequity is perceived, the employee will feel ill at ease and probably try one of two things. First, s/he may reduce his or her own inputs. Secondly, s/he may increase his or her own outputs. Inequity may arise from faulty perception in which case the manager needs to correct the inaccuracy. If inequity exists, the manager needs to examine the situation carefully and find a remedy.

*Reinforcement theory* is based on concepts of how people learn. Most people remember hearing about Pavlov's dogs being taught to salivate at the ringing of a bell because they connected the bell with being fed. That type of "learning" is called classical conditioning as it is a trained stimulus-response reaction. The model that describes human behavior is known as *"operant conditioning."* In this case the expectation of a consequence determines a person's behavior. B.F. Skinner made the concept of *"behavior modification"* very popular in literature and in the work environment. Behavior modification depends upon various types of reinforcement techniques with the basic belief that you tend to get the behavior you reinforce. Literature discusses four basic reinforcement techniques as follows:

- *Positive reinforcement*: A technique used to increase the incidence of a desired behavior. Telling someone they are doing a good job or giving someone a raise are examples of positive reinforcement.
- *Negative reinforcement*: This is also designed to increase the incidence of a desired behavior. If someone walks into the class late and the teacher jokingly chides him or her by saying, "Good afternoon, Yousuf Jan, nice that you could make it..." the student will likely be embarrassed into coming on time next time. On the other hand, the student may love the extra attention and continue to come late.
- *Punishment*: Designed to decrease the incidence of an undesired behavior, punishment does not fit in well with today's values and may breed frustration and resentment. Examples of punishment include scolding someone in front of his or her peers or sending someone home from work. Naturally, there are some incidents which do deserve immediate punishment such as violence in the workplace.
- *Extinction*: This strategy also serves to decrease the incidence of an undesired behavior. Extinction entails simply ignoring a given behavior and hoping it will disappear. It is often an appropriate response for a minor behavioral problem.

*Process theories and satisfaction.* Process theories focus on *"how"* people are motivated. These theories tend to identify specific needs or values that are most conducive to satisfaction with one's job. According to experts, process theorists focus on how a person's expectations for specific outcomes associated with their performance, influence his/her performance. Of course, motivation theorists are interested in how individual behavior is energized, directed, maintained, and stopped. Process theories include Adam's equity theory, Vroom's expectancy theory, Skinner's reinforcement theory, Locke's goal setting theory, and they are central in understanding process theories.

*Content theories and satisfaction.* Content theories are about *"what"* motivates a person. These theories attempt to specify the particular needs that must be attained for an individual to be satisfied with his or her job. Two theories are most prominent in the study of content theories; Maslow's Need Hierarchy theory and Herzberg's Motivator-Hygiene theory. Maslow's Need Hierarchy theory is categorized in a defined order to include physiological needs, safety needs, belongingness and love needs, esteem needs, and self actualization needs. Maslow's theory suggested that satisfied needs are not motivators. As lower level needs are satisfied, they no longer drive behavior, and, consequently, higher order needs take over as the motivating force. Unlike Maslow, Herzberg's Motivator-Hygiene theory argues that job satisfaction and dissatisfaction result from different causes and that satisfaction depends on "Motivators" while dissatisfaction is the result of "Hygiene factors." Motivators deal with aspects of the work itself, which include work, promotion, achievement, responsibility, and recognition. Hygiene factors include working conditions, interpersonal relations, company policies and salary, and supervision.

There are many other concepts and thoughts that lead to a motivational work environment; goal setting and empowerment are two factors. There has been much research on the usefulness of concrete goals in motivating employees to higher productivity. Studies conclude that employees with challenging, concrete, measure-able goals tend to be more productive than those who do not have these goals. Employees also need feedback on how they are doing as they try to attain their goals. *Self-efficacy* refers to one's perception that he or she is able to do a given task. If a person has concrete goals that he or she accepts, believes they have the ability to do the job, and are receiving adequate feedback from their supervisor or through self-monitoring techniques, then this person is likely to have a higher degree of motivation than when these variables are not present.

### *Motivation and Employee Commitment*

Empowerment is a key managerial concept and it delegates much of the traditional management authority to employees who are doing the work. One can see how empowerment fits right in with Herzberg's job enrichment theory. Empowerment provides the "motivators" that Herzberg identified. High achievers love the additional challenge and participation. But, does every worker in every culture want to be empowered and shoulder more decision-making responsibility? Most likely not; therefore, one needs to act situationally. It is through creating meaningful jobs, personal and collective accountability, empowerment, and other job enrichment strategies that coaches and managers can create and increase an employee's affective, continuance and normative commitment. According to Myers and Allen (1997, p. 11), there are three components to commitment which are as follows:

- *Affective* commitment refers to the employee's emotional attachment to, identification with, and involvement in, the organization. Employees with a strong affective commitment continue to stay with the organization because they *want* to do so.
- *Continuance* commitment refers to an awareness of the costs associated with leaving the firm. These employees stay with the firm because they *need* to since the cost of leaving would be too high.
- *Normative* commitment reflects a feeling of obligation to continue employment. These employees feel that they *ought* to remain with the organization due to their acculturation and socialization.

Affectively committed employees tend to continue their employment with the organization because they want to do so. One affectively committed colleague mentioned that going to work for her was a pleasure because after eighteen years of work, her colleagues and co-workers became her second family; such feelings and outcomes can also lead to normative commitment as well. Affectively committed employees demonstrate their dedication to goals and shared values through their loyalty to the organization. Continuance (or "calculative") commitment refers to a person's awareness of the costs if one is to leave the organization. Employees whose primary link to the organization is based on continuance commitment remain because they need to do so. Continuance commitment represents an employee's dedication to the survival or continuance of an organization as it appears to be the best option at the time. Continuance commitment is about staying with the organization because leaving is not an attractive choice. Normatively committed employees feel that they ought to remain with the organization since the company or their bosses have enriched their lives and they want to pay them back. Normative commitment is basically about the employee's belief regarding his or her responsibility to the organization and colleagues. These employees tend to believe that it is the right and moral thing to show loyalty and stay with the organization.

Affective commitment, as stated above, is the employee's emotional attachment and involvement with the organization. Besides specific organizational and individual characteristics which cause affective commitment, such commitment also develops on the basis of work experiences that employees find rewarding or fulfilling. Evidence also suggests that the fulfillment of individual (as opposed to universal) needs is important in the development of affective commitment. *Perceptions* also play an important role in the development of employee's commitment to the organization. Employees who believe their organizations are supportive tend to become affectively committed. Employees who recognize that they have made major investments that would be lost if they were to leave the firm develop continuance commitment. Employees who think that "loyalty" is expected of them become normatively committed. Therefore, management of commitment requires that organizations manage employee perceptions.

Commitment can impact employee turnover, which can be voluntary or involuntary. According to Griffeth and Hom (2001), *voluntary turnover* means that employees freely choose to leave the job. Voluntary leaves are undesirable since the people leaving might be very productive and experienced. Voluntary turnover can be functional or dysfunctional. *Functional* turnover represents the exit of substandard performers. *Dysfunctional* turnover represents the exit of effective performers who cannot be easily replaced. Dysfunctional quits can be grouped into avoidable and unavoidable quits: *Unavoidable* quits represent those employee separations that employers cannot control, such as terminations due to childbirth, full-time care for relatives, family moves, acute medical disability, and death. Of course, *avoidable* ones are those that the employer can and should control to reduce functional or talented employee turnover. *Involuntary turnover* represents employer-initiated job separations over which leavers have little or no control, such as dismissals or layoffs.

Involuntary leaves or exits are desirable since employers do not want to keep low performers in the organization. Griffeth and Hom (2001) offer the following steps for diagnosing turnover problems:

1. Determine the voluntariness, functionality, and avoidability of turnover cases.
2. Subtract out involuntary, functional, and unavoidable quits from the overall quit rate to ascertain the rate of undesirable turnover.

3. If possible, benchmark turnover rate to industry rates.
4. Estimate the personnel cost of turnover.
5. Determine whether potential retention strategies are cost-justified.
6. Attempt to benchmark turnover costs.
7. Evaluate the potential for other kinds of turnover costs.

The overall functional purpose of motivational theories, especially job enrichment, is to reduce employee turnover, enhance employee retention, increase employee commitment, and provide meaningfulness of work so as to counter-effect negative outcomes such as decreased productivity, high turnover, poor attendance, and low employee morale and employer ratings. If it is known that talented employees who are not content at a particular organization or with their specific jobs, then they are more likely to leave the organization, causing more employee turnover and retention challenges.

## Attendance in the Workplace

A work environment that is motivational, pleasant and empowering can increase productivity, and make everyone feel welcome and proud to be a part of it. Such a work environment is likely to result in high employee satisfaction levels where people are likely to come to work with elevated levels of energy and enthusiasm. However, when this is not consistently the case in a specific workplace, employee satisfaction levels and attendance are likely to be low.

Most employers, of course, are doing everything possible to make sure the productivity of their employees and firms are high. Employee discipline is one last resort for correcting performance challenges and behavioral problems in the workplace. Of course, employees can be disciplined for many different reasons, including theft, low performance, absenteeism, and behavioral concerns. While managers and coaches should be prepared to effectively deal with a number of different violations that require discipline, a common concern seems to be employee absenteeism and tardiness.

It should be acknowledged that some absenteeism is inevitable in the workplace. Therefore, coaches and managers should plan to be flexible and professionally accommodate involuntary absences and tardiness. Absenteeism is not all bad and it cannot be totally eliminated. However, excessive absences, which include tardiness, can hurt the organization by creating more work for those who do show up every day. Unscheduled absences that are not managed effectively can create much undue stress and eventually decrease departmental morale. There are generally two types of absences in the workplace that managers and coaches should be aware of and assess on a regular basis. First, there are *involuntary* absences such as being sick, the car not working, the babysitter canceling, taking care of a sick parent, driving the kids to school, etc. Such absences or causes of tardiness cannot be corrected at all times. However, these involuntary absences often do not become a trend since most professional employees want to do a good job and are not willing intentionally to be absent. If they do become a habit, then most employees and managers are able to work out an alternative plan or a more flexible schedule (such as telecommuting or temporarily working at home) to prevent involuntary absences from turning into a departmental problem. Second, there are the *voluntary* absences that take place because employees are not really looking forward to going to work. Employees who are dissatisfied with their jobs, coworkers and managers are likely to be absent from work more often than those who are happy and satisfied. Managers and employees must recognize that absenteeism can be expensive and should try to reduce voluntary absences. Some of the reasons stated for being absent or coming to work late have included the following:

1. Remember, one day I came to work but I was actually scheduled to be off that day. Well today, I thought I was actually off.
2. The train was passing and we could not get through.
3. My dog was upset and crying when I was about to leave for work.
4. The telemarketer kept me busy and I did not want to be rude.
5. When my alarm went off, I was half a sleep and nobody tried to wake me up on time.
6. I had stayed at work for one extra hour yesterday and thought that it would be okay if I was late today. I thought all businesses were closed on the New Year Holiday.

Studies show that absenteeism tends to be high on Fridays and Mondays as some individuals "voluntarily" plan to make their weekends longer. This type of absenteeism must be measured, assessed and prevented before it becomes a trend in the department. As stated by French (2007, p. 201), a study of 300 human resource managers found that small firms spend about $60,000 and large firms spend more than $1 million on average in paid sick time for unscheduled absences each year. Of course, employee absenteeism and tardiness are not necessarily the major areas of cost to the U.S. employers since theft and fraud by employees are estimated to be around $400 billion each year. Nonetheless, excessive absenteeism can have major direct and indirect negative consequences to an organization. Studies through the Research Institute of America have estimated that one-day of being absent from work by an administrative staff can cost a company over $100 in reduced productivity. From a comprehensive perspective, absenteeism tends to hurt the U.S. economy by at least $40 billion each year.

Absenteeism in the American workplace is a major issue for small, medium, and large organizations. For most organizations, their absenteeism rates tend to vary about 2 to 12 percent each month. Absenteeism can be calculated by determining the number of lost days during a given month, multiplying it by 100, and dividing the totals by the average number of employees for that month and the total number of days worked during that period. Studies have shown that unscheduled absences have increased over the last decade in many organizations, and managers should proactively take corrective actions to prevent it from taking place in their department. Such consistent and systemic employee absences could be caused by high levels of employee dissatisfaction with one's job, department, salary, benefits, or tasks. The assessment of such trends can be a good learning experience for the organization and its managers.

Scheduling flexibility can reduce involuntary absenteeism. However, this option may not always be available for all organizations and managers. Companies must assess their absenteeism rates, keep track of it be measuring it each month, provide incentives for workers that do not use their sick days, and discuss any excessive sick days with the employee to see what can be done to immediately correct this trend.

Managers should make sure that their attendance policies are clear, fair and regularly communicated to all employees. Furthermore, they should notice absenteeism trends and immediately discuss it with employees before it goes too long. Managers must be caring and cognizant of special and mitigating circumstances. Absenteeism control options can include, but are not limited to, offering incentives for those with perfect attendance, expecting good attendance from everyone, disciplining absenteeism trends, and providing a positive work environment for all employees. Having a clear and concise policy tends to assist in the reduction of absenteeism. For example, organizations that require a note or a certificate from the doctor's office for multiple days of being out of work tends to have lower absence rates than those that do not have this requirement. Also, firms that do not have a policy regarding reimbursement of unused sick days are likely to have higher absenteeism rates since some people feel that sick days are an entitlement and must be used. So, it might be effective to reward people for unused sick days as a form of positive reinforcement and to proactively stay focused on positively influencing performance. Overall, managers and coaches should regularly monitor, keep track of, and assess employee tardiness and absences, and take corrective actions as needed to prevent any excessive trends from negatively impacting the department's productivity or employees' morale.

## Discipline and Performance Management[31]

Human resources management usually refers to the practices and policies managers need and use to carry out the personnel aspect of their management job, specifically, the acquiring, training, appraising, rewarding, disciplining, terminating, providing a healthy work environment, and fair treatment of their company's employees. Besides training and developing employees, managers also must know about equal employment opportunity, affirmative action concepts and practices, employee rights as well as disciplining and terminating employees as part of their managerial responsibility and authority. *Authority* is a positional and legitimate right of managers to make decisions in the department, to direct the work of others, and to delegate tasks to employees. Using their knowledge of human resources and authority of their position, managers can use their skills to fairly guide people's behavior and, thereby, employees' performance. Many large organizations tend to have clearly-written job descriptions that can serve as an initial contract between the employee and the organization, while the employee is being hired. Some organizations might have official employment contracts, which often are required in a detailed manner in some countries around the world. What is important to consider is that employers must not take employment contracts lightly, be they explicit or implicit; employment contracts should clarify the job's expectations, rules and policies, and the required standards as to fairly communicate to existing and incoming employees. Managers should use the

---

[31] Originally published in "*Privatization and Market-Based Leadership*," by Llumina in 2006.

communicated and formal standards for objectively and fairly interviewing, hiring, developing, and appraising employees.

Fairness and consistency in communicating expectations to employees are extremely important in managing their performance and development, especially in a diverse workforce. According to Kim and Mauborgne (1997), having a "fair process turns out to be a powerful management tool for companies struggling to make the transition from a production-based to a knowledge-based company, in which value creation depends increasingly on ideas and innovation." It is factually proven that a "fair process profoundly influences attitudes and behaviors critical to high performance," as "it builds trust and unlocks ideas." Through the implementation of a consistent and fair process, managers and organizational leaders "can achieve even the most painful and difficult goals while gaining the voluntary cooperation of employees affected" (Kim and Mauborgne, 1997). It also is clear that without a consistent and fair process for developing or disciplining employees, even outcomes that are favored by employees can be extremely difficult to achieve. Dessler (2001) states that it is necessary for employers to institute appropriate "disciplinary and discharge procedures that will survive the scrutiny of arbitrators and the courts" (p. 248). Dessler writes that three principles contribute to perceived fairness in business settings: engagement, explanation, and expectation clarity (2001, p. 249).

1. *Engagement* requires involving individuals in the decisions that affect them by asking for their input and allowing them to refute the merits of one another's ideas and assumptions.

2. *Explanation* requires ensuring that everyone involved and affected should understand how and why final decisions are made and the thinking that underlies such decisions.

3. *Expectation clarity* means making sure that all employees know the standards by which they will be judged and the penalties for not living up to the standards.

Disciplining employees for misconduct, low performance, or not meeting the stated requirements in a timely manner can be one of the most difficult parts of a manager's job. Yet, a proper and systematic process can certainly make the job easier in order to benefit the manager, the employee, and the organization. Disciplining employees is a reality of life and most managers are likely to face it at one time or another. The purpose of discipline is to make sure employees are behaving according to the written, documented, and stated work-related rules and regulations. An initial step for both managers and employees is to understand that employees have rights and they must be given proper and timely feedback on their performance in the workplace. All employees and customers in the workplace have rights, and are thus entitled to a fair, safe, respectful, and healthy work environment. This understanding can lead to respecting employees for their work, taking lessons about performance management and coaching employees, attending appropriate workshops, understanding the company's rules and policies with regard to discipline and termination, and being an effective manager.

Before moving forward with the discipline process, a manager must clarify the problem. The manager should make sure the performance problem or misconduct statement is clear. One must avoid generalities and never translate performance shortfalls and misconducts into attitudinal or personality problems. Managers should also make sure the problem description is specific, observable, documented, and factual. Also, it is important to proactively answer the "when," "what," and the "impact" aspects of the problem to clearly state the issue. The clearer the problem description, the easier it will be to communicate and discuss the issue with the employee.

Once the problem statement and its description is clear, one can begin resolving it. Overall, with regard to disciplining employees, it is best that managers not jump into making irrational decisions based on emotional outbursts. For effectively disciplining employees, managers should follow a progressive disciplining process in order to make employees aware of their shortfalls or misconducts, so they can immediately begin work on improving it. So, progressive discipline is about effectively communicating with employees about their performance, being fair to employees, and respecting their rights. Gary Dessler writes that "a fair and just discipline process is based on three pillars: rules and regulations, a system of progressive penalties, and an appeals process" (2001, p. 253). These pillars or rules are needed in order for managers to be consistent and fair in developing and disciplining their employees. With regard to progressive discipline, Dessler writes that "penalties may range from oral warnings to written warnings to suspension from the job to discharge" (2001, p. 253). Similarly, an effective and consistent appeal process goes smoothly when a progressive discipline process has been followed and implemented by each manager. Many experts and managers recommend using a progressive discipline without punishment process by gaining the employee's acceptance of the documented and expected rules and policies, while reducing the punitive nature of the discipline itself (Dessler, 2001, p. 254). The discipline without punishment process, mentioned by Dessler, includes the following steps:

1. Issue an oral reminder about the standards and the fact that the employee's performance is not aligned with the expectation.
2. Issue a formal written reminder that the performance deficiency or problem must be aligned with the expected standard.
3. Give the employee a paid one-day "decision-making leave." The employee can think whether he or she would like to continue with the job or find another position that better fits his or her desires, skills, and competencies. Upon returning to work, the employee meets with the manager and provides a decision on whether he or she will follow the expected rules and policies to meet the expectations.
4. If the behavior is aligned with the expected standards for the next full year, then all records are purged from the employee's file. Otherwise, if the behavior or performance problem is repeated, then the employee is dismissed.

### Progressively Disciplining Employees

An effective discipline process allows some flexibility in exceptional circumstances. *Progressive discipline* is a proactive approach to enhancing each employee's performance, letting employees know how they are doing, and being fair in allowing employees to either meet the expectations or find another job. Through a standardized progressive discipline process and proper factual documentation, managers can greatly enhance employee retention as well as the probability of correcting work-related problems and treating employees fairly, while also reducing the chances of legal liability for the organization. A video entitled *Legal and Effective Progressive Discipline,* made available by Coastal Human Resources, provides a six-step process for effectively dealing with disciplining employees (Progressive Discipline, 2005): counseling the associate about the problem, oral warning, written warning, suspension, termination contract, and termination. The general steps and considerations suggested for progressively disciplining employees who are not meeting the expected work-related standards are as follows:

*First: Initial counseling session to clarify the problem and expectations.* An employee must be effectively counseled immediately (not months later) if his or her performance or behavior is not satisfactory. This initial step is very important and must be properly planned to make sure the employee is treated fairly, and that the expected standards are communicated effectively. Through effective discussion and communication with the employee, oftentimes this initial counseling can eliminate the problem, thereby leading to better or more satisfactory performance.

*Second: The oral warning.* If the initial step does not eliminate the problem or enhance performance, then the manager must escalate the seriousness of the problem by meeting with the employee and orally warning him or her about the problem and expected standards. For example, a manager can say: "Deena, this is an official oral warning directly related to what was discussed at the initial counseling session about you wearing inappropriate skirts and thereby not following the company's dress code. You must adhere to the company's standards when it comes to proper hygiene and dress code. Your use of strong perfume and the short skirt do not adhere to the company's dress code standards as you can see in the employee manual." It is the manager's responsibility to indicate to the employee what the expectations are and help the employee meet the expected standards. Furthermore, the employee should be reminded of the possible consequences if the performance does not improve or behavior does not change to meet the expected standards. Once the employee clearly understands the problem, the expectations, and possible consequences of continued behavior or status quo, the oral warning session can come to a close. The manager must document this session's material by writing down what was discussed and why, what the expected standards were, and what may happen if the expectation is not met. This should be kept with the manager in case more follow-up sessions are needed.

*Third: The written warning.* If the problem or performance has not changed through the initial counseling and oral warning, then the employee must be warned officially in a written format. Every detail must be written comprehensively, clearly, succinctly, and with the specific consequence if the behavior is not improved as stated in the written warning. The written warning form must state the problem, the expected standard, and that the employee will be suspended or terminated if the behavior does not change immediately.

*Fourth: Place employee on suspension.* If the behavior or performance does not improve, the manager can terminate or suspend the employee as agreed upon in the written warning. Suspension is recommended when the manager wants to provide the employee a chance to personally think and reflect on whether the employee wants to continue working with the firm. The suspension must state the problem, the reason the employee is being suspended, the expected standard when the employee returns to work, and the next consequence which will be termination if the behavior does not change or improve as expected. Furthermore, the employee and the manager must jointly sign a new written warning and termination contract—the contract can be signed when the employee is being suspended or when the employee returns to work, depending on the standardized policy.

*Fifth: Final written warning or termination contract agreement.* Both the employee and the employer jointly agree on the expected standard and sign a contract that if the behavior does not improve immediately, the employee will be terminated.

*Sixth: Terminate the employee.* If the employee does not live up to the expected standard, then respectfully terminate the employee; clearly state why the employee is being terminated. Employees must be terminated correctly and respectfully; otherwise, it can cause major morale disruptions in the workplace. The termination of an employee often can be disruptive to the existing employees; therefore, managers must take extra caution to make sure morale and productivity are not impacted too negatively in the department.

The above steps should be handled professionally, respectfully, and privately with the employee. The word "privately" does not mean that a manager should not have a witness. As a matter-of-fact, for steps two through six, it is best to involve another manager or someone from the human resources department in the disciplining session. It is always best to have an objective third party present; however, the third party should be an objective person such as another manager or someone from human resources (preferably not the employee's colleague who works in the same department or division). As mentioned before, disciplining an employee can be stressful and time-consuming. However, effective and progressive discipline can be a great way to let employees know that their performance is not meeting the expectation and they must improve. A progressive discipline process can focus managers on the facts of each situation, objectives or the expected standards, solutions to eliminate the work-related problem, and actions needed to meet the expected standards. Gary Dessler (2001, p. 254) offers the following discipline guidelines to all coaches, managers and human resource professionals:

1. Make sure the evidence supports the charge of employee wrongdoing or performance challenge.
2. Ensure that the employees' due process rights are protected. Make sure the employee has sufficient opportunities to tell his or her side of the problem.
3. The discipline should be consistent and in alignment with the way management usually responds to similar incidents.
4. Adequately warn the employee of the disciplinary consequences of his or her alleged misconduct.
5. The rule that allegedly was violated should be "reasonably related" to the efficient and safe operation of the particular work environment.
6. Management must fairly and adequately investigate the matter before administering discipline.
7. The investigation should produce substantial evidence of misconduct.
8. Applicable rules, orders, or penalties should be applied "evenhandedly" and without discrimination.

9. The penalty should be reasonably related to the misconduct and to the employee's past work history.
10. Maintain the employee's right to counsel.
11. Do not rob the employee of his or her dignity.
12. Remember that the burden of proof is on you (the manager) since employees are considered innocent until proven guilty.
13. Get the facts and do not make decisions on hearsay.
14. Do not act or make decisions when you are angry since it is very difficult, if not impossible, to act objectively and sensibly in such moments.

It is important that managers and their firms give employees appropriate vehicles for allowing them to express their concerns, opinions, and frustrations without receiving or perceiving retaliation. Such a process can help managers gather the right information about improving the work environment for all employees, thereby creating an inclusive and safe workplace. One important element of a good work environment is fairness to all employees; or having an effective discipline process to deal fairly with problems and performance deficiencies. An effective discipline process attempts to be fair to employees while allowing them sufficient opportunities to fix the problem. An effective discipline process is accompanied with proper discharge and termination processes.

### *Discipline without Punishment*

Discipline is about correcting behavioral or performance-related problems and misconducts in the workplace. Some managers do not like to enforce discipline when employees are not performing or behaving as expected, and no one likes to be the target of it. This result is probably because most traditional discipline approaches require punishing the employee for behavioral problems. With punishment, some employees learn not to get caught by managers for doing what is disliked, instead of attempting to correct the problem and behaving as expected. While punishing the employee to correct a problem can lead to success in the short-term, it may only gain compliance to please the boss and not necessarily commitment to doing a good job. With the practical "discipline without punishment" concept, managers understand and learn how to handle one of the toughest issues any manager faces in managing employees' behavior. Discipline without punishment is very much like using appropriate situational leadership styles where the manager provides either less or more direction to the employee depending on his or her level of readiness and maturity to perform correctly the specific task. In essence, situational leadership is about disciplining employees without punishment in order to take care of the task at hand, guide or develop the employee to correctly perform the task, and enhance the manager's relationship with the associate.

Every organization is likely to have employees that occasionally show "discipline problems." If these misconducts and problems are handled incorrectly, as explained by the concept of discipline without punishment, and "when discipline is equated with punishment, even a small problem with only one person can ruin the entire team's morale and productivity" (Discipline without Punishment, 2005). When discipline issues are handled incorrectly, discipline has the possibility of causing a "battle of wills," with anger and hurt on both sides. As experienced in the workplace, for long-term purposes, not much is gained with many of the traditional discipline approaches, because most employees do not respond progressively better when they are treated progressively worse for a performance issue or a misconduct.

Using modern approaches and respectful examples, the discipline without punishment scenario provides effective ways to use discipline for a healthy department and long-term productivity. It should be understood that workers do not change their attitudes and personalities, but they can change their behavior in the workplace when asked by the organization and managers. Changing employee behavior is the essence of discipline without punishment since misconducts in the workplace tend to be a behavior problem. Discipline without punishment requires that managers first get the individual to admit there is a problem, and then coach the employee on how to solve his or her misconduct or performance-related problem. Discipline without punishment shows how managers:

⇒ Use the steps of focusing on the problem, gaining the employee's agreement to change, identifying strategies for improvement, and following-up to make sure the behavior is changed to discipline employees for lasting improvements in the workplace.

⇒ Prevent a discipline problem from turning into an attitude problem for the employee, and a morale issue for the rest of the workers in the department.

⇒ Keep personality differences, which often have nothing to do with the problem at hand, out of a discipline situation.

⇒ Handle discipline respectfully so self-esteem and feelings of self-worth are kept intact because the employee's long-term growth and development are important for productivity and healthy relationships.

⇒ Delegate the responsibility for taking care of the problem on the shoulders of the problem owner, the employee. *Discipline without punishment* requires that managers put the responsibility for a discipline problem right where it belongs—on the shoulders of the employee.

There are many situational variables, such as the employee, the manager, the problem, the environment, the culture, the relationship of the employee with the manager, and other such factors that must be considered when disciplining employees. While considering the situational variables, one should follow a standardized process to help the employee improve his or her behavior and performance in the workplace without hurting morale or causing negative or ill feelings. Discipline without punishment provides four steps for managers to achieve the goal of helping employees correct behavioral or performance-related problems. The four steps offered for discipline without punishment are (Discipline without Punishment, 2005):

1. Focusing on the problem at hand. Focus on the issue that is causing the problem and not the person. Stay away from personality related concerns or your likes or dislikes of the person. Discuss the specific work-related problem so it can be fixed. To avoid generalities and vague statements, managers should clarify the specific problem and perhaps write it down before discussing it with the employee.

2. Gaining the employee's agreement that there is a problem and that it must be changed. The employee should at least agree to change or that a change is needed. Furthermore, he or she should agree that it is his/her responsibility to correct the problem.
3. Identifying appropriate strategies for improvement jointly with the employee. These strategies should either eliminate the problem or at least improve the performance to a satisfactory level as agreed upon.
4. Following-up to make sure the problem is eliminated and the behavior is improved. Take correct action as appropriate. When the behavior is improved, this provides an opportunity to further develop the individual and the relationship.

The four steps for disciplining employees without punishment is one effective approach to correcting behavioral, work-related problems in the workplace, without causing too much stress to employees, or personally being stressed each day as the manager of the department. It is understood that the manager is running the department and not the other way around, so managers should not stress themselves. Because some discipline incidents or approaches tend to be negative and cause friction between the manager and employees due to a lack of effective communication, a few managers simply avoid facing the problem until it becomes a huge issue and can no longer be avoided. Such tendencies and procrastination of discussing problems and performance-related issues with employees can cause much undue stress, frustration, and hostility. Discipline without punishment offers an effective approach to address most behavioral and performance-related problems immediately in a mature, professional, direct, and task-focused manner, while attempting to jointly "brainstorm" on possible solutions that the employee can use to improve the situation. It must be remembered that the problem "owner" is the employee and consequently he or she is responsible for taking care of the problem. Managers can use the situational leadership styles of telling the employee what to do, selling the employee on the solution, participating with the employee on coming up with a solution, or delegating the task to the employee as per his or her level of readiness and maturity for the specific task or issue. Just like effective leadership, disciplining is not always reserved just for poor performers; rather, it is something that managers should do consistently with all employees, when needed, in order to create an inclusive, productive, and safe work environment for all. With this mindset and paradigm, disciplining employees requires effective leadership, management, and coaching skills. Effective coaches, managers, and leaders know that solving the immediate problem or performance challenge is one immediate opportunity for improvement, while developing the employee and a good relationship with him or her is another major objective for the department's long-term success. Managers must be cautious to not always strive for gaining immediate benefits at the cost of long-term success. Managers should work as coaches to enhance long-term performance.

Perhaps, some of the steps from the *Practical Coach* can apply to disciplining employees without punishment in order to effectively fix problems and enhance performance. A manager's responsibility, as a coach and as a leader, is best fulfilled when he or she maximizes long-term value for his or her department, organization, and society through the use of available resources and effective discipline management approaches. Effective managers jointly and collaboratively work with their employees to increase each worker's commitment to the job, enhance his or her performance on each task, and maximize each associate's long-term value to the organization. The discipline without punishment approach, when applied correctly, can correct most behavioral and performance-related problems in the workplace without having to resort to progressive punishment or employee discharge and employment terminations. However, when all else fails, one can resort to progressive discipline, which can lead to employee discharge and termination if the problem is not resolved correctly in the required or agreed upon time.

**Employee Discharges and Terminations**

When employees are not able to perform their tasks and duties successfully, managers must intervene to help and provide them the needed resources so they can live up to the expectations. Since most large organizations give employees about 60 days notice during layoffs and plant closings, managers should provide sufficient opportunities for employees to enhance their performance. If such efforts do not increase the employee's performance or eliminate the problem, then the employee can be discharged and his or her employment can be terminated with the organization. Dismissal, which must be taken very seriously, should be a last step in the discipline process after all reasonable efforts have been made to correct the problem. It is a fact that dismissed employees may take their cases to court, which can cost the manager and others in the organization much wasted time and resources. Managers should double check and ensure that sufficient evidence exists to justify the dismissal. Dessler (2001) writes that "the best way to handle a dismissal is to avoid it in the first place" (p. 256). In the event an employee is dismissed, it should be done respectfully, and a clear reason should be provided for the dismissal. Some common reasons for dismissals can include, but are not limited to, the following (Dessler, p. 256):
1. Unsatisfactory performance.
2. Misconduct.
3. Lack of qualification for the job.
4. Elimination of the job.
5. Changed requirements for the job.
6. Insubordination.

While disciplining and dismissing employees is not an easy task for managers, they must be consistent, professional, respectful to the employee, and factual. It is the manager's responsibility to make sure a standardized and consistent process is followed with each employee so it is fair, and that it is perceived as such. Researchers often mention how studies conducted by Connie Wanderg *et al.* (1999), in their article entitled "Perceived Fairness of Layoffs Among Individuals Who Have Been Laid Off: A Longitudinal Study" in the journal of *Personnel Psychology*, have shown that dismissed employees who were given full explanation for their termination were more likely to perceive their layoff as fair, endorse the terminating organization, and indicate that they did not wish to take the past employer to court (Dessler, p. 257)

Managers should take every possible step to avoid mistreating employees and wrongfully discharging, terminating or dismissing them. According to Dessler (2001), a "wrongful discharge occurs when an employee's dismissal does not comply with the law or with the contractual arrangement stated or implied by the firm via its employment application forms, employee manuals, or other promises" (p. 257). Managers can avoid wrongful discharges when they follow their company's stated rules and policies and when they effectively state their expectations to employees from the outset in the employee's employment process. Once again, it is best to remember that the best way to avoid wrongful discharge claims is to avoid discharges by helping employees meet the stated standards and expectations. Dismissals and discharges can cause much undue stress on both the employee and manager. Dessler writes that "managers run double their usual risk of suffering a heart attack during the week after they fire an employee." Studies have concluded "that the stress associated with firing someone doubled the usual risk of a heart attack for the person doing the firing, during the week following the dismissal" (Dessler, p. 258). When a termination becomes a necessity, managers must proceed cautiously and strategically since it can be devastating to employees, even if the employee is warned many times prior to the dismissal. While most employees handle dismissals effectively, some might become disoriented and even resort to violence. Professor Dessler (p. 258) offers the following guidelines for managers who are terminating an employee.

1. *Plan the termination session carefully.* Speak with the human resources department to make sure every step is being followed properly and all the paperwork or forms are completed in advance. Do not let the employee know about the termination over the phone. Find a neutral site for the termination session instead of holding it at the manager's office. Also, have the phone numbers for the employee assistance program personnel and security officials ready in case they are needed.

2. *Get to the point.* Inform the person immediately about the purpose of the session and make it quick.

3. *Describe the situation.* Briefly and factually state the reason that the employee is being terminated. Remember to not attack the person…simply focus on the performance problem or the reason he or she is being terminated. Emphasize that the decision is final.

4. *Listen with empathy.* Continue the interview until the employee is reasonable and speaks calmly about the reasons for his or her termination and future steps.

5. *Review all elements of the termination package or the severance package (if any).* The manager or human resources specialist can describe the severance payments, benefits, and other relevant support material available for the employee.

6. *Identify the next step.* Inform the employee what he or she should do next. Let the person know if there is an Employee Assistance or Outplacement Program available to help him or her with resume preparation or to look for jobs outside of the organization.

Some large organizations do offer outplacement services as part of their severance package. Outplacement services could include outplacement counseling, which according to Dessler (2001) "is a systematic process by which a terminated person is trained and counseled in the techniques of conducting a self-appraisal and securing a new job that is appropriate to his or her needs and talents" (p. 259). The outplacement program is simply a service which can provide retired or terminated employees with suggestions for dealing with the process of securing a new job. Such programs also can offer advice on determining appropriate jobs, resume development, going to employment agencies, and preparing for interviews. Upon the termination and dismissal of employees, human resource personnel can conduct an exit interview with the employee to gather his or her insights on some of the challenges and problems facing the organization. Exit interviews could elicit information on how the person was hired, oriented, trained, developed, and promoted to various jobs during his or her employment. Furthermore, questions can deal with the fairness of salary, ethics, morale, communication, employment relations, the style of management, the direction of the company, what they liked about their job or organization and what they disliked, and the way their decision to leave the organization or the dismissal was handled.

## Globalization[32]

Today's coaches and managers must also be concerned about local and cross-cultural norms and mores of their employees. In other words, coaches and managers must become aware of globalization trends and how they can impact local practices, and vice versa. In order for the concept of globalization and localization to succeed in any market, it is important for all coaches and managers to understand that both concepts are interdependent but not necessarily mutually exclusive. This means that a local factor will increase and expand to become a global factor. It is not logical for the one factor to take place without influencing the other. The local factor creates the global phenomena. Both concepts are dependent on each other. Therefore, vice-versa, a global issue will affect a local issue, and they can simultaneously impact each other. As one example, the recent concept of globalization is driven by banking and technology as a requirement for the ease of transactions in the local and global market. Bankers, clients and the everyday consumers require the ease of global transactions. However, the originating concept of globalization goes back to the Byzantine era of the Romans and their people.

Globalization and localization is far reaching, and includes the rising sea levels due to ocean warming on the North American continent, which will affect a small village in Asia and its neighboring countries. The warming of the ocean temperature also affects the reduced viability of the salmon swimming upstream to spawn and produce eggs. The salmon need cooler water temperatures in order to spawn successfully. The reduced salmon population then decreases the availability of salmon in the consumer market, which affects the profits of fishermen operating in the seafood market. The warming sea temperature also reduces the reproduction of tuna fish for the Sushi market, which affects the Japanese culture of sashimi dining as well as the sashimi business market. The warming of the earth in the northern hemisphere has far reaching consequences from the eastern Asian market to the

---

[32] Coauthored with B. Cassandra Grant, Nova Southeastern University.

western market of the Americas. Hence, a local phenomenon in Antarctica can have far-reaching global effects.

There is no one definition for the term "globalization," for to do so means ignoring the various applications, meanings and use for this term that is used worldwide. In other words, the term globalization is often used differently in different contexts (Mead, 2005, p. 250). There is the current phenomenon of global warming; a phenomenon in one country is related elsewhere due to the global factor of "cause and effect." The melting ice caps in Antarctica due to the warming of the earth by a mere 1 to 2 degrees, affects the rising sea levels in Southern Asia. The phenomenon of "cause and effect" applies in business as it does in nature. The term "no man is an island" can be aptly applied to countries globally and the global effect we have on each other medically as well as otherwise. An illness in Africa if not cured as an epidemic while in its early stages, quickly becomes an endemic for the rest of the world. Examples of such global medical phenomenon include mad cow disease, SARS epidemic, as well as the bird flu crisis. These medical issues made their way to many countries in less than five years. The ongoing issue of the HIV/AIDS virus has become a borderless medical disease that began many years ago and is now a global problem. However, for the purpose of narrowing this concept, globalization can be aptly described as a worldwide effect that is not local in nature due to its cause and effect on people, society and business ventures. Globalization is a phenomenon created by local factors, which increases and crosses borders thus affecting the global market.

In order to pinpoint where globalization began, Richard Mead has utilized the 1970s as the recent point of origin as a set of processes that have historical and cultural roots (2005, p. 251). However, one can also go as far back as the Roman era, and to Carthage which was Rome's rival, the Hellenic world as well as the Chinese Dynasty (Mead, p. 247). One can discuss the Chinese silk trade in business and the Roman Empire's influence on current society in politics, specifically the ruling Roman council known as the Senate, hence the U.S. Senate and its 100 members, two for each state of the Union. This example is also applicable to the United Kingdom's ruling council, the House of Parliament.

There is the loss suffered from globalization as governments lose control over local decision-making processes for their countries, as decisions made by the European Union affects the citizens of the United Kingdom (Mead, p. 254). The local Prime Minister and the House of Parliament are powerless to the overriding decisions of the European Union. Alternatively, global implications can and often do rival local conditions. One can no longer be concerned only with local rivals; the global condition often affects the local market. For example, the global conditions of oil affecting the local conditions and prices of gasoline is the current and most classical example. There is also the diversification of labor by the Japanese Toyota market to capitalize on international production by diversifying to different locations (Mead, p. 253). This has resulted in the Japanese automobile manufacturer outperforming the American Ford automobile production line in sales and consumer appeal. By globalizing their production and making structural changes, the Japanese have been able to take advantage of the development of information technology (Mead, p. 253). A structural change that Ford is now trying to accomplish at the expense of thousands of job losses and a $12.7 billion dollar loss in profits as revealed in the media during the early part of 2007 (Bunkley, 2007).

What does all of this mean for the expatriate manager or coach who has to function in a local market affected by global conditions? It means adapting, learning and changing with the market. The expatriate manager must look to his/her local market of employees as well as consumers for queues and guidance as s/he learns the culture and the customs in order to succeed in the global market. Many corporations prefer to utilize local managers in the global market, as the local manager knows the local culture best. Therefore, in order for the expatriate manager to succeed globally in a local market, the expatriate manager is expected to be highly skilled in multiculturalism and be able to adapt and come up to speed in a minimal amount of time. For example, the expatriate manager must understand the requirement of a two-hour siesta in Spain from noon to 2 p.m., and the requirement of a 20 to 30-minute break for tea around 2 p.m. in the afternoon in the United Kingdom. These cultural practices are unheard of and frowned upon in the United States, where productivity and being driven overrides the human factor of taking time out for self during business hours. In the U.S., utilizing office hours solely for producing tangible work related results is the norm. The expatriate manager and coach must remove this American concept and expectation if s/he expects to succeed in a global or international market outside of the United States.

## Coaches and Cross-Cultural Management Concerns[33]

Leaders exist around the world. While there are many universal traits that leaders around the globe may share, there are also many motivation strategies, influence techniques, norms, and mores that are not universal at this time. As such, coaches, managers and leaders should be careful and sensitive to the needs of their diverse and cross-cultural employees and colleagues. Leaders, managers and coaches must always remember what the balloon salesperson said to the little boy at the carnival, that "It is not the color or the size of the balloons that make a difference. It is what is inside that makes them go up." Effective leadership and coaching is about objectively applying relevant principles in a sensitive manner with each employee in order to make a positive difference in their achievement of high performance.

Dr. Yuka Fujimoto and Dr. Charmine Hartel, authors of the 2006 article entitled "A self-representation analysis of the effects of individualist-collectivist interactions within organizations in individualistic cultures; Lessons for diversity management," are experts in the areas of diversity management, culture, values, attitudes, disability, and self identity processes and outcomes. These authors state that in modern times, diversity within organizations presents both an opportunity and a challenge within the context of business efficiency, innovativeness and competitiveness. It is important for a company to create an environment where the full range of skills and knowledge of its diverse workforce are being employed to major effect. Many companies within the Asia-Pacific region are striving to achieve this goal through cross-cultural management. In this context, organizations that

---

[33] Article summaries prepared by Steven D. Cooke, B. Cassandra Grant, Fernanda Gazmuri, and Carolina (Maria) Ayala, Nova Southeastern University.

operate with an openness with respect to cultural and racial differences are more likely to be effective. Individualist-collectivist interaction (ICI) is what lies at the basis of cross-cultural communication, but although this is considered key in management, there does not appear to be enough literature explaining which factors would aid in the fostering of such relationships/interactions – which would thus lead to an organization maintaining its competitive edge. The authors also state that expatriate individuals exposed to cross-cultural experiences and diverse management practices should reflect this need, while utilizing and enabling "the full use of the range of skills and talents available to ensure affective and behavioral alignment." The article goes on to state that research has indicated that cultural diversity (comprised of individualists and collectivists) – and the coexistence of racio-ethnic and values dissimilarities - within an organization is likely to lead to increased creativity, problem-solving skills and a higher degree of cooperative behavior which often proves beneficial within an organization. Prejudices related to the above-mentioned dissimilarities, would be "individual experience of work, group dynamics, employee attitudes, and employee behaviors" (Fujimoto & Hartel, 2006). Initially, individuals create stereotypes in their mind, but as they work more closely together, these stereotypes are replaced by a stronger understanding and knowledge of the other person. An open mindset is therefore more effective within the context of cross-cultural management practices.

Cultural alienation is also a factor that creates prejudice and negative outcomes to ICI. When these prejudices are overcome, ICI will function more effectively. Similarity attraction (leaning towards people who have similar ideas and values) is also something that needs to be overcome. Supervisors who exercise similarity attraction may find that they are alienating people who are dissimilar to them and, in the process, producing unfair performance appraisals. Hence, the author states that "although organizations recognize the importance of diversity management, there is still a gap between recognition and action...differences in self representation associated with IC orientations create different prejudicial tendencies" (Fujimoto & Hartel, 2006). In conclusion, it is by taking full advantage of the differences in cognitive processes of people from different cultures – therefore, eliminating or moderating these prejudicial tendencies - that an organization can be truly successful.

The fostering of cultural diversity is an issue that we are constantly being faced with in today's business and working world. The authors mention several instances where diversity created positive outcomes within organizations, one of which is the following: "...increasing cultural diversity within a Hong Kong shipping operation led to the need to foster management skills in dealing with cross-cultural sensitivities and hiring in countries with different labor laws" (Fujimoto & Hartel, 2006). Furthermore, "an American operation in China outlined their keys to success as maintaining an open mindset for different management practices and minimizing value judgments about Chinese ways of business" (Fujimoto & Hartel, 2006). However, in the practical world, one has to watch out for the pitfalls (such as negative behavioral outcomes) that are created in the process of fostering cultural diversity. One example given by the authors is that "...research showed that workgroups consisting of Chinese (collectivists) and Netherlanders (individualists) produced greater profit but reported low job satisfaction, organizational commitment and higher rates of turnover. These findings stress the importance of developing diversity-oriented HRM so that cognitive benefits of diversity [i.e. a culturally diverse workforce] are increased and affective and behavioral costs are minimized" (Fujimoto & Hartel, 2006).

### Managing and Mentoring Expatriates

The 2005 article entitled "A needs-driven approach to expatriate adjustment and career development: a multiple mentoring perspective," written by John M. Mezias, and Terri A. Scandura, featured in the *Journal of International Business Studies*, discusses the importance of mentoring expatriate managers and their firms. The article cites the importance of assigning the aid of multiple mentors for the purpose of adjustment and development prior to the expatriate being sent overseas for global assignments. Premature expatriate departures and unsuccessful repatriation obstructs knowledge transfer, decreases local managers' confidence in the corporation's confidence and discourages other managers from accepting international assignments. This loss in knowledge from not successfully sending expatriates home once the assignment has been completed are stated at a 10% loss of the expatriate managers dues to resignations from their firms shortly upon completing their assignments. The statistics state an additional 14% leave within 2 to 3 years upon returning home from their assignments. The article quotes the costs associated with the loss of knowledge and the loss of expatriate managers for the multinational corporations within the U.S. for these corporations, ranges from $2-$2.5 billion. The authors further discuss how international mentoring may improve expatriate adjustment, development and retention, which may affect the outcome of international strategy and the importance mentoring may have on preventing lost opportunities of transferring gained knowledge. Mentoring expatriates may aid in developing a competitive advantage through knowledge transfer versus the challenge of trying to gain an understanding of inferred/tacit knowledge, while adjusting to living and working in a foreign country with a different social and cultural context.

In order to be successful in the global market, the expatriate manager will need training beyond academia; the expatriate will need mentoring. What does this mean? In order to ensure the expatriate manager's global assignment is successful, the corporation will need to ensure that the expatriate manager is instructed in the norms of the culture he/she will be working in. How is this accomplished? The corporation will need to have a program in place that will instruct the expatriate in the norms as well as the idiosyncrasies of the culture. These instructions will need to include the perspectives, tastes, trends, and approaches of the unfamiliar culture. According to experts, "Instructions will need to include learning how to adapt to living in other cultures, and learning how to interact with foreign colleagues as equals" (Apud, Johnson and Lenartowicz, 2006, p. 527). Beyond the mentoring program, "corporations should have culturally sensitive policies in place for the expatriate, such as the ability to keep in touch with co-workers in the host country, and encourage host country managers to provide assistance and support" (Mezias and Scandura, 2005). By keeping in touch with the host-country on a regular basis, this aids to foster the transfer of knowledge to the host country, as well as ensures the expatriate has a solid support base with the host country. Otherwise, the expatriate can become immersed in the culture and lose sight of the bigger picture of being able to balance the expatriate role with the role of remaining grounded in the purpose of the corporation's assignment.

The term "Stockholm syndrome" has usually been utilized in reference to held hostages becoming immersed in their plight and identifying with their captor. However, this syndrome can be utilized in other situations. The situation of an expatriate manager becoming immersed and then identifying with the expatriate culture he/she has been placed in is also possible, and with it the potential for reverse ethnocentrism, especially if the expatriate does not have the support of the host country and begins to feel abandoned and left to cope with the assignment with no support. It would be feasible to see the potential for this adverse syndrome to become a potential end-result of the host country's unintentional cultural isolation.

Due to the perception of lack of support, the burden of assistance and support will be transferred to the expatriate, an added responsibility the expatriate would be forced to face on top of learning about the new culture. However, with the appropriate policies in place, such issues are avoidable, and allow the expatriate to focus on the job of learning about the new culture. In order to succeed in the task of accomplishing the assigned job in a positive manner, without adverse personal or psychological effects, the expatriate needs to be able to focus on learning the new culture. Without the appropriate policies in place, such oversights can translate into the expatriate leaving the corporation once the assignment has been completed, if completed, as some expatriates do not complete the assignment, which adds to the statistics of "$2-$2.5 billion in losses to the multinational corporations" (Mezias and Scandura, 2005). For example, the article discusses this type of added responsibility as protean, a Greek term, which speaks to changing/adapting form in order to fit the local circumstances and demands of the task and culture (Mezias and Scandura, 2005). Without the appropriate policies being in place, it becomes the responsibility of the expatriate to change and adapt in order to fit into the expatriate culture with no assistance of mentorship. This is a risky venture when the stakes are as high as billions of dollars in revenue losses.

Practical policies should include a monthly return-home program to ensure reconnection with the host country, especially reconnection with the support network of friends and family. The monthly return-home program also ensures refreshing and reinforcing the goals of the company as the expatriate provides progress reports to the corporation. These reports will aid the corporation to assess what is working, what needs to be improved upon and ask the expatriate what he/she needs in order to ensure the assignment is successful. The corporation's involvement in this manner will reassure the expatriate of the corporation's support and the importance of the expatriate's mind-set and well-being to the company.

Mezias and Scandura's article addressed the importance of putting in place a well thought-out policy on how to support the expatriate manager on assignment. This is a cutting-edge managerial practice as most corporations may not be aware of the importance of a similar policy. Realistically, how many corporations would have the forethought to create such a policy, unless the program/policy has been brought to their attention, or due to the results of trial and error? The results of trial and error as featured in the article can be extremely costly, and is easily preventable. A mentoring program of this nature should be the first item on the agenda once the expatriate manager has been chosen. A successful mentoring program can be outsourced to the expatriate country for the initial three months of the expatriate manager actually filling the assigned position abroad. Or, maybe the designated manager could go abroad few months before the expatriate assignment actually begins in order to understand and learn the new culture. The expatriate manager would live in-country (host country) while being mentored, and partake in the monthly return-home program as part of the requirement to utilize the support network of reconnecting with family and friends, while reporting to the corporation on the progress of the mentoring program. This would be a preview of what the process will be, once the expatriate manager has completed the mentoring program and has filled the role of expatriate manager in-country. This process will add value to the corporation as it will aid to ensure the success of the expatriate assignment. An additional option is to do an exchange program with an in-country employee who would be sent to the host country to be mentored. This in-county employee would be the expatriate manager's assistant as needed when he or she returns home to the host country on the required monthly return-home program to refresh and reconnect with family and friends. Such an exchange program would also foster a healthy camaraderie with the in-country employees as they will view their fellow employees as being given similar opportunities.

### *Skills for Global Managers*

It may seem that the globalization trend has been strongly underway for a long time, yet many companies are still having trouble finding managers who are comfortable and effective in a global environment. Even managers who are top performers often lack cultural awareness in their dealings with employees and partners overseas and lack experience managing complex processes over long distances. Why is it so difficult for human resources leaders and senior executives to develop effective global managers? Glenn Rifkin (2006) answers this question by explaining three steps companies and managers can take to prepare for the challenges of managing globally, as well as key characteristics of successful global managers.

The article entitled "*The Soft Skills of Global Managers*" by Rifkin aims to help develop a clearer understanding of the managing challenges of working across borders; to show the importance of inculcating in new global managers an awareness of and appreciation for cultural differences; and to point to the tools and support that global managers need to succeed. Managing in today's global arena requires meeting the challenge of managing people who differ in time and place, as well as culturally, socially, and linguistically. According to global strategy professor Mary Teagarden, embracing and exploiting differences among cultures begins by addressing "a headquarters' mindset" (Rifkin, 2006). That mindset involves the common assumptions by companies that they can do things abroad in the same manner as they do them domestically. Teagarden urges leaders to focus more closely on the empathic qualities of prospective global managers and to ensure that managers have had an opportunity to build an understanding of the different behaviors in the new cultures in which they will work.

Teagarden has also identified key characteristics possessed by successful global managers. Three of the most important are: a belief that differences matter;

openness to new and different ideas; and cognitive complexity, or the ability to focus on both the "hard" and "soft" metrics in an organization. Prospective global managers can focus on these factors as they assess their skills and readiness for their new assignment. Small and midsized organizations usually have a scarcity of mentoring skills to help with the first of the three factors. Concerning the second factor, Teagarden says companies too often regard globalization as a one-way street, rather than tapping into the management expertise of other regions. Cognitive complexity seems to be the most difficult factor to get right, as companies struggle to balance the need for consistent corporate practices with the need for regional uniqueness. It requires an awareness of cultures in the midst of dynamic change. It also demands a healthy dose of independent thinking among some very unfamiliar surroundings. "Soft skills" in management and "people processes" are more important for industry than capital or hardware like machinery and technology to achieve global competitiveness. An effective global business leader requires both subject matter knowledge and strong interpersonal and communication skills.

Rifkin's article cites Mary Kay Cosmetics door to door sales dilemma in China. The Chinese management team created and implemented an innovative distribution system. Being open to new ideas, Mary Kay Cosmetics replicated this concept in their global operations. "That is how you use the human supply chain very effectively," Teagarden says. The article also cites Cisco's experience to illustrate the difficulty of teaching new global managers how to balance corporate philosophy with unique local circumstances. One way to go about this is to allow new global managers to move gradually into unfamiliar cultures, such as by first working on a virtual team or—as Cisco now does—by employing "cultural ambassadors."

### *Cross Cultural Communication Tips*

In his 2007 article, Neil Payne provides several tips for effective communication in diverse cultures. Cross cultural communication can create many complications for a business. There are basic tips that can help managers and expatriates minimize misunderstandings and to maximize their cross-cultural communication skills. Payne, in his article, talked about important information to take into consideration anytime managers and coaches negotiate on a global market. In order to improve cross-cultural negotiations it is important to slow down, separate questions, avoid negative questions, take turn and listen, write things down, be supportive, check meaning, avoid slang, watch the use of humor, and maintain local etiquette.

*Slow down.* We need to be comprehensive and acknowledge that even when English, which is one of the most common languages in the world, is used in cross-cultural negotiation that does not mean that all people involved manage the language as their mother tongue. For this reason, it is crucial to speak slowly and clearly. On the other hand, it is necessary to ensure effective pronunciation in order to transmit messages the best way possible.

*Separate questions.* With the intention of maintaining a clear communication, Neil Payne explains the importance of trying not to ask double question. These complex questions can lead to a misunderstanding and usually the listener only catches one part of the inquiry. To avoid confusion it is important to maintain the language as simple as possible.

*Avoid negative questions.* Payne gives information about how different cultures have different meanings for "Yes" or "No" answers. So, we need to be careful when using these types of answers and questions to keep away from misinterpretation.

*Take turns.* It is fundamental to take time to listen and make sure everyone understands the ideas and topics presented. To continue a conversation in a global market it is important for this dynamic to ensure the correct delivery of the message involved in the conversation.

*Write it down.* Always write down those questions or doubts that can rise in the conversation. These uncertainties should be discussed to stay away from any mix-up of the information.

*Be supportive.* Neil Payne assures that for the preservation of a comfortable communication, it is important to be patient and encourage those whose main tongue is not English to speak and give their opinions. This action will create an environment of confidence and trust. As a consequence, negotiation will be productive and easier.

*Check meanings.* When communicating across cultures it is vital to check meaning. Every culture can have a different meaning for certain words and phrases; therefore, never assume that the other party understands and before continuing with the conversation, make sure to summarize what has been said in order to verify that it is clear.

*Avoid slang.* Idioms and slang are not completely understood by foreigners who speak a different language. Avoid idioms and slang.

*Watch the humor.* Every culture deals with humor differently. Some cultures take business very seriously and jokes are interpreted as disrespectful. For these reasons, using appropriate humor is important to a professional environment during cross-cultural interactions and negotiations.

*Maintain etiquette.* Cross-cultural etiquette can lead to a great business relationship or to a total business failure. Understand the other person's or party's norms and mores regarding their local business etiquette. Etiquette in business differs so much from country to country that it is crucial to learn about it before any meeting with the counterpart. Often, a lack of knowledge about the local etiquette can cause a major miscommunication.

Cross-cultural communication is about dealing with people from different cultures. It is fundamental to be aware of cross-cultural tips to maintain an efficient communication. Of course, there are many other cultural elements and nuances that coaches must be aware of and sensitive to when helping others develop. The following are some of the suggestions and implications for cross-cultural coaching, as offered by Bacon and Spear (2003, p. 244) and other experts in the field:

- Allow cultural difference to come to surface and be visible. Acknowledge differences as appropriate.
- Be aware that in any coaching or communication session, it is the message received that counts (and not necessarily the message sent).
- Use effective communication skills to better understand the coachee: pay attention to both verbal and nonverbal messages, paraphrase what you understand, confirm your understanding, and avoid prejudgment.

- Keep in mind that the other person is more likely to forgive errors than arrogance.
- Work toward creating synergy by avoiding ethnocentric mindsets and assumptions.
- Use the differences to learn and seek new solutions by exploring diverse perspectives and paradigms, and ultimately choosing a mutually-agreed upon alternative.

## *Summary*

Motivating, coaching, leading, managing, developing, retaining, disciplining, and terminating employees are realities of life in all organizations, and they are all very important elements of a manager's responsibility. Effective coaches and managers attempt to avoid employee termination, discipline, and discharge by recruiting and hiring the right individuals. Furthermore, through the creation of a motivational work environment, they develop and assist employees in achieving the stated objectives through effective leadership skills, discipline without punishment processes, and progressive discipline approaches. Effective coaches and managers are always concerned about the progressive development of their employees, and thus utilize a standardized corrective action process when performance expectations and standards are not going as expected. Effective coaches proactively help their employees become successful by getting them to use their strengths in performing what they enjoy doing. As an effective leader and coach, Dr. Randolph Pohlman believes that coaches can help their employees become motivated and successful by providing them with a vision of the future, getting them to pay attention to detail, getting things done proactively, showing a sense of humor, taking initiative, thinking strategically, getting prepared for more challenging responsibilities, and creating value for themselves and their organizations (Personal Communication, April 02, 2007).

Effective managers and coaches must be sensitive to the needs of their cross-cultural people and work strategically to make sure all their employees are as successful as they would like to be based upon each employee's qualifications, goals, abilities, and competencies. Sensitivity through effective coaching can certainly enhance employee commitment. According to William Lauffer, "Employee commitment is an attitude—separate from job satisfaction—that suggests that employees would be motivated to continue with an employment relationship as opposed to terminating that relationship" (Personal Communication, November 2006). The applicability of some of the recommendations, mentioned thus far, is evident in today's workplace. Lauffer, who is a successful practitioner, states that "most of our efforts to minimize turnover focus on building affective commitment, with some orientation toward normative commitment." Lauffer goes on to say that established supervisory practices often facilitate organizational commitment by including all team members in the decision-making process. Any hiring decision should require that each team member has the opportunity to interview potential candidates for either team member or management positions. Employment offers are to be contingent on general agreement of candidate suitability. Furthermore, according Lauffer, each year's budgeting process should include a significant amount targeted toward associate development that helps to build both affective commitment and normative commitment. Finally, managers and coaches could assess progress in these areas each year using such instruments as Gallup's Q12, which is designed to measure how much job satisfaction and commitment each employee is likely to experience as an outcome of social relationships at work, guidance and support from their immediate supervisor, and the degree to which they have autonomy and control over their work,

------------------------------

Discipline is not something managers do to poor performers. Discipline is something managers and leaders help create for all employees because they deserve a safe, inclusive, and professional work environment.

------------------------------

## *Discussion Questions*

1. Discuss two motivational theories that coaches can use to create an inspirational work environment for all.
2. What can coaches do to increase an employee's commitment to the department and/or organization? Discuss strategies for enhancing employees' affective, continuance and normative commitments.
3. What are some of the common causes of employee tardiness and excessive absences? What can coaches and managers do to effectively deal with such issues? Discuss and list five specific actions to reduce voluntary absences.
4. What can coaches do to effectively discipline employees?
5. Can employee discipline and termination cases be avoided? Discuss.
6. Why are employees terminated? Discuss some common examples or reasons. What are some guidelines for effective employee terminations?
7. Discuss the concept of Discipline without Punishment? Should managers adapt this process? Why or why not?
8. Have you ever seen managers or heard of managers who terminated an employee in a totally wrong manner as the manager allowed his or her emotions to drive the decision? Discuss your personal examples. What could have been done to terminate the employee in a dignified and respectful manner?
9. What forces are driving the trend toward globalization of management and leadership practices?
10. Are there differences between managing and leading in domestic workplaces versus an international workplace? Discuss.
11. What are your suggestions for coaching effectiveness where a manager, for the first time, is going to work in a foreign country?

# CHAPTER 13

## Rewards, Recognition Programs, and Ethics

The support of executives and managers are critically important to the success and ethical implementation of socially responsible performance management and reward systems. To create an environment that supports ethical behavior, it is extremely important to educate executives and managers in the creation of a holistic performance management program as well as in designing and executing ethical reward programs. In order for a performance management system and reward program to work effectively, high level executives and managers, as well as their employees and colleagues, should also be appropriately rewarded for exercising and modeling ethical behavior. A survey of respondents from medium to large size companies showed that 83% of them have at least one or more employee recognition or reward programs. The structure and ethical implementation of such programs can make or break the project.

Proper design and implementation of reward and recognition programs, as part of a comprehensive performance management system, can be productive and it will recover more than just its cost. Based on personal experiences of the author as a manager and a review of best practices, this practical chapter reviews various aspects of performance management systems and reward programs, as well as their ethical ramifications, and recommends guidelines for the implementation of effective recognition programs through twenty-first century managers and entrepreneurs in a responsible manner.

### Performance Management and Human Resources

The traditional methods of running a business based on feelings, goodwill, social responsibility, because of thinking that it is the right thing to do are changing to where every decision needs measurement if it is worthy of implementation, and the "it makes sense paradigm." There is always an acceptable ratio of cost that is associated with the means of achieving certain outcomes and if the outcomes produce less than the cost, then most often it would not make good business sense to follow this strategy. Today, we can measure the performance of individuals in terms of their attributes, behaviors, and the results they produce.

*Performance management* is a way of measuring and making sure that the activities of everyone in the organization are aligned with the overall shared mission, vision, and goals of the company. An appropriate performance management program determines what performance means, how it is measured, and provides timely feedback to those responsible for accomplishing the tasks. In today's complicated and changing business environment, most companies are looking for ways to gain a competitive advantage over others in their industry, and performance management is one way to gain this edge. Most performance management programs are designed to align employee activities to the firm's goals, provide useful data to make administratively educated decisions about employees, and to provide appropriate feedback to employees so they can correct their shortcomings in a timely manner and build on their strengths.

Some companies use performance management as a strategy to link employee activities (results and accomplishments) with the mission of the company as defined by the short-term goals. This means defining the prospective goals, activities that would accomplish those outcomes and other characteristics employees would need to exhibit to accomplish the strategic results. Other organizations use performance management as away of helping them make administrative decisions such as promotions, pay raises, layoffs, termination, and recognizing people for a job well-done. One area where most managers have difficulty would be administering honest performance appraisals to their employees. This is because managers do not want their employees to feel bad and/or be upset with the management. The general reasons are that "I have to work with these people day after day and I can't tell them that they are not doing well." This challenge becomes especially difficult if the relationship between employee and manager is really close where they know each other's family members by names, faces and hobbies. However, providing honest and consistent feedback is vital to the success of the individual and the organization. Therefore, it is worthy of careful and deliberate planning and time for the manager and the employee.

Dr. Stephen R. Covey, the author of *Seven Habits of Highly Effective People*, encourages organizations to use a win-win agreement to get a clear, mutual understanding, and an agreed-upon strategy up front in five areas which include desired results, guidelines, resources, accountability, and consequences. Managers should be encouraged to use a similar format with their associates as they see appropriate. Most managers use this format to discuss and clarify a new employee's responsibilities, an employee who is horizontally changing jobs for cross-functional training, or employees who receive vertical promotions and assume new responsibilities. This process normally takes place in a different time than performance appraisals. As a matter-of-fact, it is usually completed at the beginning of a review period where the employee will traditionally receive a performance appraisal at the end of that period. It is completed at the beginning to clarify and help the employee be successful and to achieve maximum development in his/her job during the given period. The performance appraisal should be specific and congruent with the goals of the firm, it should be measurable and valid, it should also be based on attainable and acceptable goals (something that the employee has received relevant training about and reflects his/her responsibilities), and last but not least, it should be reliable and timely. According to the theory of behavior modification, a behavior that is not rewarded, acknowledged, or recognized on a reliable and timely basis will have a tendency to be ignored.

Feedback is a very important part of any performance management system and should be given careful attention and consideration. Feedback to employees should be presented in such a way that it results in better performance, high productivity, higher motivation, and high morale. There are many ways to give feedback to employees and the following are some elements that should be considered in performance management:

- Give feedback right after performance; do not wait for a later time.
- Ask your employees to rate their own performance (allow enough time).
- Focus on the problem and not the person (we cannot be very successful at changing people).
- Focus on behavior or activities and not the person.
- Criticize the result and be constructive in doing so.
- Be a partner and not just a boss.

It is crucial and vital to measure and manage performance effectively because it can be the main process of gaining a competitive advantage. Performance management programs can be used strategically, administratively, and in a developmental way to help associates move from a dependence stage in their level of job maturity to an independence stage and finally to an interdependence level where they can work harmoniously with everyone in the organization. Of-course, measurement will be the key to knowing where one is and where he/she needs to go, the means of getting there, making resources available to get there, and guidelines that need to be followed in order to get there in accordance with the company goals and mission in mind.

According to Corcoran (2006), *performance management* is a system that is made up of several interdependent internal processes. It begins when a job is initially defined and ends when an employee leaves the company. Appraisals are just one part of an overall process that covers everything from recruitment and selection to goal setting, performance measurement and review, and training and development. Performance management relates to everything that takes place between these two events. A performance management system should involve the following processes (Corcoran, 2006):

- Creation of a clearly defined job description, which highlights competencies, or required knowledge, skills and abilities (KSAs) for the job. These are the building blocks of the system.
- Selecting the right people for the job based on their fulfilling the required KSAs. Concrete data from the selection process should give an indication of where gaps in KSAs may exist between what is ideally required and what the person has. This is key in beginning to performance manage the new incumbent.
- Effective goal/objective setting based on the expectations inherent with the job. These should be outlined in an introductory session, preferably during a formal induction process.
- Defining measurable performance standards. What is acceptable? What is not? How and when will the employee's performance be measured, and by whom?

- The provision of on-going coaching and feedback. Being clear about expectations and how the new employee is performing against them. This can be done on the *ad hoc* basis as work is performed.
- Holding formal quarterly and/or biannual performance discussions. These may occur on an *ad hoc* basis but should also be formalized, as a regular occurrence during the year.
- Annual performance review. Both employees and their line managers should prepare for this meeting., and should use previous reviews/performance discussions as the framework for the meeting.
- Training and development programs, and personal development plans should be agreed with the new employee to address any gaps which may exist between the KSAs required and those actually exhibited in carrying out the job. Information from the structured selection process can inform this discussion.

Performance management is about setting and achieving organizational objectives. Objectives should be *SMART*: specific, measurable, achievable, rewarding, and time-bounded. Objectives would typically include the 'what', 'who', 'how', and 'when' elements. The goals and objectives put forward by the employee in conjunction with the manager's assessment of the staff member's performance will determine to a great extent the training and development objectives.

According to Helm, Holladay, and Tortorella (2007), thinking of performance management as a complete system that encompasses goal alignment, education, communication, and continuous feedback can lead to the recognition of top performers. This recognition is important as organizations try to retain their top talent and improve the performance of all employees in an effort to positively influence the customer, client or a patient's experience. Helm, Holladay, and Tortorella (2007) mentioned that effective performance management involving a complete system of goal setting, training, communication, and ongoing feedback is a practice on which research often has important implications. However, research to date has primarily focused on one component of this topic-the link between performance and pay. Helm, Holladay, and Tortorella (2007) make the following points regarding pay and performance:

- Merit pay is a program that determines differing reward amounts according to the employee's performance level.
- Pay-for-performance programs are in place in many organizations, but only few organizations specify the goals of their performance management system, evaluate whether or not the goals are achieved, or align the goals to the organization's strategic plans.
- An increasingly large number of organizations in various industries, from computer technology to finance and retail sales to tree planting, have investigated how rewards, specifically compensation, can be linked to performance; which leads to widespread and growing development of pay-for-performance components in performance management systems.

In industries such as the healthcare, employee recognition becomes especially important because of the critical shortage of qualified workers. With a focus on the employee, Helm, Holladay, and Tortorella's (2007) study defined the performance management system to include the following:

- Setting and aligning employee goals to institutional strategies,
- Ongoing communication between managers and employees,
- Process training for employees, and
- Increasing the link between employee performance and rewards.

Lessons learned from Helm, Holladay, and Tortorella's (2007) study included the following elements:

- First, mandatory ongoing training for all employees is a key factor in ensuring that employees receive consistent messages and thoroughly understand the process.
- Second, all evaluators must be held accountable for completing timely and effective performance evaluations so that the link between pay and performance is not compromised.
- Finally, all communication plans need to explain the benefits of the SPR (single point review) to the employees and the organization as a whole.

This performance management initiative is a significant step toward achieving the institution's ultimate goal of being an employer of choice, where top performers are recognized, and for providing documented research that other organizations can learn from and use in their own performance management efforts (Helm, Holladay, and Tortorella, 2007). According to Helm, Holladay, and Tortorella, as organizations face employee turnover challenges, having a pay-for-performance system fosters retention of top performers. Additionally, as noted in the study, reporting structure in a matrix environment can be very confusing. Clarification of relationships is critical to the success of this type of program as well as to the overall success of an organization.

### Human Resource Planning Strategies

Realistically speaking, many organizations do not take the time to appropriately plan their strategy of obtaining the required labor, setting appropriate goals, implementing and evaluating the set plans. Without taking this time to proactively plan, companies may have to deal with crises management more than they would like to and that would cost them more time and money.

Human resource administrators can plan appropriately to help their companies develop and implement strategies to effectively take advantage of labor market opportunities and build on the company's strengths to compete more efficiently. Human resource professionals are required to create strategies that would allow everyone to collaborate effectively with each other in cross-functional departments. Collaboration, joint effort to produce shared results aligned with common goals, among people in different departments and offices can be a very cumbersome responsibility and take more than just time and cost. It requires planning, commitment, teamwork, knowledge, and being proactive. Collaboration should address and discuss differences while confronting them with synergistic problem-solving techniques. Of-course, the obvious outcome would be synergy— results that are greater than the sum of the efforts of each individual or department planning individually. Human resource administrators can serve as the facilitators of this long-rang planning so the efforts of all individuals are appropriately coordinated and combined to pull together toward the common goal. Since one of the main functions of human resource professionals is to satisfy and motivate employees in their workplace, employee collaboration should be used extensively to increase participation, productivity, and satisfaction.

One of the biggest mistakes one can make is to believe that he or she works for someone else. Everybody works for him/herself and should enhance the productivity and performance of "I-Incorporated." The times have changed and there is no such thing as life-time employment anymore. Employee dependence on an organization is obsolete and a thing of the past. This creates short-term employment contracts, decreased loyalty, less commitment, and in some cases total chaos if managers do not take these elements into consideration. So, the human resource administrators should plan for these variables accordingly and provide people the opportunity to grow, learn and make themselves more valuable to the company and to the society in general. The common human resource planning activities are forecasting, goal setting and strategic planning, and program implementation and evaluation.

*Forecasting* involves determining the demand for various types of human resources. Human resources professionals would attempt to extrapolate, based on past data and trends, the prospective areas of labor demand and labor shortages. Determining labor demands for specific skills that are relevant for the organization may not always be very simple or exact, but most professionals use a statistical or judgmental method. After determining the labor demands for each job category, the human resource administrators can compare the figures with the labor supply to determine labor shortage or surplus. According to these figures, the organization can make an educated decision on their prospective strategy to deal with the shortage or surplus. We have seen many companies that have been forced to "strategize for efficiency" (downsizing, right-sizing) and layoff thousands of people to cut cost. This is a difficult process which involves much cost, timing, planning, and goodwill on the part of the organization. Appropriate planning for forecasting of the labor market's demand and supply can be very helpful toward eliminating huge headaches.

*Goal setting and strategic planning* involves focusing on specific goals to overcome the prospective problems associated with the shortage or surplus of the labor market. These goals are created based on the analysis of labor supply and demand. Some of the strategies in dealing with a labor surplus may include strategizing for efficiency, layoffs, pay reduction, demotions, retirement options, natural attrition, transfers, and retraining. Some possible strategies for labor shortage may include overtime, outsourcing, using temporary help, turnover reduction, using technology and robots, and hiring part-time associates who would like to contribute to the society a few hours of their week.

Finally, *program implementation and evaluation* can take place. It is important to make sure an individual or department is responsible for making sure the plans are implemented appropriately and according to the original plans where necessary deviations are recorded and taken into account. The next major part would be to evaluate the program in terms of its contribution to the overall success of the company. All planned forecast of labor, goal setting, and implementation should be documented and reported for future administrators. The documentation process is important since many people are involved and the new template can serve future planners.

### *Rewards Systems and Feedback*

There is an increasing demand on corporations to develop reward programs that are motivating employees to work harder and faster. These programs usually educate and encourage associates to become more productive, efficient, and valuable individuals in the company in terms of the "bottom-line." However, due to the pressures related to performance and incentives, in some cases, these programs have encouraged unethical behavior as was shown in the case of Sears Automotive associates in the 1980s. Mechanics were charging customers for work that was not required and in some cases for jobs that were not even performed in order to make more money because their bonus was based on sales volumes. Ethics training programs and corporate emphasis on fairness and morality are important elements of a successful campaign aimed at increasing ethical awareness and behavior in the workplace, but it means nothing if the reward systems and incentives are not aligned with the program. A survey of individuals (managers and employees) from the retail industry, in a Fortune One Hundred company, shows that today people are better prepared to deal with ethical issues and are less tolerant of questionable practices in their firms. Nowadays, committed associates are more likely to speak out or leave the company if their values conflict with that of their firms. So, in order to attract and retain qualified and committed individuals, firms need to have appropriate pay systems that encourage and reward employees to always stay focused on producing quality products in an efficient manner and to always do the right thing.

In order to remain competitive, as an organization that is filled with a diverse workforce with conflicting goals, managers and entrepreneurs need to effectively manage the performance of their most valuable asset, people. Managers and entrepreneurs should be moving toward greater alignment between performance management and company strategies, values, and quality measures. Reward systems should be linked with goal-setting, employee development, competency measures, and team performance. This will decentralize the decision-making down the hierarchy to empower those performing the tasks. This will translate into better reward systems and better morale among employees. In order to create a competitive edge, many organizations are now doing more with fewer employees, so it is imperative that people are rewarded for using effective and ethical problem-solving and decision-making skills.

While most human resource managers agree on the value of effective reward systems, few consider how differences in the quality of reward systems and incentive programs can affect the morale and productivity of each individual. Most reward systems have been written by one individual or obtained from a traditional or generic reward program. These types of reward systems may have serious limitations that may prevent its application to the general population and they can be very costly without producing the desired results for the organization. These rewards may not provide all the information needed to motivate employees to achieve top performance on a continuous basis. The 1993 Gallup Poll found that about 33% of the American workforce would prefer a 20% reduction in their salaries if they could have the option of working fewer hours. Research has shown that those companies that have offered such options, their employees have taken advantage of it. There are many people who would like to live a comfortable life which is normally a balance between work, family, and time for oneself. Many individuals are finding out that happiness does not lie in having money, but rather in a balanced life where one prioritizes his or her time around quality and family oriented life-style. As time, technology, and people's priorities change, so should the corporate reward system.

It is important to continuously monitor the needs and wants of employees. For example, the executives of Tupperware, based in Kissimmee, Florida, are required to take thirty days on the road each year to spend time with their top 15,000 sales people. They try to cover a large portion of their sales force and not just the top five or ten sales people as done by most companies. The chairman and president of Home Depot Inc., headquartered in Atlanta, used to hold a quarterly meeting on Sunday mornings and all 23,000 employees were paid to attend and watch this forty-five minute program via satellite television hookup. The executives would answer questions and go over the growth plans and how employees are to play a part in this growth plan. At Knight-Ridder publications, they have "management coffee breaks." During this time, management would meet with twenty to twenty-five employees for about an hour to have coffee and discuss employee questions and suggestions. It has been said that if two employees are each having a penny and they exchange their pennies, then they will still each have only one penny. But, if these two individuals each have an idea and they exchange their ideas, then they will each have two ideas with the possibility of creating a third or even fourth because new ideas generate more ideas when seen from different perspectives.

In the traditional performance appraisal systems, people are normally put into categories of above average, average, or below average. This format may damage morale in the company and, thus it should be enhanced or eliminated. Rather than waste time and energy on the traditional reward systems, as part of a comprehensive performance management program, managers should consider conducting a formal job analysis that would provide relevant work behaviors and characteristics of the work environment. This information would lead to designing a reward program that would classify, compensate, and evaluate jobs based on individual and team performance.

Immediate feedback on performance can motivate individuals to change their strategy or to become more creative and adjust their methods to become high performing. In parallel with the Pygmalion effect or the self-fulfilling prophecy concept, it is appropriate for managers and entrepreneurs to assume that everyone would like do well and become a contributing part of the society or company. However, people need feedback about their performance; and, if they can see and evaluate their own performance, then they would be able and willing to take appropriate action. For example, people are often motivated to go bowling because they can get feedback instantaneously and that makes them happy. It is difficult to imagine many individuals bowling if there was a curtain between the bowler and the pins where the bowlers could not immediately see their results. This is also true of watching sports on television where viewers can see who wins and who loses as it happens. Not many people watch games that were played weeks ago since they know the results and therefore cannot be part of the game because the outcome is already known to them. So, just-in-time feedback is vital to every individual at every level of the organization and everyone wants to learn about his or her progress and stay abreast of it.

In order to create a high performance team in the 21$^{st}$ century, managers and entrepreneurs need to shift from the traditional hierarchy to a team-based management system. The basic or core elements of team structure should consist of the following:

- Work should be structured based on customer needs.
- Training programs should be provided to move to new levels.
- Rewards should be based on productivity and performance.
- Employees should get more responsibility as they become ready for them.
- No waiting for attrition or wearing out of the team.
- Cross training and different levels of skill should be required.
- Job responsibilities should emphasize results and not tasks or techniques.

It is also important to point out that after understanding the culture of the organization, managers and entrepreneurs will need to "unlearn" the traditional management practices. The new practice should develop systems of accountability and it should measure the right "KPI's" (key performance indicators). The new system should also encourage risk taking on the part of management as well as employees, and failure should be tolerated to an extent where it does not go out of control. It is believed that most people have capabilities beyond those which they are called for to complete their jobs. They can go deeper into their jobs and make better and stronger methods of getting work done more effectively and efficiently. This is a major shift from the traditional hierarchy into a team-driven management system and it will take time and planning on the part of executives. This reward program should be result-oriented and should not just concentrate on techniques because people can be creative and invent far more superior methods of accomplishing the results. Managers should keep in mind that their employees deserve to know what needs to be done and how it should be completed and they will often handle the responsibilities better than what is expected. Communication should flow horizontally, from side-to-side, and vertically, up and down, to all employees. The new pay system to reward high performance teams could (be):

- Focused on the mission of the company.
- Team-based but employee focused.
- Market driven.
- Allow for strategic decisions at the employee levels.
- Control growth of base pay.
- Compatible with the market or industry pay structure.
- Provide fair incentives for the high level executives to meet customer needs.
- Differentiate between levels of performance.

- Eliminate the "one size fits all" mentality or strategy.

The completion of job analysis should provide relevant information about key performance indicators that need to be reinforced in the reward programs. After clarifying those KPI's that need to be reinforced, human resource professionals can design the new compensation plan which should reward ethical decision-making and the output. The reward programs should be individually focused because the value of certain rewards varies between different individuals. Bob Nelson, author of "*1001 Ways to Reward Employees*" says, "Appreciation for your best people heightens morale and it enhances your corporate image." The rewards should also be matched with each individual as his or her expectations, background, response to public or private recognitions, desire for money or promotion, and desire for peer respect may vary greatly and could be influenced by his or her past.

The new reward system requires the willingness and support of management, at all levels, to move from the traditional culture of entitlement and seniority to teamwork, empowerment, and employee involvement. Everyone needs to realize that the employees, unions, government officials, and executives of the organization have the same interest in the long run which is the success of the organization in an ethical manner and in the most efficient way. So, employees should be involved actively in the issues affecting them or their work. In its most general or simplest format, the new pay in an organization can be achieved by following a strategy and performance pay process.

**Strategy-based pay.** *This is the base pay which can reinforce new broader jobs, skill development, and performance.* Base pay should be determined as a result of skill and the external market. Every job should have a base salary that is compatible with the industry or market. All jobs should be analyzed and described based on its work behaviors and characteristics of the work environment. Each position should be a little different than the previous one and should include added responsibility of new knowledge or skill. So, the base pay should be different for each job and should represent the level of skill or knowledge. All employees should be given the opportunity to learn new skills and knowledge required to take more responsibilities. Pay increases and promotions should be based on a 360 degree evaluation where each individual, even suppliers and vendors, can evaluate and recommend their co-workers for pay increase and promotions. It is extremely important that people are trained in the evaluation process and made aware of the effects of their evaluation on the person being evaluated. If conducted properly peer evaluations often are the most accurate judgments of an employee's behaviors.

**Performance-based pay.** *Includes variable pay to reinforce and encourage performance improvements by sharing the profits or benefits of improved performance.* The concept of "pay for performance" philosophy is what Frederick Taylor, the father of scientific management, practiced. However his methods did not involve people's brain but only their bodies. Today's pay for performance strategy can be an excellent strategy if it focuses on the result and not necessarily just on the means. This strategy would work great with technical and manufacturing jobs. However, jobs that require decisions of morality and ethics cannot be left alone to each individual as they represent the company and their views may not necessarily match that of the company. Moral and ethical decisions should be a concern of every stakeholder including corporate executives and management. Individuals should be given resources, training, and the means of accomplishing results within defined limitations. Such limitations can be defined by a code of ethics or the values which the company has been guided by in its day-to-day operations. Such limitations may also be represented by a number of questions that must be asked before proceeding with the decision. A question might be: does the decision violate anybody's rights, company values, societal values, laws, or professional codes of ethics? A "yes" answer means discuss the matter with others before proceeding, and a "no" answer would mean the decision is aligned with the corporate values and mission.

The future pay strategy eliminates the traditional indirect pay, because it did not expect measurable results on the investment, and incorporates it into the variable pay. The variable pay, payments that are not folded into base pay which vary according to performance, can be a great motivator for individuals and organizations should they take advantage of it. This will help improve employee morale and can provide them with ways of becoming winners and gaining self-confidence through self-affirmation. For example, managers and entrepreneurs can reward employees for their unit production of optical fibers, cookware, ceramic cores, etc. This reward should be based on quality production of each unit with increasing reward as production goes higher both in quality and quantity. People should also be rewarded for the training of other associates, mentoring, cleanliness, knowledge of other skills, and maintenance of equipment. Pay for performance also provides immediate feedback to individuals and most importantly, employees evaluate their own performance based on their units of production and other key performance indicators. Since feedback is one of the top motivators, if not the top, the pay for performance system would work great in the manufacturing environment. Managers and entrepreneurs should remember that timely verbal feedback, when coupled with a desire to change, can provide a more accurate development tool than any written document. Timely verbal feedback reinforces good performance and good managerial behavior. Managers doing a good job of providing timely and relevant feedback for good performance will have that behavior reinforced which should cause it to continue.

An example of this new pay system would be Eastman Chemical which at one time eliminated their formal appraisal program and their new system was designed to develop highly motivated employees. The executives at Eastman Chemical believed that employees need to feel like winners and that a positive feeling will give them exuberance and positive self-esteem in their personal and professional lives. Eastman Chemical received suggestions from its employees, through a survey, and prepared an employee development system with the following characteristics:

- Systematic growth of pay rates through the pay range and they are managed by the use of the learning curve concept and the use of maturity tables.
- Performance by accomplishments and contributions are important considerations in establishing individual pay.
- Long-term contributions are recognized through promotions.
- Flexibility for special recognition pay increase has been budgeted into the merit review.

Through industry benchmarking and the use of everyone's talent as well as input, managers and entrepreneurs can create the best pay system which can equip people for the twenty-first century and gain the firm a competitive edge throughout the industry. Decision-making has become increasingly difficult and more complicated in today's fast-paced business world. Therefore, an appropriate and well-designed plan can encourage and support moral behavior in today's empowered and decentralized workforce. A well-designed pay system should increase employee involvement, workforce flexibility, teamwork, learning, commitment, loyalty, and integrity in the firm. A well designed pay system will turn conflicting situations into positive results. Conflict if not managed appropriately can be devastating and negatively affect morale, teamwork, productivity, and of-course the organization's bottom-line. But, if employees are encouraged to cooperate as team-members and openly discuss their thoughts, then they can easily move from "having a point of view" to a "viewing point." In this type of a work environment, according to Thomas Crumb, author of "*The Magic of Conflict,*" a life of work can be transformed into a work of art because people feel happy and are intrinsically motivated to be involved and work harmoniously. Charles Stanly, a religious speaker, encourages people to earn their income honestly, invest wisely, give generously, and enjoy heartily. Through management's hard work and just reward programs, people will be more committed, loyal and happy at their jobs and can enjoy life.

### Why Should Rewards Have An Ethical Dimension?

The answer to the question of "Why should rewards have an ethical dimension" is that because the ends do not always justify the means. Traditionally, most rewards are based on the bottom-line results, profitability and making the numbers look right to meet expected or set targets. This type of a reward system may encourage and promote immoral behavior in the organization. The importance of money and profits become greater than trying to do the right thing. So, managers and entrepreneurs should look at the rewards from all aspects, including the motivation and incentives it provides for accomplishing the monetary results. An example of this would be the Bausch and Lomb's managers and executives who inflated their sales volume of Ray-Ban sunglasses to meet set performance standards or targeted goals. They were sending a large supply of these glasses to customers who did not need them. Some of those customers were sent two years of supplies despite the fact that they did not ask for them.

There are cases where some people have taken advantage of the system because of their passion for the reward. Ron Waver was a thirty-year old football player who played football at the University of Texas under an assumed identity during the 1995-1996 Season. He pleaded guilty of using someone else's identity and social security number to get onto the team. He says he loves football and the rewards are great for doing what you love. So, he did not feel bad about what he did. This is similar to the case of singers' Millie Vanillie. The two singers were using someone else's voice as their own. They became very famous among teenagers during the late 1980s but were finally discovered and their dreams were shattered. They took advantage of the system and betrayed people.

Joseph Jett, a Harvard MBA graduate and former Kidder Peabody bond trader, was named Kidder's "man of the year" and received Kidder Peabody's star employee "Chairman's Award" for 1993. However, in April of 1994 Jet was fired by Kidder and they accused him of faking about $350 million in profits to mask $80 million in losses through the complicated, computerized systems of trading. These fake profits, over a two year period, translated into millions of dollars in bonuses for Jett and other executives at Kidder. Regulators claim that his motive of personal gain led him to fix the numbers and report the fake profits. And as the result of the fake profits, he earned more than $11 million in bonuses during 1992 and 1993. Joseph Jett claims that he is innocent and his superiors were well aware of his trading. He argues that he could not have committed fraud because all of his trading has been documented and it has always been available to his bosses and the auditors. He says "money is important to me only as a symbol of accomplishment" (USA TODAY, May 20, 1996). A main problem with this money mentality is that it is a never ending process and it can go on forever. Success and accomplishment cannot be solely defined by money, because money can be gathered with immoral means which contradict the internal feelings of accomplishment that produce intrinsic rewards. Just because the documents are clear and everyone agrees with an action, does not make the action right. Executives need to set specific guidelines and training programs that help people look beyond the numbers for their purpose and the means of achieving those purposes. In Jett's case the system allowed room for such errors and he took advantage of it claiming he did not do anything wrong. Similar errors have been made by people at Enron, Tyco, WorldCom, and other firms in recent years.

The department of Justice reported that in 1995 about 5,506 former officers, directors, consultants, and others of saving and loans involved were convicted of fraud in the savings and loans debacle. And of the total number of people convicted, 4,157 were sent to prison. According to Louie Larimer (1996), AT&T, on October 20th of 1995, was accused of bilking millions of customers on their long distance phone calls. They were allegedly billing people for telephone calls that were never made. This lawsuit sought to recover $50,000 for each of its class members. He further states that Dr. James Thompson, a family practitioner, filed a lawsuit against the nation's largest hospital chain- Columbia-HCA Healthcare Corp. The hospital was supposedly paying bribes and kickbacks to the doctors in exchange for their referrals.

On September 25, 1995, Honda Motor Co. and some of its subsidiaries, such as the North America and American Honda, were charged with sending the popular models to those dealers who paid bribes and kickbacks. Michael Monus, former president of Phar-Mor drug chain, was convicted in September of 1995 on 109 counts of fraud. He was convicted because of using phony financial data to lure more than $1 billion in investment. William Aramony, former president of United Way, was also convicted of fraud and misappropriating funds in 1995. These few examples of fraud and immoral acts exemplify the need for effective reward programs that are designed to provide encouragement and support for ethical decisions throughout the company. According to Louie Larimer, "The process of ethical reasoning requires emotional discipline, intellectual integrity, inner reflection and the conscious exercise of free will toward a noble or just end" (1996).

### Recognition and Rewards

Traditional methods of running an organization have changed rapidly and will probably continue to do so at an even faster pace as the workforce changes. In the past, a majority of the workforce was made-up of white males and this has been changing rapidly as more women and minorities from different backgrounds are joining the workforce in the United States. It has been predicted that about 5/6th of the new workforce will be women (2/3 of the new workforce), minorities, and immigrants. This diverse group of workforce requires different sets of compensations packages. For example, in general, when compared to men, more women may prefer to have time off as opposed to working overtime for increased salary or earnings (Broadie, 1996). Also, young adults and new immigrants tend to prefer to work more often for the monetary rewards. According to Supers' 1995 international work importance study, in the book called "*Life Roles, Values, and Careers*," immigrants who had lived in the United States for a long period of time did not value work as highly as new or recent immigrants. So, the changing workforce requires new and flexible reward practices that can enhance and produce positive situations in the work environment.

Recognition programs can be geared toward both extroverts, those who need incentives to be motivated, and introverts, those who are motivated because of internal satisfaction of pride in workmanship and responsibility. Human resource professionals should design recognition programs to serve both introverts and extroverts to make the job more fulfilling. Challenging and fulfilling jobs can keep people happy and internally motivated to complete their jobs with commitment and personal integrity.

Many organizations are rewarding people based on a bonus system that can increase or decrease depending on the performance of bottom-line (profits), or sales for the company or individual. In most cases the organization will provide a basic salary and the bonus will be added based on the sales or net profit of the individual or the team. In some cases, these programs can backfire and hurt the company from the unethical behavior of one or more employees. As mentioned before, Sears Automotive used to reward their associates based on their sales volume, so some of the mechanics started overcharging people for supposedly fixing parts of the engine which they did not do. This unethical behavior was discovered by the media which pressured the company to change their bonus programs so it does not allow room for immoral behavior. Another company provided bonus for their management and full-time associates on quarterly basis. They discovered that some managers hesitated to recommend or promote eligible part-time associates to full-time and kept them at their part-time status as long as possible. They did this so they would not have to pay them a bonus each quarter because that will decrease the profits of their departments as well as their personal bonuses. So, the company had to create more policies that would prevent or eliminate this type of discrimination by certain individual managers.

There are some rewards systems that might be ethical, but can become a violation to the Fair Labor Standards Act. Fair Labor Standards Act regulates minimum wage, overtime, child labor, and record keeping issues. For example, let us say that a car salesperson had an income of $160,000 last year. Suppose during one of the weeks last year there was a threat of bad weather and hurricanes, so as the result he or she would not able to sell cars. Now, if this salesperson is paid less than minimum wage during that week, then the employer would have violated the minimum wage policy. So, in some cases an issue might be ethical but not legal and this is why all policies should be thoroughly investigated for its positive as well as its negative impact. A blue jeans company was forced by the courts to pay $180,000 in wages for back-pay because they deducted too much money from their employees' paychecks during a single week. Those deductions, which were for blue jeans uniforms that employees had to wear during work, caused some paychecks to be below minimum wage during a one-week period and that is a violation. So, it is important that human resource professionals look above and beyond the law to consider a win-win situation for the company and the individual.

## *Types of Rewards*

Cash awards are good; however the marginal utility of each dollar decreases as the award increases. Cash awards are temporary awards and the affects usually end during the next paycheck or the next day. So, cash awards in general, are not very effective in the long-term, and they are not always very popular either (Joinson, 1996). Most employers agree that they can get more mileage from noncash awards than they can from cash awards. Noncash awards are less costly and they should be given immediately, and more often, to continuously reinforce positive behavior. Research shows that every 12 cent cash award has been costing only 4 cents in recognition by noncash awards. Rewards tend to be about 38% a combination of cash and noncash, 15% cash, and 47% noncash for most large firms.

Table 13.1 – Common Recognition Programs

| Recognition Program | Percentage of Firms Using It |
|---|---|
| Years of service | 59% |
| Going "above and beyond" the job | 51% |
| Customer service | 41% |
| Cost saving | 39% |
| Increased productivity | 37% |

Today's employers are constantly finding different methods of recognizing their associates. These methods can range from recognizing productivity gains, to customer service and even putting an effort to make a new project or product work. According to Carla Joinson (1996), a survey of 213 companies reported using one or more of the programs listed in Table 13.1, and years of service was ranked first among the awards.

## *Rewarding for Performance*

It is extremely important that rewards are perceived as fair and just in the eyes of the beholder or those receiving it. Fairness in pay and rewards appear to be the key factor in providing an environment that motivates people to believe in their superior's actions and policies. It is obvious that each manager would like to reward his or her productive employees, however, surveys show that top performers do not always receive top pay for their efforts and performance. According to Carla Joinson (1996), a survey of more than 350,000 government employees showed that more than 50 percent believed that "some people do most of the work while others do just enough to get by." Most of the respondents did not believe that job performance was an important factor in promotion, nor did they believe that the best people rose to the top of the organization. It is true that top managers make decisions regarding pay, rewards and promotions based on employee or team performance, however, it is important that these decisions are perceived as just and fair by their associates.

The scenario of giving high performers more work and avoiding the least performers is very familiar to most supermarket managers. A stock person who completes his or her aisle or work before everyone else is usually asked to help the person who is either a slow worker or is not able to get his or her work done on time. It is a good idea to have high performers work with low performers, however, the high performers need to be acknowledged, recognized, and rewarded appropriately for their contributions. Traditionally, people with seniority are being paid higher than the new associates and this may not be very fair on jobs that do not need experience. It may even have a counter productive affect on new associates who are high performers. Usually, high performers that are not recognized properly may reduce their standards to match the average standards, meaning they are going to do the minimum just to get by until a better position comes along.

A retail store manager calculated how much time he should spend in one of his service departments, an in-store bakery. He argued that since he is the store manager, the amount of time he spends in the bakery department should be proportional to the amount of sales they produce compared to other departments. This bakery department had about four percent of the total store sales on weekly basis. The store manager argued that he should not spend more than about two hours of his week on issues relating to this department. This type of attitude from a leader can have negative effects on people, because people are individuals and they all deserve and want special recognition for their efforts and not necessarily just performance. This is like an executive secretary that performs administrative duties and his or her contributions are not directly measurable in terms of monetary value. But, this person prepares all the meeting agenda's, appointments, speaks with associates, customers, and suppliers on daily basis. In other words, this person is the backbone of the organization and his or her level of loyalty and commitment is very important to the company. Now, if this person does not get proper rewards and recognition, then he or she may develop a negative attitude toward the company which may have an affect on the decisions of vendors as well as the internal and external customers. So, it is important that people are recognized for how they do their jobs and not necessarily just for their contribution to the bottom-line because that might be out of their circle of control or influence.

It has been documented that managers spend most of their time with two to five percent of their employees who cause many problems. So, not only the average and top performers get ignored by the manager but they also get most of the work that needs immediate attention. In general, most managers would give an important project to people who they can count on based on their past performance. Over time, these high performing people can get frustrated and may even change their performance or leave the company. This is especially true if they feel that their co-workers who are not very productive get the same reward as high performing associates. It is crucial to spend time and effort with low performers to help them get better, but we cannot afford to do it at the expense of others who are doing well. Managers should spend appropriate or evenly balanced amounts of time with each group or individual in the department in order to recognize their contributions or to help them become better performers.

### *Establishing and Designing a Recognition Program*

Designing and implementing an effective recognition program takes time and an understanding of the organization's recourses, culture, management styles, and employees. While there are no templates that might fit each organization, managers and entrepreneurs can begin by following the generic steps mentioned in Table 13.2: setting goals, mapping the strategy, developing measurement plans, planning the budget, identifying target groups and awards, identifying ethical dimensions and criteria, identifying a marketing plan, and implementing and improving the program.

Table 13.2 – Steps for Designing a Recognition Program

| STEPS | ACTIONS | DESCRIPTION |
|---|---|---|
| 1 | *Set Goals* | What are you trying to accomplish? Begin with the end in mind |
| 2 | *Map the Strategy* | Create a task force, set rules and policies, involve representatives from all groups or departments. |
| 3 | *Develop Measurements Plans* | How and where will it be measured? Company or department level. Should be simple. |
| 4 | *Plan the budget* | Take care of the administrative costs including roll-out process, training, and promotion costs. |
| 5 | *Identify target groups and awards* | Identify demographics, delivery time (2 - 48 hrs.), Variety of awards for teams and individuals. |
| 6 | *Identify ethical dimensions and criteria* | Is it encouraging the mission? Is it aligned with company philosophy? Is it rewarding the desired behavior? Do the ends justify the means? |
| 7 | *Identify Marketing Plan* | How and when is it going to be delivered? Who will be running the program? And who is going to follow-up on the promotion? |
| 8 | *Implement and Evaluate the Program* | Follow through, get feedback on benefits and side-effects, can it be made better? How long should the program last? Measure effects such as sales, profits, morale, satisfaction, turnover, and so on. |

## Guidelines for Rewards and Recognition

Since there are many layers of management with different background and experience throughout the organization, it is important for professionals to follow a systematic and flexible approach to recognition and reward programs. It is also important to train managers and supervisors at all levels to reward and recognize their people appropriately and responsibly. While it is important to treat everyone consistently because everyone has the same rights, it is even more important to remember that people have different needs and the journey toward fulfilling those specific needs are the key motivating factors. It is the journey that enlightens people and not always the destination, so people should be recognized for their achievements and they should have new goals to accomplish. Managers should try to match the reward with the individual. Some managers have used the Myer Briggs survey profile to make better decisions about different task forces, working groups, and teams. They have tried to match the task with the right teams or individuals. Perhaps, similar profiles and strategies can be used to determine the type of rewards that would match individual or team needs and desires. One should also keep in mind the piece rate or pay for performance methods as well. When it comes to goal setting, managers and entrepreneurs should consider SMART (Specific, Meaningful, Achievable, Reliable or Rewarding, and Timely) goal-setting strategies for effectively recognizing and rewarding people. Human resource professionals should always make sure that their recognition and award programs are SMART.

Besides having a SMART recognition program, organizations should use the following guidelines to develop, design, and deliver fair reward programs.

***Train managers and supervisors about rewards.*** Research shows that there is about a twenty-five percent misunderstanding between managers and associates as to what is important in the organization. Some managers are afraid to give timely feedback to low performers and that might be why they are performing poorly. It has been said that honesty is the best policy, and honest feedback can create many opportunities for managers and employees. Feedback appears to be the number one motivator and this can be seen from watching sports on television. Some people are watching sports for long periods of time because they are able to receive feedback on a continuous basis. This immediate feedback can reinforce many positive thoughts and may encourage people to become "couch potatoes."

The immediate feedback process can be a great motivator which appears to be true in the case of bowling. What if there was a wall in the middle of the lane and the bowlers could not see the pins falling, there would be no immediate feedback, and the player probably would not experience the same effect as getting feedback immediately.

Results and goals should also be communicated to all associates as they become available. These goals should be set reasonably high and should be communicated to everyone on how they can accomplish these results. Rewards should be designed to create and recognize many winners, not just the top performers. For an example, ask a group of people to choose a partner and try to have an eye contest from a close distance. Let them know that the first person who blinks, loses and should sit down; and after one minute see how many pairs are still competing. Normally, there would not be too many pairs still standing up. However, if you tell them that the next contest will be for one minute and all winners will get some type of a reward, this time you will see many more pairs, almost one-hundred percent, who are going to become winners and this is because the first time you did not give them a set time limit or goal. So, communicating the set targets to associates can make a difference as long as they can see the rewards as fair and achievable.

Figure 13.1 - Management Training Circle

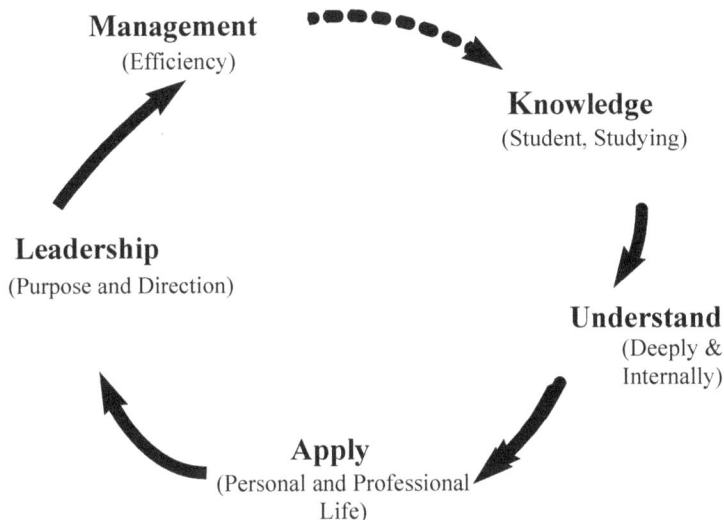

**Management**
(Efficiency)

**Knowledge**
(Student, Studying)

**Leadership**
(Purpose and Direction)

**Understand**
(Deeply &
Internally)

**Apply**
(Personal and Professional
Life)

It is also helpful to follow the "Management Training Circle" approach (presented in Figure 13.1) in training the material to the designers, executives, and managers. This approach is based on knowledge, understanding, application, leadership, and management or implementation of a new program. It is an inside-out approach and it starts with each person involved in the design and implementation of a program or reward system. They have to experience and model the program in order for it to be successful. General Collin Powel said "the greatest thing I learned is that soldiers watch what their superiors do; you can lecture them and give them classes, but it is your personal example they will follow." This is true in the organization as well, so the executives and the designers need to experience the material firsthand in order for it to make sense.

First of all, the designers, executives, and managers should have the relevant knowledge about reward programs and their purpose. Next, they should dig deeper into the purpose and the logic behind having reward programs. This involves understanding what motivates people, why it motivates them, and how it can help their purpose. Then, they should apply this material to themselves and other small groups for experimentation. The results will provide a vision of leadership that will guide people to their mission, goals, and values. After establishing and understanding their mission, goals, and values, they will be in a position to work on managing the program for efficiency. It is important that leadership or vision of the future precedes management because without a purpose it is extremely difficult and costly to be efficient, especially with people. There are very few things more costly than being on the wrong track or recovering from it. Also, being on the right track involves continuous research and updating, otherwise it will not take too long for one to get run over by others who are speeding down the competitive highway of business.

*Create flexible and creative reward programs*: It is important to keep the individual in mind when rewarding teams and groups. Reward programs should focus on teams as well as individuals in many different ways. Rewards should be based on win-win-win situations where the company stakeholders, teams, and individuals are recognized and rewarded accordingly. It is critical to match the reward with the employee so the reward can be meaningful to the person receiving it. It is also important to reward and recognize people appropriately as some individuals like to be recognized publicly while others may not want public recognition. One may draw some conclusions from Myer-Briggs type of instrument about the preference of each individual. However, everyone wants to be a winner and substandard performers can become winners if they are given proper opportunities, encouragement, and guidance. The key to finding the easiest way to get a difficult job done is to delegate the job to a lazy person and you will see the easiest way of accomplishing it. The moral of the story is that anyone can be creative in their own way if they apply themselves and if one looks at things from their perspective or frame of reference.

*Clarify standards and expectations to everyone*: Without a destination, one can be driving around for days and never get anywhere. With proper destination one can eventually get there, even if they have to stop and ask for directions. It is crucial to have standards and communicate those standards to all employees on a regular basis. Job descriptions and evaluation forms should be designed professionally and they should measure the right elements, those that are geared toward the mission\vision of the department or the company.

*Cross-functional training and agronomic*: It is essential to consider the work environment and enhance it to reduce boredom and increase creativity and involvement. Repetition can be very boring and sometimes repetitive jobs do not require the person's spiritual mind to be involved one-hundred percent of the time. A study completed by the University of Illinois showed that listening to music may increase productivity in all jobs (Oldham et al., 1996). Sometimes it is helpful to provide job enrichment and cross-train people for different jobs and/or departments. This can reduce cost of overtime, increase morale and job satisfaction, and keep people involved as a team. This would also help to find the right people for the right jobs, especially during the busy times.

*Align rewards with company mission and values*: It is important that reward programs are on parallel paths with the corporate culture of an organization. All rewards should be geared toward the mission and values of the company. Goals and objectives are short-term strategies that focus people to strive for the purpose or mission of an organization. The long-term purpose and mission of the company should be communicated to all parties and they should not be sacrificed at the expense of short-term goals. It is important to emphasize ends as well as means; otherwise some people will create unethical means of accomplishing the results.

*Encourage experimentation and individuality*: Managers should be encouraged to try new methods of rewarding and recognizing people to keep them creative, innovative, happy, and satisfied. People get tired of becoming "employee of the month" and getting to park at the employee of the month's parking lot as its reward. So, managers should try to experiment and find out what works in the organization and how it can be altered again and again. Managers should also be recognized for their efforts regardless of positive or negative results. Some incentives are designed based on good intentions, but they may not work realistically because people abuse the concept. For example, one company recognized their associates for creating "raving fans" and this could be done by going above and beyond the call of duty to satisfy a customer or if a customer wrote a complimentary letter or complimented the manager for having such a great employee. This recognition program got out of control because employees started asking customers for written letters and compliments which defeats the purpose of the incentive. So, even a well-intended reward program may have some "side-effects" that need to be taken into consideration in the designing stage of the program.

### *Summary*

Many organizations are going through what they might call reengineering, restructuring, downsizing or outsourcing, or even rightsizing. No matter what they call them, it still refers to a process that is supposedly eliminating waste and creates a "flatter" or less hierarchical organization. Management levels and hierarchies are being eliminated to reduce red-tape and increase the speed of decision making. People at all levels are expected to be prepared, flexible, and to respond faster than ever before. Changes can create many ambiguities at all levels of the organization, especially at the lower levels of management who are responsible for motivating and getting the job done with and through people. Managers are expected to match rewards with individuals and to direct individuals toward accomplishing company objectives. The difficulty occurs when personal and professional objectives do not match. So, most companies have various types of organizational reward programs that recognize and reward good employee performance.

These organizational rewards should be structured in such a way that it recognizes and enhances performance as well as the efforts of each individual. These programs should convey a message of getting the ends with ethical means. These programs should be concerned with how the results are accomplished and the results should be evaluated accordingly. In order to make sure the reward programs are designed and implemented properly, managers and executives should receive training and education to deal with these issues properly. They should try to set goals that stretch people's performance capability and goals so that employees can accomplish them and get rewarded for it in a timely manner. Everyone wants to become a winner and managers should try to help them become winners personally and professionally. This will create win-win-win situations for managers, associates, and the company. Overall, any reward and recognition program should be a part of an integrative and comprehensive performance management system that is strategically aligned with the organization's mission and vision statements.

## Discussion Questions

1. How are rewards and recognitions programs related to performance management? Discuss.
2. Why should managers and coaches consider the ethical implications of their rewards and recognition programs?
3. What is the role of managers, coaches and human resource personnel in the area of ethics and reward programs?
4. What types of rewards and recognitions are typically offered to employees?
5. Mention and list five rewards that the new generation of employees might desire in their ideal workplace? Why would the offering of these rewards create a motivational work environment?
6. What can managers, coaches, and human resource personnel do to create a motivational work environment and an organizational culture in the service industry that consistently encourage high performance?
7. What can the members of a locality (city, village, or province) do (in terms of rewards and punishment) to make sure their political leaders are motivated to serve the interests of the public, and not their own self-interests?

# CHAPTER 14

## Problem-Solving and Leadership

For the twenty-first century firm, the true sustainable advantages and a long-term competitive edge come from the success of each individual manager and employee within the organization. These managers and employees should become proactive leaders in order to be effective coaches. These coaches can then be effective business managers in their departments, organizations and industries. In order for the cycle of productivity and development to continue, the business leader's goal should be to create managers and coaches with the requisite skills to compete effectively in national and global markets by focusing on what is important and by managing priorities.

This section provides more information about leadership, which requires communication, time management, integrity, character building, ethics, and problem solving skills for all managers and employees if they are to effectively learn, think critically, innovate, and to create value for their organizations and themselves. The first step towards empowerment and excellence through an empowered workforce is achieving the goal of appropriately educating the workforce to manage priorities based on importance. The second step is to empower employees to think for themselves so they can take advantage of every opportunity as they become better prepared to meet the competitive challenges of their day-to-day operations while balancing the most important activities. Having effective time management and problem solving skills are a good start toward independence and empowerment. Furthermore, effective coaching and leadership is a continuous process of learning, developing, influencing, and character building through the creation of a trusting relationship as well as the timely management of stress, change and conflict.

### Problem Solving Approaches[34]

The "Communication for Problem-Solving" method, when practiced, could enhance, clarify and significantly improve the communication process. All of us 'communicate' in some way since our styles and manners are cultural. The professional leader or coach learns the language and technique of professionalism. For this technique to be used effectively, one must accept these basic assumptions:

---

[34] This material comes from *"Managing Workpalce Stress and Conflict amid Change"* by Mujtaba and McCartney, 2007; Llumina Press.

1. People are generally well-meaning and don't want to hurt other people.
2. The difference between positive and negative communication is strategy.
3. Anger is a natural emotion. When it is 'managed' constructively, it 'clears the air' and promotes growth.
4. Usually, attempts to solve a problem are done by accusations. It is necessary to forget about blame! Who is wrong and who is right is not the problem.

The issue is to solve a problem for the benefit of all, i.e. try a win-win situation. As long as we live, there will always be problems, so it is important that we master this skill. There are two principle factors to consider when there are problems; we must learn how to accuse effectively (i.e., how to make the proper statement about the problem) and how to react or respond to accusations. Now, learn the rules and put them into practice!

### *Rules for the Accuser (i.e. how to accuse) are:*

1. The purpose to the accusation is to solve a problem.
2. Accusations should be made one at a time.
3. Accusations should be specific and not vague.
4. Accusations should be accompanied by specific suggestions for change.
5. There should be no exaggerations.
6. Do not use any insults.
7. Watch the tone of your voice; it may carry insult.
8. Watch the frequency of the accusations. Nobody likes a nagger!

### *Rules for the Accusee (i.e. how to respond) are:*

1. An accusation should never be denied.
2. Do not counter-accuse.
3. Do not interrupt the accuser.
4. Do not use the accusation as a pretext for initiating a destructive response, especially of past events.

There are some other general rules to remember for effective communication and skill-building and the following are some of them:
1. Avoid the invitation to fight.
2. Remember that people's memories are constantly distorting and their perceptions of events are real to them.
3. All human beings have faults and also strong opinions. There are faults that you will have to accept, but there are other faults that may have to be discussed. You must also agree to disagree!
4. Avoid unfair techniques, such as;
   - Blaming the person for something they can't help.
   - Silence.
   - Switching the subject.
   - Analyzing as if you were a psychiatrist.

5. Don't make assumptions or try to 'read' the other person's mind. Always test your assumptions with the other person.
6. Be positive about long-range intentions and sincerity and respond positively.

You must develop a 'mind-set' of professionalism and learn from your mistakes. Communication for problem-solving is just one of the many techniques for effective communication, growth enrichment and maturity. The key is to practice effective communication at all times. Practice! Practice! Practice!

Communication is the key to success; whether it is individual, group, electronic, motivational or within a large organization. We all need to convey messages and receive information in order to function as human beings. We now know that to be successful and to lead people within teams, groups and organizations, effective communication is the key!

### Understanding and Solving Problems

Peter Senge (1990), author of *"The Fifth Discipline,"* said "Real learning gets to the heart of what it means to be human." He further continued to say that "Through learning we recreate ourselves; through learning we become able to do something we never were able to do; and through learning we re-perceive the world and our relationship to it." After all, it is through learning that we extend our capacities to create, to be part of the generative process of life. Senge emphasized that "There is within each of us a deep hunger for this type of learning." We can continue and say that through learning we can become better problems solvers for our organizations. The workplace has many challenges due to its fast-paced requirements and changing rules in order to remain competitive. Such complex changes require a competent workforce that can anticipate and proactively solve problems. Educated employees should be developed to think for themselves when it comes to tackling and solving problems to speed up the process in better serving the organization's relevant constituencies. The following are some relevant considerations for developing your problem solving skills.

*Do We Really Have Problems?* You know that you have been in the corporate world too long if you think that you never have any problems in your life, just "issues" and "improvement opportunities." In reality, most issues and improvement opportunities are problems that need to be taken care of accurately, productively, and urgently in order to remain rational, sensible, and competitive. Herman Melville once said that "a smooth sea never made a successful sailor" which means that through determination to constantly become better and make meaningful contributions we can overcome these issues and become better managers. Without these issues and opportunities, our lives would be very boring and repetitive. As a matter of fact, most managers spend close to eighty percent of their time solving problems. Yet, most of these managers were not taught how to solve management problems. They had to learn through *heuristics* - trial and error.

*Defining the Problem and Its Owners:* One can define a "problem" as the gap between the real and the ideal in goals while attempting to overcome challenging issues and improvement opportunities in the daily work environment. Furthermore, we can define problem owners as those who have unmet goals and objectives. Issues and improvement opportunities can be looked at as problems and problems can be seen as opportunities for improvement in order to maintain a positive attitude and outlook on life. Some problems are opportunities to simply improve while others are opportunities for turning wrongs into rights. Solving problems quickly and accurately is an art and a science that needs structure, practice, experience, intuition, and discipline. Solving management dilemmas and problems is no different than solving any other difficult problem. Often a problem exists when there is a discrepancy between what is actually happening and what should be happening. The first thing you need to do is determine exactly what the problem is and who owns it. A question that can guide one in determining who owns the problem is to ask, "Whose needs' are not being met."

*Process or People Problems?* Researchers have found that about eighty to eight five percent of problems are process or systems related, and about five to fifteen percent are people related. Only fifteen percent of associate's performance problems are due to lack of training; the other eighty five percent are due to lack of feedback, task interference, and negative consequences. So, find out the source of the problem and then plan for the appropriate solution since training people on communication or motivation may not be the solution to process related challenges. Neither is empowering untrained people to resolve challenges that are beyond their abilities and/or level of comprehension.

*Convergent and Divergent Approaches to Problem-Solving:* The *convergent* approach is the structured, logical, purposeful and deliberate method of solving problems. Most scientific researchers use this method to analyze the problem and find solutions to them in a formal way. This way others can follow the same procedure and get the same results. The advantages are consistency and standardization while the disadvantages might be "red tape" and eliminating the human factor, which can be disastrous at times. The *divergent* approach is the creative, innovative, customized, situational, and spontaneous method of solving problems. It states that no two situations are alike and each situation may require different ways of solving the problem. What works for one person may not necessarily work for another person under the same circumstances. According to experts, creativity diverges from the straight-and-narrow path that convergent thinking requires one to follow. Advantages of the divergent approach are the human factor and situational attention while the disadvantages can include cost, uncertainty, and lack of direction. The convergent approach integrates divergent thinking to problem solving in dealing with problems that take a significant chunk of a manager's time and effort. Regardless of which approach is used, a manager should:

*Focus on what is important:* It is critical to separate what is urgent and important from things that are urgent but not important. Pareto's Law states that eighty percent of the results flow from twenty percent of activities. So, some activities have much more impact than others and one should focus on these high leverage activities. The Pareto principle tells us that eighty percent of problems are caused by twenty percent of subordinates. Obviously we do not want to spend eighty percent of our time with twenty percent of our associates that constantly keep causing problems. This will cause managers to keep putting out fires and there will be no time to plan for future important activities. Proactively focusing on what is important will reduce the need for putting out fires, and increase one's time to appropriately *plan* future strategies; *organize*, train, and prepare people as well as resources to get the job done; *lead* people in the right direction, and *control* the unpredictable circumstances as they arise.

*Delegate appropriately*: Appropriate delegation means fully preparing people to the point where they can competently do the job without needing anyone's help. Most people cannot let go of things they feel comfortable doing and things that they enjoy doing. However, as a manager you cannot keep doing all the tasks by yourself and be successful. J. C. Penny once said, "the wisest decision I ever made was to let go when I realized that I couldn't do it all by myself anymore." Proper delegation requires mutual understanding between the manager and the associate with regards to the desired outcome, guidelines and boundaries of what to do and what not to do, resources available to accomplish the desired outcome, responsibility and accountability for the successful progress of the task, and the consequence of effectively performing the task. If the way a job is being done is too complex or time consuming and if you think there might be better ways of doing it, then delegate the job to the laziest person in your department and soon you will discover the easiest way of getting it done.

*Listen empathically*: There are four methods of communication which are reading, writing, speaking, and listening. According to most workshop participants, listening is the most important of all four methods. Ironically, it has also been the most neglected one in the education and training arena. Most people do not receive much training in listening and consequently need to improve their listening skills. It is a skill that almost everyone can improve upon to help eliminate misunderstandings. Managers should listen empathically with their eyes and heart for more than just words. The highest level of listening is empathic listening, listening with the eyes and the heart for *feelings* and *emotions*. It is a way of seeing things from the other person's perspective, the way he or she is seeing it. Empathic listening requires you to avoid autobiographical responses while trying to understand the message. Autobiographical responses also discourage people to open up and tell you their feelings and thoughts.

*Do not take other people's monkeys*. Bill Oncken, in his article co-authored with Donald L. Wass and titled "*Management Time: Who's got the monkey?*" published in *Harvard Business Review* in 1974, stated that a monkey is a problem or the next move a person needs to make when the dialogue breaks. Problems are like monkeys and taking too many monkeys can rob you of your valuable discretionary time. Often managers seem to run out of time while their subordinates seem to run out of work. This is because managers are taking their subordinates' monkeys for various reasons. Oncken and Wass suggest five rules with regard to taking care of monkeys. First, monkeys should be fed or shot; otherwise it wastes the manager's time and resources. Second, the monkey population should be kept below the maximum number that the manager can handle during a given period of time. Third, monkeys should be fed by appointment rather than having to hunt for them. Fourth, monkeys should be fed face-to-face or person-to-person over a telephone rather than email and written documents. Fifth, every monkey should have a scheduled "next feeding time" and an assigned "degree of initiative." Effectively following these rules will reduce a manager's problems and allow him/her to spend more time focusing on what is important. According to Oncken, the best way to reduce procrastination and increase the urgency and importance of a project is to delegate it to subordinates.

*Avoid becoming an automatic answering machine.* Managers can and do face problems many times daily and they must provide answers to them accurately and quickly. The repetition of solving these problems and experiences can cause managers to automatically respond and solve the employee's problems without fully listening to his or her concerns. Consequently, this tendency can cause anger, resentment, feelings of not being heard, not being part of the team, and dissatisfaction on the employee's part. Some managers carry this tendency to their home lives as well and try to be problem-solvers. This tendency can ruin personal relationships and cause bad listening habits. There are many conscious and unconscious habits that can be very disturbing to employees and becoming an automatic answering machine is one of them. Many of these habits are unconscious and stem from the natural tendency to solve problems quickly because of the mindset that "we are managers and it is our job to provide the answers." This mentality has been reinforced by the fast-paced work environment and the managers' expertise and experience. While managers may have total familiarity with most problem situations because of repetition and the nature of an employee's job, the employee does not know this and may think the manager doesn't care about his/her problem. While some of these habits are unconscious and routine, others are purposeful, some are trivial, some are therapeutic, and some are caused by the personality traits of the manager.

### Using IDEAS to Solve Problems

The IDEAS model is a structured (convergent) problem solving process for identifying and solving a problem. Instead of waiting for a solution to pop into your head from up above, the IDEAS model can help get you to the best solution one step at a time with available resources. IDEAS helps you think critically and creatively to investigate the problem, develop alternatives, examine and evaluate proposed alternatives, accept and administer the chosen alternative, and survey the results for success of current and future opportunities. Edward de Bono, the guru of creative thinking in his 1991 book "*I Am Right You Are Wrong?*", wrote that "the most effective critical thinking is actually creative thinking - the ability to generate alternative solutions. There is a need for attention to thinking that is productive, constructive, generative, and creative. Reactive thinking and problem solving will not equip people to improve society." This is why a manager needs to proactively focus on planning and preparing others in order to avoid putting out fires and solving problems. The IDEAS model helps you solve significant problems and the following are the five steps of problem solving:

*1. Identify and Investigate the Problem.* Once a problem has been identified, the problem-solving process begins. It is important to make sure the right problem has been identified. So, the first and foremost important step is to *define the problem* statement accurately and clearly. Solution imagineering is the second step to identifying and investigating the problem. *Solution imagineering* involves mentally seeing the problem solved and its prospective results accomplished. The accomplished results can clarify the objectives of solving the problem. This can also be accomplished through brainstorming or "Six Hat Thinking" principles. The third step is to *investigate the real cause* of the problem. Often, the real cause of the problem is hidden underneath the surface. Just like an iceberg has its major parts under the water and its tip above the water, real causes of the problem can often be hidden under all the symptoms. A cause-and-effect diagram can be used to brainstorm and diagnose the real cause of the problem. Always measure twice and cut once because if you are solving the wrong problem, things will get worse. You cannot climb to the right place if your ladder is leaning against the wrong wall.

2. *Develop Alternatives*. Most people are able to form a solution to general problems based on their intuitive senses as soon as they come in contact with the problem. The truth of the matter is that most often solutions are based on past experiences and developed paradigms instead of facts surrounding the current issue or problem. While one may intuitively have the solution in mind, it is best to generate several other alternatives through brainstorming or "Six Hat Thinking" which is another form of brainstorming for creativity, formality and discipline. The main purpose of this step is to generate ideas, and the first rule of any brainstorming session is not to evaluate ideas as they are being generated.

3. *Evaluate and Examine Alternatives*. Upon successful generation of several workable alternatives, one must evaluate and examine them for cost and benefit analysis as it pertains to all stakeholders. One must analyze them, and then attempt to evaluate their benefits with regards to all stakeholders and check their alignment with one's personal and professional values. After summing up the values and costs, one may determine whether to pursue an alternative or keep searching for better solutions. There are many roads that can lead you from here to your destination. However, the shortest road is the *"straight path"* which you should travel.

4. *Accept and Administer an Alternative*. The chosen alternative should solve the problem efficiently, productively, and with the least cost being imposed on the stakeholders. The alternative that respects everyone's rights and maximizes the benefits to everyone involved should be chosen and implemented. Implementation takes time, resources, planning, budgeting, and organizing all the related elements. The way a solution is implemented can make all the difference in the world because a solution is no better than the worst action taken to implement it. Implementation requires proper planning, organizing, control, and execution. Remember, implementation is an *IMP*ortant *LE*adership ele*MENT* because knowledge by itself does not produce anything. It is properly applied or executed knowledge that produces results including power.

5. *Survey the Results and Suggest Improvements*. Once a decision is implemented, it is very important to follow through and examine the actual results. This can serve as an educational experience and as a confirmation tool to make sure the original root cause of the problem is eliminated. Upon close examination of the results one should take proper action and do what is necessary.

Always make a decision and proceed. It is through convergent and divergent problem solving techniques that managers discover new opportunities, alternatives, and better methods. However, it is through determination, persistency, and decision-making abilities that managers get results and make things happen. We live in an imperfect world and our decisions need to be made in a timely manner with the available information. Because of deadlines, problem solvers will inevitably need to make decisions through "*satisficing*" with the limited information in the allotted time, and they will need to become effective problem-solvers and coaches.

## Trust Building Traits

There are many leadership traits and characteristics that are important for effective coaching and performance management. However, such traits as trust are mandatory as they can make or break a person's career and level of influence with others. In the special issue of Harvard Business Review in January 2007 (pp. 15-25), in an article entitled "*Moments of Truth: Global Executives Talk About the Challenges that Shaped Them as Leaders,*" the editors asked business leaders in various settings what they thought was the most important leadership quality and how they have been personally tested? The commonly cited leadership traits and characteristics that shaped them as leaders were the following: humility, energy, intuition, vision, perspective, passion, conviction, and learning. While the traits and characteristics of humility, energy, intuition, vision, perspective, passion, conviction, and learning are very important for effective leadership, they cannot make a person a leader or a coach unless he or she has developed a high level of trust with his or her followers.

Bacon and Spear (2003, p. 16) state that "Coaching relationships are made, not born." According to Bacon and Spear, coaches need to build trust with coachees by showing confidence, caring and acceptance. So, trust is having faith and confidence in the ability of those whom you interact with on a daily basis. The best way to build trust is to demonstrate compassion, courage, and honesty in all your interactions for the right reasons and at the right times. A person of integrity and high character is trustworthy and influential. S/he can become a great role model and do many great things for others by being compassionate, courageous, and honest. You build trust by doing what you say you would do (DWYSYWD) 100% of the time. Consistency is the key to building trust by always DWYSYWD. If you read DWYSYWD backwards, it still says "Do What You Say You Would Do."

Trust is a factor in both one's personal as well as professional life with colleagues, customers and supplier relationships. According to James Masciarielli (1998), there are three major components of transforming people we know into people that we know intimately (Byrnes, 2007[35]). For example, a supplier must communicate with customers constantly, trust them (and be trusted by them), and provide value to their products and services. The formula is as follows: $R = T + V + D$; that is, relationship equals trust plus value plus dialogue (Masciarielli, 1998). Masciarielli identifies five sets of skills to support his theory: positioning, hunting, coaching, leading, and framing.

*Positioning* – How clearly do you convey the value that you, your team and your company bring to the table? Can you articulate a clear and lasting impression to different audiences, and do so in 30 seconds or less? Positioning is about knowing your values, credibility and message and being able to communicate all of this so that people understand where you're heading and what you hope to contribute. In other words, do your counterparts see you as you want them to see you?

---

[35] Contributed by Thomas J. Byrnes, Nova Southeastern University.

*Hunting* – How well (and how often) do you create and identify new business opportunities? People with good hunting skills take the initiative to look for exactly what they want and then make plans to go after it.

*Coaching* – When you coach, you listen, nurture, advise, and help others achieve their goals. You do whatever you can to bring out the best in people the best performance, highest commitment, and greatest results. Thus, coaching allows others to gain value from you.

*Leading* – If you have worked hard at the previous three items, you've earned the right to contract with others to help you achieve your objectives. Leading means motivating others to work with you to achieve your goals, it is about getting things done through others and stimulating the most effective actions for groups.

*Farming* – This suggests maintaining and harvesting all that value you've been creating and demonstrating. It means knowing when to tap people for the "3 Is": *introductions* (to desired contacts and prospects), *information* (to help with your positioning and hunting) and *ideas* (to help with any of the other four keys). "Farmers" keep relationships current, tilling the soil for present and future value. They sow, nurture, and reap" (Masciarielli, 1998). All of these attributes are essential elements of a solid customer relationship management system.

Trusting behavior, with customers, occurs when a person relies on another, risks something of value, and attempts to achieve a desired goal (Byrnes, 2007). The extent to which any behavior might be considered an act of trust would be determined by the amount of risk faced by the customer, as well as the extent to which a customer has to rely on the performance of the marketing entity. A cognitive state of trust exists when one person assumes without adequate evidence that the other's behavior will not confer unacceptably negative outcomes upon him. Further, a trusting individual bases the assumption on perceptions of the other's knowledge, competence, and motive. Trust is important to the success of a partnership. With trust as a precursor, a customer becomes loyal to a firm and forms a commitment to that firm. Trust is a core ingredient of successful coach-coachee, leader-follower, and buyer-seller relationships.

Trust is a building block for effective communication with one's friends, colleagues, employees, vendors, and suppliers. The flow of communication between you and everyone you come in contact with is greatly affected by the level of trust that exists between you and them. If the trust level is high, you have an environment that supports open and honest communication. It is up to you, as a leader, to help build an environment of trust with everyone around you. When people feel comfortable and safe from being judged prematurely and incorrectly, they are more willing to open up and speak their minds. If the trust level is low, then the opposite becomes true. So, you can make or "break" the level of trust between you and your friends, colleagues, and peers through your character. Remember, who you are as a person communicates much more loudly, persuasively and eloquently than anything you write, say or do. To become a person of strong character, you need to be consistently compassionate, courageous, and honest in all of your dealings with people.

### *Honesty*

Honesty is always telling the truth. It has been said that "honesty is the best policy," and of course, many believe this to be true, even in today's society. As you may also believe, honest people tend to persevere and become the heroes and role models in the long-run. People are internally motivated and subconsciously obligated to be honest and tell the truth. Shakespeare once wrote, "Every man has his faults and honesty is his. He is more honest than wise." He further wrote, "What a tangled web we weave - when we at first practice to deceive."

We should always remember that any deviance from the truth will cause more dishonesty and larger burdens of guilt to our subconscious minds, which can drive a person to high levels of self-imposed stress faster than anything else. So, remember that the truth will always set you free, and, as a result, you will never become a "prisoner of your own conscience." People who have experienced the most horrible conditions and the most inhumane treatments by prison guards during political wars go on to live great lives. However, not many people can live happily with themselves if they have been less than honest to themselves and those who care about them. Psychologists call this cognitive dissonance, which is basically the cacophony, disharmony, or discord between your beliefs and actions which are subconsciously recognized by the human mind that naturally wants to be honest and do the right thing.

Living purposefully and happily is the mission of everyone alive. There is no escaping this mission, it started shortly after we were born and will end when we die. While we do not have much control over our birth or death, we do have control over the happiness of our lives. Happiness is not something one can purchase or buy, but it is rather a journey or a process of how one lives on a day-to-day basis. Honest living can be a major determinant of the happiness in your life. Honesty is something you have total control over, and it is your choice at any moment in time. So ride the road of honesty in your journey towards happiness, make sure you do not get off temporarily, and know that it is a straight path and there are no twists, turns or curves. Remember, honesty is your vitamin for good health, happiness and success in life. And the best and most prescribed vitamin for an "honest person" is "B1." The metaphorical vitamin ("B1") simply says to be one; to be an honest person.

### *Courage*

John McCain, U.S. Senator, defines courage as a single occurrence or "that rare moment of unity between conscience, fear, and action, when something deep within us strikes the flint of love, of honor, of duty, to make the spark that fires our resolve" (Reardon, 2007, p. 58). While courage can certainly be shown in cases that are matters of life and death, for business professions courage is often a series of calculated risks that one must take to achieve managerial or organizational goals. Kathleen Reardon explains that "People who become good leaders have a greater than average willingness to make bold moves, but they strengthen their chances of success – and avoid career suicide – through careful deliberation and preparation" (2007, p. 60). Reardon emphasizes that courage in the business environment is not an inborn trait. Courage in the business environment or workplace is a skill that can be acquired by any employee, coach, or manager through a series of decision-making processes and continuous learning that can be improved over time. Courageous business leaders take calculated risks and make decisions according to a strategic process termed the "courage calculation." According to Reardon (2007), "courage calculation" is a method or approach for making success more likely by avoiding rash, quick, emotional, unproductive, or irrational actions and behaviors. The courage calculation, according to Reardon, is made up of the following six concrete processes that employees, managers and coaches can use to be courageous in business: set primary and secondary goals, determine the importance of achieving them, tip the power balance in one's favor, weigh risks against benefits or doing a cost-benefit analysis, select the proper time for taking action, and develop contingency plans as second and third options. For example, in regard to goal setting, one should be clear about what success is in the high-risk workplace and whether success is obtainable. Reardon (2007, p. 63) further recommends asking other questions, similar to the following, to determine an appropriate course of action:

1. Why am I pursuing this step now?
2. Am I contemplating a considered action or an impulsive one?
3. How long would it take to become better prepared? Is that too long?
4. What are the pros and cons of making a decision at a later date?
5. What are some of the political challenges? Can they be removed, avoided or effectively dealt with in a timely manner?
6. Can I do certain things now to create a better foundation for a courageous action later?
7. Am mentally and emotionally ready to take such calculated actions?
8. Do I have the needed expertise, management skills, communication skills, track record, and credibility to make this work at this time?

Of course, those who are able to honestly answer these questions are likely to take an appropriate action and act courageously when it is called for in a given month or year. Research shows that "those who act courageously in business settings have an instinct for opportunity…they read situations quickly, but they are never reckless" Reardon, 2007, p. 63). The point is that courageous managers and coaches tend to plan and prepare themselves for taking calculated risks in order to achieve their goals and develop their people. Coaches and managers should set appropriate goals, determine the importance of achieving them, tip the power balance in their favor, do a cost-benefit analysis for each alternative, select the proper time for taking "calculated actions," and develop contingency plans. These are the foundations of courage in business which can be used by everyone, including managers and coaches.

In general, courage is always doing what is right. Every person has his or her own definition of courage and most associate it with not having fear. While this can be one way of seeing or recognizing some courageous individuals, it is not always true. Courage is not the absence of fear, but rather the presence of fear that forces a person to do what is right, at the right time and for the right reasons. Courage is a state of mind that encourages you to take action regardless of your fears because your reasons are so strong that your fears become meaningless. This is when you realize that the fear within you for taking action is nothing compared to the fear you feel for not taking action. People often experience either the pain of discipline or regret.

Compared to the pain of regret, the pain of discipline is much smaller and much more enjoyable. Aristotle said it over 2,000 years ago that "a truly courageous person feels fear at the right time, for the right reasons and in the right way." A truly courageous person fears nothing but fear itself. S/he has fears of not being able to provide for his or her family or make the right decision during the moment of truth when s/he is being tested for the strength of his or her character. A truly courageous person knows that if s/he is less than honest about his/her thoughts and feelings, then they will come back to haunt him/her by finding a place in the roots of his or her thoughts and feelings.

Therefore, a truly courageous person consistently goes the extra mile and puts the necessary extra effort to do what is right in the first place. A truly courageous person settles for nothing less than the best s/he is capable of doing or becoming. The great motivational speaker, Tony Robins, once said, "To be all we can be, we must dream of doing more; and to do all that is possible, we must attempt the impossible." Truly courageous people fear that someday they might settle for less than their best and consequently work harder and smarter to better prepare so their fears do not become reality. Truly courageous people know their limits and their capabilities with regards to their goals, wants, and needs because they constantly test, challenge and improve their physical, mental, spiritual, and emotional faculties. As Tony Robins says, "you can only know how far you can go by going too far," therefore finding your limitations is not a sign of failure but an opportunity to use your strengths and improve your weaknesses. This author's mother often mentions an Afghan saying that "one should not extend his/her legs beyond the boundaries of his/her own carpet" which basically means that you should always know your limitations and boundaries so you do not hurt yourself. Runners know how fast they can run and they improve gradually through consistent practice and patience without hurting themselves by overworking and expecting quick results. Coaches should remember that truly courageous people know their values, know what they want and why they want them, and do what is right at the right times and for the right reasons.

### *Compassion*

Compassion is always showing that you care. Being compassionate and professionally sincere toward others communicates caring, value and security. Being compassionate is a state of mind that is nonjudgmental and being sincerely concerned for the wellness of others. Being sincerely compassionate is extremely important for building and growing your "circle" of influence and leadership. This requires patience, perseverance, determination, and caring. Unfortunately, the urgency-driven world of business and politics can cause people to make quick judgments about others and be discourteous to them. This type of behavior and autocratic style of leadership can stop effective communication, erode trust, and promote a world of fear. A world where your leadership influence will become nonexistent and you will have no followers.

Therefore, effective leaders and coaches know how to be compassionate and consistently show concern for people. They are patient with people but condemn and reproach wrong behavior. Effective leaders and coaches have determination to get what they want and consistently do the right things to achieve their goals. However, effective leaders and coaches also understand that time is on their side and patience is their offensive weapon and artillery. Thomas Edison, the great inventor, once said, "Everything comes to those who wait but it comes faster to those who hustle while they wait." Working hard and hustling to achieve results cannot only get you positive results but can also educate you simultaneously. Any occupation or job can have many lessons and principles for our lives. For example, through gardening and farming people have learned that "we reap what we sow." Besides learning about sowing and reaping, farmers learned about tending and keeping. The most important lesson of all would be patience and how it can pay off at the end of the season. So, be patient and compassionate with people in order to build trusting relationships and enjoy a happy life. After all, a life without compassion will have no love and a loveless life would be no better than a life of misery and frustration. A sign said it well,

*"Only one life that soon will pass - only what's done with love will last."*

As a coach, may you witness more love than you currently see, acquire more love than you deserve, and provide more love than humanly possible. And, may you always have a high level of trust as a coach to effectively manage conflicts, so you and your colleagues can enjoy a productive personal and professional life.

## Change, Conflict, and Stress Management

The fast pace of today's work environment has created many workaholics who might be successful professionally but personally they have a "bankrupt" life since they have forgotten about effectively balancing their time with family members. Perhaps, such work life is another variable playing into the high divorce rates in most countries and cultures. The fast pace of today's work world has caused changes in people's eating patterns as well. Instead of eating meals jointly with family members, friends and colleagues many families and individuals have been conditioned to eat in between work or other activities. As a matter of fact, according to a USA Today survey in August 2005, the most popular places to eat on the go were in front of the television set (60% of the respondents), in the car (42%) and at work (40%). Fifty years ago, most traditional cultures did not encourage people to eat by themselves since eating was a social time for family members to talk and converse with one another. Because of such interpersonal conversation opportunities, there was little need for psychiatrists and psychologists which are highly in demand today by many individuals because they are the only professionals who will listen to one's modern day problems…provided that they are paid. In previous centuries, when children and teenagers faced a difficult task they usually approached a family member for advice. Today, most teenagers listen to strangers on the internet and their behaviors are often driven by the actions and trends of television stars. While television icons and chat-room respondents on the internet may not always be good role models, many youngsters feel comfortable listening to them and doing what they do. These are major changes for parents and children who are brought up with traditional family values. They will have to effectively deal with these changes as well as the impact of such changes on their children and grandchildren. While many changes can be out of one's immediate control, one can be properly prepared to deal with them according to one's personal priorities and values. Even then, the most prepared individuals would have to show flexibility in choosing the best course of action for moving forward and achieving one's predetermined worthwhile goals in a changing world. Changes in modern times might be a bit more challenging for those who are not brought up with them; therefore, the new generation must develop skills to effectively deal with new changes as they too might have been conditioned by societal or organizational cultures that do not always welcome change.

Dynamic change is a constant in today's work environment. As such, using good sense, learning the latest data, and adapting to the current facts are essential ingredients for sustainable and positive change. In the twenty-first century environment, due to new technologies, change keeps picking up speed in all industries and professions. It is best to think of technological change as something that keeps multiplying on a continuous basis. Still another source of this rapid change is knowledge or information which seems to be doubling about every four to five years. Some of the commonly addressed sources of change for businesses can include changes in leadership, management, organizational structures, products, services, customers, customer demands, and location of where the firm produces or offers its products.

Because of rapid changes, new knowledge and doubling of information about every few years, the future promises much more change than has been experienced thus far. What is interesting to know and keep in mind during difficult moments is that change has no conscience and it does not play favorites. Yes, it is also true that change can quickly or slowly destroy organizations that do not adapt to the new circumstances. Pritchett states that high-velocity change calls for major shifts in behavior: "More specifically, we must think differently. Reorder our priorities. Develop faster reflexes. Give the culture an entirely new set of responses. We can't afford to ignore change and just do what comes naturally. We must face and do what works." We should welcome change with pleasure and enjoyment since it is inevitable. Steve Chandler, author, said "There is a huge difference between pleasure and enjoyment. Enjoyment always involves the use of a skill and facing of a challenge. Put more enjoyment into your life. Increase your skills, face challenges." Similarly, for effective change and stress management, increase your skills and face the challenges proactively. As the saying goes, luck is simply the intersection of preparation and opportunity. Increase your luck by acquiring the relevant knowledge regarding change, conflict and their effective management.

Mankind has never before experienced so many changes in such a short period of time, and this change, characteristic of our modern century, is a very pervasive one. Life itself is a process of change and adaptability. Our modern century of technological marvels and social revolutions has thrust upon us many unbearable conditions and consequences, some of which rage above our deepest sentiments and comprehension. Society today is bombarded on all sides with a series of drastic changes within all social institutions, and the degree at which these change factors and agents assault our minds and lives is overwhelmingly inexhaustible.

Managing change is a tactical and strategic affair which becomes increasingly dangerous and difficult as the number of change variables and agents increases. This is further complicated by conflict which is inherent in all human social affairs. Conflict is unavoidable in human affairs, and as such, serves as the bottleneck of progress! One of the major aims in change management and conflict resolution seems to be that of eliminating conflict. This is an almost impossible task we set for ourselves whilst our differences remain as individuals. It is fully within our nature to agree and disagree with each other, and our added knowledge and information of today have both increased and decreased the threshold for disagreement under various circumstances.

Change is a frightening social and psychological experience when it requires entering new spheres and situations. Moreover, change today has a significantly wider scope than it did decades ago, as the factors of globalization and cultural diversity have become fundamental principles and paradigms upon which change is prefabricated. One must now have a variety of skills and a wider knowledge base to manage or even comprehend change as it takes place within the context of cultural and social conflicts. The cross-cultural aspects of change and conflict further complicate their management and resolution.

Change is a social process because it is the human element that gives life and significance to change in any setting. Therefore, when managers and leaders consider change within their institutions or organizations they need to take a decisively behavioral or human approach to the management of change. Change is one of the most dominant characteristics of today's hard-pressing business environment in which fast-paced technology and high level competition are pushing individuals and organizations into new situations and environments. Entering into new competitive and social arenas can be highly stressful for employees and this amidst resulting conflicts internal and external to the organization. As a result of this awareness, managers and leaders must make change and conflict management a major part of their training and responsibilities. Teaching employees about the nature of change and its significance can be a first step in the process of effectively managing change.

Change is natural and expected within our lives. It is the nature and dynamics of change that can become stressful or cause conflicts, resistance and fear in us. The problem therefore is not change itself, but unplanned change. As human beings we like to plan and be able to manage our every aspect of life and living. Planned change is the catalyst around which we approach life; our education, training, socialization, communications, etc. However, life seems to offer more of the other for which we can be wholly unprepared to manage or accept; unplanned change. The field of strategic management has offered managers and leaders considerable knowledge in the area of planning; both short-term and long-term. However, planning for change is not an easy task, and this further complicates managing change. Change in today's society can offer many advantages as well as disadvantages, and this will depend on the degree of change, the context in which change unfolds, the scope of change, the mindset, knowledge base and skills of the individual undergoing change, the type of information and education the individual possesses, the source or sources of change, and the cultural and social experiences of the individual. Culturally, change can be a very destructive force, especially when assimilation of one's values, beliefs, customs, etc., becomes the major consequence. It is this aspect of change that becomes very stressful for both individuals and groups. All forms of change have cultural and social overtones that affect organizational progress and performance. Managers and leaders must become attuned to the fact that change within organizations means change within the social contexts of employees' work and lives. The field of industrial psychology still holds great knowledge benefits for those who would examine the effects of change in work environments and change management across all organizational boundaries. Furthermore, the lack of management initiatives and programs to deal with change and conflicts in immediate organizational settings are grossly lacking in 21$^{st}$ century institutions. Usually, we choose to react to change only when it arrives, and this is where conflict and resistance become major issues. We must prepare for change and then we will be better able to manage it within all contexts.

Conflict is inherent in all human affairs and this seems evident even from the onset of human history when we consider life from a Creationist perspective. Conflict seems to be part of the imperfect mind and nature of man as he strives to make decisions as to wrong or right, and those having to do with the allocation and distribution of limited resources. Conflict strives from individual differences; personal, social, psychological, cultural, physical and even the gender-related biological differences within our specie. Human conflict has both micro and macro origins; generated between individuals, groups, institutions or larger society, races or cultures. The nature of conflict as it exists within our lives rests heavily on our knowledge of selves and others and in our ability to foster tolerance and adapt to change within all contexts effectively.

Leaders of the 21$^{st}$ century must practice being effective supporters in counseling their subordinates to deal with change and in managing conflicts. It is important that managers and leaders of the 21$^{st}$ century do not strive to be or exemplify themselves as propagators of radical or mass social and organizational changes, but rather as facilitators in the change process. This will better enable them to address resistance as well as to deal with conflict. Conflict and change management should be practiced alongside each other for the best result, since they are closely interrelated and change and conflict strive from and feed on each other. Managers and leaders of today's institutions and organizations must possess a wide knowledge base and familiarity with cultures and individuals' social values in order to effectively arrive at the heart of conflict and uniquely address issues and problems. Cultural diversity as an initiative of 21$^{st}$ century organizations has added much complexity to change and conflict as individuals from varied backgrounds and societies encounter each other in active working relationships.

Conflict like change cannot be avoided, it can only be dealt with, and managers and leaders must become aware of this fact. Our differences as individuals serve to perpetuate change and conflict; our language, ethnic and social differences, etc. Knowing this fact, life then is best seen as a process of adapting to change and dealing with conflict, and the best way we can approach this is by effective change management and conflict management. The field of conflict resolution has not done much for us as a society, and this is immediately evident in the widespread social problems we experience today. One of the grave issues is the speed at which social change takes place; so rapid that it is best termed social revolution. Social revolution has perpetuated conflict throughout all corners of our society and this conflict is multiple in character. There are conflicts which are gender-based, generational-related, economic-based, racially-based, culturally-based, and the list goes on. The rate at which change is taking place at all levels of our society is alarming and as such evades our ability and comprehension to deal with it effectively. The rapid nature of change has affected our ability to address conflicts across the board as we struggle to deal with several issues at once. This puts a strain on individual knowledge and scope, as well as on the limited resources we have available including time to resolve many conflicts. Resulting from this is the need for effective stress management. Stress is a major factor of social and other related problems in individuals and organizations. In fact, it seems to be a major health issue in highly developed and industrialized nations more than in any others.

The relationship existing between stress, change, and conflict is one which becomes quite obvious when we consider the fact that they usually arise simultaneously within social contexts or situations or proceed immediately out of each other's existence.

Change in today's society is alarmingly fast-paced and this is the major issue which most individuals seem to find difficult to confront. As human beings we like to feel comfortable in a safe zone where stability guarantees us certain psychological and social needs. Change can disrupt our lives and wreck our world into disaster, especially when change has the characteristic unpredictability it does in our technologically advanced society. The 21$^{st}$ century society has the highest degree of uncertainty that our civilization has witnessed throughout generations thus far, and with individual knowledge of this fact, our resistance to change should come as no surprise. Change can be drastic and dramatic, devastating, devouring, disastrous, and destructive. Such change where culture, religion, way of life, survival, and life itself are crushed is the most fearful and problematic, causing severe cultural, social and psychological stress and damage. Stress is created by change and change can cause conflict; in the meantime, conflict can cause change and further stress. The variables of change, stress, and conflict have an interdependent relationship and they tend to impact one another; change in one can cause a positive or negative impact on the others.

Managers and leaders of 21$^{st}$ century institutions and organizations must not impose change without consensus, and when such change is introduced, implementation in an incremental manner is the best method or approach. Too much change too fast and in too little time can upset progress by affecting individual satisfaction, performance, concentration, skills, and ability to cope with tasks and responsibilities. Therefore, it is important to educate individuals about any change and make them aware of the type of change and how it will affect them. This will reduce stress as well as conflict and the resistance to change.

As a civilization, we have perhaps individually and collectively experienced more of the devastating and negative side of change than the positive one. Dramatic change has shaped our entire progress, destiny and century. Positive change is what we seek and require as individuals and when this fails to show itself we are confounded and stressed. When we plan change it often involves less stress and conflict. Managers and leaders of the 21$^{st}$ century must invest heavily in fostering and promoting positive change to motivate employees and deal with conflicts. Change can be the source of new growth or the precursor of failure and losses.

While management is a very useful tool, the value of managers coaching employees for maximum productivity amid major change must be emphasized. Due to the changing demographics of the business world such as more competition and the introduction of new technologies, organizations are discovering that traditional tactics of management are no longer enough to remain competitive. As such, coaching is coming to be recognized and practiced as an effective tool to increase morale, performance and the bottom line through the success of each individual associate. For example, it has been proven that employee commitment increases when there is a strong, positive relationship between the manager and his/her employees.

### Ethics and Character Building

As a coach or manager, you must always be concerned about ethics and fairness of your decisions and actions. For example, due to your socialization in the society thus far, you probably have had a good amount of reading on the basics of ethics, leadership, stewardship, morality, and social responsibility. As such, you have formed a good understanding of them based on your experiences and thoughts. However, most people do not really take the time to understand the true meaning of values, ethics and morality because of their busy schedules.

*Values* are core beliefs or desires that guide or motivate our attitude and actions. What one values drives his/her behavior. Some people value honesty or truthfulness in all situations while others may value loyalty to a higher degree in certain situations.

*Ethics* is the branch of philosophy that theoretically, logically, and rationally determines right from wrong, good from bad, moral from immoral, and just from unjust actions, conducts, and behavior. Some people define ethics simply as doing what you say you would do or walking the talk. Overall, ethics establishes the rules and standards that govern the moral behavior of individuals and groups. It also distinguishes between right and wrong conducts. It involves honest consideration to underlying motive, to possible potential harm, and to congruency with established values and rules. *Applied ethics* refers to moral conclusions based on rules, standards, code of ethics, and models that help guide decisions. There are many subdivisions in the field of ethics and some of the common ones are descriptive, normative, and comparative ethics. *Business ethics*, more specifically, deal with the creation and application of moral standards in the business environment.

*Morals* are judgments, standards, and rules of good conduct in the society. They guide people toward permissible behavior with regard to basic values. Consider the following dilemma and how the terms values, ethics and morals actually apply here:

A thief, named Zar, guarantees that you will receive the agreed upon confidential information from your competitor in five days. Zar is professing a *value* – he/she will deal with you honestly because you as the customer are very important to his/her business. When Zar has delivered the proper documents within the agreed upon time (five days), one can say that Zar has behaved *ethically* because he/she was consistent with his/her professed values. The following year you ask Dar, who is a competitor to Zar, and he makes the same promise as Zar by professing the same values, to get the same information from your competitor for this year. Five days later, Dar only delivers part of the information which is not totally accurate and in the meantime Dar is blackmailing you for more money. If Dar does not get more money then he will be going to the authorities and to the competitor to report this business dealing. Now, one can say that Dar has behaved *unethically* because his actions were not consistent with his professed values. Finally, one can conclude that all three parties involved in stealing insider information have acted *immorally* as judged by majority of the population. Overall, values are professed statements of one's beliefs, ethics is delivering on one's professed values, and morals are actions of good conduct as judged by the society that enhance the welfare of human beings.

Understanding values, ethics and morals while using ethical principles, each organization can form a framework for effective decision-making with formalized strategies. The willingness to add ethical principles to the decision-making structure indicates a desire to promote fairness, as well as prevent potential ethical problems from occurring. Corporate ethics programs are part of organizational life and organizations can use such sessions to further discuss the meaning of values, ethics and morals in the context of their businesses. Their organizational codes of ethics should protect individuals and address the moral values of the firm in the decision-making processes. Corporate codes of ethics are not merely some manuals for how-to-solve problems. They are tools which can empower everyone in the organization to say, "I am sorry that is against our policy or that would violate our company's code of ethics." This also will increase personal commitment of employees to their companies because people do take pride in the integrity of their corporate culture. So, be ethical, be fair, and build a great character for yourself and your organization.

Great coaches build character for themselves over time through consistent, goal-oriented actions and behaviors. A person's character is not something that is given by parents, teachers, and community leaders, but rather it is something that is chiseled through certain consistent behaviors and positions that one takes in life to positively influence others toward becoming contributing members of the society. In other words, nobody is born with a specific and predestined character. Character is built through one's day-to-day actions, reflections and personal beliefs. *Building Character: Strengthening the Heart of Good Leadership*, a 2007 Jossey-Bass book[36] by Gene Klann, provides managers and leaders the means and methods of developing their characters through example, education, experience, evaluation, and environment. It benefits organizations to develop their current and prospective managers and leaders using realistic practices and guidelines mentioned in the book. The author's rich background and experiences have made the contents of the book to be of lasting value to the personnel who plan to be leaders of their organizations or for those who are leaders and want to develop behaviors that further make them shine. Reading this book can be an asset to practicing managers and leaders of industry and governmental agencies. The following are some of the review statements and testimonials available online by various leaders and experts who have read the book:

- "Leadership successes, or failures, are the result of moral and ethical choices...the choices of character. All who lead—or want to lead—should open this book and dig in."
- "There is no shortcut to building leadership character! However, Gene Klann's book Building Character is excellent at organizing one's behaviors

---

[36] Book review contributed by Ghulam Mujtaba, Kabul University.

and creating awareness of the best practices to achieve your desired character outcome."

Gene Klann has provided examples of different leadership characters and has generally supported his means and methods of the character development by providing the results of surveys and interviews, which make the book very interesting to read. Klann's book explains the roles of leaders, which are motivating, inspiring, and influencing people. The book further describes how leadership roles differ from the roles of managers, which deals with planning, designing, directing, controlling, and tracking execution. The author suggests that good leaders should learn various methods of influencing people so they can be and become contributing members of their society. Klann explains the five influential attributes of the leaders, which are courage, caring, optimism, self-control, and communication. The book mentions that leaders can develop if they decide to do so. In other words, leadership is not necessarily an inborn trait, but rather, leadership qualities can be developed through persistent learning as well as effectively motivating, inspiring, and influencing others. The book discusses methods of self-control, self-improvement, and stress relief, including stress management, eating habits, jogging, walking, swimming, and other types of physical and mental exercises that tend to make leaders feel good both intrinsically as well as extrinsically.

What is interesting about *Building Character: Strengthening the Heart of Good Leadership* is that the author has included review questions at the end of each chapter. The questions make a leader reflect and think about the content of the chapter as well as the application of each section to one's personal and professional lives. The appendix parts of the book include lists of personnel values, assessing leadership character, a checklist of good leader behaviors, and leadership character scenarios. The review of these topics and applying the author's recommended methods will certainly benefit those who are leaders and want to develop their leadership character or for those who wish to be leaders and want the invaluable training. This book is a great book for all existing and aspiring entrepreneurs, managers and educators in the fields of business and leadership. It could also be used as a supplementary reading for students and faculty members who are discussing basic leadership and management topics in the undergraduate programs.

Overall, *Building Character* is an excellent book for all coaches, managers and leaders who want to develop other leaders within their organizations. This book offers every coach, entrepreneur and manager a practical guide to develop character in leaders at all levels to make their organizations successful through effective leadership. Klann emphasizes that character plays a critical role in leadership through the Five E's—Example, Education, Experience, Evaluation, and Environment. As a leader, one can be the kind of a leader that will serve as an example for his or her followers. Local, national and global leaders should consistently use honesty, compassion, and courage to build trust with people.

### Summary

Effective leadership is about coaching and *coaching* is about problem-solving and developing trusting relationships with employees so people can jointly clarify expectations and departmental goals thereby leading to specific action plans for their achievement. Coaching is not an innate skill, but rather it is learned. It occurs through one's life personally and professionally. Effective coaching is the process of letting people know that what they do matters to you and to the organization. Furthermore, it is about letting them know that you are there to help them be the best they can be as their success is important because it matters to you. It is also about being sincere, specific and to the point about both good and poor performance so employees can take personal responsibility for their achievements. From this perspective, coaching is and it can be one of the most important functions managers perform because it communicates performance levels, expectations, importance of the tasks and responsibilities, and it communicates a caring attitude. When effective coaches and managers see good performance, they say it and praise it. One should not let poor performance go unnoticed; as such, when one sees poor performance one can privately communicate with the person while making the discussion positively geared toward future performance. Leaders and coaches need to practice the "*Two Minute Challenge*": state what you observed; wait for a response; remind the person of the goal; ask for a specific solution; and jointly agree on the solution and its implementation.

To be effective problem-solvers, leaders and coaches must always be mentally, physically, socially, and spiritually in good shape if they are to proactively deal with stress and be a good role model for others in society. Keep your mind sharp by learning something new each day and each week. Keep your body in good shape by exercising three to four days every week for about thirty minutes each day. Keep your spirits high by reading motivational books, enjoying the present through appreciation and living in the moment, and by having a good sense of humor. Regardless of how hectic your work becomes, to improve your overall health and fitness, try to integrate the following activities into your daily routine:

- *Stretching* is an important component of fitness often neglected, especially by men. In addition to helping prevent injury and relieving muscle tension and stiffness, stretching maintains the mobility and flexibility of your muscles and joints. This maintenance becomes especially important as you age. Try to do some stretching every day.

- *Aerobic exercises* such as walking, jogging, tennis and basketball elevate your heart rate, and are best for cardiovascular health. Aim for 30 minutes of continuous activity at least three to four times a week.

- *Strength training* subjects your muscles to greater resistance than you would normally encounter in everyday life, which makes them stronger and firmer when done on a regular basis. Examples of strength training activities include lifting weights (bicep curls, leg presses, etc.), as well as squats, push-ups and sit-ups. Do strength-training exercises that work each muscle group two to three times a week.

Regular and routine exercise should help with stress management and good health. If you get too stressed, you can always add some humor to your life by repeating and reflecting upon the "Serenity Prayer for the Stressed" that was heard from Anisa Qadir:

Grant me the serenity to accept the things I can not change. And the courage to change the things I cannot accept; and the wisdom to hide the bodies of those who "ticked" me off. And when I become a big shot, help me to be careful of the toes I step on each day as they may be attached to the "bodies" I may have to kiss tomorrow. Help me to give 100% at work: 12% Mondays, 23% Tuesday, 40% Wednesday, 20% Thursday, and 5% Fridays. And help me to remember that when I am having a really bad day at work and it seems that people are trying to "tick" me off that it takes 42 muscles to frown and only 4 muscles to extend the middle finger and tell them to BITE ME.

Have a good sense of humor, be flexible and be friendly. Due to physical and mental differences regarding interest and ability, everybody is likely to have his/her own pace for growth, development and achievements. There is no reason to rush into anything or to push others into deadlines that are not realistic for them as per their perceptions. As the statement goes, "Anyone who imagines that all fruits ripen at the same time as the strawberries knows nothing about grapes" (Paracelsus). Understanding that each person is different and every individual should determine his or her own pace is a critical component of effective leadership and coaching. Since there are many things in life that one can control, it is best to avoid the pressures of unexpected events and unrealistic expectations that are beyond one's control or circle of influence; the key is to remain calm, wear a smile instead of a frown, and let life go on in a relaxed way; for tomorrow is another new day and one should stay focused on doing what is possible rather than stressing over the impossible. According to John Quincy Adams, "Patience and perseverance have a magical effect before which difficulties disappear and obstacles vanish." Besides being patient, one must also understand that, as stated by Carl Zuckmeyer, about "One-half of life is luck; the other half is discipline - and that's the important half, for without discipline you wouldn't know what to do with luck." Besides making one's own luck, it is best to also help others capitalize on their good fortunes by being a friend and a coach to them. As a friend and coach, keep in mind how good you feel when you have encouraged and supported someone else. No other argument is necessary to suggest that one should never miss the opportunity to give encouragement to others. This is the essence of being a great coach, a caring friend, and a good leader all at once.

When it comes to being a great coach, as stated in the initial chapter, take a chance and help others grow and develop. By helping others grow and develop, you will grow. Do not always be "*A Cautious Man.*"

> Once there was a very cautious man
> Who never loved, laughed or cried.
> > He never risked, he never lost
> > He never won nor ever tried.
> And one day when he passed away
> His insurance was denied.
> > For since he never really lived
> > They claimed he never really died. (*Unknown*)

While taking calculated chances, coaches must also exercise proper discipline. Julie Andrews, actress, said that "Some people regard discipline as a chore. For me, it is a kind of order that sets me free to fly." Dr. William James, psychologist, states that "Most people never run far enough on their first wind to find out if they've got a second. Give your dreams all you've got and you'll be amazed at the energy that comes out of you." Always keep in mind that it is perfectly okay to become confused when learning new concepts and philosophies: "Until you are willing to become confused about what you already know, what you know will never grow bigger, better, or more useful," says Milton Erickson, psychiatrist and hypnotherapist. As a leader of your life, you must make a decision and lead it. Thomas Jefferson said that "A leader's job is to look into the future and see things not as they are, but what they can become." See yourself as you can be in the near and distant future on a continuous basis. Be courageous and remember that "Courage is not the absence of fear, but rather the judgment that something else is more important than one's fear," as stated by writer Ambrose Redmoon. Also, keep in mind that "You are not here merely to make a living. You are here to enable the world to live more amply, with greater vision, with a finer vision of hope and achievement. You are here to enrich the world, and you impoverish yourself if you forget the errand," said the Woodrow Wilson, President of the United States. John D. Rockefeller III, philanthropist, stated that "The road to happiness lies in two simple principles: find what it is that interests you and that you can do well, and when you find it, put your whole soul into it -- every bit of energy and ambition and natural ability you have." Don't just be a leader or a manager, be a GREAT Coach!

### *Discussion Questions*

1. What are some common problems and challenges that managers face on a regular basis in their departments? Focus on obstacles that they might face on their day-to-day basis.
2. What are some problem suggestions for busy managers and coaches? List five principles that you think are important to understand and practice when it comes to problem-solving.
3. What is the role of "trust" in a relationship with employees and colleagues? Discuss through examples.
4. How can one build trust with his/her employees and colleagues? List five suggestions.
5. What can coaches and managers do to effectively manage change, stress, and conflict in their personal and professional lives? Discuss and focus on both their personal lives as well as their professional workplace when working with their employees.
6. Describe and discuss one example of a great coach that you can emulate in your professional life. Who is he or she? What makes him/her a great coach? List and discuss his/her top five coaching qualities.
7. What are some things you can do to be an inspirational coach? List five possibilities and activities.

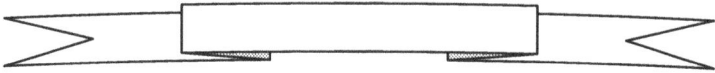

## Staying Healthy

"The best way to stay healthy is to balance one's food intake and it is best to stop eating just before the stomach is totally full. General rules for eating are to: have a healthy breakfast, share your lunch with friends and colleagues, and give a large portion of your dinner to your enemies."

*Afghan Proverb (as cited by Farhad Jamasi)*

## Positive Attitude

"The remarkable thing we have is a choice every day regarding the attitude we will embrace for that day. We cannot change our past. We cannot change the fact that people will act in a certain way. We cannot change the inevitable. The only thing we can do is play on the one string we have, and that is our attitude."

*Charles Swindoll*

## The Meaning of Success

"To laugh often and much; to win the respect of intelligent people and the affection of children; to earn the appreciation of honest critics and endure the betrayal of false friends; to appreciate beauty; to find the best in others; to leave the world a bit better, whether by a healthy child, a garden patch or a redeemed social condition; to know even one life has breathed easier because you have lived. This is to have succeeded."

*Ralph Waldo Emerson*

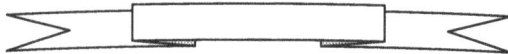

# CHAPTER 15

## Cases for Coaching and Performance Management

Coaching and performance related cases can serve as laboratories for the application of theoretical concepts and long-term retention. The following pages provide a number of cases, dilemmas and scenarios for individual and group discussion purposes. Read each case and answer the questions factually based on your understanding of the concepts and based on your further research on each topic. You can look at relevant textbooks, articles and relevant websites for the definition of the terms and understanding of the concepts. Always support your thoughts and answers with recently published articles and examples from the workplace. In your analysis and discussions with colleagues (face-to-face and online), please use constructive criticism for reflective thinking and development purposes.

Be constructive as constructive criticism is basically offering valid and well-reasoned opinions about the work of others, usually involving both positive and negative comments, in a friendly manner rather than an oppositional one. In collaborative work, this kind of constructive criticism is often a valuable tool in raising and maintaining performance standards in the department, institution and/or society. Constructive criticism includes a balance of analysis and feedback. Critical thinking and constructive criticism can help identify relevant issues to focus on during team discussions. One must use logic, patience and objective data to support one's point of view. Unfortunately, due to the overuse of poorly written negative and nagging comments, some people can easily become defensive even when constructive criticism is given in a spirit of good will. Keep in mind that constructive criticism is more likely to be accepted if the comments are objective and focused on the work or agenda rather than a person's personality or background. That is, attacking personality issues and ethnocentric traditions must be avoided in order for effective collaborations to take place among diverse teams.

Culturally sensitive individuals can adopt a passive, nonviolent attitude if they view a situation as personal, pervasive, or permanent in order to effectively collaborate with others on the team or group. Other individuals may adopt an aggressive response, but such aggression must be professional, objective and to the point. One must keep in mind that constructive criticism can be easily misinterpreted and aggressive exchanges often spiral out of control, resulting in "flaming" responses. Effective interpersonal communication skills can be helpful to assess a responder's frame of mind or paradigm. During initial exchanges or when encountering defensive individuals, effective criticism calls for softer language and inclusion of positive comments. It is best to remember that when a speaker strongly identifies with contentious areas (such as politics or religion), non-offensive criticism can become challenging. So, be careful in your discussions and use constructive criticism to get your points across to diverse team members and colleagues.

For a standardized and formal process, unless suggested otherwise, you can use the following suggestions for analyzing each case:

1. Review and thoroughly read the case and several other recently published articles related to this topic. Provide a brief summary of the case (or topic). Discuss the dilemma, the challenge or problems that are apparent.
2. Next, clearly state one main Problem or Opportunity Statement facing you in this case. Remember that the Problem or Opportunity Statement must be in the case or in its questions.
3. Provide at least one good alternative to solve the problem, enhance performance (capitalize on the opportunity) or enhance the work environment. Justify your alternative.
4. Offer an implementation plan and relevant steps for the stated alternative (preferably using a table or Gantt chart).
5. Provide an overall summary and discuss what employees, managers, and firms can learn from the lessons offered in this case.

Overall, the analysis can be in the American Psychological Association (APA) format. If relevant, you can include data, tables, figures, models, and graphs as such visuals make the material easier to read and more interesting. Make sure to label your visuals appropriately. Make sure to provide full references at the end of your analysis.

## Case 1: Rising Star and Promotion

Jim Hector is a rising star in FirstEx Company. He has earned a series of fast-track promotions with increasing senior management responsibilities. He first started in sales, quickly moved into sales management and then took an opportunity to become operations manager for his region. Presently, he is Sales Director for the Southeast section of Texas. He is looking to move into a more senior sales position. Through the grapevine he has heard of such a position. This senior sales position is at the current level of his boss in his home town of Colorado. Moving back to Colorado is something he and his wife always wanted to do; however, the promotion is truly the motivating factor not the location.

His dilemma is with his boss, Beth. He is uncertain how Beth currently views his performance and whether she will support him in his quest for this senior sales position. Over the past year, Beth has been preoccupied with personal problems and has not given him adequate feedback on his job performance. He would really like to bypass her and reach out to a more top level senior executive and informal mentor, Tom. He realizes that this would be frowned upon in his organization. He would be expected to follow the chain of command, speaking first to Beth. Still, mentoring is encouraged within the organization and he would really like the opportunity to get Tom's perspective on the situation. Since he has not received much support from Beth he is not sure how to approach her. He wonders if she will try to block him or promote him. Jim really wants this promotion. If he does not get it, he feels he has no choice but to change organizations.

### *Discussion Questions:*
1. As a coach what is the first step that you would take with Jim?
2. What is the central problem of this case?
3. What are the fact and assumptions of the case?
4. Identify strategies that Jim could use in approaching his boss, Beth.
5. In what ways could Jim utilize the advice and support of his mentor, Tom?
6. How is Jim able to communicate his intentions, while at the same time, gaining, support of Beth and Tom?

### Case 2: Managing Time and Priorities

The suggestions on managing activities in the allotted time are extremely valuable regarding the age-old business issue of time management. More than ever, application of time management philosophy and techniques during critical times at organizations will drive one's success and increase value for one's department and colleagues. Without steps to cultivate and maintain good work habits, time-management efforts will be defeated. The following tips may help one stay on track:
1. Conquer the clutter.
2. Defuse distractions.
3. Know thyself.
4. Eliminate redundancy.
5. Group and separate.
6. Share the burden.
7. Seize the moment.
8. Emulate others.
9. Make work fun.

Making everyone's time and work fun in a professional and productive manner is an important element of effective coaching. Introducing a bit of fun into your work will make the day easier for you and your customers. Challenge yourself to process one hundred pieces of paper every day for five days. Have a friendly contest with a co-worker to see who can process the most billing statements in an hour with no mistakes. If possible, flip your morning and afternoon schedules for a change of pace.

### *Discussion Questions:*
1. Are there people in your department that can use time management skills? What causes one to lose track of time and priorities? Make a list of five things that one can do to better manage his or her time.
2. The average person spends too much time on many mundane things on a daily basis because their urgency-driven world works that way. If this is the

case with one of your employees, how can you coach or influence this person to use some of the above time management activities? Discuss.

3. What does "having fun" mean in a professional work environment? Can "having fun" lead to a productive workplace? Discuss the value of having "fun" in the workplace and describe what companies and coaches are doing and can do to make the workplace a bit more "fun."

## Case 3: The Well-Paid Receptionist[37]

*The Well Paid Receptionist*, a case provided by Roland B. Cousins in 1992, discusses the trials and tribulations of how an entrepreneur goes about making a start-up business successful by bringing about a competent receptionist as the first employee of the firm. As one reads Cousins' 1992 case, it becomes clear that the key issues are related to the employer's values. The focus is on the high salary received by the office receptionist, named Cathy Brannen. Therefore, the problem or opportunity statement is to determine what should be done to make sure the receptionist's salary matches his/her job responsibilities.

The start up of a business is with no exception a risky endeavor. This statement is no less valid for Mr. Harvey Finley, founder and CEO of Troupville Business Systems. Mr. Harvey encountered serious doubts and uncertainties by those to whom he approached with his entrepreneurial idea years ago. It was a venture that had no promising results since the town had just recovered from a recession. Despite the lack of confidence demonstrated by others, Harvey was determined to pursue his goal. Along with the uncertainties of a new business, comes the insecurity of whom to hire. This is perhaps the most important step to assure value over time (VOT), after all, the employees are the most *valuable* resources of any corporation, as it is clearly demonstrated in the Cousins' case: *The Well- Paid Receptionist*. The tendency of any efficiency savvy company (especially a start up) is to want to hire "jack of all trades," a person that has great confidence, initiative, that knows no boundaries to the job description and is willing to "pull the wagon" with the same eagerness for success as its proprietor. It is no less accurate to say that the compensation that is usually attached to this position (more so for a new business) do not always correlate with its expectations, usually because there is a lack of financial security with a new venture. With all these "concepts" in mind, and after numerous attempts to employ the right person for the "jack of all trades"/secretary position, Mr. Harvey hired Cathy Brannen. Seven years later, Ms. Brannen continues to show the same enthusiasm for her job as she did during her initial interview. She has proven repeatedly that she is an asset to the corporation and has crossed her job description boundaries numerous times in order to offer value for all the parties involved in the daily business transactions of the company. Her total compensation, though not tempting at the time of hire, has become "overgenerous" since it includes the 2% of sales offered as a pay compensation for her base salary discrepancy. Ms. Brannen's current "overgenerous" compensation has recently caused a dilemma and disturbance for Harvey and alternatives to the "problem" are being contemplated.

---

[37] Coauthored with Katty Guevara and Furqan Nasri, Nova Southeastern University.

It is not unusual to overreact with amusement and disbelief when hearing about a $127,614.21 salary for a secretarial position. One may even be skeptical about the credibility of the source but nevertheless; it is imperative to keep in mind that even though the job description describes a secretary, the position that has been filled so successfully is that of "jack of all trades." This is the dilemma that Harvey is encountering; his tunnel vision has focused on Cathy's salary and not on the *raison d'être* of his success. The wake up call to his torment (Ms. Brannen's salary) came just as he was getting ready to come up with some alternatives to this "problem" before it got even more out of hand. The distraught manager overheard a cheerful exchange between Ms. Brannen and a client and suddenly, he froze. It was evident that the well-deserved success his company had enjoyed had a lot to do with the value driven approach Ms. Brannen had taken from the start. Upon the realization of the "intangible values" of a corporation it becomes clear for any proactive manager to take advantage of the opportunities it yields and maximize value over time.

It is evident that Cathy Brannen had an incentive to excel and go the extra mile at work. After all, "she would largely determine the success or failure of the firm." Her input and dedication to the well being of the firm had substantial profitable impact on her own interests. She had a measurable incentive (2% of sales) to perform beyond the highest expectations. The goals were set at the beginning, and therefore started a desired behavior. The consequences that followed the envisioned performance maintained and reinforced the desired behaviors, making the existence of both parties (corporation and employee) beneficial to the other.

Another alternative suggests that the employer reinforce the importance of having a learning organization. Employees will receive the message that they are given autonomy and therefore responsibility over their actions, they are being held accountable for the results and have a "say" and impact on the organization. They need to be made aware that they are not merely employees that they are seen as an essential asset to the firm. This environment stimulates empowerment and a "personal mastery" among all employees. This alternative would not work in the long run because there is no "measurable benefit" per se to the employee, unlike Ms. Brannen. When the employee sees a direct quantifiable gain it is more enticing and stimulating to the employee. A third and fourth alternative would be to recommend the empowerment of employees. Though, a certain degree of distrust and suspicion can be generated among subordinates when approached by management about efficiency, maximizing productivity, empowerment and "mutual benefits." These terms are not "acoustically pleasant" to the employee because historically the manager is not genuinely interested on the personal benefits of the employee, only on its own. Productivity is generally perceived as more work-same pay. It is often perceived as a direct measure of financial success. But when employees directly relate the production of their work with the quality, feel good about themselves and what they "produce", the results are *beneficial* to both the employer and the employee. These alternatives would offer added value, but probably not have long-term perspective when if implemented as an only option. A fifth alternative reinforces a basic principle of value over time (VOT), which is that people will continue to perform and act according to what they value. Keeping in mind that VOT is much more than maximizing shareholder's wealth will help organizations adopt a systematic use of value driven management and avoid "quick fixes" and managerial fads.

As can be seen from the above paragraph, there can be many alternatives available to effectively deal with the situation involving such a high salary being paid to a receptionist. Many individuals in the organization may not feel this is fair since many of them have better titles but are earning less money. As such, something must be done in order to maximize value over time for everyone. Let us discuss and evaluate three specific alternatives.

*Alternative one.* One alternative is to offer Ms. Brannen a sales position and have her work on commission. As a sales person, her salary would not be capped and it would be more in-line with other employees. This could also head off potential salary issues with other employees. The bonus has the potential of being a value destroyer in the company.

*Alternative two.* The next alternative would be to promote her. She could be given the option of being an executive assistant or an executive receptionist. Or, she could become a Vice President of sales or customer relations. This case describes her as fulfilling both positions, which could be a bit unfair. The Troupville industry average salary for executive secretaries is in the $22,000 to $25,000 range. A good receptionist earns less than $20,000. If two people were hired to replace Ms. Brennen, it would cost the company $45,000. That would be three times less than the project salary for Ms. Brannen in the current year. Because of her exceptional performance, her salary should stay pretty much close to her current earnings. Depending on what she accepts, a fair compensation strategy could be agreed upon so she can maintain her current standards of living and still be motivated to continue doing a stellar job.

*Alternative three.* Another alternative is accepting Ms. Brannen's resignation. After presenting two alternatives that would keep Ms. Brannen still employed in the company, if she decided to resign and look for employment elsewhere, Mr. Finley would be forced to accept her resignation. It would be apparent that what Ms. Brannen values is the extremely high salary that she was receiving and this is what was driving her actions. Some people enjoy their work, others the atmosphere, others the challenge, these are a few examples of Value-Driven Management (VDM) assumptions, "what is valued drives action."

### Influential Values

Although all standard value drivers are interrelated and cannot be considered as islands, the most relevant value drivers that affect this case are owner values, and individual employee values. To a lesser extent organization's cultural values, and customer values are also contributing to this case; however, their impact may not be strong enough to warrant detailed discussion. Let us examine each of the contributing value drivers in light of the case at hand.

*Owner values.* Owner values focus on profitability and return on investment. Whether it is private or public corporations, ownership values are extremely important. Interestingly, they conflict with other value drivers more often that any other set of values (Pohlman and Gardiner, 2000). Initially, Harvey made some critical mistakes. He was focused too much on the tactical side of revenue generation and was not keeping a watchful eye on the financial statements of the company. He waited too long to recognize the issue and allowed it to exacerbate into such a high impact item. Instead of taking a positive proactive approach, and creating a compensation strategy, he let initial contracts prevail. He has forced his own hand

and is now in classic reactive management situation. Now that he is faced with this problem, there is a risk that he might lose flexibility and open-mindedness and may be prone to passive, reactive style. A very strong motivating factor in Owner values is the desire to make a profit which in return can impact organizational and employees' values. This case also highlights that the employer was focused on increasing profits. In this particular situation, a cherished employee is affecting the financial results of the company. The dilemma is what course of action to take? Should the company get rid of the employee to get short-term gains? However, if the long-term perspective is kept in mind then the termination of this well-liked employee could give rise to disruption of the work routine and lowering of other employees' morale. Both these factors affect the overall productivity and negatively affect maximization of Value Over Time since Cathy is well liked by her colleagues, customers and suppliers.

*Employee values.* Every employee possesses a set of personal values, which affect his/her decisions and actions in the workplace. In a broad sense, if these personal values are supportive of the organization's values then the employee will be quite successful in his/her professional life. This is quite clearly exemplified by Cathy's actions and behavior in the company. Her personal values are very supportive of the organizational values; there is no clash and hence she is perceived as the stellar worker and there is a good role model for others. Even though Cathy is not part of the technical sales force, she does not hesitate to take on the task of answering customer's questions. Her cheerful and upbeat disposition has enabled her to develop strong rapport with the customers. Her behavior has definitely had a positive impact on creating long-term value for the organization. On the flip side, one can say that by accepting an unusually high compensation for a receptionist, her salary has detracted from the short-term creation of value.

*Customer values.* If we examine the Customer Values from a Value Driven Management perspective, we must ask ourselves what consequences would arise from her termination. She has forged really good working relationships with customers of the company; as such, we may lose some valuable customers, if she were no longer with the company. In the short term, loss of a couple of clients due to Cathy's absence can be absorbed by the corporation as there has been steady growth in customer base and revenue. Cathy used to play an integral role of presenting the company's image to all customers, either in-person or over the phone. With her departure, one would expect to see a negative impact on the creation of long-term value over time.

This case is a true human resource compensation dilemma. The model that the owner tried to follow is that of a competent organization. However, he did not perform any checks and balances as the organization grew. In competent organizations, employees' salaries are tied to their ability to create value for the organization (see *"In Search of Excellence"* written Tom Peters and Mike Waterman in 1984). In this case she was creating value for the company by marketing the products to prospective customers, answering their queries and presenting a very professional image of the company. Although these are value added activities, her primary role was that of an office worker and administrative assistant. Her salary should reflect the value which she has created for the company i.e. directly proportional to the contributions. An obvious alternative would be to terminate Cathy to maximize short term value. This approach, however, would be very reactive and has a high risk of lost productivity associated with it. It will cause long-term loss of value as well. Another alternative would be to reduce Cathy's salary to industry standards. Although it seems viable, this choice also will have a negative impact on long-term value over time. Cathy will most likely not accept the pay cut and might very well leave. This in turn would cause a loss in productivity and also affect customer value drivers. While implementing VDM concepts, Harvey should look into profit sharing plans for compensation. Instead of measuring the performance of the whole corporation, these plans measure performance of a department or group. In this case he could chalk out a profit sharing plan for employees and make different tiers. By placing her in a top bracket, he can ensure her motivation will be high (Smith and Rutigliano, 2003).

Table 14.1 – Well Paid Receptionist Implementation Possibilities

| Possible Action Steps | Who | When |
|---|---|---|
| Research partnership options. | Company attorney | ASAP |
| Investigate and identify incentives for partnership. | HR / company attorney / Comptroller | After partnership options research is completed |
| Conduct analysis to see how much partnership is worth in financial potential. | HR/Comptroller | During the partnership options research |
| Analyze which partnership options are best for Cathy and company. | HR / Attorney / Comptroller / Harvey | Immediately after research |
| Redefine Cathy's job responsibilities and job description. | HR / Harvey / Cathy | After agreeing on partnership options |
| Determine whether new receptionist should be hired or if Cathy will continue as "front person." | HR / Harvey / Cathy | After agreeing on partnership options |

It is a tough decision to be made, but Harvey will have to make the decision. The best alternative the seems to maximize value over time for the employees, owners, and customers is choice number two where Cathy is promoted to a higher position so the organization can continue to benefit from her hard work. Another option is to include her in some sort of a profit sharing plan to maintain her current salary. Profit sharing is not a foreign concept when companies try to attract top class talent. It is a means of providing incentives to the employees to take ownership of their tasks and excel at them. This would create value for the company, e. g. early releases of products, quick time to market, both resulting in larger market share. Profit sharing allows employers to offer a lower base pay and substitute a portion of the base pay by a percentage of the profits. Naturally the benefits to employees is the potential of earning more than their base pay, and the incentive to the company is reduced labor costs during economic down turns, since incentive pay is not part of base pay (Lanning, 2003).

What Harvey cannot, and must not, do is isolate the salary problem to her alone. As is evident from the case study, some other employees are making far less money than her. She is fulfilling all the requirements of her job and exceeding expectations by continuing to extend herself and help out in other areas. She is doing more than a receptionist's role. It is partly due to her excellent rapport with customers that the company is increasing its business. Her salary ought to be base-lined to sales originating from her work, not the total sales of the whole company. As the leader of the company, Harvey has the imperative to build a positive workplace that promotes organizational loyalty and encourages talented salespeople to attain high performance targets. Each employee's performance measurement must reflect the organization's business strategies and financial goals. Compensation should reflect the employee's performance level and his or her contributions to the organization's success.

There are many alternatives available to solve the dilemma of the Well Paid Receptionist. However, the best choice which maximizes value over time for relevant stakeholders seems to be to keep Cathy in the organization while paying her a comparable salary to her current compensation. Perhaps, Harvey can introduce a new performance-based plan for everyone in the organization. By taking concerted actions towards implementation of performance-based compensation, Troupville Business Systems will align compensation with business goals and management objectives, and thus ensure maximizing the organizational performance. The implementation of this decision should be done in conjunction with Cathy and then publicly announced as agreed upon. It should be done within one month or less.

### Discussion Questions:
1. What influenced Kathy to become so successful? How did Cathy become so wealthy? Discuss.
2. Did Mr. Harvey make the right decision to hire Cathy with a 2% bonus plan?
3. What are some effective alternatives to deal with Cathy's salary? If you were the owner, what would you do and why?

### Case 4: Coaching Plan for a Management Team[38]

Among physician executives in the United States 35.6% report that they counsel physicians for disruptive behavior at least daily, weekly, or monthly (Weber, 2004). These behavioral problems have substantial impact on healthcare delivery systems and negatively influence patient outcome and physician practice harmony. This fallout also influences hospital relationships and may alter patient referral patterns; some can even result in undesired legal actions. However, disruptive doctors are frequently excellent physicians and the dilemma facing medical practices is the risk of losing a quality practitioner versus keeping a personality that creates operational headaches and harms financial results.

To remain competitive, medical service organizations, whose service product is the care provided by clinicians, must find the means to proactively modify the possibility of disruptive behaviors. Some organizations have developed a process for managing disruptive physicians employed by them. The processes address administrative management and include suggestions for professional counseling. The purpose of this discussion is to review the literature regarding this problem and to introduce a coaching plan to support existing management plans.

---

[38] Prepared by Keith S. Meredith (M.D.), Jay Martin, Brain Renaud, and Rafael Gonzalez (M.D.), Nova Southeastern University.

In the current medical practice climate physicians are under a great deal of stress that did not exist one to two decades earlier. These stressors include flattened or declining compensation in the face of increased productivity, increasing costs (including liability coverage and other overhead expenses), declining public esteem, and increased performance expectations with administrative demands for quality and healthcare cost management. The changes required to meet these new challenges often lead to rising frustrations and unmet expectations (Silverstein & Kornacki, 2000). All too often these emotions are expressed in inappropriate behaviors which negatively impact healthcare provision, staff morale, and, occasionally, patient outcome (Keogh, 2004).

To expose the full nature of the problem of the disruptive physician, the American College of Physician Executives recently reported a survey of physician executives (Weber, 2004). This questionnaire, answered by over 1600 physician leaders, revealed the ubiquitous extent of behavioral problems in otherwise high functioning physicians. Only 4% of respondents said problems with physician behavior never occurred; nearly 57% replied that the inappropriate behavior was directed toward clinical subordinates (nursing staff, pharmacists, etc.); over 82% of episodes were the result of disrespectful behavior from the physician to the victim; 70% of events were committed by the same physicians over and over again; over 50% of events were described as the result of frustration over organizational changes or resistance to teamwork; and more than 60% of respondents replied that physicians were treated more leniently than other employees because of their stature.

Among the management tools recommended by authors suggesting positive approaches, coaching, mediating, referring and disciplining were noted (Keogh & Martin, 2004). The purpose of this discussion is to develop a coaching plan designed to positively influence behavioral change among this challenging and mission critical resource. Change requires time, personal effort and commitment as well as support from the coach. Management and coaches must remain committed to developing their staff (such as doctors, nurses, physician assistants, administrators, and other healthcare workers) when deficiencies are noted, such as when poor communications skills and an inability to effectively cope with stress disrupts the workplace, the practice, and relations with hospital administration. The specific behavioral issues to address with a coachee can include ineffective and negative based communication, elimination of emotional outbursts, improved teamwork and better conflict resolution skills. To best address, for a hypothetical example, a disruptive physician issue let us utilize Zeus and Skiffington's four phases of coaching (Zeus & Skiffington, 2002):

*1. Establishing the coaching relationship.* Having identified the issues detrimental to the organization and the physician, the medical director will meet with the physician and discuss the need to establish a coaching relationship. The key here is to clearly communicate the reasons for and the benefits of such a relationship. Before leaving this stage the parties will ensure that they have created a win-win agreement both parties can support as well as a commitment of resources by the medical director. Resources, aside from the medical director, include other physicians, management, human resources, medical affairs and an employee assistance plan to name just a few.

*2. Action Planning.* The medical director and physician having discussed, in great detail and at great lengths, the behavioral issue(s) and possible underlying causes, will agree on a plan of action, follow-up and time-line for completion. The action plan may include outside behavioral counseling and education. It is also reasonable to discuss consequences should the coaching goal not be reached.

3. *The coaching cycle.* Having agreed to regular follow-up, the medical director and physician will meet regularly to discuss progress, obstacles to progress and any difficulties either party is encountering. Feedback, support and encouragement from the medical director are critical as well as understanding how the physician feels about progress they are making. Through these discussions, resistance can be identified and addressed appropriately.

4. *Evaluation and Follow-up.* Determining the end of the coaching relationship can often be difficult to ascertain. Ideally through the coaching cycle both the medical director and physician will agree that sufficient progress has been made and that the relationship can become less formal. It is important however to continue follow-up meetings at appropriate intervals with the physician to ensure "slippage" does not occur.

In many organizations the physician is the most valued human resource, acting as the primary service provider and as the frontline representation to partnered hospital administrators. Although a complete different subject, physicians' recruiting and retention has become a general problem for most organizations; having to deal with the problem of a disruptive physician in the midst of the scarcity of this particular human resource makes coaching an essential tool. The goals of this coaching plan are the following:
- Help the coachee identify and accept the behaviors that motivated actions;
- Engage with the coachee in a sustained and monitored relationship, by which ongoing evaluation and follow-up will help determine the progress achieved;
- Create a supportive environment by formalizing with the coachee a win-win agreement; and
- Create the appropriate open communication environment to align the coach's effective listening and the coachee's lesser resistance for counseling and educational intervention.

It is the expected solution to this coaching exercise to effectively change the coachee's behavior to one that allows full participation and healthy interaction with peers and fellow workers in the day to day performance of the noble work that patients require.

Also expected from this coaching exercise is to obtain the side benefits of improved teamwork in the affected unit, to improve the relationship with affected peers, to improve job satisfaction in the context of reduced conflict, and to help create the environment of a coaching-oriented culture. All these are acknowledged as general coaching benefits.

### Discussion Questions:
1. What seems to be the main issue in this case?
2. What are some examples of "disruptive behaviors" that can apply to professionals in the medical industry? Discuss five examples.

3. Do you agree or disagree with the planned solution to effectively deal with disruptive behaviors with medical professionals? Discuss.

## Case 5: Coaching an Employee who does not follow Procedures[39]

Let us assume that this case is an ongoing situation within an existing company. Employee X is working in the accounts receivable department of a "for profit-company." She is a good worker in an overall sense. Her work is done on time and she does not typically seek assistance from her supervisor. Employee X makes decisions that often short-cut company processes that are in place. This is an important issue in a highly structured environment such as accounting. She feels that as long as the work is being done, why should it matter if she did not follow procedures? The behavior persists despite several discussions with Employee X about adherence to the established rules. Employee X has now applied for the leadership position in the group. This creates a conundrum for the department management. The leadership position the employee has applied for requires adherence to and support of the processes in place as well as the support of upper management. Alternatively, should Employee X not get the position, she may react badly, leading her to incite dissatisfaction in her current group. It is the purpose of this case to clarify the issues involved and discuss how the tools of coaching and influence might be used to achieve a mutually beneficial solution.

Once a potential candidate for coaching has been identified, one of the first questions to evaluate is whether coaching will realistically lead to a desired outcome. Guttman (2004) offers an approach for this evaluation that suggests gathering as much raw data as possible about the candidate. He also further explains that the candidate has to be willing to recognize not only the consequences of changing the behavior, but also the consequences on not changing. Guttman believes that the successfully coached person is one who is willing to change their behaviors; that attention only to self-awareness is not sufficient. Frisch (2005) elaborates on this idea in his concept of "emotional resilience." Emotional resilience suggests that people are secure enough within themselves to hear and evaluate honest feedback. Each of these is an element that is necessary for a successful coaching interaction. Once it is determined that the candidate can be coached, the approach to this person becomes critical. Maher has pointed out that it is important to ensure positive intent when embarking upon a coaching interaction (Maher, 2001). She suggests that one approach to focus on the employee's behavior is to talk about the effect of this behavior on the organization (Maher, 2001).

It is necessary when attempting to influence others that one understands what their wants and needs are (Vengel, 2000, p. 17). In many employer–employee relationships, control or the lack thereof, often are issues. Geisler points out that fear may be generated by a sense of employee powerlessness (Geisler, 2005). Understanding and responding to human complexity in the workplace is one of the great challenges for leaders and managers (Miller, 2003).

---

[39] Prepared by Trish Hagan (M.D.), Mack Hinson (M.D.), and Bonita Durazo, Nova Southeastern University.

Another area that a good boss and coach must understand is why a certain employee is under performing. Jana Madsen writes, "Assuming every employee has a clear understanding of what is expected of them, there are two reasons individuals under-perform. They are either not equipped for success (e.g. employees may not have the resources - cooperation, training, equipment, etc. - or adequate time to complete quality work) or do not possess the desire to succeed. In order to manage these situations and individuals, you must first assess which of these reasons apply. Those individuals who lack motivation or fail repeatedly require coaching" (Madsen, 2005). While developing a complete understanding of the situation by the coach is critical, it is not necessary to produce the solution for the coachee. Being the problem solver does not necessarily allow the coachee to develop his/her own mastery of solution processes (Brent, 2004). Starr pointed out that the difficulty with the problem-solving mindset when he noticed "directiveness is inhibited over time" (Starr, 2004). She goes on to note that the "coaching relationship is built on equality" and that part of the coach's job is to "encourage ownership" and responsibility for the coachee (Starr, 2004).

Important for the coach, the coachee and the entire team is that the coach continue to reward other team members who are performing and not solely focus on the individual who is failing to meet the set standards. "Individuals that consistently demonstrate a strong work ethic and above-average skills need feedback and guidance as well. If you ignore them - or worse yet, "reward" their hard work by strapping them with more responsibility - they won't remain your top performers for long" (Madsen, 2005). One can see how important this would be in the close-knit accounts receivable department.

It is the view of the authors that Employee X represents an opportunity for coaching in a positive way. Although her behavior is at times at odds with established company policy, she is acting in a way she believes to be beneficial for the company. It seems that this is an opportunity to identify and build on the strengths of Employee X as well as identify and develop coping mechanisms for her weaknesses. Based on accumulation of data based on a series of direct observations, it seems that Employee X's behavior is often motivated by a lack of control. This is a non-typical reaction to the process guidelines under which the accounts receivable department operates. These processes are in place to ensure uniformity and efficiency, which they in fact do provide. However, the side effect is that motivated employees feel constricted by the strict policy guidelines. The goal of coaching for Employee X will be to help find constructive ways to channel this motivation and to minimize the frustration inherent in a policy based environment.

Zeus and Skiffington outline a coaching process that involves four phases: establishing the coaching partnership; action planning; a coaching cycle; evaluation and follow-up (2002, pp. 59-82). The first step is to reach an agreement with Employee X that coaching would be beneficial to her. This could be framed in terms of improved job satisfaction and improved performance. The action planning cycle would then follow. An initial approach might be to work on ownership issues (Zeus and Skiffington, p. 130). Several of the exercises in this section of Zeus and Skiffington assess the level of commitment of the employee to the coaching process. It also may present a forum for the discussion of trust and of fears that may exist. One approach to an employee whose behavior is at odds with company policies might be a series of exercises that focus on self-awareness (Zeus and Skiffington, p. 143). For Employee X, this might have a two-fold purpose. Firstly, enhanced self-awareness might help her to identify and deal with her frustrations in a more positive way than subversion of the present system. Secondly, should Employee X be promoted to a managerial position, improved self-awareness would help to make her a more effective leader. One would expect that there would be several cycles of discussion and evaluation of actions in order to solidify the behavior patterns. One of the most important aspects of any coaching process is to define success in a priori way. It is critical that at least part of this answer be supplied by Employee X. She has the largest stake in the coaching process. A self-selected goal is a more powerful motivator to the coachee.

Employee X has demonstrated through her efforts at successfully completing projects that she is highly motivated. The opportunity to present her with a plan will present an opportunity to frame the coaching process in a positive and affirming light. Assuming that Employee X consents to a coaching arrangement, her superior would begin to work on ownership and self-awareness issues. One hopes that the effect of these interactions would produce a change in behavior. From the management point of view, it would be beneficial to see Employee X following company policies. It would also be advantageous to create an avenue of consultation for Employee X when she feels that company policies are not sufficient for a given task. Finally as outlined previously, the accomplishment of a final goal will be much more powerful if Employee X determined the goal. In the end, Employee X, the work group and the company all stand to gain from this plan.

### *Discussion Questions:*
1. What seems to be the main issue in this case?
2. How can such behaviors affect the department and future of the organization if allowed to continue? Discuss.
3. Do you agree or disagree with the planned solution to effectively deal with Employee X? Discuss the benefits and possible side effects of the proposed solution.

### Case 6: Staying Lean and Healthy

Effective coaches and managers will be less stressed because they proactively manage their activities and themselves based on their predetermined and worthwhile goals. Nonetheless, due to deadlines and the fact that sometimes we all take on (or are delegated to by our superiors) more functions than can be handled at one time, stress management techniques can be helpful in maintaining productivity. Enclosed are simple suggestions that can dramatically effect how you operate as an individual or as a team member during hectic (stressful) times in your organization.

*Diet.* Make an effort to eat more fruit, vegetables, and whole grains as a replacement for some of the high fat snacks and meals. Limit your caffeine intake.

*Sleep.* The above suggestion on diet (especially the caffeine part) will definitely impact your ability to be successful with sleeping.

*Exercise.* This does not necessarily mean running, aerobics, or weightlifting. Get up and move after sitting for more than two hours. Stretch, breath deeply, take a short walk, use the stairs... but take a few minutes every two hours or so and move to keep the blood flowing and your mind sharp.

*Think positively.* Have the attitude of "We are almost there... and we have our goals directly in sight." Flush negative or useless things out of your mind, and replace them with positive, forward-looking feelings.

*Think teams and team members.* Ask for help and help your colleagues as they attempt to become stress-balanced and healthy. Finally, it is no secret that all of these work very closely together as a sure-fire package for success. Look closely... diet, sleep, exercise, a positive attitude... it's so simple, and it's so within your reach to do! Again, trust the process as the experts would not suggest anything to you that they would not do themselves

### *Discussion Questions:*
1.  The suggestions mentioned above require that you commit to believing in yourself and what you stand for and what you want from your day. Remember, only you can ultimately drive yourself across the finish line. If you are not already, which of the above suggestions can you apply in your life? When and how? Discuss.
2.  What are some of the things that you are doing to stay healthy? Discuss your five best behaviors?
3.  How can you influence others to stay healthy? Discuss two strategies.

### Case 7: Harassing[40] the "Intern"

Jodi is a twenty-two year old undergraduate student at one of the local universities pursuing a degree in business. At career services, Jodi discovers that there is an internship offered by the local government. A few days later Jodi decides to fill out the application and within a couple of weeks she is asked to come in for an interview. Three days later, Jodi hears the good news and takes the offer.

The following week she begins her internship. Jodi and Diana conduct several meetings in order to put the manual together. Throughout these meetings the director of the department, Mr. Finely, is also present. Mr. Finely, who is also fairly new to the department, is in his early fifties, and appears to be more of a father figure to Jodi. His work within the department, as well as the local government, is highly regarded.

Within two months of her internship, the director asks Jodi to assist him with several of his projects. Feeling honored, Jodi eagerly helps and soon realizes that Mr. Finely is always asking her to help him with his presentations. During the course of the projects, Mr. Finely comments on how well dressed Jodi always is and how well she maintains her posture. Jodi feels that his compliments are very friendly and takes them in a light and innocent manner.

Finally her internship comes close to the end and the director asks her out to lunch and leaves it up to her to decide when and where to go. Jodi finally thinks to herself and decides to go to a local restaurant nearby the following day. Later that

---

[40] Original version published in *Workforce Diversity Management: Challenges, Competencies and Strategies*, 2007 by Llumina Press; coauthored with Bina Patel.

afternoon, Jodi sends the director an email confirming their lunch appointment for the following day. She waits for an answer from the director, but does not get one; so she assumes that lunch may or may not be on for tomorrow. Later that evening, Jodi receives a phone call from the director. Surprised to hear from him at her home, Jodi confirms the lunch appointment and asks why other interns were not invited. The director claims that since they will be working there on a full time basis, they will be treated to lunch another day. While Jodi continues to think, the director begins to ask her several questions, such as "what kinds of movies do you like?", "what is your family like and how many siblings do you have?" Before Jodi begins to answer, she realizes that his questions are becoming more and more personal. She feels that he is interested in her, specifically when he states that he "would like to spend more time with her." The situation becomes very uncomfortable for Jodi, who quickly makes an excuse to hang up. She decides to tell Diana about the conversation the following day, as well as deciding to quit her internship. Diana asks Jodi to file a formal compliant as this becomes a sexual harassment case. Months later, Jodi receives news from Diana that the director has been forced to resign.

### Discussion Questions:

1. Who requires coaching in this case? How would you go about coaching this person? Discuss.
2. Should Jodi have quit her internship? Could Jodi have avoided the situation? How? What should one do when faced with this situation?
3. Should the director be fired based on his comments towards Jodi? Discuss the actions taken against the director. Should he have been forced to resign based on this incident? Could there have been other reasons for this resignation?

### Case 8: And Then, She Cried[41]

Precariously overlooking the precipice of 40 years of age, Brenda began to rethink her career. Sure, she had been an up-and-comer for a decade, but the glass ceiling was beginning to show itself and the "Boy's Club" mentality of her company hierarchy was no longer shrouded in secrecy. The higher Brenda climbed in the organization, the more she disliked the view, and wondered if there was any room left for advancement. Frustrated, confused, and uncharacteristically emotional, she contemplated a job change amidst a flurry of internal dialogue.

On the other side of the office, Larry was rummaging through the sports section studying up for a verbal sparring match with his boss, David. "Hey Dave, did you see that Ohio State game last night? Wow, what a heartbreaker! Bet that quarterback had a rough night," Larry commented for all to hear. David would counter with some quirky sports anecdote and the couple would head for lunch. Although relatively new to the organization, Larry had his own agenda, and it involved a position senior to Brenda.

On Friday, David called Brenda into his office and gave her a project that was due for presentation on Monday morning. Having flawlessly executed similar

---

[41] Contributed by Gina H. Harris, Nova Southeastern University.

projects in the past, Brenda was not concerned about turnaround time or the final product. However, since this was unfamiliar territory for Larry, David suggested assigning a portion to Larry to "get his feet wet." Brenda agreed and met with Larry that afternoon to discuss his role. At the close of business on Friday, Brenda and Larry had a mutual understanding of each person's responsibilities and duties. On Monday, it was a different story.

Brenda sat down with Larry on Monday morning prior to the presentation only to find that Larry did not complete his assignment. Instead, he spent the weekend watching an endless amount of college and professional football so he could be primed for conversations with David. There was no time to readjust prior to the presentation, and Brenda had to decide whether to throw Larry under the bus or work with what she had. Being a consummate and experienced professional, Brenda did the latter and planned on discussing Larry's faux pas or blunder with David after the meeting. Unfortunately, when the inquiries began, Brenda was flat-footed in her responses and Larry's contribution was called into question. Rather than taking the high road, Larry concocted a falsehood and commented Brenda withheld important information because she wanted Larry to look bad in front of senior management. What's worse is that the men in the room seemed to believe Larry's story! Aghast at Larry's accusations and management's response, Brenda's ire and frustration got the better of her. She calmly tried to explain the truth, but the bubbling caldron of mixed emotions inside was too much to bear…and then, she cried.

Is crying the ultimate sin in business? According to Dr. Lois P. Frankel (2004), women tend to show emotion more easily than men and often substitute tears for anger. From childhood, girls are taught it is unacceptable and unladylike to be angry, thus some women have difficulty processing anger and it sometimes manifests itself as tears. Unfortunately, crying is often construed as weakness, lacking control, and being inept. Despite significant social evolution, there is simply no room for crying in business (Frankel, 2004). Not only does it make women seem weak, it makes men uncomfortable. So what should Brenda do?

Brenda should explain to the meeting attendees that she has strong feelings about the issue, excuse herself from the meeting, and regain composure (Frankel, 2004). She can represent at a later time and explain her side of the story, but it is not necessary to explain why crying entered into the picture. At a later time, Brenda should examine the elements of the situation and the triggers leading to her outburst. One such trigger to explore may involve being Larry's scapegoat. It was simple for Larry to lay blame on Brenda for his shortcomings, and because of the office environment, Larry was easily able to sway management to his way of thinking. Brenda needs to address this issue immediately.

Some women tend to allow themselves to be the scapegoat in order to let their boss, husband, friend, etc… look good. Certain women are not bothered by this, but the women who take issue with this sort of behavior should diplomatically let the respective parties know that scapegoating will not be tolerated. Parties should be put on notice that women like Brenda are unwilling to sit quietly and let scapegoating unfold. Brenda should make this clear to Larry, and David should be made aware of the situation. Although this may not change office behavior, it certainly provides pertinent information about the organizational environment and what will and will not be tolerated.

Now 41 years old, Brenda is happily employed with another institution.

### Discussion Questions:

1. Have you ever cried at work? If so, what were the circumstances? How did you recover and what would you do differently next time?
2. Is there gender bias in your workplace? Have you observed it in other organizations?
3. In your opinion, is the glass ceiling still intact in today's corporate culture?
4. As a man, how would you feel if a co-worker cried? What does this emotion convey to you?
5. Was Brenda working in a hostile environment?
6. What is sexual harassment and explain its main elements.
7. What mistakes did Brenda make in this scenario?
8. How does this case study help you and what lessons have you learned from it?

### Case 9: Managing Change

The real test of an effective coach and manager, especially these days, is how well he or she copes with personal, professional and cultural change. The rate of change has been increasing rapidly over the last three decades. In 1975, Alvin Toffler wrote a famous book, *Future Shock* which spoke about the ever-increasing rate of change and how the need to cope with so much change actually makes people ill. The father of social psychology, Kurt Lewin, described change as a three step process:

1. *Unfreezing* the old way of doing things. Unless you can show people the benefit of changing, it will be hard to convince them to invest the time and effort required.
2. *Moving* toward the change by introducing new behavior.
3. *Refreezing* new behavior. Unless you stabilize and monitor the changed behavior, people will drift back to the old way of doing things.

But why are people so resistant to change anyway? The hardest thing about implementing change is to get through the natural resistance that people have to change. There are several reasons for this phenomenon and habit is one of them.

*Habit.* It is very easy to just keep doing things the way you've always done them, especially if there seems to be nothing wrong with the results of the old habit. This is the "if it is not broke, why fix it" mentality.

*Fear of the unknown.* Habit and tradition are comfortable. When people are not sure what will happen if they change the way they do things, resistance sets in.

*Fear of losing something.* When employees are afraid they may lose a benefit or even a perquisite, they get anxious and dig in their heels against change.

*Investment of past resources.* When people or even organizations have invested time and resources in the old way of doing things, they are reluctant to change.

*Fear of inadequacy.* Sometimes employees feel that they are not capable of learning to do things a new way-this is particularly true in matters concerning technology. If they fear they will not be successful, they will try hard not to change.

These are a few of the primary reasons people resist change. How can managers overcome this resistance? Managers should begin by understanding that when they ignore the factors that affect the people involved in the change, the resistance usually accelerates.

### *Discussion Questions:*
1. Have you encountered a major change in your workplace in the last ten years? Discuss and state some of the challenges for people who were impacted by this change? What were some effective strategies for people who successfully dealt with it?
2. What can coaches do to make change easier for people to accept?
3. Should managers use "Push" or "Pull" related behaviors to help others accept a major change? Discuss using a specific change.

## Case 10: Compliant Resolution Using the "ALERT" Strategy[42]

Effective coaches know how to resolve problems and challenges with difficult internal and external customers. Effective coaches use certain strategies to make sure they resolve any problems and obstacles in a standardized manner. The "ALERT" method will demonstrate how to effectively deal with challenging customers as well as how to diffuse further complaints and conflict from arising. The acronym "ALERT" stands for:

- *A* - Acknowledge, Attentive
- *L* - Listen & Stay Positive
- *E* - Empathize (Apologize/Relate)
- *R* – Respond, Resolve Quickly, Refer (KISS = keep it simple stupid)
- *T* - Take Control, Thank the customer.

*Acknowledge*- Acknowledging the customer means being attentive. In a "walk in" situation it is important to focus your attention on the customer. Using good eye contact and an attentive body language demonstrates that you value the customer. In a busy situation when you are handling multiple tasks, you want to face the customer and tell him/her "Sir/Madame I will be with you shortly." While on the telephone, acknowledging the customer means using his/her name at the beginning and end of call. It also means not doing several other tasks while on the telephone. In acknowledging the customer you also want to smile or sound pleasant and positive on the phone. Sighs and noise will frustrate the customer.

*Listen*- When a customer calls, do not interrupt him or her. You want to allow the customer to speak so that you can get as much information as possible. Interrupting customers before they finish their statement will only frustrate them. When listening, paraphrasing key points of what was said ensures you understand. In using good listening skills it is best to ask questions like "As I understand, you mean "xyz"") or "Let me make sure that I understand what you said" and then repeat the statement or question.

---

[42] Coauthored with Lamoy Coburn, Nova Southeastern University.

*Empathize-* In this stage an employee will choose to either empathize or apologize to the customer, which is a judgment call. Empathy means that you show concern for the customer's feelings, thoughts, or attitudes. Using statements like "I understand your concern" or apologizing for any errors or hold time are useful techniques. Empathizing statements such as "I understand your concern/frustration and let me make it right for you," or relating to the situation can be effective in handling customer calls/complaints.

*Respond-* This step requires a great deal of knowledge or critical thinking skills in how to address and resolve the issue. Respond by answering questions in a positive and polite manner, placing extra emphasis on the time it will take to resolve the issue. If the issue cannot be resolved by you, do not be afraid to get the customer another employee with more knowledge and experience. If you are unable to diffuse or resolve the issue, a customer may ask to speak to a manager; do not challenge the customer by saying "my manager will tell you the same thing," just keep it simple and get your boss or simply transfer the call to the manager. When you do resolve the issue, keep the conversation as simple as possible. Do not overload the customer with more information than needed. Keep it simple means addressing the issue at hand and providing the customer with a resolution to handle the situation in the future. When a customer calls the wrong department or has to be referred to someone else, make sure that you maintain a list of contacts in each department of the company. You may want to email or call the person first to let them know that you are referring a call. Do not give incorrect information, verify with another party if you are unsure of the information. Whatever the case, focus on the issue, keep the conversation simple, and resolve the issue as quickly as possible.

*Take Control-* Be confident about your position; remember that you are the trained specialist. After the resolution takes place be sure to ask "is there anything else that I can assist you with" to ensure that all the customer's needs are met. Taking control also means following-up with the customer. This can be done by sending the customer an appreciation letter, email, or making a phone call.

### *Discussion Questions:*

1. How does your organization deal with challenging employees and customers? What can a coach do to effectively resolve problems with challenging internal and external customers? Discuss.

2. Can the "ALERT" strategy be useful for you as a manager in the workplace? If so, how? Discuss how a coach can use this strategy in a real world scenario.

### Case 11: The "Cross Dressing" Employee[43]

A federal judge ruled that the Winn-Dixie grocery store chain did not violate any federal law when it terminated a long-time employee, a truck driver, who dressed as a woman when he was away from work. The case was brought as a sex discrimination case pursuant to federal anti-discrimination law. The employee, an employee-at-will, worked for Winn-Dixie for twenty years. The employee crossed-

---

[43] Coauthored with Frank Cavico, Nova Southeastern University.

dressed on his own time as a way to relieve stress and express his feminine side. The issue was brought to Winn-Dixie's attention by the employee himself, who mentioned his feminine proclivity during an annual employment review. The terminated employee contended that his employer discriminated against him because of his sexual orientation. Winn-Dixie claimed it acted in its own best interest as a business, and fired him in the belief that, if word got out, some customers would shop elsewhere. The terminated employee eventually got another job hauling stock for a pet store chain. He asked the American Civil Liberties Union to represent him with his appeal to the U.S. Court of Appeals.

### *Discussion Questions:*
1. Do you agree with the decision of Winn-Dixie's management to terminate this employee? Why or why not?
2. If one of your male employees wishes to wear female clothing, is this a problem for you when he or she is not working? How would you coach one of your managers who is concerned about the possibility of this situation?
3. Should managers be concerned about what employees wear when they are not in the department or in the workplace? Discuss.

### Case 12: Working for a "Bad" Boss

Many public and private institutions are now focusing on developing leaders that are not only knowledgeable about what is going in their fields, but also critical thinkers and learners who are competent about how to lead, manage and create new means of making their organizations successful. For example, Nova Southeastern University's value proposition statement is *"Beyond the classroom,"* and *"Bringing life to learning,"* as they focus on imparting knowledge and the "know how" application of what makes their learners and graduates successful in their fields of expertise. Similar to NSU's philosophy, the Quantum Institute of Leadership Program, as explained by a colleague named Richard Morales, teaches coaches and leaders more than what they must "know;" as they teach and facilitate what coaches, leaders, supervisors, and managers must "do" in the workplace in order to be successful. Of course, the leaders of such modernized organizations understand that knowledge is the basis of action, but knowledge is not always translated into action and that is the purpose of being a coach: to impart and translate knowledge into goal-oriented actions.

Unfortunately, there are some individuals who graduate and earn prestigious degrees from well-known schools, only to become ineffective managers in the workplace. Take the case of Roy-bird's boss, who happens to have a college degree that qualifies him to be a "Master of Business" and a qualified manager, but he is considered to be an ineffective leader by most of his employees and the department is not performing as they could be.

This is basically a dilemma for an upcoming coach and critical thinker. Have you ever had the opportunity to work for someone who is considered and perceived to be an "ineffective" or a "bad" leader? Let us say that your colleague, *Roy-bird*, is facing a situation where he is working for this type of a leader. This boss that Roy-bird is working for lacks coaching skills, has no referent or personal power, does not trust his people (Roy-bird included), is perceived to always look for ways to "screw" his competent employees, thinks "accountability" equals punishment, motivates by using "or else" moratoriums, is scared of his own boss, and operates with a "cover my behind" mentality. This boss is so ridiculous; he is like a cartoon character. The worst part is that everybody, from the youngest employee in the department to the most experienced individuals, sees right through him and, frankly, hates him and his leadership style. In essence, over thirty people, whose lives are affected directly by this manager's decisions and actions do not want to work for him. Consequently, morale is low and the performance targets are not being met. It is the most frustrating situation Roy-bird has ever faced in his twenty-year career, and he is caught right in the middle. He needs your help and recommendations.

***Discussion Questions:***

1. What are some typical behaviors of bosses and managers who are perceived to be "ineffective" leaders and managers?
2. What are the best means of influencing "ineffective" leaders and managers? Discuss.
3. What can Roy-bird and his colleagues do to improve their work environment, to be enthused about going to work, and to meet their performance goals?
4. Discuss and coach Roy-bird and his colleagues on what they should do to improve their existing circumstances.
5. What can educational institutions do to create better leaders who are able to effectively apply their learned knowledge and expertise into action as competent coaches?

### Case 13: Employee with a Poor Attitude[44]

Susan is a receptionist in a plant that manufactures large airplane parts. The office is only a small part of the factory and one set of rules govern all. For example, time cards are used for both factory employees and office staff. The manager handles daily operations in a military fashion by keeping detailed charts on each employee's attendance and performance. Personnel are called in if they do not adhere to the strict standards set forth by management. Susan feels her work is picked apart by the manager and as a result, she has adopted an attitude of doing what is necessary, but nothing more. She does her work correctly and cannot be faulted for the content, but her demeanor is cool and not inviting to the public. This causes friction with the manager because he feels Susan is not fulfilling her receptionist duties. Although Susan is aware that her attitude has changed, she tells the manager she doesn't know what he means and asks for clarification. This is where the problem occurs – the manager cannot clearly define poor attitude, even though he knows it when he sees it. Since Susan's work is carried out, he does not have reason to let her go. Both are displeased with each other, but neither knows how to handle it.

***Discussion Questions:***

---

[44] Contributed by Marikay Concannon, Nova Southeastern University.

1.  Can managers focus on an employee's attitude issues? Discuss your reasons and logic.
2.  How can the manager relate Susan's attitude to her work?
3.  Does attitude make a difference if the work is being done?
4.  What are the effects of a poor attitude?

## Case 14: Organizational Culture and Management Influence[45]

Richard Meads (2005), in chapter four of his book, entitled *International Management: Cross-Cultural Dimensions,* expands on the topic of Organizational Culture, which is very closely linked to organizational communication. Organizational communication deals with the importance of understanding how individuals in each department communicate. Proper communication from each department is essential to the proper functionality of the entire organization. A lack of communication or too much communication can cause confusion and conflict. An organizations culture may determine the structure and success of their communication. Misunderstanding a company's culture may cause a disorder with the communication and ultimately their productivity and functionality.

Mead begins by stating that there is no formal definition for Organizational Culture because the term is so broad. The term culture in itself is open to interpretation and changes depending on nationality and region. Therefore, the same would apply for an organizations culture. There is no defining the term into one statement because it will change per company and nationality. However, it is possible for an organization's culture to fall between the two boundaries.

*Organizational cultures* can be referred to as being Structural or Experiential. The term *Structural* naturally means having a set order, rules and regulations. An organization that follows the structural flow is more likely to be planned and implemented by their management. Therefore, management influences and implements all the rules and regulations for the company. Companies, coaches and managers that follow this structure are less likely to rely on their employee's opinion to make certain changes to the organization. Management and coaches would determine all changes and structure of the organization regardless of the national culture or opinion. It is quite discouraging to know that an organization would function with this structure.

An *Experiential* organization is on the other side of the spectrum. This term refers to a structure that is based on the relationships that are held in the company. Experiential structures are based on the country's nationality, market factors, cultural values, and other personable factors. Managers and coaches in this type of structure would be interested in the opinions of the members of the company. They would also be concerned with the affects that their decisions would make on the members. There are few companies that freely maintain this type of structure.

In reality it is mentioned by Mead that an organization's culture is mainly influenced by coaches' or management's past experience with decision-making and by the national culture. Most coaches and managers would enjoy managing a company using the Structural process. This way they would be able to rationalize

---

[45] Coauthored with Solange Beckford, Nova Southeastern University.

their planning and professional factors for the company. Employees on the other hand would prefer to be apart of an Experiential structure because they would feel more empowered. The worst thing a coach or a manager could do is force a particular culture in an organization. This would be detrimental to an organization's survival. Managers and coaches should study the culture of the organization before implementing any set structure.

Mead also describes two ways to analyze an organization's culture. The *Positive analysis* refers to management having an open relationship with the members of the organization. In this system, managers and coaches will maintain positive relationships with employees and they will communicate openly with everyone. This type of relationship will allow employees to feel empowered in the company. On the other hand, an organization that has a *Negative analysis* will have the complete opposite relationship with their employees. Management will not be as open and willing to assist employees in the company. With this form of analysis, employees will feel as though they are not a part of the decision-making process. This will eventually cause them to be less interested in the company and more interested in doing just enough work to maintain a position with the company.

There is also a Strong and Weak analysis that is also used when viewing organizations. A company that is perceived as having a *Strong analysis* will show cohesiveness. The members will share like beliefs, values and attitudes. This will allow employees and coaches to communicate easily with each other causing a successful and open environment. If the company's analysis is *Weak*, then it is viewed as having a closed communication and the members rarely share any common factors.

These four factors can then be coupled as a pair for organizations that have a mixed cultural analysis. For instance, if a company has a positive and strong culture it means that the organization has an open environment for communication in which individuals share the same opinions, values and believes. Regardless of the structure of the organization, managers and coaches usually strive to have a positive and strong analysis because companies are usually more productive and functional under this form of analysis. According to researchers, "Management focused on developing, maintaining, and ensuring that the organization members have healthy and productive values. In other words the pivotal strategy is to ensure that the culture is strong (Harung and Dahl, 1995, p. 13)." A culture that has a negative and strong culture is most feared by managers and coaches. This analysis refers to environments in which the employees are united against the decisions of management. This analysis is the breading ground for employee strikes and walkouts. These events would be detrimental to the organization.

In many cases the culture can change but the degree and method of change is determined by management. Companies that have structured goals and open plans will have an easier time changing their culture because they already have an idea of where they envision the company. Opening this vision to the members of the group will allow them to be apart of that particular goal and the planning process. "Our focus was on building an organization committed to managing for the mission, managing, for innovation, and managing for diversity (Hesselbein, 2002, p. 2)." Starting channels of new communication methods with members of the organization will cause a tremendous positive affect. Allowing people to voice their opinions in a formal setting is the easiest way to recognize the main issues in the organization. New technology can sometimes cause a culture shock in an organization but it can also bring group members together to experience a positive change in the company. Setting up positive images and permanent emblems around the environment will manifest an optimistic atmosphere.

A company may have a general culture but most companies also have sub-culture just as any other national culture. "Managers and consultants make comparisons and contrasts between organizational sub-cultures in order to assess organizational relationships and differences in efficiency (Mead 2005, pp. 84-85)." Sub-cultures are easily developed in departments. An earlier reference was made to the separate departments in an organization and how they communicate. It is normal for each department to have their own culture depending on the management and structure of those departments. It is normal to assume that the accounting department usually has a formal structure and introverted personalities. The marketing and sales departments are mainly filled with extraverted people who are creative and entertaining. Despite the fact that the head management has a formal structure, the sub-culture departments can be filled with informal structures. As long as these departments are openly communicating with each other the company will be successful. When a specific culture has been manifested in an organization it is imperative for management to select hired candidates that will not conflict with the cultural structure. This is not a reference for an opportunity of racism but an opportunity of maintaining a productive environment.

Positive growth is easier to accomplish when everyone is on a common path. When a group of individuals share common factors, the learning process and technological advancements in an organization will be effortless. It is important for an organization to manifest positive visual symbols that will reinforce the company's culture. This could be as simple as posting the company's mission statement on hallways or doors. A new positive internal motto can be developed and reinforced everyday to everyone. Developing creative ways of encouraging members of the company to communicate their concerns or opinions will facilitate a change in the member's perspective. A company is nothing without the assistance and support of their employees. Positive company image comes from within the company and then reflects through the service given to customers. Maintaining a positive and open structure that is flexible to change will allow continuous growth, and a positive consumer image.

### Discussion Questions:
1. What is organizational culture? How is it created? Formally or informally?
2. What type of an impact can managers and coaches have on the organizational culture of the firms? Discuss.
3. Should leaders and coaches attempt to develop a strong organizational culture or keep it weak? Discuss the pros and cons of each.

## Case 15: Developing Ownership and Commitment[46]

An important and mission-critical element to the success of the coach/coachee relationship is the development of mutual ownership of the coaching process. Without this interaction, the interactions needed to create the desired transitions from current values, beliefs and behaviors to those that are desired, by either the organization or the individual coachee, cannot occur. The intended sustained change that happens as the result of intense self examination and subsequent evolution will be replaced by a non-lasting superficial self-evaluation which will result in minimal and possibly short-lived modifications. This result, then, will have wasted valuable resources in time and money, will be frustrating for both coach and coachee, and will deliver the erroneous message that the coaching process is unlikely to deliver successful change.

In "*Taking Ownership*," Zeus and Skiffington (2002) provide an excellent discussion of the issues pertinent to the understanding of the process of evaluating and developing ownership as the coach. It offers clearly described insights into the barriers to ownership and proscribes methods to evaluate and manage these barriers. All this is accomplished by focusing the coach on the behavioral dynamics of both the coach and the coachee. The coaching process is a demanding experience for the coachee. He or she must be willing to critically evaluate him/herself and do so openly and honestly. This can be quite uncomfortable for some, especially with a coach who may be a stranger. In addition, the coachee must be willing to accept the process as a learning and growing experience and not consider it a performance critique. This degree of positive introspection is fundamental to the coaching process and is critical to the coachee taking ownership of it. "The core ingredients of taking ownership are commitment, trust and pride," according to Zeus & Skiffington (2002, p. 130).

*Commitment.* The coaching process is a risky one for the coachee. While the potential for the accrual of long-term benefits to the coachee is significant, the risk faced by the coachee is the unknown that lays in the future outcome of the process. The coachee must be willing to submit to a careful scrutiny of not only existing behaviors, but to create real and sustainable transformation, closely held beliefs, values, and assumptions must also be laid bare. This means that the coachee must be willing to enter a committed coaching relationship without knowing what the outcome of the process will be. The development and care of this commitment is the responsibility of the coach and, to ensure success of the process, it cannot be unilateral. To accomplish this, the authors describe several specific steps that the coach can take to lay this crucial coaching foundation. They offer as a guide a "cycle of commitment" to illustrate the impact that a successful effort to create commitment can have on the change process (Zeus & Skiffington, 2002, p 131). This cycle is characterized by the continuous flow between "Commitment to possibilities," "Growing trust," "Increased commitment to goals," "Commitment to action," "Change," and recycling to "Commitment to possibilities" again. They offer a method to initiate the cycle.

1. *Establish reliability and predictability.* This is the responsibility of the coach. The coach must present him/herself as professional, experienced, credentialed and capable. Offering a clear understanding of the needs of the

---

[46] Coauthored with Keith S. Meredith (M.D.), Nova Southeastern University.

organization or the individual coachee suggests the coach's commitment to the success of the coachee.

2. *Assess the coachee's and organization's needs.* Rather than selling the coach's skills and previous success rates, the coach needs to use techniques of informed listening and developing questions that clearly seek to understand the client's needs. Careful framing of the coachee's needs by a process of exploration and collaboration rather than by advising and providing answers builds consensus and creates a growing relationship. This also allows the coachee to realize that the coach is focusing on their needs and not the coaching process as its own agenda. Finally, summarizing the outcome of these discussions by making expectations clear will decrease the coachee's performance anxiety. Mentioning that change is difficult and takes time will relieve some of this pressure.

3. *Assess the coachee's level of commitment.* Determining the coachee's vision and values is fundamental to understanding his/her commitment. The authors offer an approach to gaining these insights by exploring their previous behaviors to understand the way earlier obligations were treated and by using an assessment tool to quantify their current commitment level.

4. *Formalize the commitment process.* The use of a formal coaching contract and having the coachee sign off on this document is recommended as a method to solidify this two-way relationship.

*Fear.* Fear is a specific barrier to commitment. We all have fears and it is a powerful determinant of behavior. Fear, and its less powerful relative anxiety, can significantly influence performance and effectiveness. Anxiety, however, is also a natural emotional response to change, and if managed well, permits an appropriate transition through change. The authors discuss several fears, which if recognized and managed, may be mitigated or managed. These include fear of success, fear of failure, and fear of change. The authors also offer an example of a fear assessment tool (Zeus & Skiffington, 2002, p 137).

*Trust.* Zeus and Skiffington suggest that trust implies distrust, in the same way that opposites suggest or define each other. That is, we understand hot because we understand cold. In this context, trust is an emotional skill that implies an acknowledgement of the risk, and, therefore, of distrust. In order to trust the coach and the coaching plan, the coachee must accept that there is a risk of being betrayed by the process. But the growing commitment between the two and the acquisition of positive gains will allow trust to gain on its opposite. The behaviors of the coach can significantly influence gradual growth of mutual trust between the coach and the coachee. Avoidance of defensive responses, personal attacks and unnecessary criticism is critical. Further, developing a clear understanding of confidentiality parameters will also limit unneeded concerns and minimize trust erosion. Zeus and Skiffington also suggest the value of coach self-trust to the expression of a trustworthy demeanor. These expressions will be interpreted by the coachee as self-confidence without arrogance and genuine concern for the coachee with a willingness to develop an unencumbered emotional bond. Mechanisms to display trust in this relationship include the willingness to openly discuss the value of trust and exhibiting behaviors that command trust. The later includes staying on task by focusing on the coachee's agenda, tackling complex issues without judgment, and offering unwavering support during the coachee's journey through the process. Overall, "it is important for coaches to accept that coaching interventions are unlikely to succeed in an atmosphere of distrust and fear; trust should be built on commitment and commitment should be strengthened by trust...Fear sits outside the equation" (Zeus & Skiffington, 2002, p. 141).

*Pride*. Pride is the final key ingredient to the ownership formula. Without pride the coachee will not take complete ownership of the coaching relationship and will not completely embrace the need for it or engage in the effort. The risks are simply too high. The coach must ensure that the coachee has the opportunity to express his/her feelings. In this setting the coachee must acknowledge the gift of the coach. In the world of martial arts, this is the reason students bow to their master. The bow they receive in return is an acknowledgement of mutual respect, mutual obligation, mutual trust, and pride.

The chapter *"Taking Ownership"* in Zeus and Skiffington's work on coaching nicely discusses the importance of commitment, trust, and pride to the coaching process (Zeus & Skiffington, 2002). Just as coaching is an interaction which requires that both parties participate, so too does taking ownership. They describe a cycle of commitment and offer approaches to assess and optimize these foundations for ownership of the coaching process. Incorporating these concepts as useful adjunctive techniques of a well considered coaching plan is strongly recommended.

### *Discussion Questions:*
1. What is commitment and why is its development important in the workplace? Discuss.
2. How do managers usually develop commitment in their employees? Discuss five techniques or strategies that you have been familiar with or have witnessed.
3. Can the following commitment building process be formalized? If so, how?
   a. Establish reliability and predictability.
   b. Assess the coachee's and organization's needs.
   c. Assess the coachee's level of commitment.
   d. Formalize the commitment process.

### Case 16: Developing Managerial Self Awareness[47]

Zeus and Skiffington (2002) emphasize the importance of understanding an individual's level of self awareness in addressing coaching situations. To avoid confusion, Zeus and Skiffington note that the term "self awareness" is used in a variety of ways in modern times, and they define their understanding as "the state of being aware of our emotions and the thoughts and behaviors accompanying them" (2002). Without exploring the dangers of or difficulties created by a lack of self awareness, the authors bolster the inclusion of this topic by citing research by Kilburg that shows "a significant positive relationship between managerial self awareness and managerial performance" (Skiffington & Zeus, 2002).

---

[47] Coauthored with Jay Martin, Nova Southeastern University.

As a general overview of this complex facet of life, Zeus and Skiffington suggest that a coach's decision to concentrate on developing a coachee's self awareness depends upon: "the coach's skill in this area, the coachee's capacity for insight and awareness, and the extent to which a lack of this quality may be impacting on the coachee's growth and skill development" (Skiffington & Zeus, 2002). Aside from these factors, the coach must ensure that a safe, open environment has been cultured to ensure that the coachee will feel free to speak his/her thoughts and feelings throughout this process. No good can be achieved if both participants are not actively engaged. Zeus and Skiffington suggest several techniques to employ in efforts to promote or induce self awareness: Promoting awareness in the present, as opposed to historical situations or future dreams; Owning one's feelings, rather than displacing them; Awareness of choices, which includes claiming responsibility for our decisions; and Understanding the state of our ego, life scripts, and games employed, all based upon transactional analyses.

1. Promoting awareness in the present is designed to encourage reflection, heightening the individual's awareness of the environment, their feelings and thoughts as well as memories. The exercises suggest that spending a few moments each day reflecting will enhance awareness.

2. Owning one's feelings is designed to change an individual's perspective, as evidenced by their speech. As noted by many experts, speech is a good indicator of an individual's perspective and level of active participation in a process. Those that tend to express emotions or thoughts under the guise of 'we,' 'the group,' or 'everyone' are not taking ownership of their own thoughts and feelings. By practicing control of their speech, altering previously group based comments to individual thoughts and feelings, ownership and justification of an individual's thoughts and feelings will naturally develop.

3. Awareness of choices will develop, it is suggested, by walking the coachee through the decision making process. The coach should ensure that the coachee understands the process within which a decision is being made, assist the coachee in identifying and prioritizing their competing choices, and finally assist in developing a plan that will allow the coachee to achieve their goal. This step builds directly from the ownership of one's feelings and implies acceptance of responsibility for their decisions. It is crucial that the coach reinforce a supportive environment at this stage.

4. The final techniques suggested by the authors relate to fostering further self awareness in the hopes it will inspire further behavioral change. The authors suggest three ego states (child, parent, or adult) that the coachee should be able to identify or relate their activities to and subsequently learning how to improve their actions by consciously understanding which ego state is most productive (adult). Coachees may also be struggling with life scripts, messages that have been reinforced through a significant period of the coachee's life, which they unconsciously accept as reality (e.g. "You'll never succeed"). Similarly, coachees may have developed a habitual response to stresses or situations, which the authors name games. These latter two techniques are useful in furthering the coachee's awareness of the bases of their perspectives and developing more constructive, mature methods of working through challenges.

The benefit of promoting self awareness in employees is two-fold. It will encourage happier employees and provide an organization with an agile, creative, empowered workforce. The most effective techniques can be employed to engender such development, but it requires properly trained and experienced coaches to properly employ these techniques. Each situation, each employee or coachee requires a tailored approach that considers the individual in question.

Zeus and Skiffington revealed several techniques that could be employed to address certain deficiencies that may be exhibited in an employee's self awareness. Each supplies methods and approaches to apply when broaching the topic with the coachee, suggested exercises and thought provoking questions for reflection which when properly managed should promote a deeper self awareness. Although time consuming and seldom noted as a primary responsibility of management, coaching improved self awareness should be considered one of the most worthwhile uses of time available.

### Discussion Questions:
1. What is self awareness?
2. Why is self awareness important of managers and coaches? Why is self awareness important for the coachee?
3. What are the benefits of understanding and reflecting upon the following techniques which are suggested by Zeus and Skiffington: 1-Promoting awareness in the present, as opposed to historical situations or future dreams; 2-Owning one's feelings, rather than displacing them; 3-Awareness of choices, which includes claiming responsibility for our decisions; and 4-Understanding the state of our ego, life scripts, and games employed, all based upon transactional analyses?
4. What are some practical means of creating self awareness? Discuss.

# CHAPTER 16

## Exercises for Coaching and Performance Management

Performance and behavioral related exercises can serve as laboratories for the application of theoretical concepts and long-term learning. Read each exercise and follow or answer its relevant directions or questions.

### Exercise 1: Effective Coaches in My Past Life

Everyone has benefited, to some extent, from the guidance, assistance and leadership of effective coaches during one's socialization in the society at an early age, at school, at one's initial job, during advancement opportunities, during challenging times, during changes, and during happy times. Effective coaches can be personal or professional at any stage in one's life. Effective coaches are those that work with others by describing the problem (as they see it), helping you see the problem, clarifying their expectations, encouraging and helping one in generating possible solutions, agreeing on a specific action plan, and following up as needed to make sure the problem is solved and performance enhanced. Effective coaches help you go through these procedures without you knowing that it was a process.

Think of your past experiences related to effective coaches and write a few of these experiences, the people associated with them, and characteristics that made these individuals great coaches based on your perceptions. Try to think of the answers to the following questions as you reflect upon great coaches in your life.

1. What are the specific situations from ten to twenty years ago in your earlier years (or recent events) where someone very effectively coached to assist you become a better performer, to help you perform tasks correctly, and/or to guide you toward achieving your full potential?
2. Write the specific event(s), the dates when they happened, and the name(s) of the individual(s) doing the coaching.
3. Now, select one of the most impactful coaching experiences for deeper reflection / discussion. What made this individual an effective coach? What characteristics made him/her effective in the specific coaching event? Can you adapt some of these characteristics?

## Exercise 2: Analyzing Values

Each person is unique and may define himself or herself differently as per his or her set of values. As such, it is important that each person takes some time to examine his or her group membership qualities and values. To get you started on this reflection process, answer the following questions.

1. How would you describe yourself and your coaching qualities to another person who does not know you at this time? Write a brief biography of yourself for a two minute introduction to a group of people which includes your peers, industry leaders, your parents, and your children. This biography will be used by the master of ceremony for your introduction.

2. For deeper reflections, discuss values, how values are acquired, where values are acquired from, the power of values, how values are used, how values can change over time, and why values are important. You can also mention how a person's values can impact one's behavior in the workplace, society and life. Explore and determine your list of values (could be personal and/or professional), write them down and briefly discuss why these values are important to you. List your values in a prioritized order with one representing your most important value.

## Exercise 3: Influencing Others

Effective coaches are successful because they know how to influence their employees and colleagues. In other words, to be successful, one must be able to influence others without any formal authority. Influence is important for every person in society, especially for managers and coaches who are trying to maximize the productivity of their people and departments. You may want influence because you want to see your ideas implemented more often, get more support for various projects, build better relationships, be a more savvy politician, conduct effective seminars and conferences, make more decisive decisions, handle conflicts in a more collaborative manner, and/or to better understand people.

This exercise offers you an opportunity to think about where in your life you want more influence. Answer the following questions and be prepared to discuss these thoughts with your colleagues.

1. Who are some of the worst influencers that you know of through personal experience or media? Who are some of the best influencers that you have seen in your personal or professional life?

2. Mention one experience where someone influenced you very effectively to do something that was beneficial to you and to him/her (the influencer). What made this example so effective? What strategies were used to bring about such an influence over you? Discuss.

3. When used by others to influence you, are you more comfortable, and responsive to, Pull behaviors or Push behaviors? Discuss why?

4. When used by you to influence others, are you more comfortable using Pull behaviors or Push behaviors? Discuss why?

5. In what areas of your life and with whom do you want to have more influence? Managers, colleagues, teammates, family, friends, others? Think

of one or two examples that you would want to influence about one or two individuals either in your personal or professional life. Find out what is important to this individual, determine his or her needs, and clarify what type of a strategy might work best in order to effectively influence this person. Would it be better to use Push energy behaviors with this person or should you use more Pull energy behaviors? How about a combination of both Push/Pull behaviors?

## Exercise 4: Communication Styles and What Would You Do?

People tend to automatically "size you up" and have a first impression of who you are in the first ten seconds based on your physical appearance and non-verbal messages. And the way you communicate with others can have a great impact on your level of influence with them and whether the first impression is confirmed or disconfirmed. Alan Vengel (2000) presented four styles of communication (the authoritarian, the analyzer, the visionary, and the supporter) that coaches can use to help them better communicate and influence others, not just by *what* they say, but also by *how* they say it. The *authoritarian* prefers to be in control, makes decisions quickly, focuses on the task at hand, is face-paced, prefers brief, well-organized communication, and wants to be in charge. The *analyzer* prefers to deal with facts and confirmed information, makes careful and logical decisions, tends to have a slow pace, is reluctant to decide without having all of the facts at hand, and wants to be "in the know." The *visionary* individuals prefer to see things holistically and deal with the big picture, make decisions fast and impulsively, focus on ideas rather than little details, want to share the vision with everyone, tend to be fast-paced, and want to be in the middle of every major issue. The *supporter* prefers to deal with other individuals, sees the relationship when making decisions, tends to be more cautious when making decisions that involve other people, often seeks input from multiple parties, and wants to be "in the loop."

1. What is your dominant style of communication? The authoritarian, the analyzer, the visionary, or the supporter? Which style works best for you? How do you know?
2. Which style of communication is best for coaches? The authoritarian, the analyzer, the visionary, or the supporter? Why?
3. What is your reaction to the authoritarian, the analyzer, the visionary, and the supporter styles of communication?
4. What is your dominant style of communication? Do you need to adapt other styles of communication?
5. Which style of communication do you think would better influence others in your life? Discuss.

Read each of the following situations and determine how a coach should approach this associate and coaching opportunity. What style of communication would work best for coaches when responding to the following scenarios?

*Scenario A.* You are going to a meeting and walking in the hallway on a Monday afternoon. While almost in the middle of the department, you hear an employee (Jasmine) speaking rudely to one of her colleagues and everyone in department is able to see this situation unfold in the front of their eyes. You have noticed and heard such complaints about Jasmine in the last month from other managers. What should a coach do in this case and what communication style would work best in taking care of this situation and coaching Jasmine?

*Scenario B.* Yousuf has been working in your department with you for over ten years. He has always outperformed performance standards and met everyone's highest expectations. Currently, Yousuf is working with a team of medical doctors with a secretive and state of the art research that, if successful, can produce millions of dollars to the company later next year. Yousuf is very busy with this project that was assigned to him by you. However, now you also want him to prepare a four-hour workshop for over one hundred physicians so they can effectively deal with or manage rude behavior when working with patients and nurses. What should a coach do in this case and what communication style would work best in coaching this associate?

## Exercise 5: The Cross-Cultural Training Project

You have been working in the human resources department of your organization as a trainer for over six years. Most of your colleagues know that you have always wanted to work on a specific project regarding cross-cultural training of managers. You have some expertise and a great interest in this area, but prefer more development when the opportunity comes up. Your academic degree is in international management, which should make you a qualified candidate for this project. You find out that the company has decided that cross-cultural training is a priority this year as they want to better prepare managers for effectively dealing with expatriates in the workplace. One day, another colleague tells you that your boss is about ready to assign this project to another person, Farzana, who has been in the department for only three years and has a college degree in teaching elementary school children. You are not clear about any other specific qualifications on Farzana, but you feel that you are more qualified to lead this project. Furthermore, you know that leading this project can help you gain more insights into cross-cultural competency issues and demonstrate to everyone in the firm your expertise in project management.

Tomorrow, you are having a meeting with your boss, Belqis, about your progress on an existing project. You will probably have some time to discuss your interest on the cross-cultural training project. You can influence your boss through various methods, including effective communication and coaching styles while asking open-ended and focused questions, asserting, summarizing, and/or offering incentives. How will you prepare and what would you do?

1. What would you do? How would you approach this situation with your boss?
2. What would your goal be in this meeting?
3. What influence strategies might you use to increase your probability of being considered for this project? Discuss.
4. Have you ever encountered such an experience? What worked and what did not work?

## Exercise 6: Becoming a Practical Coach

Effective coaches encourage, inform, praise, raise awareness, collaborate, set clear expectations, serve as role models, empower, help, challenge, serve as vehicles for change, remove barriers, and enable others to reach their full potential. Also, skilled managers and coaches never let good or poor performance go unnoticed. When effective coaches and managers see good performance, they say it and praise it. One should not let poor performance go unnoticed by saying it privately to the employee and making it positively anchored toward future performance. *"The Practical Coach"* can use the *"Two Minute Challenge"* with the following steps:

◊    First, state what you observed.
◊    Second, wait for a response.
◊    Third, remind the person of the goal.
◊    Fourth, ask for a specific solution.
◊    Fifth, jointly agree on the solution and its implementation.

Effective managers jointly and collaboratively work with their employees to increase each worker's commitment to the job, enhance his or her performance on each task, and maximize each associate's long-term value to the organization.

*Exercise directions.* Take a few minutes to identify a person you currently supervise or a person who needs coaching due to poor performance. Try to think of one or two tasks which are assigned to this person who needs coaching and developing.

Think of how you will apply the coaching concepts and skills you have learned to the tasks with this person. You may want to review the coaching approaches (working one-on-one, guiding individuals to learn for themselves, and orchestrating resources and learning opportunities), coaching steps (*planning, supporting, communicating, leading, and following-up to make sure expectations are met*), and the following coaching principles.

a)    Forging a partnership,
b)    Inspiring commitment,
c)    Growing skills,
d)    Promoting persistence,
e)    Shaping the environment.

Write down your thoughts and discuss or practice it with another colleague to see how realistic this strategy might be; furthermore, seek your colleague's recommendations on what else can be done to make sure such a coaching session goes smoothly.

## Exercise 7: Being a Major Business Leader

Effective coaches get to know each individual in order to maximize individual and organizational performance through individuals, groups and processes. We can start by getting to know our own motivations first.

As an exercise, you are asked "If you could sit next to any business leader or effective coach on a plane, whom would you choose and why? What would you talk to him/her about? If you could be a coach (as a chief executive officer) of any company for a day which one would you choose and what would you want to accomplish at the end of your day?" In other words, if you could be the top leader of any company for a day which firm would you choose and, more specifically, what would you want to accomplish at the end of your day with regard to performance management and coaching and developing people? Discuss your answers.

### Exercise 8: Clarifying the Problem Statement

Before moving forward with the discipline process, a coach or manager must clarify the problem. The coach or manager should make sure the performance problem or misconduct statement is clear. One must avoid generalities and never translate performance shortfalls and misconducts into attitudinal or personality problems. Managers and coaches should also make sure the problem description is specific, observable, documented, and factual. Also, it is important to proactively answer the "when," "what," and the "impact" aspects of the problem to clearly state the issue. The clearer the problem description, the easier it will be to communicate and discuss the issue with the employee. For example, try to determine which of the following statements are specific (factual) and which ones are general (judgmental) – explain your thoughts:

1. Nauzaneen's performance with the clients' portfolio has not been acceptable for 2005.
2. Yasmeen's attitude is really bad and causing too many problems in the department. She knows that she has a bad attitude and so does everybody else.
3. This organization cannot put up with an unacceptable attendance record and overall tardiness as has been demonstrated by Mateen and his brother Nadeem.
4. Fiza's work with the clients over the last two years has been extremely poor, perhaps because of his assertive approach with their employees. They don't like him at all.
5. Zaki has left twenty minutes earlier for lunch three times during the past week and this has caused several employees to stay late in order to take care of customers.
6. Joseph had three errors in his one-page report this morning, and those errors made the firm look unprofessional.
7. Laila had a negative cash flow in her register five times this week by at least $10. The average register shortage tends to be less than $1 in the company. Therefore, Laila's record is unacceptable.
8. Mariam, the prettiest girl in the department, came to work every day last year and has submitted all her reports on time.
9. Sangar, who is considered to be a "trouble-maker" in the department, has never been late on his projects…but usually leaves 20 minutes early for lunch on Mondays, Wednesdays and Fridays to play basketball for two hours. When he returns to work in the afternoon, on a few occasions as per two comments from his colleagues, he has been a bit too "sweaty."

10. Yusof is a great candidate for an upcoming promotion. However, he is likely not to get it unless he volunteers for community work on behalf of the company each week to be recognized for his contributions. Last year he refused to do any volunteer work stating that he has to spend most of his time taking care of his elderly parents.

Once the problem statement is clear, one can proceed in resolving it. With regard to disciplining employees, it is best that managers not jump into making irrational decisions based on emotional outbursts. For effectively disciplining employees, managers should follow a progressive disciplining process in order to make employees aware of their shortfalls or misconducts so they can immediately begin work on improving them. So, progressive discipline is about effectively communicating with employees about their performance, being fair to employees, and respecting their rights.

**Exercise 9: Responding to Associates**

As discussed with managers at workshops provided to Publix Super Market Managers during the 1990's in the state of Florida, effective coaches provide clear, concise, sincere, and practical suggestions at the right times and for the right reasons while being calm and development-oriented. Being calm and appropriately responding to associates can make or break your coaching effectiveness. Listed below are several statements your associates made to you while assigning tasks to them on a busy day. For each statement, check the best response for you to make as a coach (manager) when your objective is to communicate empathically and understand the message behind the words while making sure the job gets done. Be prepared to reflect upon and clarify the reasons for your responses.

1. *Can't you find another victim to do the dirty work?*
   _____ a. Why do you feel this is dirty work?
   _____ b. Yes, but you are the best person for the job.
   _____ c. No. I am asking you to do it today.
   _____ d. This is not dirty work. It is important.
   _____ e. Do you feel that you are a victim?

2. *Wow, I'm not sure I can do that task successfully by myself.*
   _____ a. Well, okay. I will give it to someone else tomorrow.
   _____ b. Sure you can. Try it. I will be available if you need me.
   _____ c. Why do you feel you cannot do it?
   _____ d. I really think you can, or I wouldn't ask you to do it.
   _____ e. What does success really mean to you?

3. *But don't you want me to finish yesterday's assignment first?*
   _____ a. No. This is more important and it needs to be done today!
   _____ b. Can you work on them both simultaneously?
   _____ c. Which do you feel is more important?
   _____ d. No. Our priorities have changed and we need your help.
   _____ e. You are still not done with yesterday's task!

Of course, there may never be any cookie cutter answers that fit every scenario in today's complex world. The *situation* determines how you respond to the associates while coaching them or when assigning or delegating tasks. For example, emergency or rush jobs tend to require a more direct response. However, the best response occurs when you and the associate come together and work out a solution agreeable to both of you for the current situation and future development. In the real world, associates do what makes sense to them! Be sure to use patience and *empathic* listening skills as you seek to understand your associates when assigning tasks to them.

### Exercise 10: Cultural Orientations and Assertiveness

Sometimes our behavior is influenced by our culture. Understanding culture can help us to keep it from being a source of conflict when we encounter people who see the world differently than ourselves. Every culture is unique and has many elements that must be considered when learning about them. Understanding culture and its importance in shaping what we believe can help us to recognize when cultural differences are the cause of our conflict.

As one example of cultural differences, experts on anthropology and culture tend to explain that there are differences in time systems around the globe. For example, two major systems are monochromic and polychronic time orientations. *Monochronic time* includes paying attention to and doing only one thing at a time; *polychronic time* orientation means being involved with many things at once. In monochronic cultures, time is experienced and used in a linear way. Monochronic time is perceived as being almost tangible: people talk about it as though it were money, as something that can be "spent," "saved," "wasted," and "lost." Because monochronic time concentrates on one thing at a time, people who are governed by it don't like to be interrupted. Monochronic time seals people off from one another and, as a result, intensify some relationships while shortchanging others. Time becomes a room which some people are allowed to enter, while others are excluded. Monochronic time dominates most business in the United States. Polychronic time is characterized by the simultaneous occurrence of many things and by a great involvement with people. There is more emphasis on completing human transactions than on holding to schedules. Proper understanding of the difference between the monochronic and polychronic time systems will be helpful in dealing with the time-flexible Mediterranean peoples. In monochronic time cultures, the emphasis is on the compartmentalization of functions and people. In polychronic Mediterranean cultures, business offices often have large reception areas where people can wait. Polychronic people feel that private space disrupts the flow of information by shutting people off from one another. In polychronic systems, appointments mean very little and may be shifted around even at the last minute to accommodate someone more important in an individual's hierarchy of family, friends, or associates. Some polychronic people (such as Latin Americans and Arabs) give precedence to their large circle of family members over any business obligation.

*Exercise dilemma.* Let us say that an employee from a polychronic or collectivistic culture, such as India, does not appear to work as long as other employees in your company. S/he leaves work at 5:00 PM and comes to work exactly at 8:00 AM (but not earlier). S/he has a large family and needs to spend time with the children. As such, s/he does not "appear" to be as motivated for a possible promotion as several other employees who have voiced their desires and expectations regarding an upcoming promotion opportunity. Since this "Indian" employees does not seem as outspoken, assertive, or aggressive as others in the department, several of the executives believe that s/he is not interested in the promotion or in joining the management ranks. However, you believe that this "Indian" employee is a very productive person and uses his/her time very efficiently and lives a balanced life. S/he, due to the polychronic time orientation socialization, is able to manage multiple projects simultaneously and has never complained about too much work. While s/he comes to work on time and leaves on time, on several occasions s/he has worked more hours to help others in the department meet their project deadlines. S/he has performance and productivity records just as good as everyone else and has more experience in this profession than anyone else in the department. Therefore, s/he deserves the promotion and, despite his/her calm and smooth approach, would be a very good manager.

How do you go about coaching this employee to "stand out" and be "perceived" as a key competitor for this upcoming management position. Discuss and outline your plan of action.

### Exercise 11: Getting Suggestions: The "Feed-Forward" Activity

The *"feed-forward"* exercise, created by Dr. Marshal Goldsmith, is one way to simply listen and get feedback. You try to get two suggestions from another person for an area of concern and offer two suggestions to each colleague you visit on his/her concern. This exercise requires:
–   Letting go of the past.
–   Listening to suggestions without judging.
–   Learning as much as you can.
–   Helping as much as you can.
–   Learning practical points to help you be a great coach and an ethical leader.

*Exercise directions.* In few short minutes, while interacting with your colleagues, try to get as many suggestions as you can on how to resolve one current or prospective challenge you may encounter. Remember to simply say "thank you" for each suggestion and move on to the next person. No need to say "good idea," "bad idea" or "I have tried that before" type of statements. Once you have received at least one or two suggestions from each person, then circle two that you can implement and will work on during the next two months. Select a "coaching buddy," someone you can communicate on a weekly basis to discuss your progress and or challenges in the achievement of your goals or the implementation of these suggestions.

## Exercise 12: Conducting an Organizational Audit on Training

The purpose of a training and development program (for employee growth and development) audit is to assess what the organization is communicating to its employees, customers, vendors, suppliers, governments, third parties, unions, and the society in general through its advertisement, printed material, service to employees and customers, website material, phone messages, etc. Employee growth and development audits, through an effective training and development program, can be seen as the assessment of both efforts that an organization is putting forward and the actual results it is achieving from the training initiatives and programs.

The goals of a training and development program audit are to achieve a comprehensive learning experience that enables learners and managers to see how various employee growth concepts can be applied in the work environment. Such an audit provides best practices and some unique ways that modern organizations are working to develop and retain employees.

You can brainstorm some potential criteria that a team of consultants could use to evaluate the training and development efforts of an institution (government or the private sector). Initially, for example, you may think of evaluating their website or the employee manuals, and the philosophy of upper management (i.e. Are they really focused on the growth and development of a culture that values their most important asset, their human resources?). You may ask such questions as:

1. What does the organization's website communicate about their training and development programs?
2. What does the website communicate about their mission and commitments to employees, customers, vendors, suppliers, government, unions, third parties, stockholders, the environment, and employees?
3. What are the current organizational values and philosophies? Does the organization "walk its talk" in terms of living their own stated values and policies?
4. Do their benefits and work scheduling practices recognize the needs of diverse employees (scheduling plans, religious accommodations, spousal health insurance for all employees, day care, flextime, job sharing, etc.)?
5. What types of training initiatives and development programs does the institution or organization offer? Who gets trained and how? Who conducts the training? What does the training cost? How are its outcomes measured?
6. What seems to be the motivation for training and development initiatives? (employee growth, productivity, legal compliance, avoiding lawsuits, recognition of the need to have employees who relate to and understand target customers, etc.)

It is important that you develop appropriate and personalized criteria for the organization that you are auditing. As consultants and researchers, you should measure the company's performance against their mission, philosophies, and established criteria; and, keep in mind that the established criteria can be updated as per the new information and discoveries during your research, interviews and visits with the company.

Modern organizations should do all they can to retain productive and experienced employees by providing teamwork and interpersonal communication training. Employee retention in modern society can be very important, especially when the unemployment rates are low and when firms are competing for the best talent. As a team of consultants, you can develop additional criteria that address how well an organization recognizes and responds to the differing needs of its existing employees and customers. Attracting and hiring competent and diverse employees is a good start, but keeping them there may require a lot more than just having a few training and development workshops or initiatives. The firms must have an organizational culture that values its human resources, its people, by putting them first.

As consultants, your job is to focus on evaluating the organization's training and development efforts against established criteria (developed specifically for this organization with the competitors in mind) rather than on a long organizational history. The consultants are required to develop a list of recommended actions that the organization can take to benefit from the existing or prospective training and development programs. The consultants may recommend that the organization should offer a training program on leadership, management, or communication; needs to recruit more diverse employees; change their holiday and vacation policies; get diverse customers; send employee abroad to learn about their international customers; enter into new markets; conduct a survey of their employees as per their gender, age or religious backgrounds to see how satisfied they are at this time; provide diversity training to all managers and employees; and/or enhance their website to reflect a positive image of the firm. If you have a number of recommendations for the firm, try to put this into a Gantt chart, showing how and when each task should be accomplished. Overall, provide an introduction for your project, a body for your project along with all the specifics, findings, and recommendations, and finally offer an overall summary. Some items such as surveys or standard questions for interviews and other supplementary material can be included in the appendix of the report.

Overall, as a consultant team, you may take the following steps to serve as a group of experts for completing this project on organizational training and development program audit:

1.  Determine which type of an organization, institution or department you would like to audit. It is best if this institution or organization is a medium-sized firm or has about 500 to 1,000 employees.
2.  Call several specific firms and get an agreement from an employee, an official, or a manager who is willing to cooperate with you on this research during the allotted time.
3.  As a team, conduct as much research about this firm as possible before officially meeting with anyone in the firm about the actual project. Use the firms' website, their competitors' websites, and official company manuals to find the best practices in the industry. You can look at their published reports and training manuals. In addition, you can find material from secondary sources online or at the local library.
4.  Determine your established assessment and evaluation criteria for assessing the training and development initiatives of this organization or institution. Be objective to determine if this organization should receive a grade of A

(excellent), B (good), C (satisfactory or average), or D (below standard) for their organizational training and development audit when evaluated with the established criteria and compared with competitors in the industry. Provide sufficient reasons for your grading of this organization and support it with objective information.

5. Prepare your interview questions and survey instrument for your primary research. This could include about five to ten critical questions. The answer could then be assessed or evaluated as per industry standards.
6. Conduct the interview and visit (or distribute the surveys as per your plan).
7. Analyze your findings and debrief.
8. Find more information as needed or according to any existing gaps.
9. Prepare your final professional report, recommendations and presentation to the company officials and your colleagues.
10. Unless told otherwise, use the American Psychological Association (APA) guidelines for the formatting and referencing of this 6-10 page report. Include surveys, interview questions, and other supplementary material in the appendix of the report.

**Exercise 13: The Way We See Me**

The purpose of "The Way We See Me" exercise, which is a commonly used self assessment tool by most communication experts, is to clarify how you see yourself and understand how others see you. This will help you capitalize on your strengths and create a plan to strengthen your weaknesses or areas of opportunity during your interaction with others. As a result, discuss the following questions: How can you use the results? What are you going to do to improve your communication? What can others learn from your findings? Discuss things you can do to improve your overall effectiveness with your colleagues, friends, and family members.

You may choose to use the following suggested steps to conduct your research and prepare your paper.

| Step | Guidelines | Research Notes |
|------|-----------|----------------|
| 1. | Create a purpose and plan for the study and determine your target population. Distribute surveys to your audience and collect within the allotted time. | Discuss in the "*Introduction*" part of your research document. Guarantee confidentiality of the individual results to the target. |
| 2. | Complete the survey on your own behalf and determine how you see yourself. | Discuss this on the "*How I See Myself*" section of your research. |
| 3. | Analyze the data and discuss how others see you. | Discuss this in the "*Result*" section of your research. |
| 4. | Compare your own evaluation with the evaluation of others. Discuss differences (may use the Johari Window as a guideline). | Discuss this in the "*Comparison of Results*" section of the research. |
| 5. | Discuss the results and how you will apply the results to improve your communication and interaction with others to accomplish your goals. | Expound on this in the "*Application and Goals*" part of your research. |
| 6. | Summarize your learning from this experience and the overall results of the survey. | Discuss this in the "*Summary / Conclusion*" section of your research. |
| 7. | Finish your research document. Make it a good learning experience. | Tell everyone your main findings. |

**Directions: The Way We See Me Survey**

Please take a few minutes and check (√) your understanding of how the following characteristics apply to me. The results will remain confidential - so please be honest, as the cumulative responses will be used for research and improvement purposes.

*One*: How well do the following words apply to me?

| | Not at all | Slightly | Moderately | Rather well | Extremely well |
|---|---|---|---|---|---|
| 1.  Self-confident | | | | | |
| 2.  Tactful | | | | | |
| 3.  Irritable | | | | | |
| 4.  Quiet | | | | | |
| 5.  Emotionally variable | | | | | |
| 6.  Serious | | | | | |
| 7.  Energetic | | | | | |
| 8.  Well-adjusted | | | | | |
| 9.  Cooperative | | | | | |
| 10. Prejudiced | | | | | |
| 11. Unpredictable | | | | | |
| 12. Selfish | | | | | |
| 13. Leader | | | | | |
| 14. Considerate of others | | | | | |
| 15. Good natured | | | | | |
| 16. Tense | | | | | |
| 17. Open to criticism | | | | | |
| 18. Aggressive | | | | | |
| 19. Creative | | | | | |
| 20. Sense of humor | | | | | |
| 21. Responsible | | | | | |
| 22. Ambitious | | | | | |
| 23. Mature | | | | | |
| 24. Open - Easy to approach | | | | | |
| 25. Attractive | | | | | |

*Two*: Please state three of my specific strengths and three specific weaknesses!

## DON'T QUIT

When things go wrong as they sometimes will.
When the road you are trudging seems all up hill.
When funds are low and debts are high.
And you want to smile, but you have to sigh.

When care is pressing you down a bit.
Rest, if you must, but don't quit.
Life is queer with its twists and turns.
As everyone of us sometimes learns.

And many a failure turns about
When he might have won had he stuck it out:
Don't give up though the pace seems slow --
You may succeed with another blow.

Success is failure turned inside out --
The silver tint of the clouds of doubt.
And you never can tell how close you are.
It may be near when it seems so far:

So stick to the fight when you are hardest hit --
It's when things seem worst that you must not QUIT.

(*Unknown*)

"Happiness is when what you think, what you say, and what you do are in harmony"
(*Mahatma Gandhi*).

# ℬℐℬℒℐℴℊℛ𝒜ℙℋ𝒴

Abiodun, Raimi (2007). Review of "Social Intelligence: the New Science of Success" in *Workforce Diversity Management,* by Bahaudin G. Mujtaba. Llumina Press. United States.

Albrecht, Karl (2006). *Social Intelligence: the New Science of Success.* Jossey-Bass.

Aquinis, H. (2007). *Performance management.* Pearson Prentice Hall; Upper Saddle River, New Jersey.

Allen, P. (2005). Workable solutions, *Benefits Canada,* 29(7) 17-22.

Apgar, M. (1998). The Alternative Workplace: Changing Where and How People Work, *Harvard Business Review,* pp. 121-136.

Apud, S. J., James, P., & Lenartowicz, T. (2006). Cross-Cultural Competence in International Business: Toward a Definition and a Model. *Journal of International Business, 37, 4,* 527 (2006). Can also be retrieved from: http://www.jibs.net/

Arond-Thomas, M. (2004, July). Resilient leadership for challenging times. *Physician Executive, 30*(4), 18-21.

Arond-Thomas, M. (2004, September). Understanding emotional intelligence can help alter problem behavior. *Physician Executive, 30*(5), 36-39.

AstraZeneca Pharmaceuticals LP, 1800 Concord Pike, P. O. Box 15437 Wilmington, DE 19850-5437

Barnes, C. (2004). *Get Your Ducks in a Row.* Overland Park, KS: Warrington Press

Bartol, K. M., & Srivastava, A. (2002, Summer). Encouraging knowledge sharing: The role of organizational reward systems. *Journal of Leadership and Organizational Studies, 9, 1,* 64-76.

Bacon, Terry R. and Spear, Karen I. (2003). *Adaptive Coaching: The art and practice of a client-centered approach to performance improvement.* Davies-Black Publishing. Palo Alto, CA.

Barnum, P.; Liden, D. R. And DiTomaso, N., 1995. Double Jeopardy for Women and Minorities: Pay Differences with Age. *The Academy of Management Journal.* Vol. 38, # 3. June.

Baylor, Kenneth (2005). *French and Raven: The Study of Social Power.* Unpublished manuscript. United States, Nova Southeastern University (2005).

Becker-Reems, E. (2001). Synergy in motion: The board chair and CEO relationship, a high-performance organization needs a winning team. *Trustee,* 24-28. Retrieved March 14, 2005, from http://www. Pubmed. com.

Bergquist, W., Lazar, J. (2004). Alignment coaching: a broader perspective on business coaching, *Performance Improvement,* 43(10) 16-23

Bluckert, P. (2005). The similarities and differences between coaching and therapy, *Industrial and Commercial Training,* 37(2/3) 91-97.

Bielous, Gary (1995). Seven Power Bases and How to Effectively Use Them. *Supervision,* 56, 10, 14. Retrieved on August 11, 2005, from http://edelpage. the-mooseboy. com/7000/seven_power_bases. html

Booher, D. (2005). Call it as you see it. *Leadership Excellence,* 22(2), 19.

Bowater School of Management and Marketing (2006, September 29). *Lecturer in Human Resource Management.* Retrieved February 7, 2007, from http://www.deakin.edu.au/buslaw/bowater/staff/fujimoto_y.php

Boyatzis, R. E.; Melvin, L. S.; and Blaize, N. (2006). Developing sustainable leaders through coaching and compassion. *Academy of Management Learning & Education,* Vol. 5, No. 1; pages 8-24.

Branham, L. (2005). Are you engaged? *Leadership Excellence, 22*(12), 12.

Bristol-Myers Squibb, 345 Park Avenue, New York, NY. www. bms. com

Broadie, Ben (1996). Use technology to untangle wage attachments. *HRMagazine*, April. p. 57 - 60.

Brown, RB., & Brooks, I. (2002). Emotion at work: Identifying the emotional climate of night nursing. *Journal of Management in Medicine, 16*(4/5), 18 pp. Retrieved March 5, 2006, from http://0proquest. umi. com. novacat. nova. edu/pqdwebdid=288010171&Fmt=4&clientId=17038&RQT=309&VName=PQD: Proquest

Bruins, Jan (Spring, 1999). Social Power and Influence Tactics: A Theoretical Introduction-Social Influence and Social Power: Using Theory for Understanding Social Issues. *Journal of Social Issues.* Retrieved on August 24, 2005, from http://www. findarticles. com/p/articles/mi_m0341/is_1_55/ai_54831706/print

Buckner, K. & Sandholtz, K. (2003). Beyond juggling, *T & D.* 57(3)68-71.

Buckingham, Marcus (2007). *Go Put Your Strengths to Work: Six Powerful Steps to Achieve Outstanding Performance.* Free Press, United States.

Bunkley, Nick (January, 2007). *Ford Loses Record $12.7 Billion in '06.* Retrieved on January 31, 2007 from the following URL: http://www.nytimes.com/2007/01/25/business/25cnd-ford.html?ex=1327381200&en=6fc08f5f537a8aa6&ei=5088&partner=rssnyt&emc=r ss

Bureau of Labor Statistics, U. S. Department of Labor (2006)

Bureau of the Census, U. S. Department of Commerce (2006)

Byrnes, Thomas J. (2007). *Buyer Sellter Trust and Confidence in Relationship Marketing.* Unpublished Dissertation at Nova Southeastern University.

Carbonara, Peter (August 1996). Hire for Attitude, Train for Skill. *Fast Company*, Issue 04, p. 73.

Chevalier, R. (2007). *A Manager's Guide to Improving Workplace Performance.* Foreword by Marshal Goldsmith. *AMACOM:* American Management Association. New York.

Cavico, F. & Mujtaba, B. G. (2008). *Legal Challenges for the Global Manager and Entrepreneur.* Kendal Hunt Publishing Company. United States. ISBN: 978-0-7575-4037-0.

Cellich, C., & Jain, S. (2004). *Global Business Negotiations- A Practical Guide.* South-Western. Mason, Ohio: South-Western, part of the Thomson Corporation.

CG Publisher (n.d.). *Charmine E. J. Hartel.* Retrieved February 8, 2007, from http://charminehartel.cgpublisher.com/

Chang, J. (2005). Fighting for balance *Sales and Marketing Management*, 157(4) 43-44.

Chapman, Alan (2005). SWOT Analysis. Retrieved on December 3, 2005, from http://www. businessballs.com/swotanalysisfreetemplate. htm

Checkland, P. (1999). *Systems thinking, systems practice.* New York: John Wiley & Son.

Cherney, Jay K. (2005). Appreciative Teambuilding: Creating a Climate for Great Collaboration. Retrieved July 7, 2005, from: http://www. teaembuildinginc. com/article_ai.htm

Chubb Inc. Group of Insurance Companies, 15 Mountain View Road, Warren, New Jersey (USA)

Clark, Donald (2000). *Leading and Leadership*. Retrieved on August 11, 2005, from www. nwlink. com/donclark/leader/leaderled. html

CMOE Development Team (2005). The Power of Effective Coaching Skills. Retrieved October 7, 2005, from http://www. buzzle. com/editorials/text6-13-2005-71525. asp

Coaching Guide for Special Olympics, 2007. *Coaching Guide for Special Olympics: Principle of Coaching*. Retrieved on January 25, 2007 from: http://www.specialolympics.org/Special+Olympics+Public+Website/English/Coach/ Coaching_Guides/Principles+of+Coaching/default.htm.

Coaching, (1994). A World of Diversity. Workshop on Diversity and Coaching by Coleman Management Consultants, Inc.

Coaching for Results, (1999). A workshop by The Odyssey Group & Human Energy Resources.

Corcoran, C. (2006, December). Performance Management: Conducting Appraisals. *Accountancy Ireland, 38* (6), 42-45.

Conger, J. (2002). The new age of persuasion. In F. Hesselbein & R. Johnston (Eds. ), *On leading change* (1st ed., pp. 127-140). San Francisco, CA: Jossey-Bass.

Cousins, Roland B. (1992). *The Well Paid Receptionist*. Retrieved on January 20th from the Huizenga School website: http://secure.huizenga.nova.edu/5012web/cases/

Crandall, D. (editor), (2007). *Leadership Lessons from West Point*. Jossey Bass an

Crum, T. F., (1987). *The Magic of Conflict: Turning a Life of Work into a Work of Art*. Touchstone; Simon and Schuster.

Daft, R. L. (2004b). Theory Z: Opening the corporate door for participative management. *Academy of Management Executive, 18*(4), 117-121. Retrieved February 19, 2005, from ProQuest database.

Daniels, S. (2005). Leadership principles. *Leadership Excellence, 22*(4), 10.

Delbecq, A. (2001, Sep)."Evil" Manifested in Destructive Individual Behavior. *Journal of Management Inquiry, 10*(2), 221-226.

Dessler, Gary (2001). *A Framework for Human Resource Management*. 2nd edition. Prentice Hall.

Discipline without Punishment. A CRM Learning Video. 2215 Faraday Avenue. Phone: (800) 421-0833. Also made available by the Performance Systems Corporation: The Walk the Talk Company. Retrieved on 10, 06, 2005 from: http://www.crmlearning.com/product.cwa?isbn=111472V

Dupont, Kay (1997). Handling Diversity in the Workplace. AMI Publication. Forwarded by Dr. R. Roosevelt Thomas.

Edmondson, AC. (2004, March). Learning from mistakes is easier said than done: Group and organizational influences on the detection and correction of human error. *The Journal of Applied Behavioral Science, 40*(1), 66-90.

Edmondson, Vickie C. 1998. How to Succeed in Business without Being White. *Journal of Business & Entrepreneurship.*

Edmund, Heery and Mike Noon (2001). *A Dictionary of Human Resource Management*. New York: Oxford University Press.

Educational Kit, (1999). *Think Ability*. President's Committee on Employment of People with Disabilities. See "A message from the chairman Tony Coelho."

Foley, R., & Wurmser, T. (2004). Culture diversity / a mobile workplace command creative leadership, new partnerships, and innovative approaches to integration. *Nursing Administration Quarterly, 28*(2), 122-128. Retrieved April 12, 2005, from Infotrac database.

*Fortune*, 1997. The New Black Power: The Players, August 4. p. 82.

Foster, C. & Harris, L. (2005). Easy to say difficulty to do: diversity management in retail. *Human Resource Management Journal, 15*(3). pp. 4-17.

French, W. L., (2007). *Human resource management*. Sixth edition. Houghton Mifflin Company. Boston, New York.

Frey, H. William, (1999). Minority Majorities. *Written in American Demographics Books*. Page 6.

Fournies, F. (2000). *Coaching for Improved Work Performance (revised and updated edition)*. United States: McGraw-Hill.

Fournies, F. (1987). *Coaching for Improved Work Performance*. United States: Liberty Hall Press imprint of McGraw-Hill.

Frankel, L.P. (2004). *Nice girls don't get the corner office 101. Unconscious mistakes women make that sabotage their careers*. New York: Warner Business Books.

Frisch, M. (2005). Coaching Caveats: Part 2: Characteristics of the Coachee, *HR. Human Resource Planning*, 28(3)14-17.

Frito Lay Inc, A PepsiCo subsidiary, PO Box 660634, Dallas, TX (USA)

Fujimoto, Y., & Hartel, C. E. (2006). A self-representation analysis of the effects of individualist-collectivist interactions within organizations in individualistic cultures; Lessons for diversity management. *Cross Cultural Management, 13*(3), 204.

Gardner, H. (1991). *The unschooled mind: How children think and how schools should teach*. New York: BasicBooks.

Gardner, H. (1993). *Multiple intelligences: The theory in practice*. New York: BasicBooks.

Gardner, H. (1983). *Frames of Mind*. New York: BasicBooks.

Gardner, H. (1995, September 15). *A cognitive view of leadership*. Retrieved April 6, 2003, from EBSCO Web Site: http://web15.epnet.com/citation.asp?tb=1&_ug=dbs+0%2C1%2C2%2C3%2C5+In+e n%2D

Gardner, H. (1999). *Intelligence reframed*. New York, NY: BasicBooks.

Geisler, D. (2005). The next level in employee empowerment. *Quality Progress*, *38*(6), 48-52.

Gibson, James L., Ivancevich, John M., Donnelly, Jr., James H., and Konopaske, Robert (2006). *Organizations: Behavior, Structure, Processes, 12*th Edition. McGraw-Hill/Irwin: NY.

Gilbert, Dennis and Kahl, Joseph A. (1993). *The American Class Structure: A New Synthesis*, 4th Edition. Wadsworth Publishing: Belmont, CA.

Goldberg, R. (2005). Resistance to coaching, *Organizational Development Journal* 23(1) 9-17

Goldsmith, M. (2004). Expand your coaching. *Executive Excellence, 21*(10), 11-12.

Goldsmith, Marshall (Spring 2003). Helping Successful People Get Even Better! *The Journal for Quality and Participation*, Spring 2003, 26,1.

Goldsmith, Marshall (2004). If They Don't Care, Don't Waste Your Time. *Fast Company*, 84, 2004, 93. Retrieved October 14, 2005, from http://pf. fastcompany. com/magazine/84/mgoldsmith. html

Goleman, Daniel (2006). Can you raise your social IQ? *The Gainesville Sun: Parade*. Sunday, September 3, 2006. Pages 10-13.

Goleman, D. (1995, October). Know Thyself. *Emotional Intelligence* (1st, pp. 46-55). New York: Bantam Books.

Gomez-Mejia, L. R.; Balkin, D. B.; and Cardy, R. L. (2001). *Human resource management*. 3rd edition. Prentice Hall. New Jersey.

Gordon, G. E."The Dilemma of Telework: Technology vs. Tradition", in *Telework*: Present situation and future development of a new form of work organization, North-Holland, Amsterdam, 1988, pp. 113-136

Graves, Earl G. 1997. *How to Succeed in Business without Being White: Straight Talk on Making It in America*. Black Enterprise Publication.

Griffeth, Roger W. and Peter W. Hom (2001). *Retaining valued employees*. Thousand Oaks, CA: Sage Publications.

Griffeth, R. W. (1985). Moderation of the effects of job    enrichment by participation:  A longitudinal field experiment. Organizational Behavior and Human Decision Processes, 35, 73-93.

Griffeth, R. W., Hom, P. W., & Gaertner, S. (2000). A Meta-analysis of Antecedents and Correlates of Employee Turnover:  Update, moderator tests, and research implications for the next millennium. Journal of Management, 26(3), 463-488.

Guttman, H. M. (2004). Are you coachable? *Executive Excellence, 21*(6), 11-12.

Guttman, H. M. (2004). Conflict management. *Executive Excellence, 21*(1), 13.

Guttman, H. M. (2005). Power listening. *Leadership Excellence, 22*(2), 18.

Harung, H.S. and Dahl, T. (1995). Increased productivity and quality through management by values: a case study of Manpower Scandinavia, *The T.Q.M Magazine,* 7 (2), 13-22.

Helm, C., Holladay, C. L., & Tortorella, F.R. (2007, January/February). The Performance Management System: Applying and Evaluating a Pay-for-Performance Initiative. *Journal of Healthcare Management, 52* (1), 49-63.

Hersey, Paul & Campbell, Ron (2004). *Leadership: A Behavioral Science Approach.* Leadership Studies Publishing: Escondido, CA.

Hersey, Paul (July 2004). *Personal Communication on Situational Leadership.* One-week workshop by Dr. Hersey and facilitators of 'The Center for Leadership Studies." Escondido, CA. July 11-18. Phone: (760) 741-6595.

Hersey, P.; Blanchard, K.; and Johnson, D., (2001). *Management of Organizational Behavior.* Eight edition. Prentice Hall. ISBN: 013-032518X.

Hersey, Paul (1984 & 1997). *The Situational Leader.* Escondido, CA. The Center for Leadership Studies. ISBN: 0-931619-01-7. Phone: (760) 741-6595.

Hesselbein, F. 2002: The key to cultural transformation. In Hesselbein, F. and Johnston, r. (eds). *On Leading Change.* San Francisco: Jossey Bass, 1-5

Hopkins, E. Willie (1997). *Ethical Dimensions of Diversity.* Sage Publications: Sage Series on Business Ethics.

Hughes, Richard, Ginnett, Robert & Curphy, Gordon (2002). *Leadership: Enhancing the Lessons of Experience.* McGraw-Hill: NY.

Hymowitz, Carol (2007). Managers lose talent when they neglect to coach their staffs. The Wall Street Journal, B1, March 10, 2007.

Institute of Medicine. (2001). *Crossing the Quality Chasm* (1st). Washington, DC: National Academy Press.

Institute of Medicine. (2001). Building organizational supports for change. *Crossing the Quality Chasm* (pp. 111-144). Washington, DC: National Academy Press.

Johnson, W. D., & Johnson, F. P. (2003). *Joining together: Group theory and group skills.* Boston, MA: Pearson Education, Inc.

Joinson, Carla (January 1996). Reward your best employees. *HRMagazine,* April. p. 49-55.

Jones, Gareth R. and George, Jennifer M. (2008). *Contemporary Management (5th* Ed.). New York, NY: McGraw Hill.

Jones, Tom E. (2005). Breakaway Management: Changing the Behavior of Underachievers. Retrieved on October 14, 2005, from: http://www.breakawaynow.com/underachieve.html

Kaplan, R. S. 2007. What to Ask the Person in the Mirror. *Harvard Business Review*; Special issue on "The Tests of a Leader," January 2007; pages 86-95.

Karoly, L. A., Panis, C. W. A., The twenty-first Century at Work: Forces Shaping the Future Workforce and Workplace in the United States, *The Rand Corporation,* 2004.

Kaschub, M. (2002). Defining Emotional Intelligence in Music Education. *Arts Education Policy Review, 103*(5), 9-15.

Keogh, T., & Martin, M. (2004, September). Managing Unmanageable Physicians: Leadership, stewarship, and disruptive behavior. *Physician Executive, 30*(5), 18-22.

Kibort, PM. (2005, November). I drank the Kool-Aid - And learned 24 key management lessons. *Physician Executive, 31*(6), 52-55.

Kim, C. W. and Mauborgne, R. (August 1997). Fair Process: Managing in the Knowledge Economy. *Harvard Business Review*. Pages 65-66.

Kinsman, M. (2006, Feb 12). A workplace culture valuing balance boosts retention. *Knight Rider Tribune Business News.*

Koch, G. C., Gable, W., & Ellig, J. (1993). *Introduction to Market Base Management.* Fairfax, VA: The Center for Market Processes.

Kroll, K. M. (April 2007). Let's Get Flexible: Despite challenges, companies are getting more flexible with their total compensation packages. *HRMagazine*, Vol. 54, No. 4, Pages 97-100.

*Incentive Compensation and Employee Ownership.* (1999). 3rd Edition. National Center for Employee Ownership.

Lanning, Michael (2003). *Delivering Profitable Value.* The DPV Group, LLC.

Lamb, Annette & Johnson, Larry (2004). *Are You an Effective Leader?* Retrieved on September 6, 2005, from http://eduscapes. com/sms/management. html

Larimer, V. Louie (1996). Implement ethics programs. *The Colorado Springs Business Journal,* Vol. 7, p. 41.

Lazar, J. & Bergquist, W. (2004). Alignment coaching: a broader perspective on business coaching, *Performance Improvement* 43(10) 16-23.

Lipman-Blumen, J. (2002). The age of connective leadership. In F. Hesselbein & R. Johnston (Eds. ), *On Leading Change: A Leader to Leader Guide* (1st, pp. 89-102). San Francisco: Jossey-Bass.

Ludeman, K., & Erlandson, E. (2004, May). Coaching the alpha male. *Harvard Business Review, 82*(5), 58-67.

Ludeman, K. & Erlandson, E. (2004). Coaching the alpha male, *Harvard Business Review*, Reprint R0405C p. 58-67

Lyman, A., Great Place to Work Institute, Inc, April, 2004

Madsen, J. J. (2005). Managing the FM Team. *Buildings.* 99(8), 34-37.

Maher, S. (2001). The case for a coach. *Association Management, 53*(4), 78-85.

Manion, K. (2005, September). Finding physician fulfillment. *Physician Executive, 31*(5), 32-35.

Marren, Patrick (2004). In Search of Mediocrity. *The Journal of Business Strategy*, 25,1.

Marvel, K., Gunn, W., & Brezinski, KL. (2004, September). Push and pull: Resolving differences in opinion during meetings. *Physician Executive, 30*(5), 44-48.

Masciarelli, James P, (1998). Are you managing your relationships? *Management Review*, 87, (4), 41-46.

Mathis, R. L. and Jackson, J. H. (1988). *Personnel / Human resource management.* 6th edition. West Publishing Company. New York.

Mead, R. 2005: *International Management: Cross-Cultural Dimensions*, Malden MA: Blackwell Publishing 84-85.

Meredith, KS. (2006, March). Approaching Destructive Behavior. *Article Review: GMP 5640 with Dr. B. Mujtaba.* Unpublished manuscript, Nova Southeastern University.

Meyer, J.P. & Allen, N.J. (1997). *Commitment in the workplace: theory research, and application.* SAGE Publication. California.

Meyer, J.P.,Irving, P.G, & Allen, N.J. (1998). Examination of the combined effects of work values and early work experiences on organizational commitment. *Journal of Organizational Behavior, 19*(1), 29-52. Retrieved November 7, 2006 from Nova Southeastern University database.

Meyer, J.P., Stanley, D. J., Herscovitch, L. & Topolnytsky, L. (2002). Affective, continuance, and normative commitment to the organization: A meta-analysis of antecedents, correlates, and consequences. *Journal of Vocational Behavior (61)*, 20-52. Retrieved November 7, 2006 from Nova Southeastern University database.

Meyer, J. & Allen, C. (1991). A three-component conceptualization of organizational commitment. *Human Resource Management Review*, 1, 61-89.

Meyer, J. P., Allen, N. J. and Smith, C. A. (1993). Commitment to organizations and occupations: extension and test of a three-component conceptualization. *Journal of Applied Psychology*, 78, 538-551.

Mezias, J. M., & Scandura, T. A. (2005). A Needs-driven Approach to Expatriate Adjustment and Career Development: a Multiple Mentoring Perspective Cross-Cultural Communication and the Expatriate Manager: *Journal of International Business, 36, 5*, 519-538 (2005). Can also be retrieved from: http://www.jibs.net/

Miller, L. (2003). Personalities at work: understanding and managing human nature on the job. *Public Personnel Management*, *32*(3), 419-434.

Mindtools (2005). SWOT Analysis. Retrieved on December 3, 2005, from http://www.mindtools. com/pages/article/newTMC_05.htm

Mitchell, A. J., Balancing Act, *Diversity & The Bar*. September/October 2003.

Mujtaba, B. G. (2007). *Cross Cultural Management and Negotiation Practices*. ILEAD Academy Publications; Florida, United States. ISBN: 978-0-9774211-2-1. Website: Ileadacademy.com.

Mujtaba, Bahaudin G. (2007). *The ethics of management and leadership in Afghanistan (2nd edition)*. ILEAD Academy. ISBN: 978-0-9774211-0-7. Davie, Florida USA. ISBN: 978-0-9774211-0-7.

Mujtaba, B. G. (2007). *Workpalce Diversity Management: Challenges, Competencies and Strategies*. ISBN: 1-59526-548-1. Llumina Press.

Mujtaba, B. G. and McCartney, T. (2007). *Managing Workplace Stress and Conflict amid Change*. Llumina Press, Coral Springs, Florida, USA. ISBN: 1-59526-414-0.

Mujtaba, B. G. (2007). *Mentoring Diverse Professionals (2nd edition)*. Llumina Press. ISBN: 1-59526-444-2.

Mujtaba, B. G. (2006). *Cross Cultural Change Management*. ISBN: 1-59526-568-6. Llumina Press, Tamarac, Florida.

Mujtaba, B. G. (2006). Coaching for performance and productivity: the value of having managers coach employees for maximum productivity. *Smart Business Journal, 2*(7).

Nikandrou, I., Papalexandris, N., & Bourantas, D. (2000). Gaining Employee Trust after Acquisition: Implications for Managerial Action. *Employee Relations, 22*(4), 334-355.

Oldham, R. G., Cummings, A., Mischel, J. L., Schmidtke, M. J., Zhou, J. (1996). Can personal stereos improve productivity? *HRMagazine*, April, p. 95-99.

Olson, M. H."Remote Office Work: Changing Work Patterns in Space and Time", *Communications of the ACM*, 3, March 1983, pp. 182-187.

Padilla, Amado M. (2002). Online Readings in Psychology and Culture, Unit 3, Chapter 3. Retrieved on March 24, 2006, from http://www. ac. wwu. edu/~culture/padilla. htm.

Patterson, Arthur (2006). Personal Communication, March 21, 2006.

Payne, Neil (2007). *Ten Tips for Cross Cultural Communication.* Exine Articles on the Web. Available at: http://EzineArticles.com/?expert=Neil_Payne

Peak Experiences (2005). *Power and Influence*. Retrieved on August 11, 2005, from www. peak. ca/articles/power. html

Perry, Michael (October, 2006). *Rising Seas Could Leave Millions Homeless in Asia*. Retrieved on January 31, 2007 from the following URL: http://www.commondreams.org/headlines06/1009-06.htm

Peters, T. and Waterman, R. (1984). *In Search of Excellence*.

Peterson, David B. and Hicks, Mary D. (1996). *Leader as Coach: Strategies for Coaching and Developing Others*. Personnel Decisions International. ISBN: 0938529226.

Pfifferling, JH. (1999, Mar). The disruptive physician. A quality of professional life factor. *Physician Executive, 25*(2), 56-61.

Pierce, J. L., & Dunham, R. B. (1992). The 12-hour work day: A 48-hour, eight-day week. *Academy of Management Journal*, 35, 1086-1098.

Pierce, J. L., Newstrom, J. W., Dunham, R. B., & Barber, A. E. *Alternative Work Schedules.* Boston: Allyn and Bacon, Inc. (1989).

Pitney Bowes Inc., World Headquarters, 1 Elmcroft Road, Stamford, CT (USA)

Plum International Inc. (2003). A Workshop on FOCUS Coaching. Website: www.pluminternational.com. Phone: (800) 870-9490 or (954) 938-5370.

Pohlman, R. A. and Gardiner, G. S., (2000). *Value Driven Management, How to Create and Maximize Value Over Time for Organizational Success.* (NewYork) Amacom.

Profiles in Diversity Journal. A publication for sharing diversity information. Volume 1, number 2. Summer 1999.

Progressive Discipline, (2005). *Legal and Effective Progressive Discipline.* A 23 minute video. COASTAL Human Resources. Available through Video Training, Inc.; Phone-(800) 600-1555 or (206) 682-1555.

Raines, C. & Ewing, L. (2006). *The Art of connecting: How to overcome differences, build rapport, and communicate effectively with anyone.* AMACOM: New York.

Ramsey, R., (2000). Do you need a personal coach? *SuperVision*, 61(7).

Ramamoorthy, N., & Flood, P. (2004). Individualism / collectivism, perceived task interdependence and teamwork attitudes among Irish blue-collar employees: A test of the main and moderating effects. *Human Relations, 57*(3), 347-367. Retrieved March 23, 2005, from ProQuest database.

Ratzburg, Wilf (2005). *Organizational Power: Power Defined.* Retrieved on September 3, 2005, from www. geocities. com/Athens/Forum/1650/htmlpower. html?20053

Rausch, E. (2003). Guidelines for management and leadership decision. *Management Decision, 41*(10), pp. 979-988. Retrieved November 18, 2004, from ProQuest database.

Reardon, K. K. 2007. Courage as a Skill. *Harvard Business Review*; Special issue on "The Tests of a Leader," January 2007; pages 58-64.

Rifkin. G. (2006, June). The soft skills of global managers. *Harvard Management Update, 11(3).* Retrieved January 27, 2007, from http://hbswk.hbs.edu/archive/5370.html

Riggio, R.E., Murphy, S.E. & Pirozzolo, F. (2002). *Multiple intelligences and leadership.* Mahwah, NJ: Lawrence Erlbaum Associates, Inc.

Reid, J. & Hubbell, V. (2005). Creating a Performance Culture. *Ivey Business Journal*, March/April 2005. Retrieved on November 7, 2005, from http:/www. iveybusinessjournal. com

Rollo, James (2001). Performance Management: A pocket guide for employee development. Competitive Advantage Consultants Inc. and Goal QPC Publications. Website: www. goalqpc. com; Phone: (800) 643-4316.

Schaufeli, W., & Bakker, A. (2004). Job demands, job resources, and their relationship with burnout and engagement: a multi-sample study, *Journal of Organizational Behavior* 25(3) 293.

Schein, E. (1992). *Organizational culture and leadership.* San Francisco, CA: Jossey-Bass Company.

Schmitt, J, Baker, D., Bad Times: The Impact of Changes in Work Schedules on Productivity Growth, *Center for Economic and Policy Research*, November 2004.

Senge, P. (1990). The fifth discipline: The art & practice of the learning Organization. New York: Currency Doubleday.

Shellenbarger, S. How Some Innovative Employers Are Embracing Flexible Scheduling, *The Wall Street Journal*, November 17, 2005.

Siegall, M. & McDonald, T. (2004). Person-organization value congruence, burnout and diversion of resources, *Personnel Review*, 33(3)291

Silverstein, B. (2007). *Evaluating Performance: How to Appraise, Promote, and Fire*. Harper Collins Publisher, New York, NY.

Silverstein, J., & Kornacki, M. (2000). *Leading physicians through change* (1st ed. ). Tampa, Fl: American College of Physician Executives

Simons, George and Zuckerman, Amy J. (1994). Working Together: Succeeding in a Multicultural Organization. Revised edition. Crisp Publications.

Sing, C."Does Telecommuting Make Economic Sense for Companies? Proceedings of the 29th Annual Hawaii International Conference on System Sciences, 1996.

Sketch, Edward (2001). Mentoring and Coaching Help Employees Grow. *HR Focus Vol 78, no. 9*, 1, 11-15.

Sloan, A. P. Foundation, The Role of the Corporation, 630 Fifth Avenue, New York, N. Y. (2005)

Smith, B. and Rutigliano, T. (2003). *Discover you sales Strengths*.

Society for Human Resource Management, 1800 Duke Street, Alexandria, Virginia, 2004. (SWRM).

Society for Human Resource Management, Southwest Human Resource Association (SHRA), Marshall, MN. August, 2005

Spring, T. Florence (2002). *French and Raven's Source of Power*. Retrieved on August 22, 2005, from http://profsfp. cegepsth. qc. ca/lblain/cours_management/auteurs/french_and_raven. htm

Starr, J. (2004). The manager's role in coaching. *Development and Learning in Organizations*, *18*(2), 9-12.

Sternberg, R. J. (2003). *Wisdom, intelligence, and creativity synthesized.* New York: Cambridge University Press.

Sternberg, R.J., Grigorenko, E.L. (2003). *The psychology of abilities, competencies, and expertise*. New York: Cambridge University Press.

Sternberg, R.J., & Kaufman, J.C. (2000). *The evolution of intelligence*. Mahwah, NJ: Lawrence Erlbaum Associates, Publishers.

Stone, Florence M. (2007). *Coaching, Counseling & Mentoring: How to Choose and Use the right Technique to Boost Employee Performance* (2nd ed.). American Management Association. New York.

Sturdy, A. (2003, February). Knowing the unknowable? A discussion of methodological and theoretical issues in emotion research and organizational studies. *Organization*, *10*(1), 81-105.

Tangri, Ravi (2001). Approaching Change. *Chrysalis Performance Strategies, Inc.*, September 2001, 2, 2. Retrieved on November 17, 2005 from http://www. teamchrysalis. com/AC/V2/AC22_Results_Coaching_1. htm

Thacker, Rebecca A. (1995). An Examination of the Relationship between Upward Influence Tactics and Assessments of Promotability. Journal of Management, Winter, 1995. Retrieved August 24, 2005 from http://www. findarticles. com/p/articles/mi_m4256/is_n4_v21/ai_17586349/print

The Fair Labor Standards Act of 1938, as Amended, U. S. Department of Labor, Employment Standards Administration, Wage and Hour Division, WH Publication, Revised March 2004

The Leader as Coach, 2003. *Millennium Leadership Capsules for the 21st Century 7-Part Series.* Video viewed at a Workshop by Advanced Training Source. Address: 676 N. LaSalle Suite 420. Chicago, IL 60610. Phone: (312) 440-3300 Or: (800) 525-3368. Email: email: sales@atsmedia.com.

Thilo, JL. (2004, Nov). More Coaches Needed to Advise Physician Executives. *Physician Executive, 30*(6), 58-61.

Thornton, B., Peltier, G., & Perreault, G. (2004). Systems thinking: A skill to improve student achievement. *The Clearing House, 77*(5), pp. 222-228. Retrieved February 17, 2005, from ProQuest database.

Tracey, William R. (2002) *The Human Resources glossary: The Complete Desk Reference for HR Executives, Managers, and Practitioners (2nd Ed. )* Boca Raton, FL. St Lucie Press.

Trice, H. M., & Beyer, J. M. (1993). *The cultures of work organizations.* New Jersey: Prentice Hall.

Tworoger, L. C. (2004). *The Use of Power in Organizations: An Empirical Study of Public Bureaucratic and Private Non-Profit Organizations and the Adoption of a Market Orientation.* Doctoral dissertation, United States, Nova Southeastern University (2004).

Udechukwu, Ikwukananne I. (2006). Review of Karl Albrecht's book entitled *Social Intelligence: the New Science of Success.* Jossey-Bass. *Journal of Applied Management and Entrepreneurship,* Vol. 11, Num. 3; Pages 97-99.

Varian, H, American Companies Show an Edge in Putting Information to Work, *The New York Times,* January 12, 2006.

Vengel, Alan A. (2000). *The Influence Edge: How to Persuade Others to help you Achieve Your Goals.* San Francisco, CA: Berrett-Koehler Communications, Inc.

Vroom, V. (2003). Educating managers for decision-making and leadership. *Management Decision, 41*(10), pp. 968-978. Retrieved July 18, 2004, from ProQuest database.

Wah, Louisa, (2000). The emotional tightrope. Management Review, 89(1) 38 - 43

Wang, T. (2004). From general system theory to total quality management. *Journal of American Academy of Business, 4*(1/2), pp. 394-402. Retrieved March 22, 2005, from ProQuest database.

Waldroop, J. & Butler, T. (2000). Managing away bad habits. *Harvard Business Review,* September-October 2000 (Reprint) 89-97

Weber, DO. (2004, September). Poll Results: Doctors' Disruptive Behavior Disturbs Physician Leaders. *Physician Executive, 30*(5), 6-14.

Welbourne, Theresa M., (Spring 2007). Employee Engagement: Beyond the Fad and into the Executive Suite. *Leader to Leader,* Issue 44. From the Leader to Leader Institute at: *http://www3.interscience.wiley.com/cgi-bin/jtoc/73505673/.*

Wintermeyer, K. (2005, September). Personality tests and psychological tools help predict physician behavior. *Physician Executive, 31*(5), 20-21.

*Working Mother Magazine,* September 2005

Zahorsky, D (2006). Fighting employee turnover costs, Your Guide to Small Business Information. Retrieved March 24, 2006, from http://sbinformation. about. com/od/hiringfiring/a/reduceturnover_p. htm

Zeus, P. & Skiffington, S. (2002). The Coaching at Work Toolkit: A Complete Guide to Techniques and Practices. Australia: McGraw Hill

# Author Biography

Bahaudin has spent over twenty years in learning, leading and coaching employees in the corporate arena. For sixteen years, he worked as a manager and corporate trainer in a Fortune 100 firm where coaching was the best way to serve employees and customers.

Dr. Bahaudin G. Mujtaba is currently the Department Chair for Management as well as an Associate Professor of Management, Human Resources and International Management. In the years 2003-2005, he was the Director of Institutional Relations, Planning, and Accreditation for Nova Southeastern University at the H. Wayne Huizenga School of Business and Entrepreneurship in Fort Lauderdale, Florida. As a director, he was responsible for the planning of accreditation reviews for all Huizenga School's academic programs in all locations throughout United States of America and abroad.

In administrator and faculty capacities since 1996 in academia, Bahaudin has prepared for and worked with the requirements of Southern Association of Colleges and Schools (SACS), International Assembly for Collegiate Business Education (IACBE), Association to Advance Collegiate Schools of Business (AACSB), North Central Association (NCA) / Higher Learning Commission (HLC), and the University Council of Jamaica (UCJ). Bahaudin was appointed as the Director of Business Department for Undergraduate Studies at the Farquhar Center of NSU in the year 2002. As an academic Director, he was responsible for the operation of Undergraduate Business Programs. Bahaudin has been a speaker for 'The Caribbean Area Network for Quality Assurance in Tertiary Education" (CANQATE) in Jamaica, IACBE (USA), and the Association for Tertiary Institutions in the Bahamas (ATIB) in the Nassau, Bahamas.

Bahaudin has worked with various firms in the areas of management, cross-cultural communication, coaching, customer value/service, and diversity training for over twenty years.

**Author Contact Information:**
Dr. Bahaudin G. Mujtaba
Office Phone: (954) 262-5000, OR (800) 338-4723
Email: mujtaba@nova.edu

# Contributors

**Dr. Bahaudin G. Mujtaba**
Nova Southeastern University
3301 College Avenue
Fort Lauderdale-Davie, Fl 33314
(954) 262-5000
Email: mujtaba@nova.edu

**Dr. Vickie Cox Edmondson**
The University of Alabama
Birmingham, AL 35294

**Dr. Chris R. Crumley**
Trinity University
Gaithersburg, MD 20879

**Dr. Trish Hagan**
Nova Southeastern University
Colorado Springs, CO 80919

**Dr. Keith S. Meredith**
Nova Southeastern University
Scottsdale, AZ 85255

**Dr. Rafael González**
Nova Southeastern University
Vega Alta, PR 00692.

**Dr. Mack Hinson**
Nova Southeastern University
Seattle, WA 98105

**Dr. Richard Conwell**
Nova Southeastern University
Cranberry Twp, Pennsylvania

**Brian Renaud**
Nova Southeastern University
Coral Springs, FL 33071

**Jay Martin**
Nova Southeastern University
Richmond, VA 23221

**Bonita Durazo**
Nova Southeastern University
Chandler, AZ 85224

**Gina H. Harris**
Nova Southeastern University
Coral Springs, FL  33077

**Solange Beckford**
Nova Southeastern University
Orlando, FL 32805

**Dr. Les W. Carter**
St. Edward's University
Austin, TX 78704

**Lamoy Coburn**
Nova Southeastern University
Fort Lauderdale, Florida

**Marikay Concannon**
Nova Southeastern University
Fort Lauderdale, Florida

# Other Books by the Author

1. Cavico, F. & Mujtaba, B. G., (2008). *Legal Challenges for the Global Manager and Entrepreneur.* Kendal Hunt Publishing Company. United States. ISBN: 978-0-7575-4037-0.

2. Mujtaba, B. G. and Scharff, M. M. (2007). *Earning a Doctorate Degree in the 21st Century: Challenges and Joys.* ILEAD Academy Publications; Florida, USA. ISBN: 978-0-9774211-3-8.

3. Mujtaba, B. G. (2007). *Cross Cultural Management and Negotiation Practices.* ILEAD Academy Publications; Florida, United States. ISBN: 978-0-9774211-2-1.

4. Mujtaba, Bahaudin G. (2007). *AFGHANISTAN: Realities of war and rebuilding (2nd edition).* ISBN: 978-0-9774211-1-4. ILEAD Academy, LLC, Davie, Florida.

5. Mujtaba, Bahaudin G. (2007). *The ethics of management and leadership in Afghanistan (2nd edition).* ILEAD Academy. ISBN: 978-0-9774211-0-7. Davie, Florida USA. ISBN: 978-0-9774211-0-7. Website: Ileadacademy.com.

6. Mujtaba, B. G. (2007). *Workpalce Diversity Management: Challenges, Competencies and Strategies.* ISBN: 1-59526-548-1. Llumina Press.

7. Mujtaba, B. G. and McCartney, T. (2007). *Managing Workplace Stress and Conflict amid Change.* Llumina Press, Coral Springs, Florida, USA. ISBN: 1-59526-414-0.

8. Mujtaba, B. G. (2007). *Mentoring Diverse Professionals (2nd edition).* Llumina Press. ISBN: 1-59526-444-2.

9. Mujtaba, B. G. and Preziosi, R. C. (2006). *Adult Education in Academia: Recruiting and Retaining Extraordinary Facilitators of learning.* 2nd Edition. ISBN: 1593114753. Information Age Publishing. Greenwich, Connecticut. Phone: (203) 661-7602.

10. Mujtaba, B. G. (2006). *Cross Cultural Change Management.* ISBN: 1-59526-568-6. Llumina Press, Tamarac, Florida. Phone: (866) 229-9244 or Reg. (954) 726-0902.

11. Mujtaba, G. B. (2006). *Privatization and Market-Based Leadership in Developing Economies: Capacity Building in Afghanistan.* Llumina Press and Publications, Tamarac, Florida. ISBN: 1-59526-551-1.

12. Mujtaba, B. G. and Cavico, F. J., (2006). *Age Discrimination in Employment: Cross Cultural Comparison and Management Strategies.* BookSurge. ISBN: 1-4196-1587-4.

13. Cavico, F. & Mujtaba, B. G., (2005). *Business Ethics: Transcending Requirements through Moral Leadership.* Pearson Custom Publications. U. S. A. ISBN: 0-536-85783-0.

# Index Table

# Becoming Better!

Whether you think you can or cannot either
way you will be right because the key to
unlocking your team's potential is in YOU!